EARLY PRAISE FOR

Development & Deployment of Multiplayer Online Games

"By far the most comprehensive book on specifics of multiplayer games"
— **Dmitri Dain**, Managing Director @*Amaya Software*

"Finally!"
— **Boris Taratine**, Cyber Security Programme Chief Architect @*Lloyds Bank Group*

"Looking forward to read the book when it is finished"
— **Nuno Leiria**, Senior Software Engineer @*Polystream,*
formerly Core Tech Programmer @*Lionhead Studios*

"Looking forward to read the final book. The promise is great. Finally a book on the subject that isn't outdated or vague."
— **Özkan Can**, formerly Backend Technical Director @*Blue Byte, A Ubisoft Studio*

"TCP is a complex beast and you know much more about it than I do. Thank God!"
— **Glenn Fiedler**, GDC speaker,
veteran of AAA multiplayer development, and UDP fanboy for life.

"The colossal book you are writing... looks very promising and exciting"
— **Alessandro Alinone**, Co-Founder and CEO @*Lightstreamer*

"The really useful and highly practical book. This book will be a valuable addition to the library of anyone game developer."
— **Michael Morgovsky**, Co-Founder and CTO @*Plarium*

"I've been looking for a book like this for a decade. This will be invaluable for teaching game devs the ins and outs of multiplayer development."
— **Robert Zubek**, GDC speaker, Founder @*SomaSim,*
formerly Principal Software Engineer @*Zynga*

"Even unfinished, it already is the most comprehensive reference for networking and multiplayer game development that I have ever seen, and it is constantly teaching me new things. An absolute must-have for the serious developer."
— **Matt Pritchard**, AAA veteran, author, and CTO @*Forgotten Empires*
former RTS/FPS/IoT developer @*Ensemble Studios/Valve/Disney*

'NO BUGS' HARE

Sarcastic Developer
Co-Architect of a G20 Stock Exchange
Sole Architect of a Game with 400'000 Simultaneous Players
Author of Articles in CUJ, C++ Report, and Overload

DEVELOPMENT AND DEPLOYMENT OF
MULTIPLAYER ONLINE GAMES

From Social Games to MMOFPS, with Stock Exchanges In Between

ARCHITECTURE AND PRE-DEVELOPMENT

Victorious warriors win first and then go to war,
while defeated warriors go to war first and then seek to win.

— Sun Tzu, *The Art of War,* circa 500 BC

In Part ARCH, we will discuss activities that need to be performed even before the coding can be started. It includes many things that need to be done, from formulating business requirements to setting up your source control and issue-tracking systems, with lots of critical architectural decisions in between.

DIY, (RE)ACTORS, CLIENT ARCH., UNITY/UE4/ LUMBERYARD/URHO3D

Start the reactor. Free Mars...

— Kuato from *Total Recall*

Development and Deployment of Multiplayer Online Games
Volume II. DIY, (Re)Actors, Client Arch., Unity/UE4/Lumberyard/Urho3D
by 'No Bugs' Hare

Translated from Lapine by **Sergey Ignatchenko** *(Nerds for Nerds Publishing GmbH, ithare.com)*
Illustrations and Cover Design by **Sergey Gordeev** *(Gordeev Animation Graphics, gagltd.eu)*
Editing by **Erin McKnight** *(Kevin Anderson & Associates, ka-writing.com)*
Interior Design by **Alexey Shumov**, **Alexandra Evseeva**

ISBN: 978-3-903213-15-9 (Paperback)
ISBN: 978-3-903213-16-6 (Hardcover)
ISBN: 978-3-903213-17-3 (PDF)
ISBN: 978-3-903213-18-0 (ePub)
ISBN: 978-3-903213-19-7 (Kindle)

Published by **Nerds for Nerds Publishing GmbH**
Hormayrgasse 7A/19
1170 Wien
Austria

CONTENTS

Chapter 7. Client-Driven Development: Unity, UE, Lumberyard, Urho3D, and 3rd-Party Network Libraries

ACKNOWLEDGMENTS

Family

It is customary for authors to say thanks to the family members who have supported them during the endeavor of book writing. However, while I am infinitely grateful to my family (especially to my wife, Natalia), I strongly prefer to thank them in person. To the best of my knowledge, they prefer it this way too.

Comments That Helped Shape the Book

From the beginning, this book was intended as a "crowd publishing" project. Beta chapters were published on my blog, ithare.com, as soon as they were ready (and even *before* they were ready), with the aim of receiving as many comments as possible. Overall, beta chapters from Volumes I–III got over 400 comments made by over a hundred different people. And while not all these comments were exactly useful, there were quite a few people who pointed out important not-too-clearly-explained things, forgotten-at-the-moment-but-good-to-mention technologies and use cases, and some have also taught me certain things (yes, I have to admit that if you're looking for a book written by a divinely inspired knowing-everything oracle, you've got the wrong one).

Here goes an alphabetical list of people who have made important comments during beta testing of the book and who were also kind enough to provide their details to be included:

B

Michael Bartnett from New York, United States

Robert Basler from Vancouver, Canada

Marcos Bracco from La Plata, Argentina

C

Jean-Michaël Celerier from Bordeaux, France

Oded Coster from London, United Kingdom

D

Przemysław Danieluk from Poland

Bill Dieter from Portland, United States

Matt P. Dziubinski from Warsaw, Poland

F

Nir Friedman from New York, United States

Santiago Fernández Ortiz from Madrid, Spain

Timothy Fries from Spring Hill, United States

I

Dmytro Ivanchykhin from Kiev, Ukraine

J

Nathan Jervis from Hamilton, Canada

Luciano José Firmino Júnior from Recife, Brazil

K

Chris Kingsley, from Longmont, United States

Marat Khalili from Moscow, Russia

Mario Konrad from Zurich, Switzerland

L

Ivan Lapshov from Moscow, Russia

Nuno Leiria from Lisbon, Portugal

Dmitry Ligoum from Toronto, Canada

N

Jesper Nielsen from Gråsten, Denmark

R

Nathan Robinson from Stuttgart, Germany

S

Bulat Shamsutdinov from Kazan, Russia

David Schroeder from Spokane, United States

Alessandro Stamatto from Porto Alegre, Brazil

Jon Stevens from Seattle, United States

T

Duy Tran from Ho Chi Minh City, Vietnam

David Turner from Leeds, United Kingdom

W

Jon "hplus" Watte

Z

Vadim Zabrodin from Novosibirsk, Russia

Robert Zubek from Chicago, United States

...and everybody else who made important comments but declined to be included in this list

Thanks a lot, friends: your feedback was really important to make the book better.

Special Thanks to Kickstarter Backers

This book was Kickstarted and the money raised was used for professional editing and design. There aren't enough bits in the RAM of my computer to express all my gratitude to each and every one of you. The book certainly wouldn't be the same without you (and your patience has certainly been saintly). You've been a wonderful [funding] crowd — THANKS A LOT!

Here goes the "Kickstarter Backers' Hall of Fame":

0-9

10tons.com

A

ABeardOnFire
Aled
ALEJOLP
Ander Amo
Andrew
AustinK
Dan Avram
David Antúnez
    (eipporko)
Guillaume A
Islam Aliev
Jonathan Adams
Jorge Moreno
    Aguilera
Kylie Au
Luis Armendariz
Nacho Abril
Rafael "GeekFox"
    Araujo
Scott Anderson
Sergey Annenkov
Sharad Cornejo
    Altuzar
Tomáš Andrle
Victor da Cruz
    Amaro
Wali Akande

B

Alicia Boya García
Asher Baker
Babyjeans
bmac & ingrid
botiq
bryon
Bumek
busho
Christian Bryan
ck @ bsg
Cory Bloor
D Barnard
Dan Brewer
David G. Brewing-
    ton II
Emeric Barthélemy
Frank Lyder
    Bredland
Georg Begerow
Graham Bishop
    Hidden Gorilla
    Ltd
Heiko Behrens
Hrvoje Bandov
Jasmine Bulin
Kirill Belov
Leandro Barreto
Luke Beard
Marcos Bracco
Mateus Borges
Maxim Biro
Michael Brüning
Nicholas "LB"
    Braden
Patrick B
Patty Beauregard
Richard Baister
Robert Bracken-
    ridge
Stephen Bentley

Tomas Bilek
Vincent Bilodeau
Vincent Blansaer
Vladan Bato

C

Ben Carruthers
Bulent Coskun
caj
camfurt
Catprog
Charlie
Chris Cox
Christian Corsano
ChuangTseu
Connor Carter
Dmitry Chuev
Edward Carmack
Ian Compton
Javier Calvo
Laurent CETIN
Liam Costello
Milo Casagrande
Morrison Cole
Neil Coles
Ozkan Can
P. Chaintreuil
Paul Caristino
Sam Coleman
Shawn Cassar
Stuart Cassidy

D

Andreas Drewke
Andy Dunn
Chris Downs

Ciaran Deasy
Cristián Donoso
dajomu
Dan Dudley
Daniel Dimitroff
Daniele Dionisi
 (Danguru)
dd33
Digital Confec-
 tioners
Dooks Dizzo
Jamie Dexter
Jean-Michel
 Deruty
Julien Dumétier
Justin Drury
Ken Drycksback
Kyle Dean
Matthew DeLucas
Matthew Douglass
Michael Dwan
Niclas Darville
Oliver Daff
Pat Duquette
Petar Dobrev
Tim Drury

E

Craig Edwards
David Erosa
 Garcia
Egon
empty2fill
Eric Espie
Ethereal World
Geoff Evans
Jon Edwards
Matthew Erickson

Michael Ellwood
Ryan Evans
Sebastian Eggers
Semih Energin
Vlad Engelgardt

E

Антон
 Евангелатов

F

Andrew Fox
Bruno V. Fer-
 nandes
Bryce Fite
Eric Faehnrich
Glenn Fiedler
Mad William Flint
Matthew Fritz
Rosco Farrell
Rui Ferreira
Rui Figueira
Steve "Tech-Imp"
 Fernandez
Thomas Frase
Zach Fetters

G

Arvid Gerstmann
Bart Grantham
Bernardo A. Gon-
 zalez (Jasnis)
Daniel Guilford
David Garcia (le-
 dragon-dev)
Dorian George
Evan M. and
 Nathan G.

Gerardo
Gero Gerber
giant_teapot
Jason Gassel
Jonathan Gough
Jonathan Grimm
Maxime Guillem
Philip Gurevich
Risnoddlas Gry-
 tarbiff
Stu 'BloodyCactus'
 George
Szymon Gatner
Tadej Gregorcic
Tim Goshinski
Tom Guinther

H

Adam Hill
Alex Holzinger
Alun Hickery
Andrew Handley
Andrew Holmes
Carlos Hernando
David Hontecillas
Dermot Hannan
Garry Hornbuckle
Johannes Harten-
 stein
Jez Higgins, JezUK
 Ltd
Jurie Horneman
Lars Hamre
Martin S. Hehl
Michael Hoyt
P. Halonen
Remko van Haften
Sean Hernandez

Shawn H.
Tom Hawtin
Tom Haygarth
Wolfgang Haupt

I

Christopher Igoe
Dmytro Iv-
   anchykhin
Ikrima
Improbable
Martin Ivanov
Ray Ion

J

Corinna Jaschek
Greg Jandl
JackyWongCW
Jaewon Jung
Jerry Jonsson
Jesper Geertsen
   Jonsson
Jonathan Johnson
JOS
Karl Jensen
Kenneth Jørgensen
Luciano Jose
   Firmino Junior
Rainer Jenning
Rajnesh Jindel
Randolpho de
   Santana Juliao
Robert Janeczek
Thomas Sebastian
   Jensen
Wilmot-Albertini
   Jordan

K

Allan Kelly
Andrew Koenen
Andreas Koenig
Bernhard
   Kaufmann
Bronek Kozicki
Chris Kingsley
Daniel Kirchen
DM Klein
Dongseob Kim
Ivan Kravets
Joona-Pekka
   Kokko
Kristofer Knoll
Kwaki3
Lars-Göran
   Karlstedt
Malte Krüger
Marko Kevac
Matej Kormuth
Mike Kasprzak
Patrick Kulling
Pawel Kurdybacha
Pit Kleyersburg
Roope Kangas
Shay Krainer
Vladimir "ai_en-
   abled" Kozlov
Wesley Kerr

L

Andrew Lee
Andrew Lombardi
Antony Lloyd
Callum Lawson
César Laso

Damien Lebreuilly
Daniel Ludwig
David Latham
Evgenii Loikov
Game L10N, local-
   izedirect.com
Jamie Law
Jan-Christoph
   Lohmann
Javi Lavandeira
Jeffrey Lim
Johan Lohmander
Justin LeFebvre
Justin Liew
KC Lee
LordHog
Mikola Lysenko
Mun Kew Leong
Richard Locsin
Wilhansen Li

M

Adam Mikolaj
Altay Murat
Andrew McVeigh
Angel Leigh
   McCoy
Benoit Maillot
Bradley Macomber
Brett Morgan
Brian Marshall
Chris Murphy
Dan "DMac"
   MacDonald
Fernando Matar-
   rubia
Gordon Moyes
Heather Martin

Hervé MATYSIAK
Jeroen
 Meulemeester
Johan Munkestam
John McDole
Kevin McCabe
Marcus Milne
Martin Moene
Mārtiņš Možeiko
Matthew Ma
Matthew Mckenzie
MaxHouYeah
Maximilian
 Mellhage
Michael Mayr
Michal
Michal Mach
Mike
mp3tobi
Oddur Magnusson
Richard Matthias
Richard Maxwell
Robert Masella
Ronald McCor-
 mick
Rory Marquis
Seamus Moffat
Seth J. Morabito
Shawn MacFarland
Stefan Moschinski
Thijs Miedema
Tobi Müller
Troy McAnally
Umar Mustafa
Vlad Micu

N

André Pacheco

Neves
Andrey Naumenko
Dan Nolan
Ivan Nikitin
J. Djamahl Nolen
Marek Niepiekło
Nischo
NOM
Simon Nicholass
Tivadar György
 Nagy
Tran Dang Nguyen

O

Albert Olivera
Andreas Oehlke
Bradley O'Hearne
Carsten Orthbandt
David Osborne
Jason Olsan
Jonathan
 Ogle-Barrington
Lukas Obermann
Magnus Osterlind
OakFusion.pl
Ryan Olds

Ø

Knut Ørland

P

Alex Price
Alexander Popov
Alexandru Pana
Andreas Pfau
Behrouz Poustchi
Ben Perez
David Pong

Donald Plummer
Eric Pederson
 (sourcedelica)
James Pelster
Jamie Plenderleith
Jason Pecho
Lloyd Pearson
Matt Pritchard
Maxxx Power
Michael Powers
Pablo Díaz
 Pumariño
paste0x78
Patrick Palmer
Penda
Peter Petermann
Phil Peron
Pindwin
PragTob
Rafael Pasquay
Scott Posch
Sylvain P.
Tim Plummer
Tomaso Pye
Tony P
Wayne Pearson
Yevgeniy Pinskiy
Zac Paladino

Q

Andrew Quinn

R

Agata Ratz
Anton Rogov
Chris Rice
Clay Ravin
Darren Ranalli

Denis Reviakin
Francois Rouaix
Guillermo Gijon
  Robas
James Rowbotham
Juan Rufes
Juanma Reyes
La Ruse
Maxime Raoust
Michael A. Ryan
Pasha Riger
Peter Richards
RagManX
Ralph Reichart
Rdslw
Really Good TV
reopucino
Reuben R
Ron Roff
RyanH
Scout Rigney
Valentinas Rimeika
Zeno Rawling

S

Albert Smith II
Alex Sonneveld
Alexander Ziegler
  Simonsen
Brian Sheriff
Christian Funder
  Sommerlund
Christopher Sierra
Dan Sosnowski
David Salz
David Sena
David Sheldon
Deovandski

Skibinski
Dylan "PoundCat"
  Spry
Enrico Speranza
Eric Schwarzkopf
Erik Sixt
Ewan Stanley
Fabian Schaffert
Fredrik Stromberg
Geoff Schemmel
Håkan Ståby
Harvinder Sawh-
  ney
http://sava.ninja
Jeff Slutter
Joey "TML" Smith
Jonathan Soryu
Kevin Salvesen
Kishimoto Studios
Kostiantyn Shche-
  panovskyi
Kurt "Thunder-
  heart" Stangl
Lennart Steinke
Marcin Slezak
Mario Sangiorgio
Michael Savage
Michael Schuler
Michel Simatic
Morgan Shockey
Moriel Schottle-
  nder
Nathanael See
Philip Stein
Raphael Salomon
René Schmidt
Richard Searle
Robert Singletary

Rory Starks
Ross Smith
sassembla
SemanticSiv
Sergio Santana
  Ceballos
SleepyRabbit-Da-
  vid
Spielraum Tirol
Sproing Interactive
  Media
Stef
Tania Samsonova
Tengiz Sharafiev
Tero Särkkä
Todd Showalter
Victor Savkov
Wilson Silva
Winston Joseph
  Smith
Zsolt Somogyi

Ś

Grzegorz Świt

T

Barrie Tingle
Chris Threlfo
Daniel Espino
  Timón
Diogo Teixeira
Garai Tamás,
  Gerendás András
James Tatum
Julian Tith
Matt Toegel
Nicolas Tittley
Rajan Tande

Rodney J. Thomas
Ryszard Tarajkow-
ski
Steven Turek
Test_nuke
Theo
Tim Tillotson
Tree
Troxbanv
tuntematon
Wei Tchao

U

uonyx
Urs

V

Alex Vaillancourt
Carson V
Felton Vaughn
Ken Voskuil
Sam Velasquez
Silvo Vaisanen
Thomas Viktil
Yoann Le Verger

W

Andre Weissflog
Andres Weber

Ashley Williams
Bradley Weston
Bret Wright
Chris Wine
Christian Weiss
Daniel Wipper-
mann
David Wyand
Dominik Wit
Garrick Joshua
Williams
James Wright
Jate Wittayabundit
Jonathan Watson
Jorik van der Werf
Kevin Waldock
Lee Wasilenko
Mike Watkins
Nicholas Wymy-
czak
Nick Waanders
Peter Wolf
Richard Williams
Simon Withington
Wanderer
wcampos
WeirdBeard
Games
Windbringer

X

Xenide
Xlxla
Xywzel

Y

Jason Young
Kyungho Yun
Rouzbeh Youssefi
Tim Yates
Weikie Yeh

Z

George Zakharov
Maxim Zaks
Mike Zbleka
Z-Software
Zara

*...and all those backers who decided
to remain anonymous.*

P.S. This is not the last book I'm going to launch on Kickstarter, so...stay
tuned!

INTRODUCTION

NB: This is a significantly shortened version of the introduction in Vol. I. In particular, "The Story Behind This Book," "What is This Book About?" "On LAN-Based Games and Peer-to-Peer Games," and "Recommended Reading" are not repeated here.

THE HARE AND THE PEOPLE BEHIND...

About the Author: The author of this book is a 'No Bugs' Hare from the warren of Bunnylore. He is known for being a columnist for *Overload Journal* (ISSN 1354-3172) and for his significant contributions to the software development blog *ithare.com*. As 'No Bugs' is a rabbit with a mother tongue of Lapine, he needed somebody to translate the book into human language. And of course, as the book is highly technical, to translate technical details with the highest possible fidelity, he needed a translator with substantial software development experience.

About the Translator: This book has been translated from Lapine by Sergey Ignatchenko, a software architect since 1996. He is known for writing for industry journals since 1998, with his articles appearing in *CUJ*, *Overload*, *C++ Report*, and *(IN)SECURE Magazine*. His knowledge of Lapine is quite extensive, and he routinely translates the column 'No Bugs' writes for *Overload*. During Sergey's software architecting career, he has led quite a few projects, including as a co-architect of a stock exchange for a G20 country (the same software has been used by the stock exchanges of several other countries), and as a sole original architect of a major gaming site (with hundreds of thousands of simultaneous players, billions of database transactions per year, and that processes hundreds of millions of dollars per year). As a kind of paid hobby, he also invents things: he's an author and co-author of couple dozen patents (unfortunately, owned by his respective employers).

About the Illustrator: Illustrations for this book are by Sergey Gordeev, currently from *gagltd.eu*. He is a professional animator with a dozen awards from various animation festivals, and is best known for directing a few animated *Mr. Bean* episodes.

About the Editor: Erin McKnight is an internationally award-winning independent publisher and the editor of multiple books of fiction and non-fiction from both emerging and eminent writers. She was born in Scotland, raised in South Africa, and now resides in Dallas — though this is her first time working with the Lapine language.

ON REAL-WORLD EXPERIENCES

> All happy families are alike;
> each unhappy family is unhappy in its own way.
>
> — Leo Tolstoy, *Anna Karenina*

The trigger for writing this book was realizing the pitiful state of MOG-related books. However, there was another experience that served as additional motivation to write this book.

Quite a few times, when speaking to a senior dev/architect/CTO of some gamedev company (or more generally, any company that develops highly interactive distributed systems), I've been included in a dialogue along the following lines:

— How are you guys doing this?
— Psssst! I am ashamed to admit that we're doing it against each and every book out there, and doing this, this, and this…
<pause>

— Well, we're doing it exactly the same way.

This basically means two things:

♦ There *are* MOG practices out there that *do* work for more than one game.

    ▪ Probably, there are even practices that can be seen as "best practices" for *many* games out there (stopping short of saying that all successful projects are alike).

♦ OTOH, *lots* of these practices are not described anywhere (never mind "described in one single place"), so each team of multiplayer gamedevs needs to re-invent them themselves. <ouch! />

This is where *Development and Deployment of Multiplayer Online Games* tries to come in. Overall,

> *this book is an attempt to summarize a body of knowledge that is known in the industry, but is rarely published, let alone published together.*

In other words, this book (taken as a complete nine volumes) intends to cover most of the issues related to architecting, developing, and deploying an MOG (with a few exceptions as outlined below).

Of course, given the scale of this (probably overambitious) task, I will almost certainly forget quite a few things. Still, I will try to do my best.

IS THIS BOOK FOR YOU?

CD *not* included

First, let's briefly warn some potential readers who may be otherwise frustrated.

I have to admit that this book is not one of those "how to get rich!" books. Moreover, it is not even one of those "how to copy-paste your game engine to get rich!" books. The road to launching your own multiplayer online game in a way that scales (and to getting rich in the process as a nice-to-have side effect <wink />) is anything but easy, and it is important to realize it *well before* you undertake the effort of developing your own MOG.

The road to launching your own MOG in a way that scales (and to getting rich as a nice-to-have side effect) is anything but easy, and it is important to realize it *well before* you undertake the effort of developing your own MOG.

As a logical result of *not* being a book to copy-paste your game engine from, this book does not include any CD, and neither does it include any code for a ready-to-use MOG engine. There are, of course, occasional code snippets here and there, but they're intended to illustrate the points in the text and have *absolutely nothing to do* with a ready-to-use game engine that you can use as a starting point and modify later.

There are several reasons why I am not trying to make such a ready-to-use game engine, but the main one is that trying to do so would restrict discussion to a very limited subset of easy-to-illustrate items, which in turn would narrow the scope of the book tremendously.[1]

"Nothing About Everything"

From a certain point of view, all programming books can be divided into "books that tell everything about nothing" and "books that tell nothing about everything." The former are *very* specific, but this universally comes at a cost of narrowing the scope to solving one *very* specific problem, with anything beyond this narrowly defined problem going out the window. These books are often useful, but often their use is limited to beginners for use as a learning project.

The latter type of book, the kind that explains "nothing about everything," is trying to generalize as much as possible at the cost of not going into implementation details at each and every corner.

The latter type of book, the kind that explains "nothing about everything," is trying to generalize as much as possible at the cost of not going into implementation details at each and every corner. Usually, such books are of little use for learn-by-example, but can help seasoned developers progress much further by explaining not "how to do low-level things," but rather "how to combine those low-level things into a larger picture, and how to balance them within that larger picture to get the desired result." And when trying to balance things, usually the best (and maybe the only viable) way to do so is to explain it in terms of relevant real-world experiences.

Of course, in general, the division between these book types is not that clear, and there are some books in the gray area between these two types, but this particular book belongs firmly in the "nothing about everything" camp. It correlates well with not having a CD (as mentioned

---

1   Or would force me to write MOG-engine-that-covers-everything-out-there, and even I am not *that* audacious.

above), and with being oriented toward intermediate developers and up (as mentioned below).

Prerequisite: Intermediate+

This book is targeted toward at-least-somewhat-experienced developers (or, in other words, it is *not* a "how to develop your first program" book with IDE screenshots and copy-paste examples). If your game project is your very first programming project, you're likely to have difficulty understanding this book.[2]

I would even go so far as to say that

> *The target audience for this book starts from those intermediate developers who want to progress into senior ones, and goes all the way up to CTOs and architects.*

In particular, there will be no explanation of what event-driven programming is about, what the difference is between optimistic locking and pessimistic locking, why you need a source control system, and so on. Instead, there will be discussions of how *the concept of futures* fits into event-driven programming, when the use of optimistic locking *makes sense for games*, and how to use source control *in the presence of unmergeable files*.

On the other hand, this book doesn't rely on in-depth knowledge in any specific area. To read and understand this book, you don't need to be a TCP guru who knows every tiny detail of RFC 793 by heart; neither do you need to have hands-on experience with shaders and/or CUDA; even less do I expect you to be a C++ wizard who is capable of writing an arbitrary Turing-complete program in templates, or a DB/2 expert who can predict how execution plans will be affected by adding "1=0" to "WHERE" clauses, or an admin guru able to configure BGP-based DDoS protection without consulting any documentation (BTW, to be honest, these things are beyond my own capabilities too).

Of course, 3D graphics experience may be helpful for 3D MOGs, and knowledge of network basics and sockets won't hurt for *any* MOG,

If your game project is your very first programming project, you're likely to have difficulty understanding this book

---

2   Feel free to read the book in this case, but don't complain if it turns out to be too difficult.

Both 3D games and multiplayer games are overwhelming subjects even if taken separately, so trying to learn them within the same development effort is likely to be catastrophic.

but whenever discussing the issues that go beyond "things that every intermediate-level developer out there should know anyway," I will try to provide pointers "where to read about this specific stuff if you happen to have no idea about it."

And last, but certainly not least:

> *Even if you're an experienced developer but have worked on neither single-player 3D games nor multiplayer games, it would be unwise to start with a multiplayer 3D game.*

Both 3D games and multiplayer games are overwhelming subjects even if taken separately, so trying to learn them within the same development effort is likely to be catastrophic.

That being said, I am sure that going into multiplayer 3D games is possible both from the single-player 3D game side and from the non-3D multiplayer side (the latter includes social games and stock exchanges).

HOW TO READ THIS BOOK

Conventions

This book uses more or less traditional conventions, but there are still a few things that may require some explanation.

There are those pull-quotes in the margins — the ones with my face inside a circle.

First, there are those pull-quotes in the margins — the ones with my face inside a circle. These are just repetitions of the same sentences that are already present in the text, but that reflect my emotional feeling about them. Whenever I'm describing something, I honestly believe it to be true; however, whether or not I like it is a completely different story, and I want to be able to express my feelings about the things I'm saying (and without cluttering the main text with long descriptions of these feelings).

Then there are "wiki quotes." These are intended to introduce certain terms that are more or less well known in some industries, but which may be completely new for some readers. I am not able to discuss these terms in depth myself (the book is already over the top, pagewise), and am instead suggesting taking a look at them elsewhere (as always, Wikipedia and Google being the primary candidates).

Code Samples

As is expected from a development book, there will be code samples included. Most of the samples in the code are in C++, but this certainly does *not* mean that the ideas are limited to C++. On the contrary, most of the examples (except for one C++-specific chapter in Volume V) are intended to apply to pretty much any programming language, and C++ is used as the most common programming language used for game development.[3]

Also, please note that the samples should be treated as just that, samples, to illustrate the idea. Except when mentioning it explicitly, I am not trying to teach you C++ or C++ best practices. Therefore, whenever I am facing the dilemma of "whether to make the big idea behind it more obvious, or to follow best practices," I am likely to sacrifice some of the best practices in the name of the point-at-hand being more understandable.

My Captain-Obvious Hat

With the target audience of this book being pretty broad,[4] I am bound to explain things-that-are-considered-obvious by certain groups of people (but which may still be unclear for another group). Moreover, for each and every bit in this book, there is somebody out there who knows it. So, please don't complain that "most of the stuff in this book is well known"— it certainly is and, as noted above, the whole point of the book is to "*summarize* a body of knowledge that is known in the industry, but is rarely published."

As a result, please don't hit me too hard when I'm saying things that are obvious specifically to you. I can assure you that there are developers out there who don't know that specific thing (and don't rush to name those idiots, as they're likely to know some other stuff that you don't know yet[5]).

Wikipedia

Wikipedia is a free online encyclopedia that aims to allow anyone to edit articles.

—**Wikipedia**

---

3   And also the one I know the best.

4   I admit being guilty as charged regarding an attempt to reach as many people as I can.

5   And if you already know everything under the sun, you probably should have written your own book on MOGs and spared me the effort.

I will try to include notices (like this one) whenever I know for sure that a certain section of the book is not interesting for a certain group of people (for example, my musings on graphics will certainly be way too obvious to 3D professionals).

I will try to include notices whenever I know for sure that a certain section of the book is not interesting for a certain group of people (for example, my musings on graphics will certainly be way too obvious to 3D professionals). Still, it is unlikely that I've managed to mark all such places, and I apologize for any inconvenience caused by reading stuff-that-is-obvious-to-you.

Terminology

As for any wide-but-not-so-formalized field, MOG development has its share of confusing terms (and, even worse, terms that have different meanings in different sub-fields <ouch! />). I am not going to argue "which terms are 'correct'" (it's all in the eye of the beholder, which makes all the arguments on terminology silly to start with). Instead (and taking into account that using the terms without understanding their meaning is even sillier), I am going to define how-*I*-am-going-to-use such terms for the purposes of this book.

MMO vs MOG

The very first term that causes quite a bit of confusion is the definition of "Massively Multiplayer Online Games" (a.k.a. MMOGs and MMOs).

The point of confusion lies with those games that have tons of players, but don't have all of them within one single Game World. As the games with the most players online (think CS or LoL) tend to fall in this category, it is quite an important one. In this regard, one school of logic says, "Hey, it is multiplayer, it is online, and it has a massive number of players, so it is an MMO." Another school of thought (the one that happens to take over Wikipedia's article on MMOGs[6]) says that to qualify as an MMOG, it is necessary to run the whole thing within one single instance of the Game World.

As promised, I won't argue over terminology, just noting that to avoid any potential for confusion, I will try to avoid using the term "MMO" (except for the much better defined MMORPG and maybe MMOFPS). Which means that —

---

6   Note that as of 2017, the Wikipedia article on MMOGs violates quite a few fundamental Wikipedia policies.

> *What we'll be discussing in this book is referred to as Multiplayer Online Games, even when they have massive numbers of players.*

In fact, most of the time I'll assume that we're talking about the games able to handle hundreds of thousands of simultaneous players; this is the only thing that really matters (and whether to name it MMOG or just MOG is not of much interest).

Server

In MOG world, the term "Server" is badly overloaded, and can be used to denote several different things.

One such meaning is "server," as in "physical server box"; another is a "place where players can connect" (for example, "West-Europe Server"). However, in spite of the name, the latter is actually almost universally implemented as a bunch of physical Server Boxes (usually residing within one Datacenter). To make things even more confusing, people often use the term "servers" for different instances of your Game World (which in turn can be pretty much anything: from an instance of a battle arena where the play occurs, to the whole instance of a complicated MMORPGs Game World).

To avoid unnecessary confusion, for the purpose of this book, let's name the physical server box a Server, and a bunch of physical servers residing within a single datacenter a Datacenter. As for "game world instances," we'll name each of the logically separated entities running on the physical server box a Game Server; when talking about more specific types of Game Servers, we'll say Game World Server, or Matchmaking Server, or Cashier Server, etc. Once again, it is not because "these definitions are 'right'" in any way — it is just a convention I prefer to use.

Dedicated Server

Another ongoing source of confusion with regard to MOGs is the definition of the "dedicated server." In the hosting industry, there is a very well-established understanding that it is a "server box where you have root/Administrator access"; usually such "dedicated servers" are available for rent, and the term is used to differentiate "dedicated servers" (physical boxes) from "virtual servers" (which is just a *part* of

Most of the time, I'll assume that we're talking about the game able to handle hundreds of thousands of simultaneous players; this is the only thing that really matters (and whether to name it MMOG or just MOG is not of that much interest).

the physical box, and, in some cases, such as within the cloud, can also migrate with time from one physical box to another).

On the other hand, for MOG development, there is a very different common understanding of the term "dedicated server," which roughly means something along the lines of "instance of the game that doesn't have graphics directly attached to it" (this definition is most popular among indie gamedevs and comes from P2P architectures, with an elected Client acting as a Server).

For the purpose of this book, I'll try to avoid using the term "dedicated server" at all to avoid confusion; however, if there is an occasional slip of the tongue (or whenever I am talking about renting Servers from ISPs), I mean the first definition (i.e., a "physical server box, usually rented from hosting ISP").

BYOS (As in, "Bring Your Own Salt")

In the practical world (especially in game development), for each and every "Do THIS_THING this_way" statement, there exists a counterexample…

One last thing I would like to mention before we proceed to more practical matters. There is not one single sentence in this book (or any other book for that matter) that is to be taken as an "absolute truth." In the practical world (especially in game development), for each and every "Do THIS_THING this_way" statement, there exists a counterexample illustrating that sometimes THIS_THING can (or even *should*) be done in a different (and often directly opposing) manner.

All advice out there has its own applicability limits, and so does any advice within this book. When I know of certain game-related scenarios where these limits are likely to be exceeded (and the advice will become inapplicable), I will try to mention it. However, it is extremely difficult to predict all the usage scenarios in a huge industry such as game development, so you should be prepared that some of the advice in this book (or any other book for that matter) is inapplicable to your game without warning.

Therefore, take everything you read (here or elsewhere) with a good pinch of salt. And as salt is not included with the book, you'll need to bring your own. In more practical terms—

> *For each and every decision you make based on advice in this book, ask yourself:*
> **Does This Advice Really Apply to My Specific Case?**

SETTING THE CONTEXT. VOL. I SUMMARY

In Volume I, we started at the very beginning—and, for games, the "very beginning" is the Game Design Document, also known as the GDD (discussed in Chapter 1); most importantly, we concentrated on those GDD issues that are *specific for multiplayer games* (and, evidently, there are quite a few).

Then, in Chapter 2, we proceeded to the all-important argument of "should our game be P2P or Server-based, or Deterministic Lockstep-based," and found that, considering the risks coming from cheaters (and them attacking *all* successful games), our only viable option for a multiplayer-game-with-thousands-of-simultaneous-players is Authoritative Servers.

In Chapter 3, we ended preliminaries and got to the real stuff—specifically, to communications and communication flows. First, we briefly examined[7] different communication flows between the Client and the Server from the viewpoint of latencies, input lag, and RTTs. We started from simplistic Server->Client->Server communication (which works only for slower games), and went all the way to Client-Side Prediction, Lag Compensation, and Forwarded Inputs (eventually reaching the state-of-the-art, latency-wise).

Then, we arrived at the all-important question of reducing traffic. This discussion included varied topics such as having the Client State different from the Server State and also different from the Publishable State, and Interest Management (which also has very important implications in reducing the potential for cheating), and then we tried to systematize different flavors of Compression.

Afterward, we briefly mentioned Scalability (it was just a small part of the overall discussion on Scalability; more to follow in Volume III,

---

7   Yes, thirty pages is a very brief discussion for this kind of thing.

Volume VI, and Volume IX), and examined Server-2-Server communications (including the all-important Async Inter-DB Transfer protocol; we'll desperately need it later to achieve DB scalability). And, last but not least, we discussed an Interface Definition Language; while it is possible to develop your MOGs without IDL, it provides so many advantages that I certainly advise *not* doing any serious new development without one.

CHAPTER 4.
DIY VS. RE-USE: IN SEARCH OF BALANCE

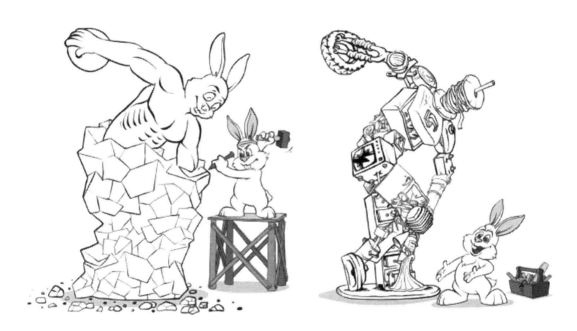

In any sizable development project, there is always the question "What should we do ourselves, and what should we re-use?" Way too often, this question is answered as "Let's re-use whatever we can get our hands on" without understanding all the implications of re-use (and especially of the implications of *improper* re-use; for really bad examples of the latter see, for example, [Hare]). On the other hand, the opposing approach of "DIY Everything" can easily lead to projects that cannot possibly be completed in one person's lifetime, which is usually "way too long" for games. In this chapter, we will attempt to discuss the question "What should we re-use?" in detail.

DIY

Initialism of Do It Yourself

—**Wiktionary**

On one end of the spectrum, there are games that are nothing more but "skins" of somebody-else's game. In this case, you're essentially counting on having better marketing than your competition.

Within the gamedev realm, the answers to the "DIY vs. Re-Use" question reside on a pretty wide spectrum, from "DIY pretty much nothing" to "DIY pretty much everything." On one end of the spectrum, there are games that are nothing more than "skins" of somebody-else's game (in such cases, you're usually able to re-texture and re-brand their game, but without any changes to gameplay; changes to meshes and/or sounds may be allowed or disallowed). In this case, you're essentially counting on having better marketing and textures/theme than your competition (as everything else is the same for you and them). This approach may even bring in some money, but if you're into it, you're probably reading the wrong book (though, if you're running your own Servers, some information from Volumes VII and IX might still be useful and may provide some additional competitive advantage, but don't expect miracles in this regard).

On the other end of the spectrum, there are game-development teams out there that try to develop pretty much everything from their own 3D engine, their own TCP replacement, and their own cryptography (using algorithms that are "much better" than TLS), to their own graphics and sound drivers (fortunately, cases when developers are trying to develop their own console and their own OS are very much few and far between[8]). This approach, while often fun to work on, may have problems with providing results within a reasonable time, so your project may easily run out of money (and as the investors understand it, running out of money will probably happen sooner rather than later).

Therefore, it is necessary to find a reasonable balance between the parts that you need to re-use, and the parts you need to implement yourself. However, before we start discussing different aspects of "DIY vs. Re-use," let's first spend some time on the all-important concept of dependency — and the closely related concept of Vendor Lock-In.

DEPENDENCIES AND VENDOR LOCK-INS

Whenever we're re-using a 3rd-party library, we get a dependency on it. Both in theory and in practice, dependencies vary in strength. If we

---

8   Even Doom engine by ID software — which I admire, BTW — didn't go *that* far.

can remove dependency, then things are not too bad (and the dependency strength depends on the amount of effort required to remove it). However, if we cannot remove dependency, it becomes an Absolute Dependency, also known as Vendor Lock-In. For the purpose of this book, I'll use the terms Absolute Dependency and Vendor Lock-In interchangeably.

Impact of Vendor Lock-Ins

First, let's note that for "Games with an Undefined Life Span" (as defined in Volume I's chapter on GDD), the consequences of having 3rd-party Absolute Dependency are significantly worse than for "Games with Limited Life Span." Having a Vendor Lock-In for a limited-time project is often fine, even if your choice is imperfect; having the very same Absolute Dependency "forever and ever, till death do us part" is a much bigger deal, which can easily lead to disaster if your choice turns out to be the wrong one.

You shouldn't count on assumptions such as "oh, it is a Big Company, so they won't go down"; in particular, while the company might not go down, they still may drop their game engine or library, or drop support for those-features or those-platforms you cannot survive without.

Moreover, usually for "Games with Undefined Life Span," you shouldn't count on assumptions such as "oh, it is a Big Company, so they won't go down"; in particular, while the company might not go down, they still may drop their game engine or library, or drop support for those-features or those-platforms you cannot survive without. While for a limited time, such risks can be estimated and are therefore manageable (in many cases, we can say with a sufficient level of confidence that "they will support such-and-such a feature three years from now"), relying on a 3rd party doing something-you-need "forever and ever" is usually too strong of an assumption.

BTW, speaking about Big Companies dropping technologies: it is often related to the question of "whether strategic interests of the engine developer (or actually, of any technology that you're considering as an Absolute Dependency) are aligned with games." Just to give two bad examples in this regard: Flash wasn't aligned with Adobe's strategy, and was effectively allowed to die; the interests of the browser-development crowd weren't (and aren't) aligned with those of game developers — and six years after all the big fuzz about HTML5 games, all we have is still a half-baked implementation (except for *emscripten*, which is a completely separate and not-really-HTML-based development). On the other hand, game engine development companies (such as Unity or Unreal) have games as their *core* business, so they're not likely to drop games overnight (however, a wider question of "whether their strategic interests are aligned with a certain platform you need or with a specific feature you need" still stands).

Weakening/Isolating Dependencies

Fortunately, there are ways out there to weaken dependencies; however (and unfortunately)

> *Measures to weaken dependencies need to be undertaken starting from the very beginning of the project.*

Otherwise (i.e., if you create a strong dependency and try to weaken it significantly further down the road), it can easily lead to rewriting of the whole thing.

To be more specific, let's first consider one of the most typical (and generally very strong) classes of dependencies: Platform Lock-Ins; and as soon as we know how to get it right, we'll try to generalize it to all 3rd-party dependencies out there.

On Platform Lock-Ins and Cross-Platform Code

When talking about Platform Lock-Ins, it is quite well-known that

> *If your game is not intended to be single-platform forever-and-ever, you SHOULDN'T allow **any** platform-specific Vendor Lock-Ins.*

If you happen to allow calls to Win32 DLLs from your C# game, you will get an Absolute Vendor Lock-In on Windows much sooner than you release your first prototype.

For example, if you happen to allow calls to Win32 DLLs from your C# game, you will get an Absolute Vendor Lock-In on Windows much sooner than you release your first prototype. A slippery road toward Absolute Vendor Lock-In always starts small, as "hey, we'll just use this single very neat feature." However, in just three months, you'll get sooooo many such neat-features-your-code-depends-on (as well as Win32-specific concepts, constants, and struct-like classes spilled over all over your code) that you won't be able to remove them without re-writing the whole thing from scratch.

In other words, if you're considering porting your game sooner or later, make sure that *all* your Lock-Ins are cross-platform. Otherwise, you'll be facing an extremely unpleasant surprise when it is time to port your game.

Non-Working Cross-Platform: Rewriting Low-Level APIs

BTW, when aiming for a cross-platform code, you should forget about the reasoning of "hey, it won't be a problem; we'll just re-write those Win32 functions that we need, later"— it *never* works in practice. Once in my career, I've seen such an attempt firsthand. There was a company that wrote a Windows-based business-level server, and it even worked (and got significant market share too). But the whole thing had an Absolute Dependency on Win32 API, with literally hundreds of different Win32 API calls interspersed throughout the code.

On a beautiful day, a Fortune 500 company decided to buy them, on the condition that they port their code onto *nix. Four months later, their porting efforts were still at a stage of "we already wrote <windows.h>, which compiles on Linux." Needless to say, the whole port never materialized (in fact, it never got any further than compiling <windows.h>).

Overall, such "port OS calls to a different OS" efforts are known to be *extremely* time-consuming; it took WINE project (aiming to do pretty much the same thing) fifteen years — and enormous efforts — to get into version 1.0. BTW, a side note about WINE: if you're going to use it to port your Win32 game into Linux, make sure to test your game under WINE *from the very beginning*; even after all those years, WINE is still very far from providing 100% compatibility with Win32, and if your code will happen to rely on those-Win32-features-that-work-differently-under-WINE, you'll have quite a bit of trouble when trying to port your Win32 game to WINE.

Working Cross-Platform: Isolation Layer

In spite of the "porting-OS-level-APIs later" approach being pretty much hopeless, there *is* a way to write cross-platform programs. The basic idea is to have a separate isolation layer, as shown in Fig 4.1:

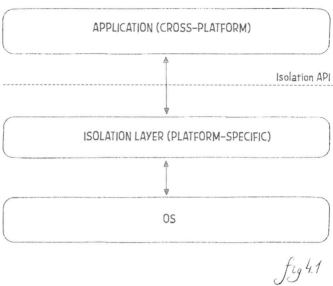

fig 4.1

I am guilty of once writing such a trivial wrapper.

However, just following the diagram on Fig 4.1 is not sufficient to enable cross-platform programs; for example, if your Isolation Layer is just a trivial wrapper exposing exactly the same parameters that were present in underlying OS calls, it won't do anything to help make your program cross-platform. I am guilty of once writing such a trivial wrapper (it was about twenty years ago, so I hope it is already past the statute of limitations) — and the experience was bad enough to prevent me ever repeating this meaningless exercise.

In practice, two approaches to make the Isolation Layer really cross-platform are known to work.

Working Cross-Platform: Isolation Layer/Lowest Common Denominator

One common approach to making the Isolation Layer work is to make Isolation API a *lowest common denominator* of all the underlying cross-platform APIs. This approach is known to work, however, when applied to app-level programming, has the following very significant drawbacks:

♦ It requires a priori and intimate knowledge of all the platforms involved (including those platforms that will be supported later).

This alone makes the approach problematic for us (=“poor defenseless game developers”).

♦ It doesn't allow us to use platform-specific trickery (that is, without introducing additional abstraction layers). As one example (and in pretty much any lowest-common-denominator library, there are tons of similar examples): while both Win32 API and *pthreads* do allow the use of mutexes in shared memory, *std::mutex* (built based on the “lowest common denominator” paradigm) doesn't allow it.

As a result, whenever I am wearing my app-level developer hat, I don't really like such lowest-common-denominator Isolation APIs; while they might work, there are usually better options (especially for a project with 1M+ total lines of code).

Working Cross-Platform: Isolation Layer/In Terms of App

An alternative way for the Isolation Layer in Fig 4.1 to provide real cross-platform capabilities is to have your Isolation API expressed in terms of what-your-App-needs (as opposed to being expressed in terms of what-your-OS-provides).

Just one example: for a Server app, it is usually a pretty bad idea to have your Isolation Layer mimic even as ubiquitous a function as file open. As soon as your Isolation Layer exposes intimate details of either *nix *open()* or Win32 *CreateFile()*, you'll have a difficult time re-implementing your Isolation Layer later. And, if you don't expose the fine details of these functions, you might be okay, but you'll have to restrict your API to be “the lowest common denominator” of the platform-specific APIs, which has its own pretty serious problems, as described above.

However, if you concentrate on what-your-Server-app needs to do, then, instead of the file open function, you may realize that all you need is the logging function,[9] which has two big advantages:

a) It will make the lives of your developers easier (and will unify their logging too), and:

b) Rewriting your logging function will be easy for pretty much *any* platform (and without an in-depth knowledge of the intimate platform details in advance).

However, if you concentrate on what-your-Server-app needs to do, then, instead of the file open function, you will provide the logging function, which has two big advantages.

---

9   Ideally, providing logging for all your types-used-within-your-app too.

And if your Server app happens to use files as persistent storage[10], you should have a separate set of Isolation APIs implementing persistent storage for your app and, once again, they should work not in terms of "opening file," but at least of "storing/retrieving an object with such-and-such-ID" (among many other things, it will facilitate the switch to a database later — and without rewriting your whole game).

Working Cross-Platform: Summary

To summarize the reasoning above:

> *Having your Isolation Layer defined in terms of Application is the best way to enable cross-platform ports later down the road.*

I've seen many attempts to go cross-platform, and can tell you the following:

◆ The only successful cross-platform attempts were those using Isolation Layer.

   ▪ Moreover, all successful cross-platform systems I've seen used either:

      • Isolation API as a "lowest common denominator" or

      • Isolation API in terms of Application needs

   ▪ And of these two, for app-level development, I clearly prefer the latter.

BTW, identifying proper Isolation APIs is not an easy task even for the "Isolation API expressed in terms of Application" approach,[11] and can easily take more than one iteration to get right (especially if you're doing it for the first time). However, if remembering two mantras (one about the Isolation API being expressed "in terms of your Application needs," and another about it being "as high-level as possible"), you do have the chance to achieve it sooner rather than later.

---

10   Usually, I *strongly* prefer databases, but in the real world pretty much anything can happen.

11   Though it is still *much* easier than looking for the "least common denominator."

Isolating Arbitrary Libraries. Isolation APIs in terms of App

By now, we've observed two ways to implement your Isolation API to enable real cross-platform development. As noted above, it MUST be done via an Isolation Layer, *plus* the Isolation API MUST either:

♦ Be the lowest common denominator among all the platforms, or

♦ Be an app-oriented API

While for app-level development I tend to prefer app-oriented APIs, I have to admit that for cross-platform development both of these approaches can be made to work.

However, when we try to generalize these (quite well-known) observations from isolating platform specifics to isolating *arbitrary* 3rd-party engines and libraries, the situation changes. As the lowest-common-denominator approach (as noted above) requires intimate knowledge of the API-being-isolated, using it to isolate *arbitrary* 3rd-party engines and libraries (and keeping in mind that they're — unlike OS APIs — changing all the time) becomes pretty much a non-starter. In other words, it is next-to-impossible to find a stable lowest common denominator for entities that may be unknown at the point of finding the denominator, and which are in a state of flux.

In other words —

While for app-level development I tend to prefer app-oriented APIs, I have to admit that for cross-platform development, both of these approaches can be made to work.

> *Pretty much the only practical way to deal with **abstract** 3rd-party dependencies is to have your Isolation API expressed in terms of your app, and not in terms of the 3rd-party library/engine.*

On "Wrapping, Then Wrapping Some More"

When talking about isolating dependencies, one common approach is to add more and more isolation layers (which can be described as "wrap, then wrap some more") until the desired result is reached.

This multi-wrapping approach might work, but its success ultimately depends on one of the wrappers being either "lowest common denominator" (which, as noted above, is mostly applicable to cross-platform development), or being expressed in terms of App layer (which applies across the board).

And as soon as one of the wrappers complies with either of these requirements, the whole multi-wrapper system effectively becomes an incarnation of Fig 4.1 (which works along the lines discussed above). As a result, I prefer not to consider multiple wrappers a separate isolation technique; from a more practical standpoint, while there are cases where multiple wrappers might be necessary, in my experience such cases are few and far between, and one single Isolation Layer is usually good enough.

Vigilance, and More Vigilance

In practice (and regardless of which of the two ways of making your Isolation API work you're using), it is not sufficient just to declare that you have an Isolation Layer and proclaim that "We're using *only* Isolation API to do these kinds of things."

Any such policy is perfectly useless unless:

◆ *All*[12] of your team members understand the policy,

◆ They understand *why* you're doing it, and

◆ Are prepared to spend some additional effort to follow the policy.

Otherwise, it is better to just throw the policy out the window[13] and admit to having Absolute Vendor-Lock In.

The slippery slope toward the mire of platform-specific-spaghetti code always starts easily and is fairly flat: "oh, we'll use this neat feature bypassing Isolation Layer just this once" and then becomes steep and enormously difficult to stop. To have any chance in an uphill battle against dependencies, *everybody* on the team who learns about such a violation should stop all other tasks and fix it ASAP. In some cases (and if the app-level feature is really necessary), support for the new feature may need to be added into the Isolation Layer, but bypassing Isolation API should be a Big Fat No-No™.

In practice, it is not sufficient just to declare that you have an Isolation Layer and proclaim that "we're using *only* Isolation API to do these kinds of things."

---

12   Okay, I'll settle for 96.7%.

13   No relation to MS Windows.

Practically, to ensure that your Isolation Layer has a fighting chance, you should at least:

♦ Write in big bold letters in your design documents that *all* the access to module X should be via Isolation Layer IsolatedX, and that all the direct access to module X is outright prohibited.

♦ Make sure that everybody on the team knows it.

♦ Try to prohibit calling APIs of the module X directly (i.e. without IsolatedX) when compiling your code on your build machine.

▪ For example, in C++, this can be achieved via using so-called *pimpl idiom* for your Isolation Layer IsolatedX, and prohibiting direct inclusion of 3rd-party header files by anybody-except-for-your-Isolation-Layer.

♦ Unless you have managed to prohibit 3rd-party APIs on your build machine (see above), you should have special periodic reviews to ensure that nobody uses these prohibited APIs. It is much, *much* simpler to avoid these APIs in the early stages than trying to remove them later (which can easily amount to rewriting really big chunks of your code).

While these rules may look overly harsh and seem too time-consuming, practice shows that without following them, chances are that you won't be able to replace that 3rd-party module X when you need to. Dependencies are sneaky, and it takes extreme vigilance to avoid them. On the other hand, if you don't want to do these things, feel free to ignore them — just be honest with yourself and realize that Module X is one of your Absolute Dependencies forever, and with all the resulting implications too.

"Two Platforms" Approach

One thing that tends to help a lot with keeping your code clean from bypassing-Isolation-Layer violations is ongoing compiling and testing of your system using two different platforms (3rd-party libraries/engines/…) at the same time. If you keep testing your game in two substantially different environments as you develop, the chance of platform-specific (library/engine/…-specific) code accidentally slipping in is reduced by orders of magnitude (and, in most cases, becomes negligible).

pimpl idiom

also known as an opaque pointer, Bridge pattern, handle classes, Compiler firewall idiom, d-pointer, or Cheshire Cat, is a special case of an opaque data type, a datatype declared to be a pointer to a record or data structure of some unspecified type

—**Wikipedia**

Dependencies are sneaky, and it takes extreme vigilance to avoid them.

The only problem with undertaking such two-platform development is that often it is unaffordable during the early stages of the project. Also, you need to make sure that platforms/libraries/engines are indeed *substantially* different (and, for example, Linux and Mac OS might not qualify as such, especially if talking about non-GUI code).

TL;DR on Vendor Lock-Ins and Isolating Dependencies

A short summary of our discussion of Vendor Lock-Ins and ways to isolate them:

◆ Vendor Lock-Ins are dangerous, especially for Games with Undefined Life Spans.

◆ Isolation Layer is The Way To Go™ if you want to limit the impact of the Vendor Lock-In.

 ▪ For isolation to work, Isolation API *should* be either:

  • The lowest common denominator between all the underlying libraries (which has significant drawbacks, especially if isolating an abstract 3rd-party library with a not-so-carved-in-stone API), or:

  • Expressed in terms of App needs (opposed to being expressed in terms of capabilities of the 3rd-party library).

 ▪ You need to be vigilant in your quest to fight Isolation-by-passing-code.

  • In this regard, the two-platform/library/engine approach tends to help a lot, though it is often prohibitively expensive in the early stages of development (and this is exactly when you need it the most).

BUSINESS PERSPECTIVE: DIY YOUR ADDED VALUE

Now, after discussing Vendor Lock-Ins (and describing ways to mitigate their negatives too), we can come back to our primary question of "DIY vs. Re-Use." First, let's take a look at this question from the business or monetization point of view. While business perspective is not exactly the point of this book, in this case it is intertwined with the rest of our discussion and we cannot ignore it completely.

From the business point of view, you should always understand what "added value" your project provides for your customers. In other words, what is that thing that you add on top of whatever-you're-re-using? What is that unique expertise you provide to your players?

When talking about the "DIY vs. 3rd-party re-use" question, it is safe to say that

> ### *At least, you should develop your Added Value yourself.*

You should always understand what "added value" your project provides for your customers.

The motivation behind the above rule is simple: If you're re-using everything (including gameplay, world map, and meshes), with only cosmetic differences (such as textures), then your game won't really be different from the other games that are doing the same thing. For your game to succeed commercially, you need a distinguishing factor (a.k.a. USP–Unique Selling Point[14]), and it is your Added Value that normally becomes your USP.[15] In general, pretty much anything can serve as an USP (including such things as marketing, or the quality of support); however, within the scope of this book we'll concentrate only on those USPs that are software-related.[16]

The rule of Added Value SHOULD be taken care of at a business or GDD level. However, even after this rule is taken into consideration, you still need to make "DIY vs. Re-Use" decisions for those things that don't constitute the added-value-for-end-users (or at least are not perceived as constituting the added value at first glance). In this regard, usually it more or less boils down to one of the three approaches described below.

---

14   A.K.A. Unique Selling Proposition, a.k.a. Unique Value Proposition (UVP).

15   While sometimes "pure luck" qualifies as a distinguishing factor, it is not something you can count on.

16   This, however, includes such things as "CRM system that allows to provide better support," etc.

The biggest problem with building your game around a 3rd-party game engine is that, in this case, the game engine becomes your Absolute Dependency.

ENGINE-CENTRIC APPROACH: GAME ENGINE AS AN INHERENT VENDOR LOCK-IN

Probably the most common approach to indie game development is to pick a 3rd-party game engine and build your game around that engine. Such game engines usually don't implement all the gameplay (instead, they provide you with a way to implement your own gameplay on top of the engine), so you're fine from the Added Value point of view. For the sake of brevity, let's refer to this "3rd-party engine will do everything for us" approach as a much shorter "Engine-Centric" Approach.

The biggest problem with building your game around a 3rd-party game engine is that, in this case, the game engine becomes your Absolute Dependency, a.k.a. Vendor Lock-In; in other words, it means that "if the engine is discontinued, we won't be able to add new features, which will lead us to close sooner rather than later."

While by itself Vendor Lock-In is not a showstopper for building your game around a 3rd-party game engine (and, indeed, there are many cases when you should do just that), you certainly need to understand the implications of this Absolute Dependency before deciding to go for it. In particular, make sure to read the *Dependencies and Vendor Lock-Ins* section above.

Engine-Centric Approach: Pretty Much Inevitable for Indie RPG/FPS games

This subsection mostly applies to indie game developers; AAA guys and gals, feel free to skip it.

NB: this subsection mostly applies to indie game developers; AAA guys and gals, feel free to skip it .

In spite of the inherent risks of having such a Vendor Lock-In on your game engine, it should be noted that there are several MOG genres where developing a game engine yourself is rarely feasible for an indie developer. In particular, this applies to Role-Player Games (RPGs) and First-Person Shooters (FPS); more generally, it applies to most of the games that implement a 1st-person view in a simulated 3D world. The engines for these games tend to be extremely complicated, and it will normally take much-more-time-than-you-have to develop them.

Fortunately, in this field there are quite a few very decent engines with reasonably good APIs separating the engine itself from your game logic. In particular, in Chapter 7, we'll discuss Unity 5, Unreal Engine 4, Amazon Lumberyard, and Urho3D — as well as their respective pros and cons, in the context of MOG development.[17]

For Real-Time Strategies (RTS), the situation is much less obvious; depending on the specifics of your game, you may have more options. For example,

(a) You may want to use a 3rd-party 3D engine like one of the above (though this will work only for games with a low-by-RTS-standards number of units, so you need to study very carefully the engine's capabilities in this regard).

(b) You may use 2D graphics (or pre-rendered 3D; see Chapter 6 for further discussion), with your own engine.

(c) You may want to develop your own 3D engine (optimized for large crowds but without features that are not necessary for you), or:

(d) You may even make a game that runs as 2D on some devices, and as 3D on other devices (see Chapter 6 for further discussion of dual 2D/3D interfaces).

For all the other genres, whether to use a 3rd-party engine for your indie game is a completely open question, and you will need to decide what is better for your game; for non-RPG/non-FPS games, and if your game is intended to have an Undefined Life Span, it is often better to develop a game engine yourself than to re-use a 3rd-party game engine; on the other hand, even when you have your own game engine, you still may use a 3rd-party 3D rendering engine, or even several such 3D engines (see the discussion in Chapter 6 for further details). Note that I'm still not arguing to DIY *everything*, but rather to develop your own *game engine* (specialized for your own *game logic*), while re-using a rendering engine (especially if it is a 3D rendering engine).

Even when you have your own game engine, you still may use a 3rd-party 3D rendering engine

And if you're going to re-use a 3rd-party game engine (for whatever reason), make sure to read and follow the *Engine-Centric Approach: You Still Need to Understand How It Works* section directly below.

---

17   My apologies to fans of other game engines, but I simply cannot cover all engines in existence.

Engine-Centric Approach: You Still Need to Understand How It Works

When introducing a 3rd-party game engine as an Absolute Dependency, a.k.a. Vendor Lock-In, you still need to understand how the engine works under the hood. Moreover, you need to know a lot about the engine-you're-about-to-choose before you make a decision to allow the engine Vendor to Lock-you-In. Otherwise, six months down the road, you can easily end up in a situation of "Oh, this engine apparently cannot implement this feature, and we absolutely need it, so we need to scrap everything and start from scratch using different game engine." <Bummer />

One thing you should never do when developing anything-more-complicated-than-two-player-tic-tac-toe is blindly believe that the game-engine-of-your-choice will be a perfect fit to your specific game. Even when the game engine is used by dozens of highly successful games, there is no guarantee that it will work for your specific requirements (unless, of course, you're making a 100% clone of an existing successful game). Instead of assuming "The Engine Will Do Everything Exactly As We Want It," you should try to understand all the relevant implications of the engine-you're-about-to-choose, and see if its limitations and peculiarities will affect you badly down the road.

Of course, there will be tons of implementation details that you're not able to know right now. On the other hand, you should at least go through this book to see how what-you-will-need maps onto what-your-engine-can-provide, aiming to:

♦ Understand what exactly the features you need are.

♦ Make sure that your engine of choice provides these features.

♦ Determine if some of the features you need are not provided by your game engine (which is almost certain for an MOG); you should at least know that you can implement those "missing" features yourself on top of your game engine.

While this may look time-consuming, it will certainly save a lot of time down the road. While introducing Absolute Dependency/Vendor Lock-In may be the right thing to do for you, this is a *very significant decision* and, as such, it MUST NOT be taken lightly.

One thing you should never do when developing anything-more-complicated-than-two-player-tic-tac-toe is blindly believe that the game-engine-of-your-choice will be a perfect fit for your specific game.

Engine-Centric Approach: On "Temporary" Dependencies

> Nothing is so permanent as a temporary government program.
>
> — Milton Friedman

If you want to use a 3rd-party game engine to speed up development, and count on the approach of "we'll use this game engine for now, and when we're big and rich, we will rewrite it ourselves," you need to realize that removing such a big and fat dependency as a game engine is usually not realistic. Eliminating dependency on a 2D engine, sound engine, even a 3D graphics/rendering engine may be possible (though will certainly require extreme vigilance during development; see the *Vigilance, and More Vigilance* section above), yet eliminating dependency on your game engine is usually pretty much hopeless without rewriting the whole thing.

Eliminating dependency on your game engine is pretty much hopeless without rewriting the whole thing.

The latter observation is related to the number and nature of dependencies that arise when we integrate our game with our game engine. If we consider a lightweight non-game-engine library such as, say, Berkeley sockets, it introduces only a few dependencies (and very simple ones at that). A 2D graphics-only engine introduces dozens of medium-complexity dependencies — which is worse, but can still be handled. However, for a typical game engine, we'll have *hundreds* of dependencies — including lots of very elaborate ones, making proper isolation of a game engine pretty much hopeless.

Moreover, for a game engine, these dependencies tend to have very different natures (ranging from mesh file formats to API callbacks, with pretty much everything else you can think of in-between). Among other things, this variety often defeats good ol' Isolation Layer techniques. As one example, isolating a mesh file that is accessed directly from the game engine (and which the game engine internals heavily depend on) is rarely feasible. And if we're talking about scripting language or VMs, which are usually embedded within the game engine, they are usually next-to-impossible to isolate.[18]

---

18   More than that, rewriting scripting language to keep it 100% compatible is very rarely feasible, as the number of peculiarities of such things is usually enormous, and for each peculiarity you can count on some of your scripts using this peculiarity somewhere (often without anybody in the whole team realizing such a dependency-on-peculiarity even exists).

To make things even worse, the better the game engine you're using, the more perfectly legitimate uses you have for those dependencies, and the more Locked-In you become as a result (all while having only Good Reasons™ for doing it).

Due to these factors, IMNSHO, the task of making your Game Logic game-engine-agnostic is by orders of magnitude more complicated than making your program cross-platform (which is also quite an effort to start with), so think more than twice before attempting it.

On the other hand, isolating just your *rendering engine* (and not the whole *game engine*), while still being very cumbersome, has significantly better chances of flying; while for 3D rendering engines, meshes and associated file formats are still going to be a Big Headache™ (and in extreme cases, you may even end up using different 3D models for different 3D rendering engines), at least scripting and logic won't cause you any trouble. As a rule of thumb, if trying to isolate a graphics engine, implementation should go along the lines of the Isolation Layer, as discussed in the *Isolating Arbitrary Libraries. Isolation APIs in terms of App* section above, which, for a graphics engine, effectively translates into implementing a Logic-2-Graphics Layer, as discussed in Chapter 6.

"RE-USE EVERYTHING IN SIGHT" APPROACH: AN INTEGRATION NIGHTMARE

When your code does nothing beyond dealing with peculiarities and outright bugs of 3rd-party libraries, it cannot possibly be anything but spaghetti.

If you've decided not to make a 3rd-party engine your Absolute Dependency, then the second approach often comes into play. Roughly, it can be described as "we need such-and-such a feature, so what is the 3rd-party component/library/... we want to borrow and re-use to implement this feature?"

Unfortunately, way too many developers out there think that this is exactly the way software should be developed. (Mis-)Perception along the lines of "hey, re-use is good, so there can be nothing wrong with re-use" is IMO way too popular with developers; for managers, it is the "re-use saves on the development time" argument which usually hits home.

However, in practice, it is not that simple. Such "re-use everything in sight" projects more often than not become an integration nightmare. As one of the developers of such a project (the one who was responsible for writing an installer) has put it: "Our product is a load of s**t, and my job is to carry it in my hands to the end-user PC, without spilling it around." As you can see, he wasn't too fond of the product (and the product didn't work too reliably either, so the whole product line was closed within a year or two).

Even worse, such "re-use everything in sight" projects were observed to become spaghetti code very quickly; moreover, in my experience, when your code does nothing beyond dealing with peculiarities and outright bugs of 3rd-party libraries, it cannot possibly be anything but spaghetti. Oh, and keep in mind that indiscriminate re-use has been observed as a source of some of the worst software bugs in development history; see, for example, [Hare] for details.

The problem with trying to reuse-everything-you-can-get-your-hands-on can be explained as follows. With such an indiscriminate re-use, some[19] of the modules or components you are using will inevitably be less-than-ideal for the job; moreover, even if the component is good enough now, it may become much-less-than-ideal when[20] your GDD changes. And then, given that the number of your not-so-ideal components is large enough, you will find yourself in an endless loop of "hey, trying to do this with Component A has broken something else with Component B, and fixing it in Component B has had such-and-such an undesired consequence in Component C," with "how to avoid robbing Peter to pay Paul" chases quickly becoming *modus operandi* for your developers.

To make sure that managers also understand the perils of indiscriminate re-use: you (as a manager) need to keep in mind that indiscriminate re-use very frequently leads to "Oh, we cannot implement this incoming marketing or monetization requirement because our 3rd-party component doesn't support such-and-such a feature"; and if such things happen more than a few times over the lifespan of the project, it tends to have a rather significant negative impact on the bot-

modus operandi

a distinct pattern or method of operation esp. that indicates or suggests the work of a single criminal in more than one crime

—**Wikipedia**

Oh, we cannot implement this incoming marketing or monetization requirement because our 3rd-party component doesn't support such-and-such a feature.

---

19   In practice, it will be like "most."

20   It is indeed 'when' and not 'if'! See Vol. I's chapter on GDD.

tom line of the company. Or describing the same thing from a slightly different perspective: <ceo-only information: to be kept secret from developers>*If your developers are implementing their own component, it is they who are responsible for this "we cannot implement marketing/ monetization requirement" scenario never happening; at the moment when you force (or allow) them to "use such-and-such library," you give them this excuse on a plate*</ceo-only information: to be kept secret from developers>.

One additional Bad Thing™ that usually arises from indiscriminate re-use is an increase in ongoing maintenance costs (which is especially bad for those Games with Undefined Life Spans). Complicated and not-too-well-defined dependencies, such as game engines, are known for changing things that break backward compatibility (especially if you got overly creative in the ways you're using them, which is usually exactly what happens in real-world development). As soon as you've found yourself in such a position, you basically have two options: (a) try to keep up with the changes, or (b) freeze everything (as freezing "just this one thing" is rarely a viable option due to interdependencies). If you have too many dependencies, neither of these options will really work: with (a), you'll spend most of your time just trying to keep up with changes of all those libraries you're re-using, instead of developing yourself, and with (b), you'll start to lag behind all those new features, which were the reason to use a 3rd-party library/engine in the first place (and while "freeze" may be fine for a single-player game released and sold once, for an MOG with an Undefined Life Span, it is rarely acceptable).

BTW, to make it perfectly clear: I'm not arguing that *any* re-use is evil; it is only *indiscriminate* re-use that should be avoided. What I am arguing for is the "Responsible Re-use" approach described shortly.

"DIY EVERYTHING": THE RISK OF A NEVER-ENDING STORY

Another approach (the one that I am admittedly prone to using <sad-face />) is to write *everything* yourself. Okay, very few developers will write the OS themselves,[21] but for most of the other things, you can usually find somebody who will argue that "this is the most important thing in the universe, and you simply MUST do it *exactly* this way, and, as there is nothing that does it exactly this way, we MUST do it ourselves."

There are people out there who argue for rewriting TCP over UDP[22,23]; there are people out there arguing that TLS is not good enough, so you need to use your own security protocol; there are people out there arguing for writing crypto-quality RNG based on their own algorithm[24]; there are also quite a few people out there writing their own in-memory databases for your game; and there are even more people out there arguing for writing your own 3D engine.

There are people out there arguing for writing crypto-quality RNG using their own algorithm.

Moreover, depending on your circumstances, writing *some* of these things yourself may even make sense;

> however, writing **all** of these things together yourself will lead to a product that will almost inevitably never be released.

As a result, with all of my dislike of 3rd-party dependencies, I will admit that we *do* need to re-use *something*. So, an obvious next question is: "What exactly should we re-use, and what should we write ourselves?"

---

21   Not even me.

22   I will admit that I was guilty of such a suggestion myself for one project, though it happened at a later stage of game development, which I'm humbly asking for you to consider a mitigating circumstance.

23   BTW, writing your own protocol on top of UDP (though usually *not* attempting to make "better TCP") is often necessary for fast-paced games; this will be discussed in Volume IV.

24   Once it took me several months of trying to convince an external auditor that implementing RNG "his way" was not the only "right" way to implement crypto-RNG, with the conflict eventually elevated to The Top Authority on Cryptography (specifically, to Bruce Schneier); it is probably worth noting that the auditor guy remained unconvinced (though he was overridden by his own management. <Phew! />).

"RESPONSIBLE RE-USE" APPROACH: IN SEARCH OF BALANCE

As discussed above (convincingly enough, I hope), there are things that you should re-use, and there are things you shouldn't. The key, of course, is related to the question of "What to Re-use and What to DIY?" While the answer enters the realm of art (or black magic, if you prefer), and largely follows from the experience, there are still a few hints that may help you in making such a decision:

Decisions about re-use MUST NOT be taken lightly.

♦ Most importantly, decisions about re-use MUST NOT be taken lightly; it means that no clandestine re-use should be allowed, and that all re-use decisions MUST be approved by the project architect (or by consensus of senior-enough developers).

♦ Discussion of "to re-use or not to re-use" MUST be made on a case-by-case basis, and MUST include *both* issues related to licensing *and* to reuse-being-a-good-thing-in-the-long-run (you can be pretty sure that arguments related to short-run benefits are already brought forward by the developer-pushing-re-use-of-this-specific-library).

◆ To decide whether a specific re-use will be a good-thing-in-the-long-run, the following hints may help:

- ▪ "Glue" code almost universally SHOULD be DIY code; while it is unlikely that you will have any doubts about it, for the sake of completeness I'm still mentioning it here.

- ▪ If writing your own code will provide some Added Value (which is visible in the player terms), it is a really good candidate for DIY. And even if it doesn't touch gameplay, it can still provide Added Value.

  - • One example: if your own communication library will provide properties that lead to better user-observable connectivity (better="better than the one currently used by competition"), it does provide Added Value (or a competitive advantage, if you prefer), and therefore may easily qualify for DIY. Of course, development costs still need to be taken into account, but at least the idea shouldn't be thrown away without consideration.

  - • In another practical example, if you're considering re-using Windows dialogs (or MFC) and, as a DIY alternative, your own library provides a way to implement i18n without the need for translators to edit graphics (!) for each-and-every dialog in existence, it normally qualifies as an "Added Value" (at least compared to MFC).

- ▪ If you're about to re-use something with a very well defined interface (API/messages/etc.), and where the interface does whatever-you-want and is not likely to change significantly in the future, it is a really good candidate for re-use. Examples include TLS, JPEG/PNG libraries, TCP, and so on.

- ▪ If you're about to re-use something that has much more non-trivial logic inside than it exposes APIs outside, it might be a good candidate for re-use.

  - • One such example is 3D engines (unless you're sure you can make them significantly better than existing ones; see the item on Added Value above).

However, when re-using 3D engines, it is usually a good idea to have your own Isolation Layer around them in order to avoid them becoming an Absolute Dependency. Such an Isolation Layer should usually be written in a manner described in the *Weakening/ Isolating Dependencies* section above (and as described there, dependencies are sneaky, so you need to be vigilant to avoid them).

- If you're about to re-use something for the Client-Side (or for the non-controlled environment in general), and it uses a DLL-residing-in-system-folder (i.e., even if it is a part of your installer, or is installed in a place that is well-known and can be overwritten by some other installer), double-check that you cannot make this DLL/component private[25] — otherwise, seriously consider DIY. This also applies to re-use of components, including Windows-provided components.

  - The reason for this rather unusual (but still very important in practice) recommendation is the following: it has been observed for real-world-apps-with-an-install-base-in-the-millions that reliance on something-that-you-don't-really-control introduces a pretty nasty dependency, with such dependencies failing for some (though usually small) percentage of your players. If you have 10 such dependencies, each of which fails for a mere 1% of your users, you're losing about $1-(0.99^{10})\sim=9\%$ of your player base (plus, people will complain about your game not working, increasing your actual losses n-fold). Real-world horror stories in this regard include such things as:

    - The program that used IE to render not-really-necessary animation, failing with one specific version of IE on player's computer.
    - Some Win32 function (the one that isn't really necessary and is therefore rarely used) was

---

25   Roughly equivalent to "moving it to your own folder."

used just to avoid parsing .BMP file, only to be found failing on a certain brand of laptops due to faulty video drivers.[26]

· Some [censored] developer of a 4th-party app replaced stock mfc42.dll with their own "improved" version, causing quite a few applications to fail (okay, doing this has become more difficult starting with Vista or so, but it is still possible if they're persistent enough).

• BTW, don't think that such failures "are not your problem"— from the end-user perspective, it is *your* program that crashes, so it is *you* they will blame for the crash. In general, the less dependencies-on-specific-PC-configuration your Client has, the better experience you will be able to provide for your players, and all the theoretical considerations of "oh, having a separate DLL of 1M in size will eat as much as 1M on HDD and about the same size of RAM while our app is running" are really insignificant compared to your players a having better experience, especially for modern PCs with ~1T of HDD and 1G+ of RAM.

• Keep in mind that "re-use via DLLs" on the Client-Side introduces well-defined points that are widely (ab)used by cheaters (such as bot writers); this is one more reason to avoid re-using DLLs and COM components (even if they're private). This also applies to using standard Windows controls (which are very easy to extract information from, which in turn enables at least grinding bots). See Volume VIII's chapter on Bot Fighting for further discussion of these issues. BTW, re-use via statically linked libraries is usually not affected by this problem.[27]

Don't think that such failures "are not your problem"— from the end-user perspective, it is your program that crashes, so it is *you* they will blame for the crash.

---

26   Why such a purely-format-parsing function has had anything to do with drivers is anybody's guess.

27   Strictly speaking, statically linked well-known libraries can also make the life of a cheater a bit easier (in particular, via F.L.I.R.T. engine of IDA debugger), but this effect is usually relatively mild compared to that big hole you're punching in your own code when using DLLs.

- If nothing of the above applies, and you're about to write yourself something that is central and critical to your game, it may be a good candidate for DIY. The more critical and central the part of your code is, the more likely related changes will be required, leading to more and more integration work, which can easily lead to the cost of integration exceeding the value provided by the borrowed code. About the same thing can be observed from a different angle: for the central and critical code, you generally want to have as much control as you possibly can.

- If nothing of the above applies, and you're about to re-use something that is of limited value (or is barely connected) to your game, it may be a good candidate for re-use. The more peripheral the part of the code is, the less likely it is that related changes will have a drastic effect on the rest of your code, so costs of the re-integration with the rest of your code in the case of changes will hopefully be relatively small.

- Personally, when in doubt, I usually prefer to DIY, and it happens to work pretty well with the developers I usually have on my team. However, I realize that I usually work with developers who qualify as "really, really good ones" (I'm sure that most of them are at least within top-1%), so once again, your mileage may vary. On the other hand, if for some functionality all the considerations above are already taken into account and you're still in doubt (while being able to keep a straight face) on the "DIY vs. re-use" question, this specific decision on this specific functionality probably doesn't really matter *that* much.

Personally, when in doubt, I usually prefer to DIY.

Note that as with most of the other generic advice, all the above advice should be taken with a good pinch of salt. Your specific case and line of argument may be very different; what is most important is to avoid making decisions without thinking, and to at least take the considerations listed above into account; if after thoroughly thinking it over, you decide that all the above is irrelevant to your game, so be it.

"Responsible Re-Use" Examples

Here are some examples of what-to-reuse and what-not-to-reuse (though YMMV really significantly) under the "Responsible Re-Use" guidelines:

♦ **OS/Console**: usually don't really have a choice about it. Re-use (and isolate your platform-specific code if cross-platform might be necessary in the future).

♦ **Game Engine:** depends on genre, but for RPG/FPS re-use is pretty much inevitable for indie development (see the *Engine-Centric Approach: Pretty Much Inevitable for Indie RPG/FPS* section above). If re-using the whole Game Engine, most likely you won't be able to avoid it becoming your Absolute Dependency, so unfortunately isolation isn't likely to help.

♦ **TCP/TLS/JPEG/PNG/etc.**: these libraries are very well-defined, very small, and easy to integrate. Usually it is a Really Good Idea™ to re-use them. Note that on the Client-Side it is much better to re-use them (and pretty much everything else) using static libraries rather than using DLLs, due to the reasons outlined above.

♦ **3D Engine**: 3D engines are good candidates for re-use (mostly because DIY is beyond the capabilities of most indie teams out there), but they will try really hard to lock you in. However, given enough effort and vigilance, you MIGHT be able to avoid being Locked-In; to keep your chances in this regard, you'll almost certainly need to isolate your 3D engine (for the specifics of implementing an Isolation Layer for graphics, see discussion on Logic-to-Graphics layer in Chapter 6).

♦ **2D Engine**: usually 2D engines are not *that* difficult to implement even for indie teams (see also Volume V's chapter on Graphics 101), which often means that depending on your specifics, there might be a realistic choice between DIY your own 2D engine and re-using (again, make sure to isolate it if re-using).

♦ **HTML rendering:** you will likely need something along these lines for i18n dialogs, and you will in turn likely need them for monetization etc. See the discussion on it in Chapter 6; examples include embedded *WebKit* or *wxHTML*. As a rule of thumb, these are very

If re-using Game Engine, most likely you won't be able to avoid it becoming your Absolute Dependency, so unfortunately isolation isn't likely to help.

bulky for DIY, and it is a Good Idea™ to re-use them (once again, make sure to isolate them via an app-oriented Isolation API).

- While you're at it — let's note that as a rule of thumb it is better to stay away from system-specific HTML controls (such as Windows/IE HTML Control). These are changing way too often, have been observed to depend heavily on the specific version which happens to be installed on the Client box, by design behave differently on different platforms, and so on.

- Keep in mind that at a certain point, you MAY need to re-write certain game-critical elements from standard UI into DIY to deal with bots. More on this in Volume VIII's chapter on Bot Fighting, but the overall logic goes as follows: in the realm of bot-fighting, we often need to obfuscate things, and using standard stuff rarely allows for necessary obfuscation. On the other hand, usually this can be changed later without rewriting the whole thing, so you *may* be able to ignore this issue for the time being (replacing standard stuff with DIY when bots start to become a problem).

At a certain point, you MAY need to rewrite certain game-critical elements from standard UI into DIY to deal with bots.

- ◆ **Core logic of your game**. This is where your Added Value is. As a Big Fat Rule of Thumb™, DIY.
- ◆ **Something that is very peripheral to your game**. This is what is not likely to cause too much havoc to replace. As a rule-of-thumb, re-use (as long as you can be sure what exactly you're re-using on the Client-Side; see above about DLLs, etc.). And, as another rule-of-thumb, isolate these peripheral pieces too.

"Responsible Re-Use": on "Temporary" Dependencies

If you're planning to use some module/library only temporarily (to speed up the first release), and re-write it later "when we're big and rich," it *might* work, but you need to be aware of several major caveats along the way. First, you need to realize that this "use temporary, rewrite later" approach, as a rule of thumb, won't work for replacing the whole game engine (see the *Engine-Centric Approach: On "Temporary" Dependencies* section above).

Second, for those-modules-you-want-to-remove-later, you certainly need to use the Isolation Layer from the very beginning — and with a proper Isolation API too (see the discussion in the *Working Cross-Plat-form: Isolation Layer* section above).

And, last but not least, you need to be *extremely vigilant* when writing your code, to avoid bypassing your Isolation Layer. Otherwise, when the "we're big and rich" part comes, the 3rd-party module/library/engine will become *that much* intertwined with the rest of your code that separating it will amount to rewriting everything from scratch (which is rarely an option for an up-and-running MOG). See the *Vigilance, and More Vigilance* section above for further discussion.

CHAPTER 4 SUMMARY

Our takeouts from Chapter 4:

♦ DON'T take the "DIY vs. Re-Use" question lightly; if you make Really Bad decisions in this regard, it can easily kill your game down the road.

♦ If you're an indie shop, DO consider using an Engine-Centric approach, but keep in mind that Absolute Dependency (a.k.a. Vendor Lock-In) that you're introducing. Be especially cautious when using this way for Games with Undefined Life Spans (as defined in Vol. I's chapter on GDD). On the other hand, Engine-Centric approach is pretty much inevitable for indie FPS/RPG games. If going Engine-Centric, make sure that you understand how the engine of your choosing implements those things you need.

♦ If Engine-Centric doesn't work for you (for example, because there is no engine available that allows you to satisfy all your GDD Requirements), you generally should use "Responsible Re-use" as described above. If going this way, make sure to read the list of hints listed in the *"Responsible Re-Use" Approach: In Search of Balance* section above.

  ▪ In particular, make sure to implement an Isolation Layer (with an Isolation API expressed in terms of app layer) wherever applicable. And make sure to be vigilant when enforcing your isolation (see the *Vigilance, and More Vigilance* section for discussion).

Bibliography

Hare, 'No Bugs'. 2011. *"Overused Code Reuse."* Overload. http://ithare.com/overused-code-reuse/.

CHAPTER 5.
(RE)ACTOR-FEST ARCHITECTURE. IT JUST WORKS.

We have this handy fusion reactor in the sky called the sun,
you don't have to do anything, it just works. It shows up every day.

— Elon Musk

Now, after we discussed DIY-vs.-re-use, we can proceed to the very heart of the discussion on architecture for multiplayer games.

Of course, there is more than one way to shoe this architectural horse. However, there is one way of architecting your system that I *strongly* prefer to all others;[28] moreover, it can be made very reliable (=“it just works”), it works very well for games, and is very familiar to gamedevs too. I’m talking about Game Loop, a.k.a. Event-Driven Program, a.k.a. (Re)Actor.

TO REACT OR NOT TO REACT? THAT IS (ALMOST) NO QUESTION

Reactor Pattern

The reactor design pattern is an event handling pattern for handling service requests delivered concurrently to a service handler by one or more inputs. The service handler then demultiplexes the incoming requests and dispatches them synchronously to the associated request handlers.

—Wikipedia

I have to admit that I am a big fan of Reactors. During my career, I’ve seen (and built) quite a few Reactor-based systems — and all of them[29] worked like a charm. One such system was a game competing on a pretty crowded market and serving hundreds of thousands of simultaneous players, and there were two relevant stories about it:

♦ Once upon a time, a pre-IPO auditor said about it: “Hey guys, your system has downtimes that are several times lower than the rest of the industry!”[30]

♦ At one point, I got the chance to look at the system built by the competitor. While the systems had pretty much identical functionality, the Reactor-based one was using fifty Server Boxes to handle 400K simultaneous players, while the competition was using 400 Server Boxes to handle around 100K simultaneous players. It means that the Reactor-based system was able to handle up to 32x more players per Server Box than the competition.

Of course, these stories count only as *anecdotal evidence*, and, of course, Reactors weren’t *the only* cause for these properties, but IMNSHO they still illustrate two all-important properties of Reactor-based systems: (a) they’re very reliable; and (b) they perform very well.

---

28   At least for *stateful interactive* systems, and the vast majority of games out there qualify as such.

29   Well, at least those that are worth mentioning.

30   For the full story, see Volume III’s chapter on Server-Side Architecture, but for the time being, even the first part of it will do.

More generally, I see Reactor-based systems (more specifically, systems based on non-blocking deterministic Reactors) as a very good tool for implementing stateful interactive systems (games included) from the following points of view:

♦ **Very clean separation between different parts of the system.** As Reactors are not allowed to interact with one another, besides exchanging messages (and these messages/RPC-calls cannot also contain messy stuff such as pointers to other-Reactor-space, etc.), clean separation is pretty much enforced. In turn, such a clean separation helps a damn lot as your system grows larger.

As Reactors are not allowed to interact with one another besides exchanging messages, clean separation is pretty much enforced.

♦ **Very reliable programs** (="It Just Works"). As Reactors are inherently protected from impossible-to-debug and inherently untestable inter-thread races, it helps *a lot* to make the system more reliable.

  ▪ In addition, an ability to find and fix problems in production (and ideally, after one single failure) is a very important part of making such distributed systems reliable. Deterministic Reactors tend to fare extremely well from this point of view too.

♦ **Very good performance in production** too. Besides the story above, there is a reason why nginx tends to perform better than Apache — and this is pretty much the same reason why share-pretty-much-nothing Reactors also perform very well. In short, thread context switches are expensive, and moving data between CPUs (which is often caused by such context switches) is even more expensive; if we account for cache invalidation, the cost of the thread context switch can easily reach 100K to 1M CPU clock cycles; see [Li, Ding, and Shen]. As a result, non-blocking Reactors, which tend to avoid most of such unnecessary jerking around, have an obvious edge. And with modern x64 CPUs spending up to 300 CPU cycles on an uncached "remote" memory read compared to 3 CPU cycles on an L1 memory read, this 100x difference means that the edge of Reactor-based programs can be quite substantial.[31]

Contrary to popular (mis)belief, Reactor-based systems DO scale, and scale well.

♦ **Very good scalability**. Contrary to popular (mis)belief, Reactor-based systems *do* scale, and scale well. Of course, we will need

---

31 NB: 300 CPU cycles and 100x numbers are for "remote NUMA node" accesses; without NUMA in the picture, the difference is more like 30–50x, which is also not too shabby.

multiple Reactors to build a scalable Reactor-based system — but this is exactly what (Re)Actor-fest architecture (the one we're discussing in this chapter) is about. Very shortly:

- For the Server-Side, as soon as we can split our Server-Side into Reactors-fitting-onto-one-single-core, we'll be perfectly fine; and as soon as splitting our Game Logic is on the agenda, it usually doesn't matter too much if we're splitting into Server-size chunks or core-size chunks (see also the discussion on splitting of seamless Game Worlds in Volume I's chapter on Communications).

- Scaling the Reactor-based Client-Side can be somewhat more complicated (in particular because of the large monolithic Client-Side State, which needs to be processed). However, certain variations (discussed in the *(Kinda-)Scaling Individual (Re)Actors* section) are known to be used by AAA gamedevs with great success (see also directly below).

BTW, Reactors are also actively used by major game development companies; from what can be said based on publicly available information, Bungie, in particular, seems to be a big fan of deterministic Reactors (see, for example, [Aldridge] and [Tatarchuk]), and very successfully so. Also, Riot Games rely on determinism too (and while they *do* use threads — from their description in [Hoskinson] it *seems* that they're using a relatively minor variation of the Reactors/Game Loops, with inter-thread interactions being very limited and well-defined).

"Almost" Before "No Question"

In spite of my love for Reactors, I have to admit that

If you're very averse to the very idea of Reactors, you can build distributed interactive system without them.

Or, in other words:

Strictly speaking, Reactors are optional —
*Though, IMNSHO, they are **extremely nice** to use.*

Most likely, if dropping Reactors, you'll still want to keep canonical Game Loop/Simulation Loop for your game (and, most likely, it will apply both to your Client and to your Server), but other than that, you can do pretty much whatever-you-want (see the *Reactors or Not — Stay Away from Thread Sync in your Game Logic* section below, though). I am still saying that you SHOULD use Reactors, but am stopping short of saying that you MUST use them.

I am still saying that you SHOULD use Reactors, but am stopping short of saying that you MUST use them.

As a result, for the rest of this book beyond this chapter, I will try to describe each of the Reactor-related topics from two different points of view. First, I will try to explain things in a generic way, without referring to Reactors, and then I will often discuss more specific Reactor-based implementation of the same thing. If you *really* hate Reactors, feel free to ignore the Reactor-based stuff; still, the generic discussion will usually stand, regardless of Reactors.

Reactors or Not — Stay Away from Thread Sync in your Game Logic

The last but not least observation in this regard. Whether you're using Reactors or not, I *strongly* insist that —

> *Using thread synchronization such as mutexes and atomics directly within your app-level code is a recipe for disaster.*

There are several reasons why it is a Really Bad Idea™. I don't want to go into a lengthy discussion here, but will just note that using thread sync within your app-level (Game Logic) code will almost-inevitably result in:

♦ Having way too many things to care about at the same time, essentially pushing developers well beyond the "magic number" of 7±2, which is the cognitive limit of the human brain (and is therefore extremely difficult to bypass). For more discussion of this phenomenon, see, for example, [Hare, Multi-Threading at the Business-Logic Level is Considered Harmful].

♦ Introducing *lots* of potential for inter-thread race conditions. And the worst thing about race conditions is that they're perfectly untestable, which means that they can sit silently for years. Just to illustrate how sneaky these bugs can be: one multi-threaded race

The Magical Number Seven, Plus or Minus Two

is one of the most highly cited papers in psychology. It is often interpreted to argue that the number of objects an average human can hold in working memory is 7 ± 2. This is frequently referred to as Miller's Law.

—Wikipedia

was found sitting for years in no less than STL implementation provided by a major C++ compiler [Ignatchenko, STL Implementations and Thread Safety].

- Moreover, such sleeping races tend to manifest themselves only under serious load (with the chance of them manifesting growing in a highly non-linear manner compared to the load), which means that they will hit you *exactly* at the very worst possible moment (for example, during Tournament of the Year or something).

- To make things even worse, whenever you're facing the race in production, there is no reliable way of handling it (except for reviewing all the relevant code, which is usually way too overwhelming). You cannot even reproduce the race, which makes all the traditional debugging techniques perfectly useless (in contrast, with deterministic Reactors, all the bugs are reproducible by definition).

♦ Mutexes (critical sections, etc.) mean the potential for blocks, which in turn means the potential for degradations both of performance and scalability.

- And just as with races, these degradations will sit quietly for a while, starting to manifest themselves only at the worst possible moment. Very shortly, as contention on mutex grows, performance and scalability quickly go out the window (and in a highly-non-linear manner).

- Also, as noted in [Henney], let's keep in mind that contrary to popular misconception, mutex is not really a concurrency mechanism; instead, the whole point of mutex is actually to *prevent* concurrency.

A few further things to note here:

♦ Even "one single mutex" visible from app-level is a Very Bad Thing™

I wrote a framework that was avoiding thread sync, except for one small callback that was called from a different thread and required access to the object state.

- A real-world story in this regard. Once upon a time, I wrote a framework that managed to avoid thread sync, except for one small callback that was called from a different thread and required access to the object state (it was effectively implementing what-was-later-named-a-Proactor-pattern, and in my back-then implementation the callback was called from an arbitrary thread). The rules governing thread sync from this small callback were very obvious to me, but were apparently very difficult to grasp for *all* the app-level programmers; overall, this small callback was responsible for *that* many bugs that it became the prime suspect whenever a bug was noticed. <ouch! /> As a mitigating factor for my sentencing, I want to say that I learned my lesson, and have avoided such callbacks-from-a-different-thread ever since.

♦ Avoiding explicit thread sync within your stateful Game Logic doesn't necessarily mean that you MUST always access the state from only one single thread (though accessing from one single thread will certainly do the trick). In general, you MAY access the state of your Game Logic from different threads,[32] but then it MUST be the job of the Infrastructure Code to perform locks *before* the control is passed to Game Logic. For more discussion on the separation between Infrastructure Code and Logic code, see the *On Separating Infrastructure Code from Logic Code* section below.

♦ Reactors are not the only way to avoid thread sync. In particular, other-than-Reactors message passing mechanisms normally do it too.

♦ The firm "no thread sync" rule above applies only to Game and Business Logic; you still *can* write infrastructure-level code using mutexes.[33] While I still *often* argue for avoiding thread-sync-beyond-queues and for using Reactors for Infrastructure Code too, I admit that using mutexes for Infrastructure Code is not too bad (and sometimes can be justified). In other words: if your primary concern with avoiding explicit thread sync is about infrastructure-level code, go ahead and use mutexes for your infrastructure — *as long as you avoid them for app-level code, such as Game Logic*. In quite a few cases (and especially if your game is successful), you'll migrate your infrastructure-level code into Reactors a bit later (I've done that myself); and BTW, it is Game Logic being clean from thread-sync that makes such later migration feasible.

Message passing

Message passing sends a message to a process (which may be an actor or object) and relies on the process and the supporting infrastructure to select and invoke the actual code to run.

—**Wikipedia**

---

32   At the cost of the potential for performance and scalability problems hitting you, but at least reliability and maintainability won't be affected.

33   Moreover, for some primitives such as Queues, you *will* almost certainly need explicit thread sync (such as mutexes, critical sections, condition variables, etc.).

♦ There MIGHT be cases when you DO need to use thread-sync at app level due to performance requirements; one particular example of it is so-called high-frequency trading (HFT). Still, keep in mind that (a) it is a *very* rare scenario, so for your usual gamedev you won't need it; (b) as it is all about nanosecond-level performance, and each context switch caused by contention on the mutex can cost you up to a millisecond(!) – you still shouldn't be using mutexes for HFT-like tasks. When talking about nanoseconds, we should at least be using non-blocking algorithms and atomics, but it is often necessary to go beyond that and exploit even-more-asynchronous-methods such as memory barriers and Read-Copy-Updates.

▪ BTW, if you happen to need heavy calculations – make sure to take a look at an asynchronous-and-mutex-free HPX. Not only that HPX usually outperforms synchronous stuff coming from dark ages of OpenMP, but in addition it can also be integrated nicely with Reactors (see also the *Offloading* section below).

ON TERMINOLOGY. ACTOR, REACTOR, EVENT-DRIVEN PROGRAM, GAME LOOP, OR AD-HOC FINITE STATE MACHINE? WE'LL NAME IT (RE)ACTOR.

There are only two hard things in Computer Science:
cache invalidation and naming things.

— Phil Karlton

With event-driven programming being known for so many years, related techniques have many different names — and with very similar (though sometimes not-exactly-identical) meanings.

Let's note that the model-we'll-be-talking-about is very close to a classical Reactor pattern (and to event-processing too); on the other hand, it exhibits certain properties of a more generic Actor model. In some sense, our Reactors are quite an "active" kind, and can initiate some actions that are not always expected from purely reactive processing; in particular, just like more generic Actors, our Reactors can send messages to other Reactors, can post timer events to themselves, can initiate non-blocking calls[34] and can request creation of other Reactors.

I like to think of these things as "Actors," but the term "Actor" is usually used in a very different sense among gamedevs,[35] and I certainly don't want to introduce this kind of confusion. As a result — after spending long sleepless nights meditating on this "how to name this event-driven thing" question — I came up with a term (Re)Actor, and this is what I'll be using in this chapter (and over the course of the remaining volumes).

Let's keep in mind that pretty much all of the following concepts are closely related to our (Re)Actors:

♦ Reactor (as in "Reactor pattern")

  ▪ Note that both "Reactive programming" and "Functional Reactive Prooogramming" are substantially different from "Reactor programming pattern."

  ▪ On the other hand, our (Re)Actor-fest Architecture is very close to the "Reactive Systems" as defined in The Reactive Manifesto ([Bonér, et al.]).[36]

♦ Actor (as in "Actor concurrency model")

♦ Event-driven program

♦ Game loop (or event loop)

♦ Finite State Machines (FSMs)

  ▪ Note, however, that when talking about FSMs, *usually* it is table-driven Finite State Machines that are implied, and these are quite different. What we're effectively doing with our (Re)Actors is defining a finite state machine in terms of

---

34 Which makes them somewhat similar to Proactors, though for our Reactors all app-level callbacks are guaranteed to be sync-free (and for generic Proactors, it depends).

35 See, for example, UE4 AActor.

36 Note that for the purpose of this book, I don't want to get into a terminological discussion of whether "event-driven" is different from "message-driven"; we'll be using these two terms interchangeably, with an understanding that both of them are concentrated on addressable recipients rather than addressable sources.

code rather than in terms of transition tables (such FSMs are known as *ad-hoc FSMs*). However, while these two representations are mathematically equivalent, they're quite different in practice. In particular, while table-driven FSMs work very well for embedded development (and other scenarios with only very few states involved), they start to fall apart very quickly as the number of states grows (due to so-called "state explosion"). For more discussion on FSMs and (Re)Actors, see the *Relation of Deterministic (Re)Actors to Deterministic Finite Automata* section below.

GAME LOOP: GAME PROGRAMMING CLASSIC

We'll start from the good old Game Loop, and will observe how just a few additional brush strokes will make it a (Re) Actor — usable for distributed programming and MOGs.

> Game loops are the quintessential example of a "game programming pattern"
>
> — Robert Nystrom in *Game Programming Patterns*

After giving our (Re)Actors a nice name, let's define how-they-are-supposed-to-work. As we're talking about games, we'll start from the good old Game Loop, and will observe how just a few additional brush strokes will make it a (Re)Actor — usable for distributed programming and MOGs.

Traditionally, most of the single-player games out there are based on a so-called Game Loop. Classical Game Loop looks more or less as follows (see, for example, [Nystrom, Game Loop]):

```
//Listing 5.GameLoop
while(true) {
  read_and_process_inputs();
  update();
  render();
}37
```

---

37   For the listings in this chapter, we'll use pseudo-code; this emphasizes an observation that most of the reasoning here will also apply to pretty much *any* modern programming language (with an obvious notion that continuation-style implementations will need support for lambdas, and some C++/C# specific trickery clearly labeled as such). In addition, some of the corresponding and not-so-trivial C++ listings can be found in Appendix 5.A.

This kind of Game Loop doesn't wait for input, but rather polls input devices and goes ahead regardless of the input being present[38]; let's name this a "simple tight Game Loop."

As discussed in detail in [Nystrom, Game Loop] and [Fiedler, Fix Your Timestep!]), in addition to the simple tight Game Loop above, quite a few different timestep schemas can be used:

♦ Fixed-timestep, with delay at the end if there is time left until the next tick (where "tick" can be either "network tick" or "monitor refresh tick"). This is the most popular timestep used on the Server-Side, and is widely used for V-Synced systems on the Client-Side.

♦ Variable-timestep tight loop. Basically, we're measuring how long the previous frame took, and using this measured time as a *next* timestep. However, as noted in both [Nystrom, Game Loop] and [Fiedler, Fix Your Timestep!], this kind of timestep can be quite fragile; in particular, updates being too long can easily make your simulation unstable (in terms of numerical analysis, it is a manifestation of a well-known effect that steps being too large can easily cause the numerical method to start diverging).

　　▪ To deal with this instability and divergence, multiple physics updates (with smaller — and usually fixed — timesteps for each) per one render can be made.

　　　　• This effectively leads to updates and renders each running with its own rate; on the other hand, such independence, if the rates are not multiples of one another, can easily lead to the movements looking visually uneven. To deal with it, some kind of interpolation/extrapolation is often used (please refer to [Fiedler, Fix Your Timestep!] and/or [Nystrom, Game Loop] for further details).

Overall, a detailed discussion of timesteps is not what we're looking at now; however, for our current purposes, it is important that:

♦ For the Server-Side, any kind of "tight loop" is usually not necessary — and is usually not desirable either. Unlike on the Client, on the Server-Side there is no argument of "hey, we need

Tight Loop

Such a loop which heavily uses I/O or processing resources, failing to adequately share them with other programs running in the operating system.

—**Wikipedia**

Unlike on the Client, on the Server-Side there is no argument of "hey, we need to use all available resources to have the game look as good and smooth as possible."

38　BTW, this is pretty close to what is often done in real-time industrial control systems.

to use all available resources to have the game look as good and smooth as possible"; it means that running "tight loop" is not really necessary on the Server-Side. On the other hand, "tight loop" tends to use more CPU cycles, and as for the Server-Side, it is us who pay for those CPU cycles — well, it is not exactly desirable.

- ▪ This makes fixed-timestep by far the most preferable option for the Server-Side.
- ♦ For the Client-Side, however, all the logic in [Fiedler, Fix Your Timestep!] and [Nystrom, Game Loop] still applies — and "tight loops" can be a Good Thing™. When designing your timestep for the Client-Side, make sure to read at least one of these sources carefully (and we'll briefly discuss issues related to the Client-Side timestep in Chapter 6).
- ♦ As we want our (Re)Actors to apply both to the Client- and Server-Side, *we need to make sure that they can handle all the different variations of the Game Loop, including "tight loop" ones.* We'll discuss "how to do it" in a jiff.

(RE)ACTOR AS A GENERALIZATION OF GAME LOOP

Let's start our discussion of (Re)Actors from the fixed-timestep Game Loop: the one that is usually used on the Server-Side (and on V-Synced Clients too). It usually looks along the following lines:

```
//Listing 5.GameLoop2
while(true) {
  read_and_process_inputs();
  update();
  post_updates_to_clients();
  sleep(time_left_until_end_of_network_tick);
}
```

This *Listing 5.GameLoop2* above can easily be rewritten (and very often *is* rewritten) into an *exactly* equivalent form of:

```
//Listing 5.GameLoop3
while(true) {
  wait_for_event();
  read_and_process_inputs();
  update();
  post_updates_to_clients();
  post_timer_event(
    time_left_until_end_of_network_tick);
}
```

Here, instead of sleeping right within our loop, we're saying "hey, please send us an 'event' that will arrive in *time_left_until_end_of_network_tick* microseconds, and will wake us up." And at this point, we're already halfway to the event-driven (Re)Actor (while staying *exactly* equivalent to the original fixed-timestep Game Loop).

Listing 5.GameLoop3 can be further rewritten into another strictly equivalent form, going along the lines of:[39]

At this point, we're already halfway to the event-driven (Re)Actor (while staying *exactly* equivalent to the original fixed-timestep Game Loop).

```
//Listing 5.Reactor
//PSEUDO-CODE
class Infrastructure {
  GenericReactor r;//MUST have react() function
  constructor() {
    //initialize r
  }
  function run_loop() {
    while(true) {
      ev = wait_for_event();
      ev.inputs = read_inputs();
      r.react(ev);
    }
  }
}
class ConcreteReactor extends GenericReactor {
  //implements some concrete logic – for example, Game Logic
  function react(ev) {
    assert ev.type == TIMER_EVENT;
    process_inputs(ev.inputs);
    update();
    post_updates_to_clients();
    post_timer_event(time_left_until_end_of_network_tick);
  }
}
```

---

39   Note that Listing 5.Reactor uses (Re)Actor terminology; however, save for names, it is
      indistinguishable from good old event-driven programming.

The code in *Listing 5.Reactor* above is once again strictly equivalent to the code in *Listing 5.GameLoop2* and *Listing 5.GameLoop3*, but, on the other hand, already represents quite an obvious example of good ol' event-driven programming(!).[40] Let's also note that for the time being, we intentionally do not discuss "how to implement delivering those timer messages" (this is system-dependent, and there are multiple ways to do it; we'll discuss some of them in Volume IV's chapter on Network Programming and Volume V's chapter on C++).

If we look at our *Listing 5.Reactor* a bit closer, we'll realize that such a (Re)Actor-based form of the classical event loop is extremely generic. First, let's note that

> ### The (Re)Actor can be used to express **any** kind of Game Loop (including all forms of tight loops).

For tight loops, we can easily say that whenever we finish rendering of the current frame, we'll ask the framework to issue the next event "right now" (see *process.nextTick()* from *Node.js* as one example of an API implementing this concept, but obviously the idea is not restricted to Javascript or *Node.js*).

Moreover, our (Re)Actor is not restricted to describing simulations and game loops.

Moreover, our (Re)Actor is not restricted to describing simulations and game loops: in addition to expressing all kinds of game loops and timesteps, our *Listing 5.Reactor* can also be used to implement those games that are not based on the concept of ticks (such games include at least social games, casino-like games, and stock exchanges). In such cases, the Server-Side Re(Actor) will just receive Events such as "a message has arrived from the Client," and the Client-Side Re(Actor) will receive the usual "key pressed" ("mouse clicked," etc.) UI Events.

Going even further, this event-driven/Re(Actor) form can (and IMNSHO SHOULD) be used to implement different entities that are not exactly mapped into Game World simulation logic. These entities include everything you need to run your multiplayer game (and which are shown on an Entities & Relationships Diagram, discussed

---

40   Strictly speaking, there is still a subtle difference from "classical" event-driven programming; for "classical" event-driven programming, we usually have one event per each user input; in the Listing 5.EventProcessor, we're assuming that it is the job of the framework to provide the current state of all the inputs and make them a part of *Event ev*

in Vol. I's chapter on GDD), from matchmaking and tournaments to payment and social gateways.

To summarize:

> *(Re)Actors (a.k.a. Event-Driven Programs) can be used to implement pretty much everything[41] from Game World simulations to Event-Driven Cashiers and Matchmaking Servers.*

This is Good News™ for us — in particular because, as we'll see in the *Advantages of (Re)Actors* section below, (Re)Actors provide very significant real-world benefits exactly for interactive distributed systems.

Other Event-Driven Systems: GUI, Erlang, Node.js, and Java Reactor

The concept of event-driven programs (which we name (Re)Actors) is not something new (and is neither restricted to games); in fact, these things have existed for a very long time. In particular, pretty much any GUI system out there is some kind of (Re)Actor.

In addition, existing event-driven Re(Actor)-like programs are not restricted to the Client-Side. Examples of Server-Side event-driven processing go back at least to Erlang (1986), with a much more recent wave of *Node.js*, JVM-based *Project Reactor*, and (to a certain extent) *Python*'s *Twisted* and *Akka Actors*. More on the relationship of our (Re)Actor-fest architecture with these event-driven systems will be discussed in the *Relation to Erlang Concurrency, Akka Actors, and Node.js* section below.

It should be noted that *goroutines* from Go programming language, while having certain similarities with (Re)Actors, are *not* equivalent to them (due to thread sync issues — and, as I said above, I am *strongly* opposing thread sync at app-level); for more discussion, see the *On Using goroutines-for-callbacks: BEWARE THREAD SYNC!* section below.

Erlang

Erlang is a general-purpose, concurrent, garbage-collected programming language and runtime system.

—**Wikipedia**

---

41   Within the realm of interactive systems, that is; applicability of (Re)Actors to HPC, etc. is a very different story, which we fortunately don't need to discuss now.

it is a universally Good Idea™ to separate your infrastructure-level code from your application-level code.

On Separating Infrastructure Code from Logic Code

In my experience, it is a universally Good Idea™ to separate your infrastructure-level code from your application-level code. There are several reasons to have this separation, including different abstraction levels, different style guidelines, and often different people developing these parts of code.

In the case of our *Listing 5.Reactor*, we'll say that it is only *class ConcreteReactor* that implements app-level Game Logic, and *class Infrastructure* (and all its internals) belongs to "Infrastructure Code." These two layers should have a very clean separation along the lines of *class GenericReactor* (and *GenericReactor.react()* function). Moreover, they will have very different requirements; in particular:

♦ App-level logic (*class ConcreteReactor*) SHOULD be perfectly cross-platform.

♦ Infrastructure code (*class Infrastructure*) MAY (and most of the time will) be platform-specific.

For (Re)Actor programs, such a clean separation will enable two all-important properties of properly built (Re)Actors. It is that

> *1. The very same Re(Actor) can be deployed on any platform.*
> *2. The very same Re(Actor) can be deployed in very different execution environments depending on your current needs.*

As the cross-platform property is rather obvious, let's concentrate on the second one. It means if you keep this very clean interface along the lines of *class GenericReactor* and *GenericReactor.react()* functions, you will be able to rewrite your infrastructure-level code (*class Infrastructure* in the *Listing 5.Reactor*) to deploy your *class ConcreteReactor* in any of the following configurations:

♦ One instance of *class ConcreteReactor* per process.

♦ One instance of *class ConcreteReactor* per thread.

♦ Several instances of *class ConcreteReactor* per thread. Some restrictions apply, and the offer is void where prohibited; in short, such configurations essentially require fully non-blocking (Re)Actors (opposed to "mostly-non-blocking (Re)Actors" that we're normally okay with, as discussed below).

◆ Completion-port-based event handling (i.e., the event is handled by any of the threads that got the event from the completion queue); note that we'll need to ensure thread sync within our Infrastructure Code.

◆ Your own hardware-aware (Re)Actor execution scheduler. The most obvious hardware-related configuration would take NUMA into account, effectively ensuring that your (Re)Actors have some affinity to NUMA nodes, both with regards to CPU and RAM. However, in some (admittedly extreme) cases, you may want to go even further; for example, I've heard of people playing with the NIC receive queue IRQ/CPU (somewhat along the lines of Receive Side Scaling/Receive Packet Steering), though this admittedly belongs in the realm of Black Magic.

◆ Web-driven event handling (see Vol. III's chapter on Server-Side Architecture for further discussion)

◆ And so on…

Most importantly, all these configurations can (and SHOULD) be achievable *without any changes to your class ConcreteReactor whatsoever*(!). In other words, (Re)Actor is (Re)Actor is (Re)Actor, regardless of how it is deployed.

This, in particular, allows us to defer decisions about deployment architecture until, well, deployment. In practice, I've observed this ability to be very useful: during development, it is very difficult to predict exact deployment configurations (and trying to account for all possible configurations leads to overengineering); however, as the number of players increases, new deployment configurations tend to emerge, and the only practical way to enable them at a later stage is to have all application-level code agnostic to deployment architecture — exactly the thing that is provided by clean separation of the (Re)Actor along the lines of *GenericReactor* and *GenericReactor.react()* function.

One real-world example in this regard. For quite a few games out there, it makes sense to run many of your (Re)Actors within a single thread (or using one completion queue), and there was quite a large game doing exactly this. On the other hand, the same game happened

(Re)Actor is (Re)Actor
is (Re)Actor, regardless
of how it is deployed.

to run weekly Quite-Important Tournaments — and ran Game Worlds of such tournaments as "single-Game-World-per-thread" (still having multiple Game Worlds per process); among other things, it allowed to raise thread priority for those-Important-Tournaments. And for the Tournament of the Year, it was run with its Game Worlds as separate processes to ensure near-perfect separation of Game Worlds of this all-important tournament. As the Game Worlds of that game were written as (Re)Actors that were completely isolated along the lines above, it allowed that large game to deploy them in these different configurations *without any changes to the Game World itself.*

Other examples of changing deployment architectures include such things as spreading your Game Server (Re)Actors over several Data-centers across the globe, support for migration of your Game Worlds to balance your Servers better, switching from optimistic-locking to a pessimistic one for Web-based deployment architectures, and even switching from a Web-based deployment architecture to a Classical one (all these topics will be discussed in Vol. III's chapter on Server-Side Architecture). Once again, having *class ConcreteReactor* tightly coupled with your *class Infrastructure* would make implementing such features next-to-impossible (that is, unless you thought of all of them from the very beginning), but with a clean separation between infrastructure code and application-level code, it becomes perfectly feasible.

Bottom line:

> *Clean separation of (Re)Actors along the lines of **class GenericReactor** and **GenericReactor.react()** is a Good Thing™.*

Advantages of (Re)Actors

I have to confess that I am a Big Fan™ of (Re)Actors.

Just in case you haven't already noticed</tongue-in-cheek>, I have to confess that I am a Big Fan™ of (Re)Actors. Compared to other models (and especially to the massively-multithreaded model with mutex-based thread synchronization), they provide the following advantages:

♦ (Re)Actors tend to enforce very clean interfaces between different parts of your system. In particular, these interfaces tend to be *much* cleaner than those interfaces that tend to arise in "component programming."

- Due to its message-passing nature, testing of (Re)Actors is also simplified; in particular, risks of finger-pointing between different-teams-developing-different-(Re)Actors are inherently lower with (Re)Actors than with other types of APIs.

♦ If properly implemented,[42] (Re)Actors also allow us to isolate "logic" from cross-platform stuff in a very strong manner.

- This allows for the re-use of *exactly* the same Game and Business Logic on different platforms (and in different deployment scenarios) without rewriting it. And benefits from having one single code base for frequently changing Game Logic cannot be overestimated (in fact, having two frequently changing code bases is pretty much guaranteed to doom one of them[43]).

- This is closely related to the above-discussed ability to deploy (Re)Actors in very different deployment scenarios, moving many decisions about threads, platform-specific APIs, etc. to deployment-time (which has been observed to be a Really Good Thing™ in the long run).

♦ (Re)Actors do not require thinking about inter-thread synchronization while writing game/business logic. IMNSHO, this alone qualifies as a sufficient reason to use them.

- As discussed above in the *Reactors or Not — Stay Away from Thread Sync in your Game Logic* section, trying to think about both inter-thread synchronization and Game and Business logic is an almost-surefire way to a mortgage-crisis-size disaster.

♦ Performance-wise, (Re)Actors tend to perform very well:

- By their very nature, (Re)Actors tend to exhibit very good spatial locality (and spatial locality is very important for performance on modern CPUs; see further discussion in Vol. V's chapter on C++).

- The non-blocking variety of (Re)Actors avoids unnecessary thread context switches, which tends to improve perfor-

---

42   Obviously, "properly" = "along the lines discussed in this chapter."

43   At least, I can say that I've seen it more than once, and didn't see any counterexamples.

mance greatly (see further discussion on the cost of context switches in Vol. V's chapter on C++).

♦ (Re)Actors can be made deterministic at a small cost (see the *Implementing Deterministic Logic* section below). And deterministic (Re)Actors provide their own set of goodies (for a more detailed discussion of these, see the *Deterministic Logic: Benefits* section below):

- ▪ Deterministic testing, including (but not limited to):
  - • Production post-factum analysis (including visual analysis of Client-Side handling of packet loss/delays).
  - • Replay-based regression testing
  - • Better overall quality of testing compared to non-deterministic tests. More on it in the *Non-Deterministic Tests are Pointless* section below.
- ▪ Server-Side features such as low-latency fault tolerance, (Re)Actor migration, and almost-zero-downtime upgrades (the latter with some reservations).
- ▪ And quite a few other things.

I REALLY hope that even with the limited list above, I've managed to convince you that (Re)Actors (a.k.a. Game Loops, Event-Driven Programs, Ad-Hoc Finite State Machines, etc., etc.) are a Good Thing™.

Phew! I probably forgot to include something important, but I hope that even with the limited list above, I've managed to convince you that (Re)Actors (a.k.a. Game Loops, Event-Driven Programs, Ad-Hoc Finite State Machines, etc., etc.) are a Good Thing™.

(Re)Actors in Game Engines

Actually, (Re)Actors and Reactor-like systems are well known in games (albeit under various names). In addition to the ubiquitous Game Loop, which, as we've discussed, is a special case of a bit-more-generic (Re)Actor, there is also *class Process* from Chapter 7 of [McShaffry and Graham] — which has obvious resemblances to our *class GenericReactor*. And then, of course, there is Bungie and its heavy use of (Re)Actor-like logic (as described in [Tatarchuk] and [Aldridge]).

Some existing systems (such as Game Loop and *class Process*) have a limited spectrum of events compared to our (Re)Actor; however, the Big Idea™ of processing local state without thread sync and without unnecessary thread context switches is still exactly the same. Moreover, quite a few of these (Re)Actor-like systems (in particular, *class Process* from [McShaffry and Graham]) are intended to be used with *cooperative multitasking,* and our non-blocking (Re)Actors described below are essentially working in exactly the same manner.

Bottom line: (Re)Actor-based architectures are very far from being something new for games; rather, (Re)Actor is merely a mild generalization of tried-and-tested practices that are successfully used in the gamedev world for generations. Two very important generalizations of (Re)Actors in the context of MOGs are that:

♦ Our (Re)Actors can be used on the Server-Side, *and*

♦ They can be used for non-simulation tasks (such as classical event-driven tasks).

Overall, I am arguing to

> ### Use (Re)Actors as a building block for your Game Architecture.

I've seen a very successful game that had its whole architecture revolve around (Re)Actors; while there were deviations from (Re)Actors at the level of Infrastructure Code, 100% of the app-level/game-level code[44] was within (Re)Actors. This was the very same game that surprised the pre-IPO auditor with its reliability, and which supported 32x more players per Server than the competition; in addition, it has survived over fifteen years on the same (Re)Actor-based architecture without a complete rewrite of its Game Logic (though updates were released every two to three weeks, and its Infrastructure Code was rewritten more than once during those fifteen years).

While it may happen that at certain places (especially when or if you need to integrate with existing code) you MAY need to deviate from (Re)Actors, I insist that by default it is a Really Good Idea™ to use (Re)Actors in *all* the places of your Game Architecture where it is possible (deviating only when there is no other way around it, which should be very rare[45]).

---

44   That is, if we don't count DB reports, which are a very separate beast.

45   As in, "a few instances per million lines of code."

For our online game purposes, there are two all-important changes that are necessary to make our life down the road easier.

TWO ALL-IMPORTANT IMPROVEMENTS TO CLASSICAL EVENT-DRIVEN PROGRAMMING: MOSTLY-NON-BLOCKING PROCESSING AND DETERMINISM

Compared to the usual event-driven programming (such as the one commonly used for Windows/Android/JavaScript/… UI programming), for our online game purposes[46] there are two all-important changes that we ought to make. While not strictly required, these changes will certainly make our life down the road easier; I'm talking about (a) (mostly-)non-blocking processing and (b) determinism.

Both of these things are really important for quite a few reasons, which we'll see below.

NON-BLOCKING PROCESSING

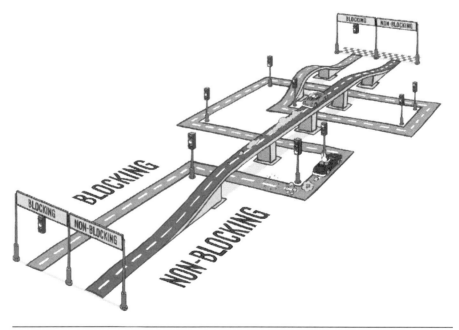

---

46   Or, more generally, distributed computing purposes.

The first issue that we need to take into account when using event-driven programming for MOG development is the sad fact that networks can be slow, often *damn* slow. Have you ever seen a GUI that hangs for a long while (like "1-2 minutes"[47]), just to spring back to life later?[48] Chances are that the code tried to make a blocking connection attempt to a Server, and there happened to be some kind of temporary Internet "black hole" on the path between your laptop and the server;[49] with the *connect()* or *recv()* call being blocking, the whole GUI is blocked while waiting for the response <ouch! />.

While merely "very annoying" for the UI client, for the Server-Side, such blocking processing of network communications is just plain unacceptable. If there is a "black hole" on the path from the Server to one of the Clients, then blocking all the Server-Side processing until it is back (or until we realize that it has disconnected) would slow things down beyond belief. Moreover, even if connectivity for *all* the Clients is good, usual round-trip times (which are normally in the 100ms+ range, and that's waiting for *just one Client*) will exceed the length of our "network tick" (usually around 20–50ms).

For the Server-Side, such blocking processing of network communications is just plain unacceptable.

Therefore,

> ## We need to have non-blocking processing at the very least for network-related operations.

In addition, the less blocking our (Re)Actor has, the less thread context switches we'll get. As mentioned above, the cost of a thread context switch can easily reach into hundreds of thousands of CPU cycles, which means that going non-blocking is a big incentive, performance-wise. Real-world stories supporting this observation range from the aforementioned nginx-outperforming-Apache to once-saying-blocking-calls-and-threads-is-all-we'll-ever-need Java[50] introducing non-blocking APIs.

---

47   This BTW happens to coincide with more-or-less typical "BGP convergence time", or "modem retrain time"; more on it in Vol. IV's chapter on Network Programming.

48   That is, if you didn't kill the process by this point.

49   If it is not a "black hole," *usually* (though far from "universally") there is some indication of connection failure coming from the Server, which SHOULD cause the Client to react earlier than in two minutes.

50   It is difficult to believe now, but there was such a point of view among Java developers that lasted up to 2000 or so.

BTW, in addition to having worse performance as such, blocking systems often tend to exhibit performance degradation as the load on them increases (this can be observed as a graph showing dependency of CPU-cycles-spent as a function of what-is-done, being worse-than-linear); in particular, it happens due to increased resource contention, which increases the number of those dreaded context switches even further. Non-blocking Shared-Nothing systems, to the contrary, tend to exhibit constant or even somewhat-improving(!) performance under the load (i.e., they may scale better-than-linearly under the load[51]); the latter happens because for a non-blocking queue-based system under the load, different portions of the work happen to be performed without a context switch, which in turn reduces overheads.

What NOT to Use — "OO" RPC Frameworks

Before getting into a discussion of "what kind of approaches or frameworks you SHOULD use," let's discuss "what you SHOULDN'T use"; I'm talking about OO-like RPC frameworks such as CORBA, DCOM, and ICE.

In the Seventies, a new concept arose in the world of distributed computing: after request-response protocols became popular, it seemed logical and neat to say "let's consider a request-response a "function call"— which led to Remote Procedure Calls (RPCs). With time, it has evolved into an "Object-Oriented" style of RPC, with Clients creating remote objects on the Server-Side and manipulating them there. All of CORBA/DCOM/ICE fall into this latter category.

Unfortunately, there is one big problem with this concept, and it is that while it *might* work for LAN (with some reservations), I have never seen this concept work reasonably well in any real-world project over WAN.

Unfortunately, there is one big problem with this concept, and it is that the concept doesn't work over WAN.

The most egregious example of "OO" RPC-based technologies and WAN that I've seen in the real world unfolded as follows. While working for a Really Big Company™, I was assigned to a project that was about to ship their CORBA-based software to customers. And the software was working (rather slow but not *too* slow) while tested within the LAN, but as soon as they started to deploy it over a trans-Atlantic

---

51   Yes, I've seen it for a real-world system.

link (which was the way it had to be eventually deployed per Business Requirements), user-initiated operations started to take as long as twenty minutes to complete. When tasked with solving this little problem of the project being utterly unusable in its intended environment (and the task was aggravated by a firm Business Requirement to keep CORBA as a transport[52]), the best we could do was relegate CORBA to a simple byte-message transport (via creating a CORBA-level API with one single function postMessage() function, taking character array as a parameter, with this array containing a message that was composed and parsed at app level).[53] Doing this reduced user waiting times by a factor of 400x(!), which decreased delays from twenty minutes to single-digit seconds; i.e., made it more or less usable for the app in question.

Problems with using "OO" RPC-based techniques for WAN-based games are twofold:

♦ By default, RPC in such frameworks is blocking. And blocking RPC is to be avoided at all costs when dealing with WAN (in particular, due to 'hanged' connections and due to latencies; see a real-world example above to see what latencies can do to your WAN app if you're using blocking calls).

  ▪ In particular, in the real-world CORBA-based system described above, that 20-minute delay was caused by several thousands of blocking RPC calls (made in the true CORBA spirit of making an object and then calling remote methods of this object to populate its fields one by one), and with each blocking call taking at least 100–120ms over the Atlantic, each thousand of such blocking RPC calls was taking at least two minutes.

  ▪ On the other hand, non-blocking RPC *is* possible with both ICE and DCOM (it is just not really popular, and not really convenient to use).

♦ Generally, the RPC-based OO paradigm as it is implemented by these frameworks doesn't support the concept of a pre-existing

---

52   Having Business Requirements like these is a fallacy (as pretty much anything that is not about interactions with users or 3rd parties qualifies as an implementation detail), but, well, it does happen.

53   NB: another way to skin this cat would be to use parameters-by-value, but it wasn't available in CORBA at that time; also, it would still be pretty much the same paradigm as the one with byte messages, merely moving marshaling from app-level to within-CORBA.

Server-Side stateful object.[54] Instead, usually Server-Side creates Server-Side objects on behalf of the Client — and then uses references by Client-Side to Server-Side objects.

- This creates severe mismatches with typical game and simulation programming models such as classical Game Loops (see, for example, Chapter 6 for a brief discussion of Game Loops on the Client-Side).

    - On the other hand, it *is* possible to use this model to emulate Game Loops (and, more generally, (Re)Actors); however, as it goes pretty much against established RPC-based OO paradigms, doing so is rather cumbersome.

- In addition, the very concept of remote references (i.e., Client-Side references to Server-Side objects) doesn't work over WAN — not at all (at the very least because WAN connections are inherently unreliable, which in turn causes so-called "server-side garbage"). While some workarounds are possible (see, for example, [Spruiell]), they tend to be ugly, unreliable, and vulnerable to all kinds of DoS attacks.

    - As a Big Fat Rule of Thumb™, a *much* better alternative is to have each request correspond to one single transaction (either over in-memory state or over DB); in addition to being free from the problems above, it tends to provide a *much* cleaner API between the layers (in particular, with messages being transactions, it has *much* fewer unwritten and poorly enforceable limitations on the allowed sequences of requests).

As a Big Fat Rule of Thumb™, a *much* better alternative is to have each request correspond to one single transaction.

---

54   Moreover, a lack of long-living stateful objects is often touted as an advantage of this paradigm, based on the misunderstanding that having objects stateless is The Only Way™ to make systems scalable. I won't go into a lengthy discussion about it here, rather noting the big difference between making middleware trivially scalable (which "OO" RPC-based stuff is actually all about), and making a whole real-world system — including database(!) — scalable. The former is easy, but it essentially does nothing except push the scalability problem from middleware to the database. The latter is never trivial, so some kind of non-trivial thinking needs to be involved anyway (and my preferred way of such thinking is via (Re)Actors and non-blocking eventually-consistent exchanges along the lines of Inter-DB Async Transfer Protocol as described in Vol. I's chapter on Communications). More on it in Vol. III's chapter on Scalability.

As a result,

> *I STRONGLY advise against using "OO" RPC-based frameworks (those with blocking RPC calls **and/or** remote references) for over-the-WAN game-like/interactive processing.*

Sure, it is possible to emulate pretty much everything over these frameworks (for example, as described for a real-world case with CORBA above), but, if doing it this way, all the added value of these frameworks is reduced to zero (and probably even below), so I don't see why I should bother with using any of them for building a distributed system over WAN.

On the other hand, let's note that RPCs as such are not necessarily evil; if RPCs (a) are non-blocking and (b) don't rely on[55] remote references, RPC can be perfectly fine. Examples of such RPCs-that-are-fine-for-gamedev include (not really surprisingly) RPCs provided by Unity and UE4 engines.

To Block, or Not to Block, That Is the Question. Mostly-Non-Blocking (Re)Actors

Non-blocking code has a pretty bad reputation among developers as being difficult to grasp and difficult to maintain. I've even seen people arguing that it is a premature optimization. On the other hand, from my experience, non-blocking code (well, mostly-non-blocking; see below) works very well from the exact perspective of readability and maintainability — though it heavily depends on what-the-task-is-we're-trying-to-solve. Let's take a closer look at the blocking vs non-blocking code in different contexts.

Non-blocking code has a pretty bad reputation among developers as difficult to grasp and difficult to maintain.

In any case, we'll be talking about the situation when we have a request that takes some time; and the question we'll try to answer is whether we want to implement this request using blocking call, or a non-blocking one.

---

55   Even better: "don't allow to create."

From the point of view of performance, most of the time everything SHOULD be non-blocking, plain and simple.[56] But if we take a look at it from the development complexity side of things, we'll see that things are not that obvious.

In practice, there are two different cases when we make a potentially blocking call, and the subtle difference between these two cases is where the whole secret of the balance between blocking and non-blocking calls can be found.

Case 1. Processing Input Events While Call Is in Progress Is Required at Logic Level

The first case for a potentially-non-blocking call arises when, according to our Business/Game Logic, we need to handle events occurring while the potentially-blocking call is in progress — and these events may affect what our Logic is doing.

For example, if we want to send our player some information, we certainly want to process inputs (from him and other players) while the information is en route; if on the Client we want to display a simple box asking "Yes"/"No," we still want to process updates-to-our-Game-World coming from the Server, and so on and so forth.

In such a case, if we'll implement our Game Logic via non-blocking calls, it will be relatively ugly (depending on the specifics of your implementation; see Take 1–Take 8 below), but TBH, it won't be *too* bad.

On the other hand, if we try to implement the same thing via blocking calls, it would mean that we'll need to have a second thread to handle these concurrently incoming events, we'll need to have some "current state" data to share between threads, we'll need to make sure to access this "shared data" *only* under mutex locks; then we'll need to make sure to release this mutex while the blocking call is in progress (so that the incoming-events-thread can access it) — and remember that we MUST NOT access (from incoming-events-thread) that data that can be mod-

The first case for a potentially-non-blocking call arises when, according to our Business/Game Logic, we need to handle events occurring while the potential-ly-blocking call is in progress — and these events may affect what our Logic is doing.

---

56   Strictly speaking, if a thread context switch is inevitable anyway, blocking code will perform pretty much the same performance-wise as a non-blocking one. OTOH, such behavior is usually platform-specific (and undocumented too), so from purely a performance perspective, you almost-never cannot lose (and are likely to gain something, at least on some of the platforms) from going non-blocking.

ified by the call itself. Then, we'll realize that queueing our incoming requests becomes tricky (or we need to give up ordering completely), and so on and so forth. This whole shared-data-based handling will become an unmanageable never-ending race-ridden non-deterministic nightmare very quickly.

Sure, non-blocking calls isn't exactly a picnic even in Case 1, but blocking calls, when applied to Case 1 (with the need to process other incoming events while the call is in progress), are much, *much* worse.

As a result,

> *For scenarios when we do need to process other input events while the call is in progress, non-blocking calls are **much** better than blocking-code-with-thread-synced-concurrent-processing, at least from code reliability, testability, and maintainability points of view.*

Case 2. No Processing at Logic level While Call Is In Progress

On the other hand, there is a rather different set of scenarios, when we MAY (or even MUST) delay processing other inputs while the outstanding call is in progress. "MAY" happens, in particular, when we can be 100% sure that during normal operation the call cannot possibly take a long time; "MUST" is more rare, but I've observed it a few times in the real world (it was necessary to avoid certain classes of races where strict syncing guarantees between different (Re)Actors were necessary).

And as soon as we can say that we don't want to process anything during the call duration — great! Indeed, linear blocking code will be simpler, better readable, etc., etc. (and, as a side benefit, we can still stay within (Re)Actors too).

The only potential drawback of blocking code in such scenarios is extra thread context switches (leading to a loss in performance). However:

♦ Even in the worst case, this is only a performance issue. In other words: we're not talking about crashes, corrupted data, wrong results, etc.

Green Threads

green threads are threads that are scheduled by a runtime library or virtual machine (VM) instead of natively by the underlying operating system

—Wikipedia

Based on the reasoning above, I suggest splitting all your calls into two broad categories: "long" ones (which are likely to last long enough to require competing events to be processed while waiting), and "short" ones, which you can afford to wait for.

♦ If you're using blocking calls sparingly, the performance hit is not too likely to be observable.

♦ If your threads have nothing to do anyway while you're processing your call, it is not a problem at all (if there is nothing to do for current thread, we will have the context switch anyway).

♦ If your Infrastructure Code can use fibers (or coroutines), then to reduce thread switching, Infrastructure Code can run several (Re)Actors within the same thread, and can implement kinda-"green threads" itself; i.e., whenever a blocking call is made by one of the (Re)Actors, your Infrastructure Code can take over control, and if there is an input event for another (Re)Actor, let this second (Re)Actor process its input while the first one is waiting for the blocking call. Note that all this can usually be implemented completely within the Infrastructure Code, and without affecting the code of any (Re)Actors involved.

As a result,

> *When we don't need to process other events while the blocking call is in progress, I tend to **start** implementation with more straightforward blocking calls (changing to non-blocking **if** performance is demonstrated to become an issue).*

From the point of view of reliability, this approach is bulletproof — and is also very straightforward and readable (that is, *as long as* we're staying within our Case #2 which doesn't require processing events while waiting). As for the performance issues that *might* result from the calls being blocking, they rarely cause trouble at the application level. Still, keep in mind that they *might* become a problem, and be prepared to go non-blocking; that is *if* you can see that a specific blocking call causes trouble. On the other hand, going into non-blocking calls for those calls-that-don't-need-processing-of-concurrent-inputs, and without any performance problems in sight IMO usually qualifies as a "premature optimization."

Blocking or Non-Blocking? Mostly Non-Blocking

Based on the above reasoning, I suggest splitting all your calls into two broad categories: "long" ones (which are likely to last long enough to require competing events to be processed while waiting), and "short" ones, which you can afford to wait for. Let's note that as soon as you have the framework for handling non-blocking calls (which you should anyway), mistakes in separating "long" calls from "short" calls are not *that* expensive (as it is possible to rewrite one call from one category to another without affecting too much of the overall code).

This is different *both* from traditional processing with its "everything is blocking just because so happened" *and* from "everything MUST be non-blocking" paradigm (which is how *Node.js* is often (mis)interpreted). What I'm suggesting is doing things in the easiest possible way, which is non-blocking for those "long" calls that may be interleaved with incoming events, and blocking for "short" calls.

This is all good — but still, it would be even better to have more specific guidelines to know where to start; to provide these guidelines, let's take a look at those interactions that can require potentially blocking calls, and see whether they're likely to qualify as "long calls" (which MUST be handled in a non-blocking manner) or "short ones" (which MAY be handled via blocking calls).

My personal experience with choosing blocking vs non-blocking processing is summarised in the following table:

Client-Side	
User Input	Non-blocking *only*
File Access	Depends
Communications with Server	Non-blocking *only*
Server-Side	
Communications with Client	Non-blocking *only*
Communications with other Servers in the same Datacenter	*Mostly* non-blocking
Communications with Servers in other Datacenters	Non-blocking *only* (see exception below)
Database/Disk	Depends

As we can see, all operations with potentially very large waiting times (this includes at least user input and all operations over the WAN) MUST handle inputs while they're in progress — and therefore MUST be non-blocking.

One possible exception to this rule applies when we have so-called "Gateway Servers," discussed in Vol. III's chapter on Server-Side Architecture; they tend to have lots of substantially independent requests going over WAN to a third-party provider (such as a payment processor or social network), and *as long as all the requests are perfectly independent*, it is okay to process these requests via several (Re)Actors, with each of the (Re)Actors making blocking calls to reach the third-party provider. Performance-wise, this approach represents a tradeoff between code simplicity and performance — but, as integration code with third-party providers tends to change rather frequently, and as performance/scalability is rarely an issue with Gateway Servers, it is often a reasonable tradeoff.

As for operations which are 100% limited to LAN, sometimes we MAY rely on LAN operations being fast enough, though I still *strongly* prefer non-blocking handling for them. On the other hand, I am much more lenient with handling local disk/DB I/O in a blocking manner; as a rule of thumb, if you're reading one single DB record or a single up-to-10K file, you can easily fit into below-1-ms range,[57] which may easily happen to be acceptable for you while keeping your calls blocking (OTOH, a dozen of such records/files at the same time can easily cause unacceptable delays).

Overall, at Game Logic level, it is all about delays:

> ***If delays are large enough,[58] we need to process concurrent events and go non-blocking. Otherwise, blocking calls may be okay.***

As we can see from the above table, for our purposes most of the calls will need to be non-blocking; hence, for the purposes of this book, let's name this approach of "handling long delays as non-blocking but short delays as blocking" as "*mostly*-non-blocking processing."

As a rule of thumb, if you're reading one single DB record or a single up-to-10K file, you can easily fit into the below-1-ms range, which may easily happen to be acceptable for you while keeping your calls blocking.

---

57   That is, if you can be reasonably sure that the file is cached, or if you're using SSD.

58   Even if it happens once-in-a-blue-moon.

Implementing Non-Blocking Processing for Games

Traditionally, for games there are three substantially different types of non-blocking operations:

♦ Waits

♦ Publishing of non-blocking state updates (and other kinda-broadcast messages; see Vol. I's chapter on Communications for discussion).

♦ All kinds of request-response point-to-point communications (these cover *both* communications between different (Re)Actors, *and* things such as non-blocking I/O etc.).

"Offloading" of the calculations to a different thread/core/Server is not necessarily typical for games, but still MAY be implemented on top of request-response communications (though, as we'll see below, special considerations for simplifying offloading, may still apply).

Waits/Timers

For a non-blocking event-driven system, whenever we want our system to "sleep," we're *not* calling a blocking *sleep()* function; instead, we're actually scheduling a timer event at a certain time, and completing our processing for the time being (pretty much as we did it to simulate Game Loop over (Re)Actor). Whenever the scheduled time comes (give or take), our Infrastructure Code (such as *class Infrastructure* from *Listing 5.Reactor*) delivers the special timer event to the object of our *class ConcreteReactor*.

It is worth noting that timers, to specify actions-that-need-to-be-performed-after-the-timer-event-fires *may* use techniques that are very similar to Take 1–Take 8 processing discussed in the *Handling Returns in Non-Blocking Way in (Re)Actors* section below.

Non-Blocking State Publishing and (Kinda-) Broadcast Messages

To have an API to perform state publishing (and kinda-Broadcast Messages as discussed in Vol. I's chapter on Communications) on the

For a non-blocking event-driven system, whenever we want our system to "sleep," we're *not* calling a blocking *sleep()* function; instead, we're actually scheduling a timer event at a certain time, and completing our processing for the time being.

Server-Side, one option is to have some kind of non-blocking *publish()* function (with a corresponding update and an optional callback on a Client side), effectively implementing so-called Observer Design Pattern (though in a remote manner).

An alternative API to publish Game World State is related to increasingly popular "synchronized variables" such as *[SyncVar]* in Unity 5 HLAPI and *UPROPERTY(Replicated)* in UE4. We'll discuss more of them in Chapter 7, but for now we need to point out one related observation: while there is nothing wrong with the *concept* of synchronized states and variables, *currently available* variable synchronization mechanisms are often too simplistic for real-world deployments with hundreds of thousands of simultaneous players (for more detailed discussion, see Chapter 7).

What applies regardless of the API chosen is that both for state publishing and (kinda-)Broadcast Messages, all the communications look like "fire-and-forget" from the point of view of the publisher/sender. It means that there is no possible reply to them and so a pretty annoying question of "what to do when reply comes back?" doesn't arise at all.

Point-to-Point Communications and Other Request-Response Stuff

Point-to-point communications can be separated into two subcategories:

♦ "Fire-and-forget" communications, and

♦ "Request-response" communications

"Fire-and-forget" is the simple one; as long we don't need *any* response back, we don't need to wait for it and, more importantly, we don't need to specify what-to-do-when-the-call-is-completed. In particular, Unity- and UE4-style void RPC calls without an option to throw an exception fit into this "fire-and-forget" pattern.

Request-Response

However, there are *lots* of real-world scenarios when "fire-and-forget" point-to-point communications are not sufficient, and we need "request-response" type interactions. These are generally quite different from state updates, and also from "fire-and-forget" communications.

As long we don't need *any* response back, we don't need to wait for it and, more importantly, we don't need to specify what-to-do-when-the-call-is-completed.

In particular, a very typical pattern is that one (Re)Actor needs to request some value from another (Re)Actor, which effectively corresponds to a non-void RPC call (and to stay within our non-blocking paradigm, we need to make this non-void RPC call non-blocking). One very common example of it is requesting something from your database (Re)Actor (again, in a non-blocking manner). Moreover, *any* kind of non-blocking request-response can be handled in exactly the same manner as a non-blocking RPC call — which covers pretty much all kinds of request-response communications (including "long" I/O requests to read disk, etc.).

Even the task of offloading some heavy calculations into a separate thread (i.e., achieving not only concurrency, but also parallelism) can be implemented "as if" it is an RPC call to a (Re)Actor sitting in that separate thread. As one example, we can be requesting other (Re)Actors (deployed to different threads) to perform SHA-256 calculations to solve a proof-of-work "puzzle" (proof-of-work puzzles as a way to mitigate certain DDoS attacks will be discussed in Volume IV); in other words, to solve the "puzzle" using multiple threads, the (Re)Actor may simply call non-blocking RPC-like function SHA256(...) multiple times.[59]

All these cases are indeed very similar from the caller's point of view. In particular, all are following the *exact same* RPC-like pattern:

♦ Do something to initiate the request. While implementation-wise it can be sending a network packet, or issuing a DB request, or starting a non-blocking file read, or posting a message into an inter-thread queue, from the caller's point of view all these things look exactly the same.

♦ Wait until the request is completed and the reply is obtained.

♦ Perform pre-defined action to process the reply.

Request-Response Complication: What to Do When the Call is Completed

In such an RPC-like request-response pattern, the first two steps are rather obvious to implement, but the third is unfortunately not. What

---

59 In fact, to achieve reasonable efficiency, it will be more complicated than that, but all the additional complexity beyond keeping offloaded chunks "large enough" SHOULD be kept within Infrastructure Code. In other words, from the point of view of the application-level code, it is still sufficient to code it as a kinda-RPC call (just keeping granularity coarse enough to avoid thrashing the system with too many RPC calls and thread context switches).

exactly should we do when the data from our request comes back? Should we call a callback (if yes, from which thread? And where should the variables-used-by-callback be stored?)? Should we change a state of some "future" (a.k.a. "promise") so that somebody who waits for this "future" gets notified, unblocked, or the callback-associated-with-the-future called? Should we just wait for a message/event with a reply, handling everything manually at app level?

In general, there are many different ways of handling this "what-to-do-on-receiving-reply" problem, but within our (Re)Actor pattern, one thing is for certain:

> *Whatever happens when the asynchronous request (such as RPC call) is completed MUST be performed in such a manner that there is no need to perform any thread sync with the rest of the (Re)Actor, even if access to the (Re)Actor state is needed.*[60]

In other words, you can write your code pretty much "as if" all-your-code-for-the-same-Reactor is always executed within the same thread.

In other words, you should be able to write your app-level code (the one that calls that non-blocking non-void RPC) pretty much "as if" all-your-code-for-the-same-(Re)Actor is always executed within the same thread (and whether it will be actually the same thread or not is not that important). And, I contend that this is the Really Good Thing™. Actually, as I've already mentioned, once in my career[61] I've deviated from this "reply-is-processed-within-the-same-thread-as-everything-else" approach; while theoretically it was okay (and there were IMHO clear guidelines how to deal with it thread-wise), it has caused *many* more problems for fellow developers than it was worth. The lesson I learned at that point was as follows: "Never ever force app-level developers to perform thread-sync";[62] since then, I've kept all my threading

---

60   Strictly speaking, there are two ways this can be achieved: either by ensuring that all-the-access to the (Re)Actor state always goes from one single thread, or by explicit thread sync *at infrastructure level*. I usually *strongly* prefer the former (and it performs better too), but the latter can also work.

61   As a mitigating circumstance, I should tell that it was about twenty years ago, when I was young and inexperienced, and that I submit myself to the mercy of the court.

62   As argued in [Hare, Multi-threading at Business-logic Level is Considered Harmful], combining app-logic with threading tends to raise the number of entities that the developer needs to consider at the same time, well above the magic number of 7±2; this, in turn, often causes cognitive overload as a result.

completely out of sight of app-level development, and found that this way it works *much* better both for infrastructure-level and app-level developers.

Another thing to understand about non-void non-blocking calls in the context of (Re)Actors is that due to the non-blocking nature of the call,

> *Other things can happen within the same event-driven object while the non-blocking call is being executed*

(also see discussion in the *To Block, or Not to Block, That Is the Question. Mostly-Non-Blocking (Re)Actors* section above).

This can be seen as either a blessing (as it allows for essentially parallel execution while staying away from any thread synchronization), or a curse (as it complicates understanding), but needs to be kept in mind at all times while you are dealing with non-blocking calls. BTW, as we discussed above in the *Case 1. Processing Input Events While Call Is in Progress Is Required at Logic Level* section, this additional complexity arises *not* because we decided to write our code in a non-blocking manner; instead, it follows from the *objective* need to perform processing while we're waiting for results of the outstanding-call-that-may-take-a-long-while.

Regardless of our motivation, handling returns from non-void non-blocking calls is quite a complicated task; moreover, there is no consensus on "what is the best way of doing it" (though recently, there is a trend towards await-style coroutines). As a result, instead of suggesting one way of handling non-void non-blocking calls, we'll discuss several different approaches, so you can choose the one that is more applicable to your specific situation (and TBH, this decision is not black-and-white, so personal preferences can play a significant role).

Handling Returns in Non-Blocking Way in (Re)Actors

Historically, in games, handling of non-void RPC calls is usually implemented either via plain messages or via simulating them on top of void RPC calls (see Take 1 and Take 2 below for details). However, while *both* messages and void-only RPC calls DO work correctly (and most

Historically, in games, handling of non-void RPC calls is usually implemented either via plain messages or via simulating them on top of void RPC calls.

importantly, without any need for app-level developers to deal with thread sync), they tend to become rather cumbersome as the complexity of your system increases. Fortunately, there are ways out there to avoid it, and this is exactly what we're about to discuss.

On the other hand, it is necessary to mention that *all* the different ways of handling returns from non-blocking calls, which we'll discuss below, are pretty much equivalent (save for different syntax). In other words, in a certain sense, all the different takes below are only about "syntactic sugar" around plain messages, so if I am saying that some of the Takes are ugly but you happen to think that they are okay, it will be more or less about personal preferences (and not about "you're doing it deadly wrong").

IDL

Interface definition language (IDL) is a specification language used to describe a software component's application programming interface (API).

—Wikipedia

For the purpose of our examples, we assume that we have some kind of IDL compiler (along the lines discussed in Vol. I's chapter on Communications), with this IDL compiler taking function definitions and producing necessary pseudo-code stubs for them (in practice, it will be stubs in whatever-your-programming-language-of-choice). To very briefly reiterate discussion from the chapter on Communications, the idea behind the IDL is to have all the inter-object communications defined in a special Interface Definition Language (see examples below), with an IDL compiler taking these IDL definitions and producing stubs (which in turn include relevant marshalling/unmarshalling code) for our (Re)Actors. We also assume that our IDL compiler (being written by us for our own purposes) *can generate any stub/skeleton code we need.*

To compare different ways of handling of non-blocking returns, let's consider the following example of a "simple item purchase"; we'll use this example to see how the code for handling this same task differs, depending on the approach.

The "simple item purchase" example scenario goes as follows. Let's assume that we have a special (Re)Actor (named Cashier) to handle all the money-related processing, including in-game purchases. Now, a request from the Client comes in to the Cashier (Re)Actor, saying that the player wants to purchase a certain item (taking tokens from his in-game account) and place it in his inventory.[63]

---

63   For the purpose of this example, we set aside the question "how has the player selected an item to purchase?" and assume that it was the result of a previous sequence of messages between the Client and the Server.

From this point on, the processing goes as shown in Fig 5.1:

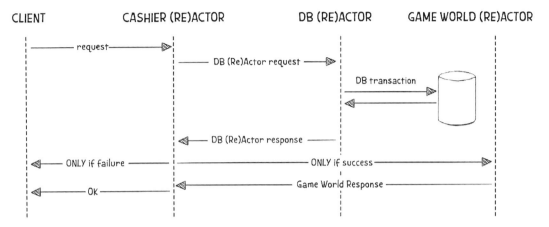

As shown in Fig 5.1, first the Cashier (Re)Actor gets the request from the Client and forwards it to the DB (Re)Actor. Then, the DB (Re)Actor performs the transaction over the database (checking if there are enough tokens in his in-game account, then subtracting tokens from his in-game account and adding an item and probably also adding an audit record — all within the same DB ACID transaction), and sends the result (success/failure) back to the Cashier (Re)Actor. The Cashier (Re)Actor gets this result and, if it is "failure," sends the reply to the Client. However, if the result was "success," the Cashier needs to send a request to the Game World (Re)Actor to add the item to the player's inventory, and only on a reply from the Game World (Re)Actor may it report to the Client that the item has been successfully added.

For the purpose of our analysis, let's concentrate on the part of the "simple item purchase" flow that is handled by the Cashier (Re)Actor. If we'd be allowed to write it in a blocking manner (and with help from the IDL compiler), the corresponding code of the Cashier (Re)Actor would look along the following lines:

```
//Listing 5.Blocking.noexcept
//PSEUDO-CODE
function purchaseItem( item_id, connection_id ) {
  user_id = get_user_id(connection_id);
  //blocking RPC call to DB (Re)Actor:
  db_ok = dbPurchaseItem(db_reactor_id,
                    user_id, item_id);
```

```
if(!db_ok)
  return false;
gameworld_reactor_id =
            find_gameworld_for_user(user_id);
//blocking RPC call to Game World (Re)Actor:
gameworld_ok = gameworldAddItem(
            gameworld_reactor_id,
            user_id, item_id);
return gameworld_ok;
}
```

Unfortunately, in practice, we won't be able to use this kind of blocking syntax for our non-blocking (Re)Actor (as we shouldn't block our Cashier while our requests to DB are processed).

Unfortunately, in practice, we won't be able to use this kind of blocking syntax for our non-blocking (Re)Actor (as we shouldn't block our Cashier while our requests to the DB are processed); however, we *are* able to use this *Listing 5.Blocking.noexcept* as a kind of "baseline" to judge readability and maintainability of our non-blocking solutions. All the essential logic we need to implement is described above within seven or so lines of code of *Listing 5.Blocking.noexcept*; anything else that we'll be adding to achieve non-blocking operation is boiler-plate code, and we need to avoid it to the fullest extent possible.

One additional observation that implicitly follows from our code being non-blocking is that there can be multiple outstanding requests to DB and Game World(s): if another request comes in while the first is being processed by a third-party (Re)Actor, we need to start processing the second request *before* the reply to the first one arrives.[64] As we'll see below, this observation has serious implications on the code (as we need to store those multiple outstanding requests somewhere, search them, etc.).

Take 1. Naïv e Approach: Plain Messages (Will Work, But Is Plain Ugly)

> IMPORTANT: *Don't worry if you think that the code in Take 1 is ugly. It is. Please skip to OO-based, lambda-based, and futures-based versions if the code in Take 1 offends your sensibilities.*

Both in theory and in practice, inter-(Re)Actor communications (as well as all the other non-blocking stuff) can be dealt with merely via

---

64   *Sometimes* processing of the second request can be delayed until processing of the first is completed, but this is a scalability killer, so it SHOULD be avoided as a Big Fat Rule of Thumb™.

introducing yet another bunch of input events. Let's say that (Re)Actor A needs to request some data from (Re)Actor B. Within our message-based "Take 1," it will be implemented as:

◆ (Re)Actor A sending a request message to (Re)Actor B (how it is delivered is a different story, which will be discussed in Volume IV).

◆ (Re)Actor B gets this request message as an input event, processes it, and sends a reply message back to (Re)Actor A.

◆ (Re)Actor A gets this reply message as an input event, and performs some (Re)Actor-specific actions.

As we can see, the logic is very simple and straightforward. However, let's see what happens when we try to implement Cashier processing of our "simple item purchase" example in this manner. To do so, our imaginary IDL may look as follows:

Both in theory and in practice, all the non-blocking calls can be dealt with merely via introducing yet another bunch of input events.

```
//Listing 5.Take1.IDL
//NB: we do need to specify types in IDL
//  even if our programming language is purely dynamic
//Client-to-Cashier:
bool cashierPurchaseItem(int item_id);
//CASHIER-to-DB:
bool dbPurchaseItem(int user_id, int item_id);
//CASHIER-to-GameWorld
bool gameworldAddItem(int user_id, int item_id);
```

After this IDL is compiled, we may get something like:

```
//Listing 5.Take1.IDLGen
//PSEUDO-CODE
//GENERATED FROM IDL, DO NOT MODIFY!
const CASHIER_PURCHASEITEM_REQUEST = 123;
const CASHIER_PURCHASEITEM_RESPONSE = 124;
const DB_PURCHASEITEM_REQUEST = 125;
const DB_PURCHASEITEM_RESPONSE = 126;
const GAMEWORLD_ADDITEM_REQUEST = 127;
const GAMEWORLD_ADDITEM_RESPONSE = 128;
//returns Msg
function cashierPurchaseItem_request_compose(
  request_id, item_id) { /* IDL-generated code */ }
//returns (request_id, item_id)
function cashierPurchaseItem_request_parse(msg)
```

```
{ /* IDL-generated code */ }
//returns Msg
function cashierPurchaseItem_response_compose(
  request_id, ret) { /* IDL-generated code */ }
//returns (request_id,returned_value)
function cashierPurchaseItem_response_parse(msg)
  { /* IDL-generated code */ }
//returns Msg
function dbPurchaseItem_request_compose(
                    request_id, user_id, item_id)
  { /* IDL-generated code */ }
//returns (request_id, int user_id, int item_id)
function dbPurchaseItem_request_parse(msg)
  { /* IDL-generated code */ }
//returns Msg
function dbPurchaseItem_response_compose(
  request_id, ret) { /* IDL-generated code */ }
//returns (request_id,returned_value)
function dbPurchaseItem_response_parse(msg)
  { /* IDL-generated code */ }
//returns Msg
function gameworldAddItem_request_compose(
   request_id, user_id, item_id)
     { /* IDL-generated code */ }
//returns (request_id, user_id, item_id)
function gameworldAddItem_request_parse(msg)
  { /* IDL-generated code */ }
//returns Msg
function gameworldAddItem_response_compose(
  request_id, ret) { /* IDL-generated code */ }
//returns (request_id,returned_value)
function gameworldAddItem_response_parse(msg)
  { /* IDL-generated code */ }
```

Note that the above IDL-compiler-generated code implies that we're using *request_ids* to match incoming replies to previously issued requests; in many cases, it is not strictly required. Strictly speaking, in some usage scenarios we *are* able to get away with replying to, say, *dbPurchaseItem()* not with a tuple (*request_id,returned_value*) as in the example above, but with a tuple (*user_id,item_id,bool*). However, the overall code won't get *that much* simpler, *and* it will become much less straightforward (without request_id, handling of scenarios such as "what if there are two outstanding requests with the same user_id," while possible, tends to be extremely tedious and error-prone). That's why I usually strongly prefer relying on *request_ids* consistently across the code instead of inventing ad-hoc solutions for each RPC call. As we'll use the same model (with *request_ids*) for *all* our Takes, this choice shouldn't affect our analysis too much.

Back to our *Listing 5.Take1.IDLGen*. As we can see, generated code actually has nothing to do with RPCs; rather, it is merely a set of functions composing and parsing messages with the format defined in IDL. As a result, our code in our Cashier (Re)Actor will look like the following (and this is where things start getting *really* ugly):

As a result, our code in our Cashier (Re)Actor will look like the following (and this is where things start getting *really* ugly).

```
//Listing 5.Take1.noexcept
//PSEUDO-CODE
//CAUTION: SEVERELY UGLY CODE AHEAD!!
const DBRequested = 0;
const GameWorldRequested = 1;
class PurchaseRqData {
  constructor(user_request_id_,
              user_id_, item_id) {
    status = DBRequested;
    user_request_id = user_request_id_;
    user_id = user_id_;
    item_id = item_id_;
  }
}
class CashierReactor {
  purchase_item_requests = new map();
    //map of request_ids into PurchaseRqData
    // we need it to account for multiple players
    // requesting purchases at the same time
};
function CashierReactor.react(Event ev) {
  switch(ev.type) {
    case CASHIER_PURCHASEITEM_REQUEST:
    {
      msg = ev.msg;
      (user_request_id, item_id) =
         cashierPurchaseItem_request_parse(msg);
      user_id = get_user_id(ev);
      request_id = new_request_id();
      msg2 = dbPurchaseItem_request_compose(
             request_id, user_id, item_id);
      send_msg_to(db_reactor_id, msg2);
```

```
      purchase_item_requests.insert(
        request_id,
        PurchaseRqData(user_request_id,
                            user_id, item_id));
    break;
  }

  case DB_PURCHASEITEM_RESPONSE:
  {
    msg = ev.msg;
    (request_id, db_ok) = dbPurchaseItem_parse(msg);
    found = purchase_item_requests.extract(request_id);
    assert found != null;
    assert found.status == DBRequested;
    if(!db_ok) {
        msg3 = cashierPurchaseItem_response_compose(
                found.user_request_id, false);
        send_msg_back_to(user_id, msg3);
        break;
      }

    gameworld_reactor_id =
                find_gameworld_for_user(found.user_id);
    msg4 = gameworldAddItem_request_compose(request_id,
                found.user_id, found.item_id);
    send_msg_to(gameworld_reactor_id, msg4);
    found.status = GameWorldRequested;
    break;
  }
  case GAMEWORLD_ADDITEM_RESPONSE:
  {
    msg = ev.msg;
    (request_id, gw_ok) =
                    gameworldAddItem_response_parse(msg);
    found = purchase_item_requests.extract(request_id);
    assert found != null;
    assert found.status == GameWorldRequested;
    msg2 = cashierPurchaseItem_response_compose(
                            found.user_request_id, gw_ok);
    send_msg_back_to(user_id, msg2);
    break;
  }
 }
}
```

If you feel that this code was beaten with an ugly stick, well, that's because it was (and if you take a look at Appendix 5.A, you'll see that the C++ version is even worse).

In *Listing 5.Take1.noexcept*, we have over 40 lines of code (over 50 for C++) with only 7 of them being really meaningful (and the rest being boilerplate stuff); this is pretty bad. Not only does it take a lot of keystrokes to write, but, *much* more importantly, it is even worse to read (the substance of what-we-want-to-do being completely hidden within that mass of boilerplate code). Moreover, the code is very fragile, making maintenance very difficult and error-prone. If such a piece of code happens once for your million-LOC game that's okay, but for a real-world game, chances are that you will need these things *much* more than once (and they will be *much* more complicated), and then it will become a quite an unpleasant problem.

In other words, for a pretty much any non-trivial case, the code style shown above will be very difficult to maintain. Yes, it is doable, but it takes *much* more effort than is really necessary. Let's see what we can do to improve it.

If you feel that this code was beaten with an ugly stick, well, that's because it was.

LOC

Lines of Code is a software metric used to measure the size of a computer program by counting the number of lines in the text of the program's source code

—**Wikipedia**

Take 2. Void-Only RPCs (A Tiny Bit Better, Still Really Ugly)

Void-only non-blocking RPCs are probably the most popular way of message passing in modern commercially-available game engines such as Unity 5 or UE4 (see also discussion on them in Chapter 7). If relying on void-only RPCs, the code on the receiving side will look less ugly than for plain messages, but the code on the sending side will still be pretty bad. Let's see how our "simple item purchase" example will look if we're using void-only RPCs to implement it.

For void-only RPCs, our "simple item purchase" IDL may look along the following lines:

```
//Listing 5.Take2.IDL
//Client-to-Cashier:
void cashierPurchaseItemRequest(int request_id, int item_id);
void cashierPurchaseItemResponse(int request_id, bool ret);
//CASHIER-to-DB:
void dbPurchaseItemRequest(int request_id,
                           int user_id, int item_id);
```

```
void dbPurchaseItemResponse(int request_id, bool ret);
//CASHIER-to-GameWorld
void gameworldAddItemRequest(int request_id,
                            int user_id, int item_id);
void gameworldAddItemResponse(int request_id, bool ret);
```

Let's note that pretty often, void-RPC IDL is part of your regular programming language (such as C# or C++), with functions designated to become RPC functions being marked with something like [RPC], [Command], or UFUNCTION(Client). In this case, those marked functions effectively form an "intra-language" IDL; we'll discuss a bit more about such intra-language IDLs in popular game engines in Chapter 7.

On the other hand, for our current purposes of handling non-blocking calls, it is not important whether IDL is external or intra-language. Whatever our IDL, after it is compiled, we may get something along the lines of:[65]

```
//Listing 5.Take2.IDLGen
//PSEUDO-CODE
//GENERATED FROM IDL, DO NOT MODIFY!
function cashierPurchaseItemRequest(
        r, //CashierReactor object
        peer_reactor, request_id, item_id) {
  //for Cashier, this is an RPC function
  // to be implemented
}
function cashierPurchaseItemResponse(
        peer_reactor, request_id, ret) {
  //for Cashier, this is an RPC stub
  // to be called
}
function dbPurchaseItemRequest(
        peer_reactor, request_id,
        user_id, item_id) {
  //for Cashier, this is an RPC stub
  // to be called
}
```

---

65   NB: this piece of code usually stays hidden from a developer's view; I still list it here to demonstrate how the whole thing works together for those not really familiar with IDL mechanics.

```
function dbPurchaseItemResponse(r,
        peer_reactor, request_id, ret) {
  //for Cashier, this is an RPC function
  // to be implemented
}
function gameworldAddItemRequest(
        peer_reactor, request_id, user_id, item_id) {
  //for Cashier, this is an RPC stub
  // to be called
}
function gameworldAddItemResponse(r,
        peer_reactor, request_id, ret) {
  //for Cashier, this is an RPC function
  // to be implemented
}
```

With this in mind, the code within our Cashier (Re)Actor will look
more or less as follows:

```
//Listing 5.Take2.noexcept
//PSEUDO-CODE
//CAUTION: RATHER UGLY CODE AHEAD!!
const DBRequested = 0;
const GameWorldRequested = 1;
class PurchaseRqData {//same as for Take 1
  constructor(user_request_id_,
              user_id_, item_id) {
    status = DBRequested;
    user_request_id = user_request_id_;
    user_id = user_id_;
    item_id = item_id_;
  }
}
class CashierReactor {//same as for Take 1
  purchase_item_requests = new map();
    //map of request_ids into PurchaseRqData
    // we need it to account for multiple players
    // requesting purchases at the same time
};
//implementing RPC functions (for prototypes from IDL):
function cashierPurchaseItemRequest(r,
        peer_reactor, request_id, item_id) {
  user_id = get_user_id(peer_reactor);
  request_id = new_request_id();
  dbPurchaseItemRequest(db_reactor_id, request_id,
```

```
                                        user_id, item_id);
        r.purchase_item_requests.insert(
          request_id,
          PurchaseRqData(user_request_id,
                         user_id, item_id));
      }
      function dbPurchaseItemResponse(r,
              peer_reactor, request_id, db_ok) {
        found = r.purchase_item_requests.extract(request_id);
        assert found != null;
        assert found.status == DBRequested;
        if(!db_ok) {
          user_reactor =
                     find_user_reactor_id(found.user_id);
          cashierPurchaseItemResponse(user_reactor,
                            found.user_request_id, false);
          return;
        }

        gameworld_reactor_id =
                     find_gameworld_for_user(found.user_id);
        gameworldAddItemRequest(gameworld_reactor_id,
                            request_id,
                            found.user_id, found.item_id);
        found.status = GameWorldRequested;
      }
      function gameworldAddItemResponse(
                            peer_reactor, request_id, gw_ok) {
        found = r.purchase_item_requests.find(request_id);
        assert found != null;
        assert found.status == GameWorldRequested;
        user_reactor =
                     find_user_reactor_id(found.user_id);
        cashierPurchaseItemResponse(user_reactor,
                            found.user_request_id, gw_ok);
      }
```

I see the code in our Take 2 as a relatively slight improvement over Take 1.

I see the code in our Take 2 as a relatively slight improvement over Take 1. From 40+ lines of code we're down to 30 or so (for C++ in Appendix 5.A, it is down from 50+ to 35); it is indeed an improvement, but with only 7 lines being meaningful, it is still about 4x overhead. Even worse, we're still managing outstanding requests in *purchase_item_requests* manually and at application-level, which is very error-prone.

Take 3. OO-Style: Less Error-Prone, But Still Way Too Much Boilerplate

Our third attempt at the "how to handle return values from remote procedure call" problem will be in an Object-Oriented (OO) style. We will create a callback class, register it with our (Re)Actor, and then it will be our Infrastructure Code dealing with most of the mechanics within. Rewriting our "simple item purchase" example in OO-style will significantly change the whole thing. While IDL will be the same as in *Listing 5.Take1.IDL*, both generated code and calling code will look very different.

```
//Listing 5.Take3.IDL, same as 5.Take1.IDL
//Client-to-Cashier:
bool cashierPurchaseItem(int item_id);
//CASHIER-to-DB:
bool dbPurchaseItem(int user_id, int item_id);
//CASHIER-to-GameWorld
bool gameworldAddItem(int user_id, int item_id);
```

For OO-style asynchronous calls, stub code generated from IDL by IDL compiler may look as follows:

```
//Listing 5.Take3.IDLGen
//PSEUDO-CODE
//GENERATED FROM IDL, DO NOT MODIFY!
function cashierPurchaseItem(r,
  reply_handle,
    //reply_handle is an object which allows
    // calling reply() function on it to send reply
    // back to requestor
    //reply_handle MAY be copied,
    // if it is necessary to postpone replying
    // until later
  item_id ) {
  //for Cashier, this is an RPC function
  // to be implemented
}
function dbPurchaseItem(r,
        dbPurchaseItemCb,
          //dbPurchaseItemCb.react() will be called when the
          // reply is obtained
```

```
           reactor_to, user_id, item_id ) {
  //sends a message, calls dbPurchaseItemCb.react() on
  // receving reply;
  // react() will receive result of the RPC call
  // on the other side as parameter
  //for Cashier, this is an RPC stub
  // to be called
}
function gameworldAddItem(r,
          gwAddItemCb,
          reactor_to, user_id, item_id) {
  //sends a message, calls gwAddItemCb.react()
  // on receiving reply;
  // react() will receive result of the RPC call
  //for Cashier, this is an RPC stub
  // to be called
}
```

Then, our (Re)Actor code will look as follows:

```
//Listing 5.Take3.noexcept
//PSEUDO-CODE
//CAUTION: VERBOSE CODE AHEAD!
//TAKE 3 IS LESS ERROR-PRONE THAN TAKES 1-2,
// BUT STILL HAS LOTS OF BOILERPLATE CODE
class DbPurchaseItemCallbackA {
  constructor(r_, reply_handle_,
              user_id_, item_id_) {
    r = r_;
    reply_handle = reply_handle_;
    user_id = user_id_;
    item_id = item_id_;
  }

  function react(db_ok) {
    if(!db_ok) {
      reply_handle.reply(false);
      return;
    }
    gameworld_reactor_id =
        r.find_gameworld_for_user(user_id);
    cb = new GameworldAddItemCallbackA(
            r, reply_handle,
            user_id, item_id);
    gameworldAddItem(cb, gameworld_reactor_id,
                  user_id, item_id);
  }
```

```
}
class GameworldAddItemCallbackA {
  constructor(r_, reply_handle_,
              user_id_, item_id_) {
    r = r_;
    reply_handle = reply_handle_;
    user_id = user_id_;
    item_id = item_id_;
  }
  function react(gw_ok) {
    reply_handle.reply(gw_ok);
  }
}
function cashierPurchaseItem(r,
  reply_handle, item_id) {
  user_id = get_user_id(reply_handle);
  cb = new DbPurchaseItemCallbackA(
        r, reply_handle,
        user_id, item_id);
  dbPurchaseItem(cb, db_reactor_id,
                user_id, item_id);
}
```

As we can see, Take 3 is less error-prone than the code in Takes 1-2 (keeping *purchase_item_requests* out of application level certainly qualifies as a Good Thing™ in this regard), but…Take 3 is still verbose, and still relatively poorly readable as a result. For each meaningful line of code, there are still about 2 lines of boilerplate stuff (make it 4 for C++); on the other hand, it is IMO easier to parse this boilerplate code out while reading than for Takes 1-2. On the third hand, and probably most importantly, if we compare the code in *Listing 5.Take3.noexcept* to our original blocking code in *Listing 5.Blocking.noexcept*, we'll notice that while parts of the code are more or less the same, these parts are reordered in *Listing 5.Take3.noexcept*; this tends to create quite a bit of confusion, and significantly reduce readability and maintainability of the code. In some programming languages (see, for example, *Listing 5.A.Take3.noexcept* in Appendix A for a C++ example) it might be possible to have the same ordering as in our original blocking code, but it often comes at the cost of the additional few lines of code.

In [Fugal], such approaches are named "callback hell." Well, I wouldn't be that categorical (after all, there was life before lambdas and coroutines), but, yes, it is indeed rather annoying (and has limited

As we can see, Take 3 is less error-prone than the code in Takes 1-2, but it is still verbose, and still relatively poorly readable as a result.

manageability). If your programming language doesn't support anything better than OO-style callbacks, you might need to use this kind
of stuff, but if your language supports lambdas, the very same thing can
be written in a significantly more manageable manner (see Take 4 and
subsequent takes below).

Exceptions

BTW, now, as we got rid of those *really ugly* Takes 1 and 2 (most importantly, any additional complexity would make them absolutely incom-
prehensible), we can start thinking about adding exception handling to
our non-blocking RPC calls.

How to handle excep-
tions that happened
between our callbacks.

The very first problem we're about to discuss in this regard is "how
to handle exceptions that happened *between* our callbacks." As one example, any of our RPC calls can run into an unreachable server or some
other communication problem; in such cases, the problem needs to be
reported to the caller. From a programming point of view, in blocking
code such situations are usually handled via throwing an exception,
and we'd like to use the same familiar concept for our non-blocking
RPC calls. On the other hand, most of the time we want to have *uniform*
handling of the exceptions, with an option to use the same exception
handler regardless of whether the exception happened *between* our
callbacks or *within* one of them.

To start comparing non-blocking-solutions-supporting-exceptions,
let's make another baseline code (once again, it will be the blocking one,
which we can compare against all our non-blocking takes). Let's consider the same blocking example from our *Listing 5.Blocking.noexcept*,
but with added exception handling:

```
//Listing 5.Blocking.except
//PSEUDO-CODE
function purchaseItem(item_id, connection_id) {
  try {
    user_id = get_user_id(connection_id);
    db_ok = dbPurchaseItem(db_reactor_id,
              user_id, item_id);
    if(!db_ok)
      return false;
    gameworld_reactor_id =
            find_gameworld_for_user(user_id);
```

```
    gameworld_ok = gameworldAddItem(
      gameworld_reactor_id,
      user_id, item_id);
    return gameworld_ok;
  }
  catch( x ) {
    LogException(x);
    return false;
  }
}
```

When trying to implement the same thing in a non-blocking manner, and on top of our Take 3, we can add another member function to all the callback objects; this *except()* function would take an exception object as a parameter. Then, if the exception has happened during the RPC call, we'd get a call to *except()* instead of the usual call to *react()*.

This leads to the following Take 3a (implementing the same thing as in *Listing 5.Blocking.except*, but in a non-blocking manner):

```
//Listing 5.Take3a.except
//PSEUDO-CODE
//NON-BLOCKING VERSION OF LISTING 5.Blocking.except
//CAUTION: VERBOSE CODE AHEAD!
class DbPurchaseItemCallbackA {
  constructor(
              r_, reply_handle_,
              user_id_, item_id_) {
    r = r_;
    reply_handle = reply_handle_;
    user_id = user_id_;
    item_id = item_id_;
  }

  function react(db_ok) {
    try {
      if(!db_ok) {
        reply_handle.reply(false);
        return;
      }
      gameworld_reactor_id =
            r.find_gameworld_for_user(user_id);
      cb = new GameworldAddItemCallbackA(
              r, reply_handle,
```

```
                                  user_id, item_id);
             gameworldAddItem(cb, gameworld_reactor_id,
                              user_id, item_id);
      }
      catch( x ) {
        handleCashierPurchaseError(reply_handle, x);
      }
    }
    function except(x) {
      handleCashierPurchaseError(reply_handle, x);
    }
  }
  class GameworldAddItemCallbackA {
    constructor(r_, reply_handle_,
                  user_id_, item_id_) {
      r = r_;
      reply_handle = reply_handle_;
      user_id = user_id_;
      item_id = item_id_;
    }
    function react(gw_ok) {
      reply_handle.reply(gw_ok);
    }
    function except(x) {
      handleCashierPurchaseError(reply_handle, x);
    }
  }
  function cashierPurchaseItem(r, reply_handle,
                                      item_id) {
    try {
      user_id = get_user_id(reply_handle);
      cb = new DbPurchaseItemCallbackA(
              r, reply_handle,
              user_id, item_id);
      dbPurchaseItem(cb, db_reactor_id,
                      user_id, item_id);
    }
    catch( x ) {
      handleCashierPurchaseError(x);
    }
  }
  function handleCashierPurchaseError(
          reply_handle, x) {
    LogException(x);
    reply_handle.reply(false);
  }
```

As we can see, our code from Take 3 became significantly uglier (and more verbose) after we added exception handling. While adding exceptions to our blocking code has taken only 4 extra LOC, our Take 3a version added 15 LOC to express the same exception-handling logic. Not fatal, but we can still do better.

BTW, there is an alternative approach for adding exception support to Take 3; namely, instead of adding *except()* function, we could add an *exception* parameter to all *react()* functions (this parameter being *null* if the exception didn't happen, and being a pointer to the exception otherwise). This alternative approach, while looking more similar to that of *Node.js* (see also the discussion of Take 4 below), won't change much "how ugly or verbose our Take 3a is"; in particular, repeated calls to *handleCashierPurchaseError()* will stay.

Our code from Take 3 became significantly uglier (and more verbose) after we added exception handling.

Cascading Exception Handlers

To allow for less-boilerplate and more-to-the-point exception handling, we need to "cascade" exception handlers one way or another. For example, we could say that:

♦ Infrastructure Code, in addition to calling *except()* when exception occurs in a remote call, also calls *except()* when an exception occurs within *react()*.

♦ There is an alternative form of constructor for **Callback* objects, taking another **Callback* as an input parameter.[66]

   ▪ Then, for **Callback* objects created with such an alternative constructor, "parent" *except()* will be called.

This leads us to the following Take 3b:

```
//Listing 5.Take3b.except
//PSEUDO-CODE
//NON-BLOCKING VERSION OF LISTING 5.Blocking.except
//CAUTION: VERBOSE CODE AHEAD!
class DbPurchaseItemCallbackA {
  constructor(r_, reply_handle_,
            user_id_, item_id_) {
    r = r_;
    reply_handle = reply_handle_;
    user_id = user_id_;
```

---

66   To do so, we'll need to derive all *Callback classes from common base.

```
      item_id = item_id_;
    }

    function react(db_ok) {
      try {
        if(!db_ok) {
          reply_handle.reply(false);
          return;
        }
        gameworld_reactor_id =
            r.find_gameworld_for_user(user_id);
        cb = new GameworldAddItemCallbackA(
                  this, /* 'inherits' exception
                    handler from
                    previous callback */
                  reply_handle,
                  user_id, item_id);
        gameworldAddItem(cb, gameworld_reactor_id,
                          user_id, item_id);
      }
      catch( x ) {
        handleCashierPurchaseError(reply_handle, x);
      }
    }
    function except(x) {
      handleCashierPurchaseError(reply_handle, x);
    }
}
class GameworldAddItemCallbackA {
  constructor(r_, reply_handle_,
              user_id_, item_id_ ) {
    r = r_;
    reply_handle = reply_handle_;
    user_id = user_id_;
    item_id = item_id_;
  }
  function react(gw_ok) {
    reply_handle.reply(gw_ok);
  }
  //no 'except()' here means that it is 'inherited'
  // from the previous callback
}
function cashierPurchaseItem(r, reply_handle,
        item_id) {
  try {
    user_id = get_user_id(reply_handle);
```

```
    cb = new DbPurchaseItemCallbackA(
            r, reply_handle,
            user_id, item_id);
    dbPurchaseItem(cb, db_reactor_id,
                user_id, item_id);
  }
  catch( x ) {
    handleCashierPurchaseError(x);
  }
}
function handleCashierPurchaseError(
        reply_handle, x ) {
  LogException(x);
  reply_handle.reply(false);
}
```

As we can see, with Take 3b, we're able to reduce the number of extra LOC necessary to implement exception handling (the one that took only 4 lines in original blocking code), from 15 to a somewhat more bearable 10 or so. However, this reduction comes at the cost of the loss of some flexibility and quite a bit of difficult-to-spot-magic. In particular, under this model, *GameworldAddItemCallbackA* being constructed from *this* or from *r* has different semantics, and the difference can be difficult to notice, leaving the potential for difficult-to-spot errors.

Bottom line about exceptions and Take3a/3b:

♦ Based on Take 3 (which is significantly better than Take 1/Take 2), we were able to introduce exceptions.

♦ It is even bearable (personally, if forced to choose between Take 3a and Take 3b, I'd prefer Take 3a as a more straightforward one, but the difference is not too great).

♦ However, it is still a long shot from the original blocking code on *Listing 5.Blocking.except.*

Take 4. Lambda Pyramid

For a long while, Take 3 was more or less the best we could use. However, as soon as we got lambda functions with closures (for C++, more or less since C++11), the whole non-blocking thing became significantly easier to write down. First, we could simply replace our OO-style classes with lambda functions. In this case, code generated from the very same IDL…

As soon as we got lambda functions with closures, the whole non-blocking thing became significantly easier to write down.

```
//Listing 5.Take4.IDL, same as 5.Take1.IDL and 5.Take3.IDL
//Client-to-Cashier:
bool cashierPurchaseItem(int item_id);
//CASHIER-to-DB:
bool dbPurchaseItem(int user_id, int item_id);
//CASHIER-to-GameWorld
bool gameworldAddItem(int user_id, int item_id);
```

...may look as follows:

```
//LISTING 5.Take4.IDLGen
//PSEUDO-CODE
//GENERATED FROM IDL, DO NOT MODIFY!
function cashierPurchaseItem(r,
        reply_handle,
        item_id) {
  //for Cashier, this is an RPC function
  // to be implemented
}
function dbPurchaseItem(
        reactor_peer,
        user_id, item_id, cb) {
  //for Cashier, this is an RPC stub
  // to be called
}
function gameworldAddItem(reactor_peer,
        user_id, item_id, cb) {
  //for Cashier, this is an RPC stub
  // to be called
}
```

Then, the relevant part of our *CashierReactor*'s code may be written along the lines of:

```
//LISTING 5.Take4.except
//PSEUDO-CODE
//NON-BLOCKING VERSION OF LISTING 5.Blocking.except
//BEWARE: "LAMBDA PYRAMID" ROLLER COASTER AHEAD!
// NOT FOR THE FAINT OF HEART!
function ifCashierPurchaseError( x) {
  if(x) {
    LogException(x);
    return true;
  }
  return false;
}
function cashierPurchaseItem(r,
        reply_handle, item_id) {
  user_id = get_user_id(reply_handle);
```

```
dbPurchaseItem(
  db_reactor_id,
  user_id, item_id,
  λ(x, db_ok) {
    if(ifCashierPurchaseError(x))
      return;
    if(!db_ok) {
      reply_handle.reply(false);
      return;//returns from current
              //  lambda function
    }
    gameworld_reactor_id =
        find_gameworld_for_user(user_id);
    gameworldAddItem(
      gameworld_reactor_id,
      user_id, item_id,
      λ(x, gw_ok){
        if(ifCashierPurchaseError(x))
          return;
        reply_handle.reply(gw_ok);
      }//end of 2nd lambda
    );//end of call to gameworldAddItem()
  }//end of 1st lambda
);//end of call to dbPurchaseItem
}
```

Compared to our previous attempts, such a "lambda pyramid" is significantly less verbose. Instead of Take 3, which has about 35 lines of code for a meaningful 11 or so, here we have just about 20 LOC total (or just about 2x the overhead instead of the previous 3x). And I'd say it is more readable, too; sure, when reading Take 4 it is necessary to skip those lambdas, but as soon as we learn to ignore them, the code in Take 4 becomes significantly closer to our Holy Grail of *Listing 5.Blocking. noexcept*. Still, there are two significant differences between Take 4 and the original *Listing 5.Blocking.noexcept*. First, with "lambda pyramid" in Take 4, there are additional indents not present in the original (which tends to cause quite a bit of confusion).[67] Probably even more importantly, these indents outline a more generic issue with lambda pyramids – the code which is *linear* in our originally blocking code, becomes *nested* with lambda pyramids; while not fatal, it doesn't help readability of the code, especially for larger code bases.

Compared to our previous attempts, such a "lambda pyramid" is significantly less verbose. And I'd say it is more readable, too.

---

67   And removing the indents is not a really good option, either — without them, finding those end-of-lambdas will become significantly more difficult, which doesn't help in sizeable projects.

In fact, Take 4 is very close to the way *Node.js* programs typically handle asynchronous calls. Actually, as we'll discuss below in the *Similarities to Node.js* section, the whole task we're facing with our non-blocking (Re)Actors (which can be described as "event-driven programming with support for non-blocking calls") is almost exactly the same as the one for *Node.js*, so there is no wonder that the methods we're using are similar. On the other hand, it doesn't mean that we can't do *better* than *Node.js*, and we'll discuss such options in Takes 5 and up.

Cascaded Exception Handling, Lambda Style

As we discussed above, Takes 3a/3b can handle exceptions. Semantically similar (though syntactically very different) exception handling can be added to Take 4 (with cascading achieved at the cost of passing exception-handling lambda down the stack):

```
//LISTING 5.Take4a.except
//PSEUDO-CODE
//NON-BLOCKING VERSION OF LISTING 5.Blocking.except
//BEWARE: "LAMBDA PYRAMID" ROLLER COASTER AHEAD!
// NOT FOR THE FAINT OF HEART!
function cashierPurchaseItem(r,
        reply_handle, item_id) {
  user_id = get_user_id(reply_handle);
  catc =
    λ(x) {
      LogException(x);
    };
  dbPurchaseItem(
    db_reactor_id, user_id, item_id,
    λ(db_ok){
      if(!db_ok) {
        reply_handle.reply(false);
        return;//returns from current lambda
      }
      gameworld_reactor_id =
          find_gameworld_for_user(user_id);
      gameworldAddItem(
        gameworld_reactor_id, user_id, item_id,
        λ(x, gw_ok) {
          reply_handle.reply(gw_ok);
        }, catc);
    }, catc);
}
```

Arguably, Take 4a is the best one so far, but while it does make the code certainly less verbose than, say, Take 3a/3b, it does not exactly qualify as "easily readable," especially compared to our Holy Grail of *Listing 5.Blocking.except.*

It should also be noted that with lambda pyramids such as those in Take 4/4a, it is still difficult to express the concept of "wait for more than one thing to complete."[68] In practice, it usually leads to unnecessary sequencing, adding to latencies (which may or may not be a problem for your purposes, but is still a thing to keep in mind).

On the other hand, as soon as we have lambdas in our programming toolbox, we can make another attempt to write our asynchronous code, and to obtain the code that is free from these limitations of "lambda pyramids."

With lambda pyramids, it is still difficult to express the concept of "wait for more than one thing to complete." In practice, it usually leads to unnecessary sequencing, adding to latencies.

Take 5. (Re)Actor Futures

While the 'lambda pyramid' version from Take 4 is indeed a significant improvement (especially over Take 1–Take 2), it is still miles away from the obviousness of blocking code, so let's see how we can improve

---

68 In fact, this problem is not specific to lambdas; for all the Takes 1 to 4a, expressing "wait for more than one thing to complete," while possible, is a Rather Big Headache™ (and quite error-prone, too).

it further. For our Take 5, we will use a concept known as "futures." Essentially, "future" (a.k.a. "promise") is a placeholder for the result of a certain operation (in our case, it can be *any* non-blocking operation). Originally, "future" is in "initial" state (also known as "non-computed"), and doesn't have any valid data; then, after the result is known, it is in a "computed" state (and can return a valid result).

For our purposes, we'll use a special type of future: the one intended to work with (Re)Actors.[69] With our *ReactorFutures*, IDL-generated code for the very same "item purchase" example may look as follows:

```
//LISTING 5.Take5.IDLGen
//PSEUDO-CODE
//GENERATED FROM IDL, DO NOT MODIFY!
function cashierPurchaseItem(r,
        reply_handle, item_id) {
  //for Cashier, this is an RPC function
  // to be implemented
}
function dbPurchaseItem(r, reactor_peer,
                        user_id, item_id) {
  //for Cashier, this is an RPC stub
  // to be called
}//returns ReactorFuture object

function gameworldAddItem(r, reactor_peer,
        user_id, item_id) {
  //for Cashier, this is an RPC stub
  // to be called
}//returns ReactorFuture object
```

And then the calling code will look along the lines of:[70]

```
//LISTING 5.Take5.except
//PSEUDO-CODE
//NON-BLOCKING VERSION OF LISTING 5.Blocking.except
function cashierPurchaseItem(r,
        reply_handle, item_id) {
```

---

69   As we'll see below, while our *ReactorFutures* are conceptually similar to thread-oriented futures such as *std::future<>*, they're still quite different in the way they can be used.

70   Note that it is also possible to write future-based code in Take 4/Take 4a style without declaring *gw_ok* in advance and creating a "pyramid" instead. However, most of the time, such a style will be too similar to Take 4/Take 4a to obtain any significant benefits from using futures.

```
user_id = get_user_id(reply_handle);
catc =
  λ(x) {
    LogException(x);
  };
//here db_ok is a ReactorFuture object
db_ok = dbPurchaseItem(
        r, db_reactor_id,
        user_id, item_id);
        //NB: infrastructure code
        //  should effectively postpone
        //  all the exceptions within
        //  until except() handler is provided
  gw_ok = new ReactorFuture(this);
    //we need to create/declare it here
    // to have something to refer to
    // within lambdas
  db_ok.then(λ(){
    if(!db_ok.value()) {
      reply_handle.reply(false);
      return;//returns from current lambda function
    }
    gameworld_reactor_id =
          find_gameworld_for_user(user_id);
    gw_ok = gameworldAddItem(
            r, gameworld_reactor_id,
            user_id, item_id);
  }).except(catc);
  gw_ok.then(λ(){
    reply_handle.reply(gw_ok.value());
  }).except(catc);
}
```

IMO, Take 5, while technically having a few more lines than Take 4/Take 4a, is significantly more straightforward and easier readable. Most importantly, there is no more "pyramid," and the code-that-was-linear-in-blocking-code once again looks linear in Take 5. Out of all the takes so far, I'd argue that Take 5 is the closest to the *Listing 5.Blocking.except* so far.

Also, with some support from infrastructure code, it *is* reasonably easy to express a "wait for several things to complete" with *ReactorFutures*; for example:

IMO, Take 5, while technically having a few more lines than Take 4/Take 4a, is significantly more straightforward and easier readable.

```
//LISTING 5.Take5.parallel
a = rpcA(r);//'a' is a ReactorFuture object
b = rpcB(r);//'b' is also a ReactorFuture object
both = new ReactorFutureBoth(r,a,b);
  //'both' is a special kind of ReactorFuture, which
  // has then() function waiting for
  // both 'a' and 'b' futures to complete before invoking
  // its own continuation
both.then(λ(){
  //...
});
```

On the other hand, Take 5 is still not ideal. In particular, handling of exceptions is still not obvious, especially when compared to *Listing 5.Blocking.noexcept*. Which means <drum roll /> that there will be even more takes down the road.

Similarities and Differences from Existing Futures/Promises

Up to now, when talking about "futures," we referred to an abstract *ReactorFuture*; now we'll try to compare it to existing implementations of futures (also referred to as "promises") in various programming languages.

Traditionally, all the functionality provided by existing futures/promises can be divided into two large families:

♦ Futures allowing to register a callback to be called when the value in the future becomes available. For such futures, a callback-registering function such as *then()*, or *when()*, is necessary. Such futures, in turn, can be further subdivided into two subcategories:

▪ Callback is *always* called within the same thread as the-thread-that-has-registered it.

▪ Callback can be called from *any* thread.

♦ Futures allowing to wait for a future value to become available, and then proceed. This is usually handled by an inherently blocking *wait()* function (or by *get()* function implicitly blocking until the value becomes available).

Out of these significantly different types of processing, for our non-blocking (Re)Actors, only the callback-called-from-the-same-thread will do. And existing implementations of futures/promises exhibit a rather wide spectrum of behavior:

♦ Futures providing only *wait()/get()* functionality (which is useless for our non-blocking (Re)Actors). C++ is particularly guilty of implementing futures this way; in particular, both *std::future<>* and *boost:future<>* provide only blocking functionality.

♦ Futures providing only *then()/when()* functionality, and providing guarantees that the callback will be called from the same thread. These are exactly the futures we want. Such behavior is typical for JavaScript and *Node.js* futures/promises.

♦ Dual-use futures providing both *wait()* and *then()/when()*. They can be used within our (Re)Actors, but care should be taken not to use blocking behavior (among other things, in distributed systems, blocking *wait()* or potentially-blocking *get()* can easily lead to rarely happening deadlocks <ouch and double-ouch! />).

    ▪ One example of dual-use futures includes C++ *folly::future<>* (NB: when using *folly:future<>*, be extra careful to provide right *Executor* to ensure that callback is executed within the same thread, or at least to provide infrastructure-level thread sync).

    ▪ Another example of dual-use futures is Java 8's *CompletableFuture<>*.

    ▪ Overall, I do *not* recommend using dual-use futures in your app-level code *directly*; on the other hand, using dual-use futures to implement 99% of your own infrastructure-code *ReactorFuture* is a very different story altogether, and is perfectly fine — as long as you don't expose blocking functionality to the users of your *ReactorFuture*.

Existing implementations of futures/promises exhibit a rather wide spectrum of behavior.

Of course, in addition to those-libraries-explicitly-mentioned-above, there are dozens of others; still, they will fall into one of the categories above — and, in general, will need to be handled pretty much along the same lines as the respective examples.

Overall, whatever you're using within your (Re)Actors:

> ● *(Re)Actor futures MUST provide callbacks.*
>
> ● *Moreover, (Re)Actor futures MUST guarantee that accessing members of our (Re)Actor from all the callbacks is fine without any thread synchronization.*

Take 5 Summary

Our Take 5 IMO represents yet another significant improvement over the previous Takes (in particular, it is closer to the original Blocking code than our other attempts, and also allows for easy handling of concurrent execution). And, just like our other Takes, it manages to avoid blocking, and doesn't require dreaded thread sync to access the state of our (Re)Actor.

On the other hand, certain constructs (like loops and try-catch blocks) are still quite confusing under Take 5. Let's see whether we can improve it further.

Take 6. Code Builder

What if we allow "constructing" the whole code tree (with all the control operators, and not just simple *then()*) using lambda callbacks as a basic building block.

When trying to improve readability of the try/catch code in Take 5, an interesting thought has crossed my mind: what if we allow "constructing" the whole code tree (with all the control operators, and not just simple *then()*) using lambda callbacks as a basic building block? Let's see where this approach has led us[71] so far. However, before looking at the code, let's note that:

♦ The pseudo-code below was reconstructed from C++ code (which can be found in Appendix 5.A); for different programming languages, YMMV.

♦ This is still a *very* experimental field; in other words: we can easily run into bugs that can render the whole Take 6 unusable at some point a bit later.

```
//LISTING 5.Take6.except
//PSEUDO-CODE
//NON-BLOCKING VERSION OF LISTING 5.Blocking.except
function cashierPurchaseItem(r,
        reply_handle, item_id) {
  user_id = get_user_id(reply_handle);
  db_ok = Future(r);
  gw_ok = Future(r);
  CCode code(
    ttry(
      λ(){
```

---

71   More specifically, Dmitri Ligoum and myself as part of the unfortunately-currently-frozen Autom project [Ligoum and Ignatchenko].

```
      db_ok = dbPurchaseItem(
            db_reactor_id,
            user_id, item_id);
    },
    waitFor(db_ok),
    λ(){
      if(!db_ok.value()) {
        reply_handle.reply(false);
        return eexit();
          //returns from the whole CCode block
      }
      gameworld_reactor_id =
            find_gameworld_for_user(user_id);
      gw_ok = gameworldAddItem(
            gameworld_reactor_id,
            user_id, item_id);
    },
    waitFor(gw_ok),
    λ() {
      reply_handle.reply(gw_ok.value());
    }
  )//ttry
  .ccatch( λ(x) {
    LogException(x);
  }
 );//CCode
}
```

Here, *ttry* is analogous to conventional *try*, and can contain a list of items — with each of the items being either a lambda function or a special *waitFor()* call; the latter (not surprisingly) will wait for a specified Future to be calculated. The whole thing within *ttry* above can be read as "execute lambda function, wait for *db_ok* to be calculated, execute another lambda function, wait for *gw_ok* to be calculated, execute another lambda"; it is very close to the natural flow of blocking code, and, well, this is exactly the whole point of our Take 6. As this sequence sits within *ttry*, it means that if there is an exception anywhere within, we'll catch it within a corresponding *ccatch*.

    Bingo! We've got original linear flow of the blocking code, and made it work within a non-blocking environment. Let's note though that there is a big difference between blocking and non-blocking code to be kept in mind: with a non-blocking code, in each of the points marked

Bingo! We've got original linear flow of the blocking code, and made it work within a non-blocking environment.

with *waitFor()*, our seemingly blocking sequence can be interrupted by a new incoming event. This, however, as discussed in the *To Block, or Not to Block, That Is the Question. Mostly-Non-Blocking (Re)Actors* section above, is *exactly* what we want from non-blocking processing: to be able to react to incoming events (with an ability to access the state of our (Re)Actor) while our request is being processed.

On implementing all those *ttry,* etc. functions above, I won't go into a lengthy discussion on "how this thing can possibly work" (as noted above, it is all about building functors out of functors, and for more implementation details, please refer to [Ligoum and Ignatchenko]). The only thing that really matters is that Take 6 is IMNSHO more readable than all the previous takes. The code, which was linear in blocking code, is still linear, and exceptions are handled in a more convenient manner than in our previous Takes (with exception handling being closer to blocking code, too).

Take 6a. Enter C++ Preprocessor

Now, let's see what we can do to reduce this verbosity, while keeping the code straightforward. And apparently it *is* possible — at least in C++, with its preprocessor. As we notice in the code above, there are quite a few repeating patterns that clutter the code, but, on the other hand, as these patterns are repeated over and over again, it makes them an ideal target for macros:

```
//LISTING 5.Take6a.except
//C++
//NON-BLOCKING VERSION OF LISTING 5.Blocking.except
void CashierReactor::cashierPurchaseItem(
  shared_ptr<CashierPurchaseItemReply> reply_handle,
  int item_id) {
  int user_id = get_user_id(reply_handle);
  ReactorFuture<bool> db_ok(this);
  ReactorFuture<bool> gw_ok(this);
  CCODE {
    TTRY {
      db_ok = dbPurchaseItem(
              db_reactor_id,
              user_id, item_id);
      WAITFOR(db_ok)
      if(!db_ok.value()) {
```

```
      reply_handle.reply(false);
      EEXIT;//exits from whole CCode,
            // not just from current lambda(!)
    }
    REACTORID gameworld_reactor_id =
            find_gameworld_for_user(user_id);
    gw_ok = gameworldAddItem(
            gameworld_reactor_id,
            user_id, item_id);
    WAITFOR(gw_ok)
    reply_handle.reply(gw_ok.value());
  }
  CCATCH(x) /* implies const std::exception& */ {
    LogException(x);
  }
  ENDTTRY
 }
 ENDCCODE
}
```

Who said that we cannot have our cake and eat it too? With Take 6a, we've got a perfectly non-blocking code,[72] which looks *very much* like our original *Listing 5.Blocking.except* (and syntactic differences such as ENDTTRY and ENDCCODE don't look too unreadable). While getting used to working with it will require some practice (as diagnostics in case of syntax errors will look rather weird, though not that much weirder than in the case of the missing '}' in the usual code), it IMNSHO is the best representation of our original blocking code so far. At the very least, it is easily and obviously readable, and

With Take 6a, we've got a perfectly non-blocking code, which looks ***very much*** like our original Listing 5.Blocking.except.

> *Code is read much more often than it is written.*
> *— Raymond Chen*

Offloading

In addition, as a very nice side effect, things such as offloading some calculations to a different (Re)Actor running on a different thread also look quite natural with Take 6/Take 6a:

---

72   Just like with all other our Takes.

```
//LISTING 5.Take6a.simple.offload
//C++
ReactorFuture<A> a;
CCODE {
  OFFLOAD {
    //calculating a which takes a while...
    a = something;
  }
  ENDOFFLOAD
  b = calc_b_here();//takes another while...
    //a and b are calculated in parallel,
    // usually on different CPU cores
  WAITFOR(a)
  do_something_else();
}
ENDCCODE
```

Offloading Caveat #1: Deep Copy Required

One significant issue that arises in the context of offloading in general[73] is that (unlike our other callbacks and lambdas), whatever we're passing to and from the OFFLOAD-ed portion of the code is supposed to be executed in a different thread. It implies that *all* the parameters that we're using within the OFFLOAD portion MUST have copy constructors that are essentially "deep copy" constructors (i.e., they MUST NOT leave references to original objects, copying all of the referenced objects instead).

While such "deep copy" constructors are fairly easy to implement, unfortunately, as of the moment of this writing, I can't provide any advice on *enforcing* this rule at compile time. On the positive side, while testing, those invalid references to the context of the original thread can be spotted. For example, it can be done by: (a) running the OFFLOAD-ed portion of the code (i.e., (Re)Actor implementing OFFLOAD) not only on a different thread, but within a different process, and (b) ensuring that all the objects on the heap (and ideally also on the stack) have different non-overlapping addresses within the "original" process and "offloading" process; in particular, ASLR *might* help with it for 64-bit processes, albeit only statistically. If done this way, then at the very moment of dereferencing of any invalid ref-

Unfortunately, as of the moment of this writing, I can't provide any advice on enforcing this rule at compile time.

---

73   ="regardless of the exact way we're implementing it."

erence, we'll get a good old access-violation CPU exception, allowing us at least to spot these bugs before they corrupt the data or generate invalid results.

Let's note that, in theory, it might be possible to guarantee that some objects are not modified at all[74] while offloading is in progress; if it is so, pointers to such really-unmodifiable objects can be kept without making deep copies. Still, unless you know how to provide this guarantee in a *systematic* manner for your whole project, *and* you cannot live without it, I have strong objections against this approach. Unless you have a very-consistent framework that provides the necessary unmodifiability guarantees (for example of such a consistent framework, see (Re)Actor-with-Extractors discussed below), you are bound to provide these guarantees on an ad-hoc basis, and ad-hoc multithreading at logic level is so much error-prone that it is going to become a disaster very soon.

Offloading Caveat #2: Keeping Portions Large

Another really important thing to remember when offloading, is that

> ### *Not Everything Is Worth Being Offloaded.*

If you try to offload something that is small (in an extreme case, adding two integers), you'll easily get your CPU cores loaded; however, it is important not to start jumping with joy (yet) and take a look at the speedup of your original thread. The point here is that with offloading, you'll likely be creating a thread context switch,[75] and context switches are Damn Expensive™. As a result,

> *When pieces you're offloading are too small, you MAY be creating load on the CPU cores without any speedup (and in extreme cases, you can even cause slowdown).*

---

74   Not even their *mutable* fields in C++.

75   Though infrastructure code MAY be able to save you the context switch, in particular, if offloading is implemented via "work stealing," but even in this case you're likely to get CPU cache population penalty — and it is CPU cache population that is usually more expensive than the context switch itself <sad-face />.

To avoid it, it is necessary to keep the pieces to be offloaded large enough. This is a well-known phenomenon in multithreading in general (i.e., even with no (Re)Actors in sight).

It should be noted that for (Re)Actor-style offloads (regardless of Take), this effect can be mitigated (by teaching infrastructure code to perform offloads within the same thread as long as it is possible), so (Re)Actor-based OFFLOADs tend to be more forgiving if you make a mistake, but offloading really small (time-wise) pieces of processing will still cause significant waste.

As a very rough rule of thumb for x64 platforms: for (Re)Actors, anything smaller than a few thousand CPU cycles is not worth OFF-LOAD-ing;[76] on the other hand, if you have 100 pieces each worth 100 clocks, you may combine them into one 10000-clock piece, which does have a chance to be more or less efficient.

For other platforms I don't have reliable data, though my educated guess is that for ARM it will have the same order of magnitude, though for GPGPU the whole picture is very, very different (with *much* smaller pieces making sense for GPGPU).

Offloading Caveat #3: DON'T Offload Unless Proven Necessary

This observation about the cost of offloads leads us to an interesting result, which many will consider counterintuitive:

> ### DON'T Offload Unless Proven Necessary.

As noted above, each and every offload has an associated CPU cost. It means that to get efficient calculations (="without burning too much power" on Client devices, and "leaving Server cores free for other tasks" on Servers), the best way to calculate is within one single thread, avoiding those expensive thread context switches.

The only reason to perform offload is if you're hitting the wall with single-core performance; in particular, if you cannot complete all the stuff you need by the end of the frame/network tick, well, you *may* need to offload some calculations (and in extreme cases, you may even have

The only reason to perform offload is if you're hitting the wall with single-core performance.

---

76   NB: for non-Reactor systems that *always* cause a context switch, the number will be significantly higher (at 10K–100K CPU clock cycles and beyond).

to use (Re)Actor-with-Extractors; see the *(Re)Actor-with-Extractors* section below). However, unless it is the case

> ***Keeping your processing single-threaded will improve overall throughput (though not latency).***

It will be especially obvious on Servers, where the Server running many (Re)Actors-without-offloads will certainly outperform[77] the same Server, but with (Re)Actors using lots of offloads.

Yet Another Offloading Caveat: Flow Control

Going a bit further into practicalities of offloads, we'll see that offload can take several different forms. A simple offload such as the one above is certainly the simplest one (and it works pretty well, as long as the number of outstanding OFFLOADs is limited). BTW, in a certain sense, such simple offload is quite similar to "data-driven jobs" as described in [Tatarchuk]: each of our callbacks (such as piece-of-code-after-*WAITFOR()* in the example above) is data-driven in a sense that the callback won't start until the data is available.

On the other hand, such simple offloading is not always the best idea. Let's consider, for example, implementing some calculation that is repeated a million times; with million being quite a large number (and each such request using at least a hundred bytes of RAM) - creating that many outstanding OFFLOAD requests is rarely a good thing to do. In these cases, I suggest using some kind of flow control to keep the number of requests in check (while keeping enough work for all the cores). Within our Take 6a, such a flow-controlled offload might look along the following lines:

```
//LISTING 5.Take6a.flow-controlled.offload
//C++
OutstandingOffloads offloads;
CCODE {
  i = 0;
  WWHILE(i.value() < 1000000) {
    WAIT_FOR_OFFLOAD(offloads,
            recommended_number_of_offloads());
```

```
    //WAIT_FOR_OFFLOAD waits until number of offloads
    // within its 1st parameter
    // drops below its 2nd parameter
    //recommended_number_of_offloads() is a number
    // which may depend on various parameters, including
    // latencies. For single-machine interactions,
    // a number such as 2*number_of_available_cores '
    // is usually not a bad starting point
  OFFLOAD(offloads) {
     //OFFLOAD(offloads) adds currently offloaded code
     //  to the list of offloads – and starts offload too
     calculate_one_round(i.value());
   }
 }
 ENDWWHILE
do_something_else();
}
ENDCCODE
```

The idea here is to make sure that at any point in time, there are no more than *recommended_number_of_offloads()* outstanding offloads. This effectively provides a form of flow control with regard to offloads, and addresses the problem of having a potentially unlimited set of outstanding offloads; instead, we're creating offloads on-demand when they become necessary (while keeping enough offloads in the system to make sure that all the available cores are busy).

Note that even in this case, you still need to make sure that pieces-of-processing-you're-offloading are large enough to be efficient.

Really Serious Stuff: HPX

Above, we discussed rather simple cases when you merely needed to get *some* stuff offloaded. However, if you happen to find yourself in a position that you need to perform *really* serious computations – you'll need somebody better-familiar-with-HPC-than-me to advise you. Still, there is one thing which even I-with-my-very-limited-experience-with-calculations can tell: make sure to stay away from C++17 STL parallel algorithms; instead – concentrate on the HPX-style futures-based data-driven style of calculations.

For more information on the futures-based computations style – make sure to watch [Kaiser], and for the library supporting it right now – see [STEllAR-GROUP].

Very very briefly – C++17 STL parallel algos (which are essentially built along the same lines as 20-years-old OpenMP) are effectively restricted to parallelizing certain *parts* of the calculation (with mandatory re-sync in between these *parts*, and each such re-sync implies a likely thread context switch). In contrast, HPX-style futures-based calculations include describing *data dependencies* at app-level *explicitly* (via futures), and letting your Infrastructure Code to do the rest. In turn, my somewhat-educated guess is that for most of the loads (and *especially* for the loads in highly interactive contexts such as games), HPX-style calculations will be able to save *lots* of thread context switches compared to C++17 parallel algos, and with thread context switch cost being in the range of 10K-1M CPU cycles – it is going to make a *significant* difference for most of use cases.

BTW, there are *rumours* that in-some-future-C++, STL parallel algos will provide future-based functionality similar to that of HPX (and then, they *might* become viable too), but as of now – we're not there yet, so if you have to do *massive* computations – IMVHO HPX is your best bet.

Last But Not Least: Implementing Offloading Is Not in Scope Now

One last note about offloading: at this point, we do *not* discuss how infrastructure code can/should *implement* offloading. What is important for us now is to provide a way to *describe* offloading at game-logic level.

Implementing offloading is a different story, which we'll discuss in Vol. V's Chapter on C++ (and which will include discussion on Single-Producer-Single-Consumer vs. Multiple-Producer-Multiple-Consumer Queues vs. "work stealing," etc.).

For the time being, we should be able to describe *what* we want to offload without specifying *how* infrastructure can/should do it. It is consistent with the whole (Re)Actor approach of the same (Re)Actor being usable in very different threading configurations (and which allows for us to choose these configurations at the time of deployment).

Take 7. Fibers/Stackful Coroutines

Our Takes 4-6 discussed above use lambdas and even more lambdas to get the non-blocking code more readable. However, it is interesting to note that it is also possible to achieve pretty much the same result without any lambdas via the use of fibers/stackful coroutines.[78]

From a practical point of view, fibers/stackful coroutines can be seen pretty much as cooperative (i.e., non-preemptive, a.k.a. "green") threads. Technically, fibers do *not* require support from the OS kernel (and can be implemented completely in userland), but, nevertheless, at least Windows provides its own implementation of fibers (see *CreateFiber()/ConvertThreadToFiber()* functions). On Linux/*nix, you MAY either use *setcontext()/getcontext()* functions to obtain the same effect (see, for example, [Vyukov]),[79] or a library such as *libtask* [Cox] *or protothreads* [Dunkels].

Using fibers/coroutines (more or less along the lines of protothreads, but glazed with C++, sprinkled with the support of IDL compiler, and garnished with futures), our fiber-based examples can be made to look EXACTLY like *Listing 5.Take6a*. Yes,

From a practical point of view, fibers/coroutines can be seen pretty much as cooperative (i.e., non-preemptive) threads.

> ***While the mechanics of Take 6a and Take 7 are completely different (the former is based on lambdas and the latter on fibers), app-level code can look*** *exactly* ***the same.***

This interesting observation goes perfectly in line with the notion that good code tends to express "*what we want to say*" while hiding "*how to do it*" as an implementation detail. IMO, it can pass as yet another indication that our code in Take 6a and Take 7 is rather good.

On the other hand, Take 7 can be further improved, compared to Take 6a (eliminating futures and replacing non-standard *TTRY* with traditional *try*, etc.):

```
//LISTING 5.Take7.except
//C++
//NON-BLOCKING VERSION OF LISTING 5.Blocking.except
```

---

78   I won't spend much time debating the differences between fibers and stackful coroutines, just quoting Wikipedia on the subject: "The distinction, if there is any, is that coroutines are a language-level construct, a form of control flow, while fibers are a systems-level construct, viewed as threads that happen not to run in parallel... fibers may be viewed as an implementation of coroutines, or as a substrate on which to implement coroutines." Well, in my books (pun intended), it translates into: "Fibers and coroutines are pretty much the same thing."

79   While *setcontext()/getcontext()* are technically made obsolete by POSIX.1-2008, they are still present, at least on Linux.

```
void CashierReactor::cashierPurchaseItem(
  shared_ptr<CashierPurchaseItemReply> reply_handle,
  int item_id) {
  int user_id = get_user_id(reply_handle);
  ReactorFuture<bool> db_ok(this);
  ReactorFuture<bool> gw_ok(this);
  try {
    db_ok = dbPurchaseItem(
            db_reactor_id,
            user_id, item_id);
    WAITFOR(db_ok);
      //inside WAITFOR, we'll
      // (a) include (db_ok, current_fiber)
      //      to the list of items we're waiting for
      // (b) make a fiber switch to one of the items
      //      which are ready
    if(!db_ok.value()) {
      reply_handle.reply(false);
      return;
    }
    REACTORID gameworld_reactor_id =
            find_gameworld_for_user(user_id);
    gw_ok = gameworldAddItem(
            gameworld_reactor_id,
            user_id, item_id);
    WAITFOR(gw_ok);
    reply_handle.reply(gw_ok.value());
  }
  catch(std::exception& x) {
      LogException(x);
  }
}
```

BTW, let's note that for Take 7, we *could* eliminate *WAITFOR* entirely (for example, via making *db_ok.value()* implicitly block until the result is known). Strictly speaking (and unlike using *std::future<>* directly) it will fly; however, when I mentioned this possibility to developers-who're-maintaining a multi-million-LOC (Re)Actor-based system, they were *very* skeptical about removing *WAITFOR*. The reason they gave (and thinking about it, I have to agree with them) is that when writing non-blocking code with callbacks being able to modify the state of our (Re)Actor, it is *very* important to know *all the points* where such otherwise-unexpected modification of the state is possible;

without such information, understanding the implications of some-callback-jumping-in-and-modifying-our-state while-we're-expecting-it-to-stay-the-same becomes extremely difficult and error-prone. As a result, *WAITFOR*s (or equivalent markers of the state being potentially changed) are a Good Thing™. For more discussion on it, see [Ignatch-enko, *Eight Ways to Handle Non-blocking Returns in Message-passing Programs*] .

C++: boost:: coroutines and boost::context

In C++-land, it is *boost::* library which provides support for stackful coroutines. While *boost::* coroutines *can* be used as a "substrate" to implement Take 7,[80] using them directly would be too cumbersome in the context of (Re)Actors (the need to think which coroutine to switch to is not something I'd like to deal with at the application level).

With this in mind, and taking into account that *boost::coroutine* depends on *boost::context* anyway, I'd probably suggest[81] trying to use *boost::context* rather than *boost::coroutines* to implement your own Take 7.

Note that at least in recent versions of boost::, *boost::context* is *not* implemented on top of *setcontext()* etc., and is a standalone library with support of quite a few platforms (both x86/x64 under (Linux or Windows) and ARM under (iOS or Linux/Android), with a few things on the side; see [Kowalke] for details), and with quite a bit of platform-specific asm within (among other things, it means quite a bit of time has to be spent on compiling it for the first time).

On Using goroutines-for-callbacks: BEWARE THREAD SYNC!

One other interesting beast that is closely related to coroutines comes from a very different programming language: *Go*. However, despite all the similarities between coroutines and goroutines, there is One Big Fat Difference™: goroutines are *not* guaranteed to be run from the same thread (not even "as if" they run from the same thread), and therefore, unlike our (Re)Actors, they DO require thread sync for the data shared between them.

---

80   Well, I didn't do it myself, but it *seems* viable.

81   Assuming that you want to use boost:: to implement an engine for Take7-style code.

It is still possible to mimic *most* of the behavior of our (Re)Actors on top of goroutines, by having a mutex in our (Re)Actors and locking it for each access to (Re)Actor, including *both* accesses from the original event handler *and* accesses from goroutine; this will effectively ensure that our (Re)Actor's react() function works "as if" it is called from one single thread. However, such an approach has significant drawbacks too: manual locking is cumbersome and error-prone, plus it will cause contention on the mutexes (which, depending on specifics, MAY become a major bottleneck). As a result, if you have any other options, I do *not* recommend using goroutines to implement asynchronous callbacks; as for these "other options," I don't know much of Go, but Go closures (without goroutines(!)) look awfully similar to usual lambdas, so Takes 4–6 look rather viable.

BTW, I am certainly *not* against goroutines in general: the reasoning above applies *only* to using-goroutines-to-handle-asynchronous-callbacks. Using goroutines as a substrate for (Re)Actors (using channels to communicate and Go's mantra of "don't communicate by sharing memory; share memory by communicating") is very much in line with the concepts discussed within this chapter, and is perfectly fine.

Don't communicate by sharing memory; share memory by communicating.

Take 8. async/await (.NET, Node.js, and not-standard-yet C++)

Yet another (and the last we're about to discuss) nice way of handling non-blocking calls requires support from the programming language — and, as of now, to the best of my knowledge, this support is provided *at least* by .NET programming languages, by *Node*.js [Harrington], and is steadily making its way into C++ too.

About C++ *await* (known in C++-land as "stackless coroutines", or *co_await*): as of mid-2017 it *seems* to be pretty well-positioned within the C++ standard committee (a.k.a. WG21), and *seems* to be likely to make it into C++20 standard; implementation-wise, it already *seems* to work in both MSVC and Clang, so if you're really adventurous (or if you're really desperate to use *await*), you *may* want to try it even though it is not 100% mature. For more information on C++ *co_await* in the context of processing non-blocking returns – see [Springfield] and, of course, [Nishanov].

On the other hand, as C++ *co_await* is not standard yet, certain details can easily change, so for our current purposes, we'll concentrate on .NET's interpretation of *async/await*. From my current understanding, .NET's *async/await* is almost-exactly[82] equivalent to our later Takes. Let's take a look at how our original *Listing 5.blocking.except* can be rewritten into a non-blocking version under C#:

```
//LISTING 5.Take8.except
//C#
//NON-BLOCKING VERSION OF LISTING 5.Blocking.except
async void cashierPurchaseItem(object sender,
                CashierPurchaseItemArgs e) {
  try {
    int user_id = get_user_id(sender);
    Task<bool> db_ok_task = dbPurchaseItem(
              db_reactor_id,
              user_id, e.item_id);
     //Task<> in C# has semantics
     // which is Very Similar to our ReactorFuture<>
    bool db_ok = await db_ok_task;
    if(!db_ok) {
      send_cashierPurchaseItemReply(sender, false);
      return;
    }
    REACTORID gameworld_reactor_id =
                find_gameworld_for_user(user_id);
    Task<bool> gw_ok_task = gameworldAddItem(
              gameworld_reactor_id,
              user_id, item_id);
    bool gw_ok = await gw_ok_task;
    send_cashierPurchaseItemReply(sender, gw_ok);
  }
  catch(Exception x) {
    LogException(x);
  }
}
```

As we can see, Take 8 looks very similar to our Take 6a and Take 7. Exactly as with Take 6a/Take 7, the flow is linear, and we're merely marking those points where the program flow can be interrupted to process intervening events (in Take 6a/Take 7, it was *WAITFOR*; in Take 8, it is *await* operator — but the idea remains pretty much the same).

---

82   We'll get to this "almost" in just half a page.

However, under the hood there is one subtle difference (going beyond purely syntactic ones). Specifically, in our Take 6a and Take 7, whenever our code runs into *WAITFOR*, we're stopping execution of this branch until the result becomes available (though we do *not* stop the thread, and MAY process new incoming events). For Take 8/C#, behavior is slightly different: at the point of *await*, .NET tries to jump to the caller and run the caller's code until the caller itself reaches *await*, and so on; only at the point of the very topmost caller (i.e., when this process reaches the event handler itself) will .NET start processing other incoming events.

Under the hood, there is one subtle difference.

Most of the time, this difference is not important, but there can be cases when the seemingly similar code will behave differently under the original Take 6a/Take 7 semantics and under *await* (Take 8) semantics. On the other hand, such cases are very, very few and far between (especially for a really non-blocking code).

Across-the-Board Generalizations

Phew! We discussed eight(!) different ways to do the same thing: handle a return from a non-void function in a non-blocking manner. Now we can try to make some generalizations.

Surprise: All the Different Takes are Functionally Equivalent, and Very Close Performance-Wise Too

Performance-wise, the differences between the different takes discussed above will be negligible for pretty much any conceivable scenario.

One not-so-obvious observation about all our Takes is that while they *look* strikingly different, they will exhibit *exactly* the same run-time behavior[83] (that is, saving for potential differences in performance, but even those performance differences will be negligible in the vast majority of use cases; see also below).

On the other hand, in spite of that functional equivalence, there is a big practical difference between different Takes; this difference comes in the form of significantly different code maintenance costs. For example, if having the choice between modifying 100 different pieces of code written in Take 1-style, or Take 8-style, I will choose the latter any day of the week.

Performance-wise, the differences between the different Takes discussed above will be negligible for pretty much any conceivable scenario. Not that they will perform *exactly* the same, but the differences are small enough to be outweighed by pretty much everything else.

Similarities to Node.js

As I have already noted, our Take 4 looks very much like Node.js. However, the similarities of our (Re)Actors with *Node.js* are not limited to Take 4. The most important property shared with Node.js is that all our callbacks/continuations (and more generally, *all* the code in our Takes) are performed from the same thread[84] as the main (Re)Actor code. In other words: whatever is going on, we do *not* need to use any kind of thread sync to access our (Re)Actor from our callbacks.

This is an extremely important property of *Node.js* (and of all our Takes). Not only does it save us from thread context switches when our code runs into an already-owned mutex, but it also simplifies debugging greatly (from my experience by orders of magnitude), and improves code reliability too.

These similarities between (Re)Actors and *Node.js* actually have very deep roots: the whole premise of our (Re)Actor and *Node.js* is very similar. Very generally, both our (Re)Actor and *Node.js* are trying to do exactly the same thing: process events, plain and simple (and to process

---

83   However, see the discussion on the subtle differences with Take 8 in the *Take 8. async/await (.NET, Node.js, and not-standard-yet C++)* section.

84   at the very least — "as if" they're called from the same thread

them one by one, without the need to care about interaction between our event handlers).

With classical *Node.js* (and our Take 4), the benefits of such an approach come at the cost of switching to an unusual-and-less-straightforward coding style. However, with Take 5, and especially Take 8 (the one with *async/await*), IMNSHO there are no more significant reasons to delay switching to the non-blocking event-processing code — at least for those scenarios when we do need to process intervening messages while waiting for the result of the "long" operation. In other words:

> *No more excuses: go mostly-non-blocking today!*[85]

Handling Non-Blocking Returns in Different Programming Languages

As you have probably noticed <wink />, most of our Takes discussed above were in pseudo-code. One of the reasons for doing it this way is because many of them can be used in quite a few programming languages. In particular:

♦ Takes 1 to 3b will work in pretty much any OO-oriented programming language.

♦ Takes 4 to 6 require support for lambdas and closures. Restrictions apply; batteries not included. For example, Python lambdas won't realistically do, due to Python's one-line lambda limitation.

♦ Take 6a requires C++ with preprocessor.

♦ Take 7 requires support for fibers/stackful coroutines.

♦ Take 8 requires very special support from language/runtime, so at the moment it can be used only with .NET, with MSVC/Clang C++, and with Node.js.

Serializing (Re)Actor State

As we'll see in the *Going Circular* section below, to exploit certain features resulting from determinism (such as production post-factum analysis and fault tolerance), we need to be able to serialize not only all the inputs of our (Re)Actor, but also its current state.

We need to be able to serialize not only all the inputs of our (Re)Actor, but also its current state.

---

85   Yes, I know I sound like a commercial.

Depending on the Take we're using, and/or programming language, it might be trivial, or not too trivial:

♦ For Takes 1-3, serialization is easy regardless of the programming language (okay, in C++ you'll need to write it manually, but it is still very straightforward). The point here is that in between processing events, the only thing that needs to be serialized is (Re)Actor state (its members, all its members, and nothing but its members).

For Takes 4-6a, lambda closures become a part of the (Re)Actor state, so we need to serialize them too. While it is not a problem for most of the programming languages with built-in reflection, it is a big problem for C++. More on serializing C++ lambda closures in the *Serializing Lambda Closures and co_await frames in C++* section below.

For Take 7, serializing state is *not* trivial at all (up to the point of being pretty much infeasible <ouch! />). With fibers/stackful coroutines, we're effectively creating new stacks and jumping between them; moreover, these stacks may remain active at the point we need to serialize our (Re)Actor(!). In turn, it means that these stacks also need to be serialized. While there is no theoretical prohibition against doing such serialization, and I even know of one approach that *seems* to work for Take 7, it relies heavily on system specifics, introduces a lot of assumptions, and is way too elaborate to discuss here.

For Take 8, the situation is not *as* bad as with Take 7 (in particular, because at least C++ *co_await* frames are stored within the heap <phew />), but is still somewhat worse than with Takes 4-6. More on it in the *Serializing Lambda Closures and co_await frames in C++* section below.

> NB: to reiterate, serializing (Re)Actor state is NOT a 100% requirement; however, it IS necessary to obtain certain very important goodies arising from determinism, as will be discussed in detail below.

Serializing Lambda Closures and co_await frames in C++

As noted above, to have all the deterministic (Re)Actor-related goodies, we need to be able to serialize those captured values within lambda closures (and for Take 8 – within *co_await* frames). For most of the programming languages out there, pretty much everything is serializable, including lambda closures, but for C++, serializing lambda captured values becomes a serious challenge.

I know of two different ways of serializing C++ lambda closures and/or *co_await* frames for Takes 4-Take 6; let's name them app-level method and allocator-based method. Both are ugly, but both *seem* to work (disclaimer: in this case, there are even less warranties than usual[86]).

The app-level method applies only to lambda closures, and goes as follows:

For C++, serializing lambda captured values becomes a serious challenge.

♦ Write and debug the code written as in the examples above. It won't give you things such as production post-factum analysis or low-latency fault tolerance, but they're rarely needed at this point in development (and if necessary, you can always go via the production route described below to get them)

♦ Add a macro such as *SERIALIZABLELAMBDA* before each such lambda function; *#define* this macro to an empty string (alternatively, you may use a specially formatted comment, but I prefer empty define as more explicit).

  ▪ NB: if using Take 6a, *SERIALIZABLELAMBDA* can be made implicit for all those *TTRY*, *IIF*, and *EELSE* macros.

♦ Have your own pre-processor that takes all these *SERIALIZABLELAMBDA*s and generates code similar to that in Take 3, with all the generated classes implementing whatever-serialization-you-prefer (and all the generated classes derived from some base *class SerializableLambda* or something). Complexity of this pre-processor will depend on the amount of information you provide in your *SERIALIZABLELAMBDA* macro:

  ▪ If you write it as *SERIALIZABLELAMBDA(int i, string s)*, specifying all the captured variables with their types once again, then your pre-processor becomes trivial.

  ▪ If you want to write it as SERIALIZABLELAMBDA w/o parameters, it is still possible, but deriving those captured parameters and their types can be severely non-trivial; on

---

86   Side note. Usually, there are exactly zero warranties, so "even less warranties than usual" inevitably gets us into the "negative warranties" range <wink />.

the other hand, I know of a custom Clang plugin that was successfully used for this purpose.

- Which way to go is up to you; both will work. The latter means saving quite a bit of work for app-level developers at the cost of significant work for the preprocessor writer, so (as always) it is all about tradeoffs.

♦ In production mode, run this pre-processor before compiling, generating those *SerializableLambda* classes, and replacing all the regular lambdas with *SerializableLambda*s.

- While we're at it: make sure that your RPC functions don't accept *std::function* (accepting *class SerializableLambda* instead), so that if you forget to specify SERIALIZABLE-LAMBDA, your code won't compile (which is better than if it compiles and fails only in runtime)

The allocator-based method of serializing lambdas (and also *co_await* frames) is based on an observation that pretty much what-ever-our-compiler-and-library-will-do-to-implement-lambdas-and/ or-*co_await* – they will still store lambda closures (as well as *co_await* frames) within the heap (and nowhere else). Very briefly, it means that

> **If we find a way to direct *all* the allocations within our (Re)Actor, including lambda closures and/or *co_await* frames into our own custom allocator – and then to serialize/restore our own allocator as a whole – from the point of view of Same-Executable Determinism (discussed in the *Types of Determinism vs Deterministic Goodies* section below) we'll be fine.**

On this way, there are two main obstacles:

- Making sure that all the allocations within our (Re)Actor – that is, including std::function<> allocations and co_await frame alloca-tions, go into our custom allocator. This can be achieved either by:
  - providing our own allocator object to all the std::func-tion<> objects+coroutine objects (which is IMO way too cumbersome at least for all std::function<> objects), or
  - redefining global *::operator new()/::operator delete()*, with *all* the allocations going into our own allocator.

- Our own global *::operator new()/::operator delete()* can further use:
  - *thread_local* to restrict each of our custom allocators to one single thread
  - and within one single thread – we can use a *thread_local current_allocator* pointer (and our Infrastructure Code will always set it to the correct "allocator for the (Re)Actor-about-to-be-called" value before calling *react()*, calling lambda continuation, or resuming execution of a stackless coroutine), so that we effectively have a separate custom allocator effectively for each of our (Re)Actors. More on this technique in [Hare, Allocator for (Re)Actors. Part III].

♦ Making sure that whenever we're deserializing our custom allocator, we're restoring *exact* values for *all* the memory addresses within (otherwise we'll have problems, in particular, with function pointers or equivalent stuff). This implies that:

- We DO need to implement our allocator directly on top of OS virtual pages (such as *VirtualAllocEx()* or *mmap()*).
- Even in this case, it is not strictly guaranteed that on deserialization, we'll be able to get the same virtual pages that were available during original run – but *usually*, if we're restoring our (Re)Actor into a standalone executable (i.e. with no other (Re)Actors in it), this does work (or at least can be made to work by restricting ranges of virtual addresses used by our allocator).
- Moreover, with ASLR in use (and we SHOULD use ASLR in production at least on the Server-Side), we'll be running into a problem that in another instance of the executable, all the addresses of the functions will be shuffled, so our deserialization (more specifically – deserializing pointers to functions) won't work. To deal with it, two approaches are possible:

ASLR

Address space layout randomization (ASLR) is a computer security technique involved in preventing exploitation of memory corruption vulnerabilities... ASLR randomly arranges the address space positions of key data areas of a process.

—**Wikipedia**

- Disabling ASLR (usually NOT recommended because of security implications)

- When serializing – we can find all the ASLR off-sets for all the code/text segments, and serialize these offsets. Then, before launching our exe-cutable-where-we-want-to-deserialize-our-(Re)Actor – we can run a tool over our executable, with the tool relocates all the ASLR-able segments to their-exact-positions-according-to-serializa-tion-image – and then delete relocation tables from the executable. This will ensure that on the second run, all the ASLR-able segments reside at *exactly* the same places as before. *Disclaimer: I didn't use this technique myself, but I heard that it does work.*

Overall, which of the methods is better for lambdas - is still unclear to me, but for *co_await* frames only allocator-based one will work, so I am going to concentrate my own efforts on it.

Also let's note that when we have *static reflection*[87] – we can hope to get a more regular way for serializing lambdas/co_await frames, but even then it is unclear whether *static reflection* will cover lamb-das and *co_await*. If you're interested in it (and IMO you should be <wink />) - please make sure to push WG21 to (a) get support for "static reflection" into C++20 (it is already planned, but internal debates about details can easily get it delayed for a while – just like already happened with *lots* of C++ features <sad-face />); and (b) push support for serialization of lambdas/co_await frames into the standard.

Why So Much Discussion of This One Thing?

By now, we've spent quite a bit of time discussing this how-to-handle-non-blocking-RPC-returns matter, and you might wonder: is this discussion worth the paper it was printed on (and, more importantly, the time you've spent reading it)?

Is this discussion worth the paper it was printed on (and, more importantly, the time you've spent reading it)?

---

87   currently scheduled for C++20, but it is still very far from being carved in stone

I certainly hope so. There are two Good Reasons™ why you need to know the intricate details for this kind of stuff:

◆ Handling non-blocking returns is one thing that is desperately needed for non-blocking processing. It covers not only RPCs, but the same logic is needed for *any* kind of non-blocking processing.

◆ For systems such as *Node.js*, it is IMO exactly this lack of support for non-blocking returns that used to impede adoption of an otherwise-perfectly-good idea of (mostly-)non-blocking processing. Recently, *async/await* (in Take 8 style) were incorporated into version 7.6 of *Node.js*, and the community already seems to be jumping for joy about this addition. Now, it is time to provide comparable mechanisms for the other programming languages.

In other words,

> *Handling non-blocking returns in a usable manner is a prerequisite for any serious non-blocking system.*

TL;DR for Non-Blocking Communications in (Re)Actors

◆ We've discussed asynchronous RPC calls in detail, and handling of timer-related messages and *any* non-blocking calls can be implemented in exactly the same manner.

◆ As our (Re)Actors are mostly-non-blocking, being (mostly-) asynchronous becomes pretty much the law (somewhat similar to the dominant non-blocking ideology in *Node.js*; see also the *To Block, or Not to Block, That Is the Question. Mostly-Non-Blocking (Re)Actors* section above for further discussion).

◆ You will probably need an IDL (and IDL compiler) one way or another (see the discussion on IDL in Vol. I's chapter on Communications); on the other hand, some game engines use what I call an "In-Language IDL" (see the discussion in Chapter 7).

◆ Ways of handling asynchronous stuff in (Re)Actors have been known for a long while, but ancient ones range from "beaten with an ugly stick" to "quite ugly" (see Take 1-Take 3b).

◆ With the introduction of lambdas and futures, non-blocking code became significantly simpler to write and understand (see Take 4-Take 5).

Ancient ways of handling asynchronous stuff range from "beaten with an ugly stick" to "quite ugly."

♦ However, lambda pyramids and futures is not the limit from a usability standpoint: we've managed to improve it (reaching significantly better resemblance to the Holy Grail of the original blocking code) in Take 6, and especially Take 6a. Moreover, Take 8 (which is "almost-ideal" for our purposes) is becoming a de-facto standard pretty quickly; currently, it is available for .NET, for MSVC/Clang C++, and for Node.js.

♦ As a nice side effect of quite a few of our later Takes, we can also easily support things such as "wait for multiple operations to complete," and explicitly parallel operations (as described in the *Offloading* section).

♦ Most of the techniques we've discussed are applicable across quite a few programming languages, notably including C++ (see also Appendix 5.A), as well as JavaScript and *Node.js*.

♦ All our Takes are functionally the same (except for a subtle difference with Take 8); it is only the syntax and expressiveness that we're fighting for.

    ▪ In particular, ALL our takes (including Take 8) allow access to (Re)Actor members from callbacks/lambdas *without any inter-thread synchronization*.

♦ To get *all* the (Re)Actor goodies in C++ (including production post-factum analysis and low-latency fault tolerance), you'll need to implement serializing lambdas, and it can get rather ugly; in other programming languages, this is rarely a problem.

DETERMINISM

Now, after we've discussed the benefits of non-blocking processing and the ways to implement it, let's take a closer look at the second very important property of the easy-to-debug (Re)Actors: determinism.

Distributed Systems: Debugging Nightmare

Any MOG is a distributed system by design (hey, we do need to have a Server and at least a few Clients). While distributed systems tend to differ from non-distributed ones in quite a few ways, one aspect of distributed systems is especially annoying. It is related to debugging.

The problem with debugging of distributed systems is that it is usually impossible to predict all the scenarios that can happen in the real world. With distributed systems, the most elusive (and therefore most dangerous) bug is the one observed only when otherwise-perfectly-valid packets (events, etc.) arrive in an unusual sequence — the sequence that never occurred to you as possible, so you didn't account for it (and didn't write a test for it either).

While it is usually possible to answer the question "what will happen if such a packet/event arrives at exactly such and such moment," making an *exhaustive* list of such questions is unfeasible for any distributed system that is more complicated than a stateless HTTP request-response "Hello, Network!" If you haven't tried creating such an exhaustive list for a non-trivial system yourself, feel free to try, but it will be much cheaper to believe my experience in this field; for any non-trivial stateful system, you will inevitably miss something (and won't notice it until you run your system in the real world).

This automatically means that even the best possible unit testing (while still being useful) inevitably fails to provide any guarantees for a distributed system. Which, in turn, means that in many cases you won't be able to see the problem until it happens in simulation testing, or even in the real world. To make things even worse, in simulation testing it will happen every time at a different point. And when it happens in the real world, you usually won't be able to reproduce it in-house. *Sounds grim, right? It certainly does, and for a reason.*

As a result, I am going to make the following quite bold statement:

> **If you don't design your distributed system for debugging and post-factum analysis,**[88] **you will find yourself in lots of trouble.**

In a certain sense, we're talking about kinda-race conditions; however, as usual, I am not going to get into a lengthy discussion on terminology. For the purpose of writing a working MOG, we don't really care whether it is "right" to call the wrong-order-of-events a "race condition" (which is in line with Wikipedia), or if the term "race condition" is reserved to inter-thread operations (per Stack Overflow, which is currently shown by Google as the preferred definition when looking for "race condition").

In many cases, you won't be able to see the problem until it happens in simulation testing, or even in the real world.

Race condition

A race condition or race hazard is the behavior of an electronic, software or other system where the output is dependent on the sequence or timing of other uncontrollable events. It becomes a bug when events do not happen in the order the programmer intended.

—**Wikipedia**

---

88 A.K.A. "post-mortem analysis," but to avoid confusion with "game post-mortem," we'll stick to the term "post-factum."

What really matters is that while debugging inter-thread races is next-to-impossible,[89] (Re)Actors — due to inherent serialization — are debuggable. Even better, it is possible to design your (Re)Actor-based distributed system for debugging, and it is not *that* difficult (though it requires certain discipline and is better being done from the very beginning). Let's discuss how we can do it.

Non-Deterministic Tests are Pointless

> Non-deterministic tests have two problems, firstly they are useless...
>
> — Martin Fowler

The observation above has a strong relation to a subtly different, and rather well known phenomenon that has been discussed quite a few times (see, for example, [Fowler, Eradicating Non-Determinism in Tests] and [Hare, Deterministic Components for Distributed Systems]):

Non-Deterministic Tests Are Useless

How many times our program fails out of 100 runs?

I won't go into too many details here, but will just note what is quite obvious: if each time our program produces different results, what are we really testing? Yes, we can try to isolate some not-exactly-determinstic results and ignore them, but as soon as our output becomes essentially dependent on something beyond our control, the tests become essentially irreproducible. Moreover, while it is theoretically possible to have some kind of statistical testing (like "how many times our program fails out of 100 runs?"), such statistical testing is usually unusable for practical purposes (in particular because the failure rate of a non-deterministic system very often depends on the specific environment, which makes any results of testing-on-the-testing-machine have an unknown relevance to production-machine-under-production-load <ouch! />).

---

89   In a general case, you cannot *debug* a multithreaded system; you need to *prove* that it will be working. For multi(Re)Actor systems using multiple threads, we're effectively satisfying this requirement by *proving* that the system will be working, provided each of the threads is working (and the latter can be debugged).

The Holy Grail of Post-Factum

As discussed above, for any MOG, whatever amount of testing you do, test cases produced by real life and by your inventive players will inevitably go far beyond everything you were able to envision in advance. It means that from time to time your program will fail. while increasing time between failures is very important, another thing is (arguably) even more important: *the time it takes you to fix the bug after the bug was reported for the first time* (preventing future crashes/malfunctions for the same reason). And for reducing the number of times the program needs to fail before you can fix the bug, post-factum analysis is of paramount importance.

The Holy Grail of post-factum, of course, is when you can fix any bug using the data from one single crash, so it doesn't affect anybody anymore. This Holy Grail (as well as any other Holy Grail) is not really achievable in practice. However,

> *I've seen systems that, using techniques similar to those described in this chapter, were able to fix around 80-90% of all the bugs after a single crash.*

Note that traditional post-factum analysis using core dumps is usually significantly *less* efficient than the techniques we'll be discussing below. This happens mostly because core dump is merely a *snapshot* of the program that has already failed (and by that point, its state is usually already damaged beyond any repair), and the techniques described below usually allow us to reconstruct a *sequence of events that have led to the failure* (and starting from a correct initial state too), which is by orders of magnitude more useful.

Portability: Platform-Independent Logic as "Nothing but Moving Bits Around"

Now let's set aside all the debugging for a moment and talk a little bit about platform-independent stuff. I know I am jumping to a seemingly different subject, but we do need it; you will see how portability is related to debugging in just half a page.

It is almost-universally a Really Good Idea™ to separate your code into two very-well-defined parts: platform-dependent and platform-independent.

In most cases, graphics, input, and network APIs on different platforms will be different. Even if all your current platforms happen to have the same API for one of the purposes, chances are that your next platform will be different in this regard.

As a result, it is almost-universally a Really Good Idea™ to separate your code into two very-well-defined parts: platform-dependent and platform-independent. Further, let's observe that your platform-dependent code will usually happen to be very-rarely-changing, and it is your frequently changing Game Logic that needs to be platform-independent. In other words, your program 99% of the time can be cleanly divided into two parts: (a) rarely changing platform-dependent infrastructure-level code, and (b) frequently changing platform-independent app-level code.

When talking about platform-independent app-level logic, a friend and colleague, Dmytro Ivanchykhin, likes to describe it as "nothing more than moving bits around." Actually, this is a very precise description. If you can isolate a portion of your program in such a way that it can be described as mere "taking some bunches of bits, processing them, and giving some other bunches of bits back," all of this while making only those external calls that are 100% cross-platform,[90] you've got your logic platform-independent.

---

90   More strictly, "100% cross-platform for all the platforms you will ever need."

Having your Game Logic at least on the Client-Side as platform-independent is absolutely necessary for any kind of cross-platform development. There is no way around it, period; *any attempt to have your Game Logic interspersed with the platform-dependent calls will inevitably doom your cross-platform efforts sooner rather than later.* We'll discuss a bit more of it in Vol. IV's chapter on Things to Keep in Mind.

Stronger than Platform-Independent: Determinism

The approach described right above is very well known and is widely accepted as The Right Way™ to achieve platform independence. However, having spent quite a bit of time with the debugging of distributed systems, I've become a strong advocate of making your app-level code not only platform-independent, but also deterministic. While strictly speaking one is not a superset of the other, in practice these two concepts are very closely interrelated.

The idea here is to have outputs of your cross-platform Game Logic[91] 100% defined by input-data plus by internal-Game-Logic-state (or, in terms of (Re)Actors, "by input events plus by state of the (Re)Actor").

The idea here is to have outputs of your Game Logic 100% defined by input-data plus by internal-Game-Logic-state.

Moreover, for most of the well-written code out there, a large part of your Game Logic will already be written more or less along these lines, and there will only be a few relatively minor modifications to be made. In fact, modifications can be *that* minor that if your code is reasonably well written and platform-independent, you may even be able to introduce determinism as an afterthought. I've done such things myself, and it is not *that much* rocket science; however, honestly, it is still much better to go for determinism from the very beginning, especially as the cost of doing so is quite limited.

Deterministic Logic: Benefits

At this point, you should have two very reasonable questions. The first is "what's in this determinism stuff for me?" and the second is "how to implement it?"

---

91 Where "outputs" can usually be understood along the lines of "new state + whatever-messages-sent."

To answer the first question, and to explain why you should undertake this effort, let's discuss some of the advantages of a deterministic system.

First, let's define determinism as we need it for our purposes:

> *If you record all the inputs of a deterministic system, and re-apply these inputs to another instance of the same deterministic system in the same initial state, you will obtain exactly the same results.*

For practical purposes, let's assume that we have the mechanics to write an *inputs-log*, which will be recording all the inputs to our deterministic logic (see the *Implementing Inputs-Log* section below for some implementation hints).

With *inputs-log* available, and armed with the definition above, we can list at least the following benefits of your code being deterministic:

♦ Your testing becomes deterministic and reproducible.

  ▪ It means that as soon as you've got a failure, you can replay the whole sequence of the events from *inputs-log* and get the failure at exactly the same place in code. If you have ever debugged a distributed program with a bug-that-manifests-itself-only-on-every-twentieth-run-and-in-a-different-place, you will understand that this single item is worth all kinds of trouble.

    • As a side effect, such 100% reproducibility, in particular, allows things such as "let's stop our execution at five iterations before the failure."[92]

  ▪ In addition, your testing becomes more meaningful; without 100% determinism, any testing has a chance to fail depending on certain conditions, and having your tests fail randomly from time to time is the best way I know to start ignoring such sporadic failures (which often indicate race-related and next-to-impossible-to-figure-out bugs).

You can "replay" *inputs-log* on your functionally identical in-house system, and the bug will be reproduced at the very same point where it originally happened.

---

92   To be fair, similar things in non-production environments are possible with GDB's *reverse debugging*; however, it is platform-dependent and is out of the question for production, as running production code in reverse-enabled debug mode is tantamount to suicide for performance reasons.

On the other hand, with 100% determinism, each and every test failure means that there is a bug in your code that cannot be ignored and needs to be fixed (and also *can* be fixed). For a more detailed discussion of the relationship between testing and determinism, see also [Fowler, Eradicating Non-Determinism in Tests].

♦ Production post-factum analysis and debugging, both on the Client-Side and on the Server-Side:

  ▪ If you can log all the inputs to your deterministic logic in production (and quite often you can, at least on a circular basis; see the *Going Circular* section below for details), then after your logic has failed in production, you can "replay" this *inputs-log* on your functionally identical in-house system, and the bug will be reproduced at the very same point where it originally happened.

  ▪ Your in-house system needs to be only functionally identical to the production one (i.e., performance is a non-issue, and any compatible device will do).

  ▪ You are not required to replay the whole system; you can replay only a failed (Re)Actor instead.

  ▪ During such replay of *inputs-log*, it is not necessary to run it using the same time scale as it was run in production; it can either run faster (for example, if there were many delays, and delays can be ignored during replay), or slower (if your test rig is slower than the production one).

  ▪ BTW, post-factum doesn't necessarily mean that we're talking about analysis only *after* the crash or assert. For example, in [Aldridge], it is described how Bungie provided play-testers with an "it is lagging now" button, and used deterministic post-factum analysis to improve handling of network-related (and not only network-related) issues within their engine. Such an ability to "analyze network performance after the fact" is a Really Big Thing™ for providing the best-possible player experience in impossible-to-simulate environments; as [Aldridge] notes, using this technique, they were able to reduce network traffic by 80%(!) compared to their previous game.

♦ Replay-based regression testing using production data:

  ▪ If you've got your *inputs-log* just once, you can "replay" it to make sure that your code is still working after whatever-changes-you-recently-made. In practice, it comes in handy in at least two all-important cases (see more on replay-based regression testing in the *On Replay-Based Regression Testing* section below):

    • When your new code just adds new functionality, and unless this new functionality is activated, the system should behave exactly as before.

    • When your new code is a pure optimization (or pure refactoring) of the previous one. When we're dealing with hundreds or thousands of simultaneous users, such optimizations/rewrites can be really complicated (including major rewrites of certain pieces), and having the ability to make sure that the new code works *exactly* as the old one (just faster), is extremely important. Moreover, when it comes to major refactoring of large and critical portions of production code, such equivalence testing is the only way I know that allows us to push such refactored code in production without taking too many risks (and without making management jump too high).

♦ Low-latency fault tolerance, (Re)Actor migration (facilitating better Load Balancing), and upgrades on-the-fly with almost-zero downtime. We'll discuss these primarily Server-Side features in Vol. III's chapter on Server-Side Architecture.

♦ Keeping code bases in sync across different platforms:

  ▪ If you're unlucky enough to have two code bases (or even "1.5 code bases"; see Vol. IV's chapter on Things to Keep in Mind for a discussion of this technique), then running the same *inputs-log* taken from production over the two code bases provides an easy way to test whether the code bases are equivalent. Keep in mind that it requires cross-platform determinism, which has some additional issues, as discussed in the *Achieving Cross-Platform Determinism* section below. Fortunately, however, for keeping code bases in sync, discrepancies between platforms, while being a headache, can be fixed relatively easily during the testing.

♦ Better fuzz testing, a.k.a. fuzzing (see the *On (Re)Actors and Fuzz Testing* section below).

♦ User Replay, though see discussion in the *On Determinism and User Replay* subsection below (in short, for cross-platform replays, User Replay is very difficult — or even impossible — to implement, at least in C/C++, mostly due to floating-point issues).

Better fuzzing.

♦ Last but not least, (almost-)determinism may allow you to run exactly the same Game Logic on both the Client and the Server, feeding them the same data and obtaining (almost) the same results. As discussed in Vol. I's chapter on Communications, almost-determinism is usually fine for implementing things such as Client-Side Prediction (i.e., full-scale cross-platform determinism is not necessary) and as we'll see below, is perfectly feasible.

  ▪ As discussed in Vol. I's chapter on Communications, Client-Side Prediction is one of the very common ways to reduce perceivable latencies, and implementing it based on (almost)-deterministic building blocks (which are the same for the Client and the Server) can save quite a bit of development time.

♦ In addition, there are also other benefits of being deterministic,[93] but these are relatively exotic and beyond the scope of this book.

If you have a good development team, any reproducible bug is a dead bug.

Coming back to the question of the importance of determinism, specifically for the debugging of distributed systems, we can make the following observations:

a) If you have a good development team, any reproducible bug is a dead bug.

b) The most elusive and by-far time-consuming bugs in distributed systems tend to be race-related.

---

93 Examples include an ability to perform incremental backup just by recording all the inputs (will work if you're careful enough), and an additional ability to apply an existing inputs-log to a recently fixed code base to see "how the system would perform if not for that nasty bug there"; the latter, while being quite esoteric, may even save your bacon in some cases, though admittedly rather exotic ones.

c) These race-related bugs are very difficult to reproduce and debug; that is, without determinism (and associated replays).

From these (and at least from my own experience, too), we can easily conclude that

> *Having deterministic components makes a Really Big Difference™ when it comes to distributed systems.*

In other words,

> *With deterministic systems (and an appropriate testing framework), all those elusive and next-to-impossible-to-locate race-related bugs are brought to you on a plate.*[94]

On Replay-Based Regression Testing and Patches

As we've seen above, one of the most significant benefits of being deterministic is an ability to record the events in production, and then run them against your updated code to look for any regressions. And if your updated code behaves *exactly* like the original one, well, we've just kinda-proven (and if you can replay a day's worth of your Server load, it usually qualifies as "damn good kinda-proof") that the behavior of the updated code indeed didn't change.

However, there is a caveat:

> *Replay-based regression testing does NOT work in practice if there are* ***any*** *legitimate changes to the (Re)Actor's behavior.*

Indeed, as soon as the very first input event is handled by your updated code differently (and this change is intentional), that's it — all the further regression replay becomes impossible. Moreover, as within each build there are usually quite a few changes, well, it *seems* to mean that pretty much any replay-based regression testing won't work.

94 Not in a sense of bugs-on-a-plate for Pumba or Timon from the *Lion King* series.

This is a pretty well known observation, and actually the reason why lots of developers give up completely on replay-based regression testing. However, with the following trick it still *might* work.

First, let's note that regardless of determinism (and more generally – regardless of pretty much *everything*) we MUST use *both* a source control system, *and* an issue tracking system. Second, let's note that modern source control systems tend to support a concept of "cherry picking" changesets for a merge. Third, *if* we're using a modern source control system, we MAY use it to organize changes to our code as a bunch of independent changesets or patches (hey, if Linus can do it for kernel, we can — and actually SHOULD, regardless of replays — also do it for most of our code); moreover, we can ensure that these changesets/patches are properly attributed to the issues in our issue tracking system.

And starting from the point where we said, "hey, let's develop our changes as a bunch of independent changesets/patches" (with patches being sufficiently small), we *can* use replay for regression testing.

Let's elaborate a bit. As soon as we're developing our MOG in this manner (i.e., with certain bunches of changes/patches being independent), and clearly attributing respective commits in our source control system too, we can split all the code changes/patches into three broad categories:

Starting from the point when we said, "hey, let's develop our changes as a bunch of independent patches," we *can* use replay for regression testing.

- Adding new functionality, with changes not activated by default.
  - For example, if we're adding a new item to the game, nobody will use it until we place the item in the Game World. But it also means that (as there were no such items in the recorded game) the code with this change is supposed to replay perfectly (effectively proving that indeed the code change did *not* change anything that it wasn't supposed to change).
- Pure optimizations/refactorings: the code is supposed to work in *exactly* the same manner as before.
- Changing existing functionality. This includes *all* the changes not listed above.

The two first categories of changes can (and IMO SHOULD) be replay-regression-tested. To do so, we can always use the procedure going along the following lines:

♦ Within our source control system, we take the snapshot of the build-that-was-used-for-recording

♦ To this snapshot, we apply all the code changes/patches that are targeted for the next release, but only those that are *not* supposed to change any existing behavior (this is known as "cherry picking" and is certainly possible if you're using *git* or *SVN*, though I've *heard* that *Mercurial Queues* allow for similar functionality).

  ▪ To identify which commits to apply – we have a script which looks at commits comments (which have to map them into issues). Identifying which issues are supposed to change behavior and which are not – is rarely a problem.

♦ After applying all such changes, we get an interim test-only build. Such an interim build is supposed to replay *everything* we were able to record in production; if the interim build cannot replay recording properly, it indicates one of two things:

  ▪ either that some changes were mislabeled,

  ▪ or that there is an outright bug within the interim build. BTW, with deterministic replay available, fixing bugs is usually trivial.

♦ If a bug (or a mislabeled commit) is found– it should be fixed in one of mainstream branches (i.e. *outside* of our interim build) – and then the interim build has to be re-built from scratch along the lines described above.

♦ After fixing all the bugs in interim build – we should simply discard it (thus avoiding all the strange problems which tend to happen if we're trying to use cherry-picking in mainstream source control).

Other code changes (those really *changing* existing functionality) will still need to be dealt with using other methods.

Of course, with this approach, other code changes (those really *changing* existing functionality) will still need to be dealt with using other methods, but apparently such code changes are usually relatively small — and, as a result, are relatively easily reviewed and tested. In a typical monthly game release, 80-90% of the code changes will be about new functionality (with regressions being replay-testable using the method above), and only 10-20% will be the changes which aren't covered by replay-based testing; IMNSHO, reducing potential for a regression by 4x-5x is well-worth jumping through the hoops to enable replay-based testing (especially as most of it is going to be done by QA folks <wink />; from developer's side we just need to make sure that all the commits are properly attributed to issues in issue tracker– which has to be done anyway).

Apparently, if your development process is rather strict about separating different commits and associating them with issues, the procedure described above has a reasonably good chance of working for you at least most of the time (and that's sufficient to catch quite a few bugs before they reach production).

On (Re)Actors and Fuzz Testing

One of the goodies that is facilitated by our (Re)Actors is so-called Fuzz Testing. The idea behind fuzz testing is simple: throw anything you can think of at the program and see whether it fails. In fact, fuzz testing can be used to find very severe and almost-invisible bugs such as Heartbleed [Karjalainen][Böck].

We need to note, however, that inputs (and states) of real-world systems are usually quite large, so real brute-force analysis is not feasible. That's why there are tools out there such as *afl-fuzz* (can be found at [Zalewski]), which use genetic algorithms to find well-hidden bugs. Okay, with our *inputs-log* we can run *afl-fuzz* quite easily in the following manner:

♦ Run our (Re)Actor while recording all the inputs into the *inputs-log* under both normal conditions and using test cases generated by IDL (see Vol. I's chapter on Communications for a discussion of IDL-based test case generation).

♦ Make a standalone program that just takes some *inputs-log* and feeds it to our (Re)Actor.

♦ Instrument this program (including our (Re)Actor) with *afl-fuzz* (or whatever other fuzzer).

  ▪ In addition, DON'T forget to instrument your program with Address Sanitizer [Serebryany and Potapenko] (and/or other error detection tools)

♦ Feed those *inputs-logs,* recorded in the very beginning, to *afl-fuzz* as *initial test cases.*

Fuzz Testing

Fuzz testing or fuzzing is a software testing technique, often automated or semi-automated, that involves providing invalid, unexpected, or random data to the inputs of a computer program. The program is then monitored for exceptions such as crashes, or failing built-in code assertions or for finding potential memory leaks.

—Wikipedia

♦ Have *afl-fuzz* run its genetic algorithm magic, mutating the *inputs-logs* and feeding them to our standalone-program-with-(Re)Actor.

♦ When *afl-fuzz* finds a bug, given the deterministic nature of our (Re)Actors, the bug is trivially reproducible. Fix it.

♦ Rinse and repeat.

It should be noted that, strictly speaking, fuzz testing MIGHT work even if your program is not 100% deterministic;[95] however, the more non-deterministic the program, the lower the chances for fuzz testing to produce any meaningful results.

On Determinism and User Replay

When your Game Logic is fully deterministic, it should be possible for the Client to record *inputs* of the game as it was played (here, *inputs* to include *both* player inputs *and* network packets coming from the Server), get a small(!) file with the record (well, both player inputs and network packets *are* rather small), and then share this file with other players. This, in turn, may help to build your community, etc., etc. Due to the ease of video capturing and sharing, such User Replay is not as attractive these days as it was 10 years ago, but you still *might* want to consider it (which *seems* to be coming more or less "for free," as you need determinism for other reasons too). And if you add some inter-active features during replay (such as changing the viewing angle and commenting features such as labels attached to some important units, etc.), it might start to make business sense.

However, unfortunately, in practice using determinism for User Replay has two very significant caveats:

♦ User Replay will normally require you to adhere to the most stringent version of determinism, which includes cross-platform determinism

 ▪ And, as described in the *Achieving Cross-Platform Determinism* section below, achieving it in the presence of floating-point calculations is currently seen as next-to-im-possible, at least for C++.

Unfortunately, in practice, using determinism for User Replay has two very significant caveats.

---

95   There are no guarantees that it will work for not-strictly-deterministic programs, but it has been seen in practice.

- On the other hand, at least for some games, it is possible to have "snapshots" of the Server state at certain intervals, and to use (almost-)deterministic replay only to simulate things *between* the "snapshots." It reduces requirements for determinism (making it a *cross-platform almost-determinism*), and *might* be achievable.

◆ When implementing User Replay as deterministic replay, you'll need to deal with the "version curse." The problem here is that the replay-made-on-one-(Re)Actor won't run correctly on a different version of (Re)Actor. As a result, you will need to:

   - Add a (Re)Actor version number to all of these files, and
   - Keep all the different publicly-released versions of the (Re)Actor within the Client, so all of them are available for replay. This *might* fly, because (a) you need to record only one (Re)Actor (such as Game Logic (Re)Actor or Animation&Rendering (Re)Actor; more on them in Chapter 6) – so you'll need to keep versions for only one (Re)Actor, and (b) the code size for each version is usually fairly small (in the order of hundreds of kilobytes).

      - Even in this case, your Animation&Rendering (Re)Actor will have external dependencies (such as DirectX/OpenGL), which can be updated and cause problems. However, as long as external dependencies are 100% backward-compatible, you should be fine (at least in theory).

      - While adding meshes/textures isn't a problem for replay, replacing them is. For most of the purely cosmetic texture updates, you may be fine with using newer versions of textures on older replays, but for meshes/animations, probably not, so you may need to make them versioned too <ouch! />.

The versioning problems, while being a really big headache, are solvable, but achieving cross-platform determinism at the very best qualifies as a "pretty tough uphill battle." Personally, I probably wouldn't even dare try reaching full-scale cross-platform determinism for a floating-point based game; OTOH, reaching cross-platform *almost-determinism*, or cross-platform determinism w/o a floating point — while still being extremely daring — *might* be doable.

In any case, regardless of the problems with deterministic User Replay, all the other benefits of making your (Re)Actors deterministic still stand firmly — *and* are very important in practice, too.

Implementing Deterministic Logic

I hope that I've managed to convince you that deterministic (Re)Actors are a Good Thing™, and that now we can proceed to our second question: how to implement such deterministic (Re)Actors?

Deterministic System: Modes of Operation

First, let's define what we want from our deterministic system. Practically (and to get all the benefits above), we want to be able to run our (Re)Actor in one of three modes:

I REALLY hope I've managed to convince you that deterministic systems are a Good Thing™.

♦ **Normal Mode.** The system is just running, not actively using any of its deterministic properties.

♦ **Recording Mode.** The system is running exactly as in Normal Mode, but is additionally producing *inputs-log*.

♦ **Replay Mode.** The system is running using only information from *inputs-log* (and no other information), reproducing exact states and processing sequences that have occurred during Recording Mode.

Note that Replay Mode doesn't require us to replay the whole system; in fact, we can replay only one (Re)Actor out of the whole thing (usually the one that we suspect is guilty). If after debugging this suspect module we find that it was behaving correctly and that we have another suspect, we can replay that other suspect from its own *inputs-log* (which hopefully was written during the same session that caused failure).

Implementing Inputs-Log

As discussed above, most (if not all) benefits coming from determinism are based on *inputs-log.*

As discussed above, most (if not all) benefits coming from determinism are based on *inputs-log*. Moreover, to be used in production, *inputs-log* MUST be extremely fast (="so fast that the performance penalty is negligible").

Implementation-wise, *inputs-log* is usually organized as a sequence of "frames," with each "frame" depending on the type of data being written. Each of the "frames" usually consists of a type, and some serialized data depending on type.

That pretty much describes implementation of our *inputs-log* from 50,000-feet, but let's discuss a few hints related to implementing required serialization in C++ (other languages are usually simpler, or MUCH simpler), and which caveats need to be avoided. Below are a few hints in this regard:

♦ Usually, we'll need to serialize both the input events and the current state of our (Re)Actor (see the *Going Circular* section below for an explanation of why the latter is necessary).

  ▪ For serializing the current state, usually, you will find that your data is still simple enough to be described by solutions #1-#3 from [Standard C++ Foundation]. And while we're at it, if serializing complex structures, make sure to use suggestions described there (BTW, while it is written in C++ terms and is not easy to understand without a C++ background, the principles behind it — including the discussion of different types of graphs — apply pretty much regardless of the programming language).

♦ As *inputs-log* is a very special type of serialization (which is usually guaranteed to be deserialized on exactly the same executable), it means that you MAY serialize your data as plain C structures; for "how to extend similar serialization techniques to C++", see, for example, [Ignatchenko and Ivanchykhin].

  ▪ Warning: don't even think of using such techniques for network marshalling; they may work ONLY in extremely narrowly defined scenarios where deserialization is 100% guaranteed to happen on *exactly* the same executable as serialization.

  ▪ If using a serialization library: given that performance is usually very important, it is usually better to use a binary serialization format. In particular, FlatBuffers is not a bad candidate for this purpose (though the dirty techniques mentioned above tend to beat even FlatBuffers at the cost of the serialization format being completely non-portable).

One idea of how we can avoid recording inputs forever-and-ever is to use circular implementation of the *inputs-log.*

Going Circular

One all-important variation of our *inputs-log* arises when we want to have a "post-factum log" (sufficient to identify the problem after the program crashed), but at the same time we don't want to write all the inputs of our (Re)Actor "forever and ever," as it will eat up too much resources (actually, any "forever and ever" in production is usually waaay too long).

One idea of how we can avoid recording inputs forever-and-ever is to use circular implementation of the *inputs-log* (either on disk, or, even more likely, in-memory). Then we can store only last-N-seconds (or last-N-megabytes) of inputs to our (Re)Actor, and use them to reproduce the last-N-seconds of the life of our (Re)Actor (right before the crash).

However, for this to work, we will additionally need to:

♦ Make sure that our (Re)Actor has an additional function such as *serializeStateToLog(InputsLogForWriting ol)*, and a counterpart function *deserializeStateFromLog(InputsLogForReading il)*.

- State serialization MAY be implemented in a manner that is consistent with serialization used for *inputs-log* in general.

- On the other hand, as serializing state is a very special case (in particular, it is going to be deserialized to *exactly* the same executable) – at least for C++ we MAY try to:

  • make sure that all the parts of our (Re)Actor use the same allocator

  • serialize the whole allocator for our (Re)Actor.

As a side benefit, this approach tends to help with serializing stuff such as lambda closures or *co_await* frames (more on it in the *Serializing Lambda Closures and co_await frames in* C++ section above).

♦ Call this *serializeStateToLog()* function often enough to ensure that the in-memory circular buffer always has at least one instance of the serialized state.

♦ Make sure that there is always a way to find the serialized state, even after a circular buffer wraparound (this can be done by designing the format of your *inputs-log* carefully; for example, a 256-bit random-looking "signature" before the state frame should do the trick).

♦ On program failure, just dump the whole in-memory *inputs-log* to disk.

▪ BTW, on Linux (which is commonly used on the Server-Side) our in-memory *inputs-log* will become a part of the *core dump* pretty much for free.

♦ On start of "Replay," find the serialized state in *inputs-log*, call *deserializeStateFromLog()* from that serialized state, and proceed with log replay as usual.

Above, we describe only one of multiple possible implementations of not-so-performance-intrusive *inputs-log*; it has an advantage that all the logging can be kept in-memory and therefore is very cheap, but in case of trouble this in-memory log can be dumped, usually providing sufficient information about those all-important "last seconds before the crash." Further implementation details (such as "whether implement buffer as a memory-mapped file" and/or "whether the buffer should be kept in a separate process to make the buffer corruption less likely in case of memory corruption in the process of being logged") are entirely up to you (="they're too game-specific to discuss here").

One very important usage of circular *inputs-log* is that in many cases it allows us to keep the logging running all the time in production, both on the Client-Side and the Server-Side. It means near-perfect post-factum analysis in case of problems.

Let's make some very rough guesstimates. The typical game Client receives around a few kilobytes per second from the Server, and user input is usually negligible in comparison. Which means that we're talking about, at most, 10kBytes/second.[96] 10MByte RAM buffer is nothing for the Client-side these days, and at a rate of 10kBytes/second, we'll be able to store about fifteen minutes of "last breath data" for our Game Logic Client-Side (Re)Actor in such a RAM buffer; this fifteen minutes of data is usually by orders of magnitude more than enough to find a logical bug. For a (Re)Actor implementing your animation/rendering engine, calculations will be different, but taking into account that all the game resources are well-known and don't need to be recorded, we can again keep the data recorded to the minimum, still enabling a very good post-factum analysis.

At a rate of 10kBytes/ second, we'll be able to store about fifteen minutes of "last breath data" in a 10Mbyte RAM buffer.

---

96   Okay, there are games out there with 20Kbytes/sec, but the analysis won't change much anyway.

For the Server-Side, there are many (Re)Actors to be run per Server box, so you will probably need much more memory to keep all those multiple *inputs-logs*. As a result, you might not be able to keep circular buffers running all the time, but at the very least you should be able to run them on selected (Re)Actors (those that are currently under suspicion, or those that are not-so-time-critical, or according to whatever other criteria you want to use at the moment).

Recordable/Replayable (Re)Actor

Now, after defining our requirements to *inputs-log*, we're in a position to rewrite *class Infrastructure* from our former *Listing 5.Reactor* to support recording and replay (and note that neither *GenericReactor* nor any *ConcreteReactor*s are affected):

```
//Listing 5.RecordingReplay
//PSEUDO-CODE
class Infrastructure {
  GenericReactor r;//MUST have react() function

  constructor() {
    //initialize r
  }
  function run_loop(log4w) {
    //log4w is null if no recording is necessary
    while(true) {
      ev = wait_for_event();
      ev.inputs = read_inputs();
      if(log4w) {
        if( log4w.needsReactorState() )
          r.serialize(log4w);
        ev.serializeToLog(log4w);
      }
      r.react(ev);
    }
  }
  function replay_loop(log4r) {
    while(true) {
      ev = Event.deserializeFromLog(log4r);
      r.react(ev);
    }
  }
};
```

If we want to run our (Re)Actor *r* while writing *inputs-log*, we're simply calling *run_loop()* with parameter *log4w* not equal to *null*. And if we feed previously logged *inputs-log* to *replay_loop()* function, we will get exactly the same processing as during the recording (that is, provided that our *r.react()* is deterministic(!)).

Implementing Deterministic Logic: Non-Determinism Due to System Calls

As now we have our *class Infrastructure*, which enables recording/replay (and noticing that it will work as expected only as long as our game-specific *class ConcreteReactor* is deterministic), the next obvious question is: what do we need to do *within the (Re)Actor itself* to ensure determinism? The answer is not too difficult: to make our (Re)Actor deterministic, we merely need to eliminate all the sources of non-determinism within our (Re)Actor. Fortunately, the list of such sources is pretty short; we'll look at them one by one.

What do we need to do *within the (Re)Actor itself* to ensure determinism?

The first very big and very common source of non-determinism originates from system calls. Even innocent looking calls such as *time()* (*GetTickCount()*, etc.) are inherently non-deterministic. In fact, pretty much *any* system call can easily lead to non-deterministic results.[97]

Dealing with System Calls: Original Non-Deterministic Code

Let's start with a simple example: a class, which implements a "double-hit" logic. The idea is that if the same NPC gets hit twice within a certain pre-defined time, something nasty happens to him. Usually, such a class would be implemented along the following lines:

```
//Listing 5.DoubleHit.nondeterministic
//PSEUDO-CODE
class DoubleHit {
  const THRESHOLD = 5;
```

---

97   Note that some C library calls MAY be deterministic (for example, *memcpy()* is deterministic, as long as you're reading your own initialized memory); however, most (if not all) kernel calls are inherently non-deterministic.

```
constructor() {
  last_hit = MYTIMESTAMP_MINUS_INFINITY;
}

function hit() {
  now = system_get_current_time();
  if(now - last_hit < THRESHOLD)
    on_double_hit();

  last_hit = now;
}

function on_double_hit() {
  //do something nasty to the NPC
}
}
```

While being trivial, function *DoubleHit.hit()* is NOT deterministic.

While this example is intentionally trivial, it does illustrate the key point. Namely, while being trivial, function *DoubleHit.hit()* is NOT deterministic. When we're calling *hit()*, the result depends not only on input parameters of *hit()* and on members of *class DoubleHit*, but also on the time when it was called (such time being obtained by *system_get_current_time()*).

Dealing with System Calls: Call Wrapping

Let's see what we can do to make our *DoubleHit.hit()* deterministic. In general, there is more than one way to achieve such determinism.

The first way is to "wrap" all the invocations of the function *system_get_current_time()*.

The first way to make our *class DoubleHit* deterministic is to "wrap" all the invocations of the function *system_get_current_time()*. "Wrapping invocations" here is meant as making your own wrapper around *system_get_current_time()*, changing the behavior of the function depending on the mode in which the code is running; more specifically, you will be adding/changing some functionality in "Recording" or "Replay" modes. Such Call Wrapping of *system_get_current_time()* can be implemented, for example, as follows:

♦ Whenever the (Re)Actor is running in "recording" mode, *wrapped_get_current_time()* function would invoke *system_get_current_time()* (and would return value-returned-by-*system_get_current_time()* too); however, it would additionally store each value-returned-by system_get_current_time() into the *inputs-log* (as a separate frame).

♦ And whenever the (Re)Actor is running in "replay" mode, *wrapped_get_current_time()* would read the next frame from the *inputs-log*, get a value out of it, and return that value regardless of the actual time (without making any system calls).

This is possible exactly because of 100% determinism: as all sequences of calls during Replay are *exactly* the same as they were during Recording, it means that whenever we're calling *wrapped_get_current_time()*, then at the "current position" within our *inputs-log*, we will always have the "frame" that was made by *wrapped_get_current_time()* during Recording.

Translating the talk above into the code, Call Wrapping of the function *system_get_current_time()* may be implemented, for example, as follows:

```
//Listing 5.call_wrapping
//PSEUDO-CODE
class Infrastructure {
  const ModeNONE = 0;
  const ModeRECORDING = 1;
  const ModeREPLAY = 2;
  constructor() {
    //initialize log4r, log4w, mode
  }
  function wrapped_get_current_time() {
    if(mode == ModeREPLAY) {
      assert log4r != null;
      return log4r.read_timestamp();
    }

    ret = system_get_current_time();

    if(mode == ModeRECORDING) {
      assert log4w != null;
      log4w.write_timestamp(ret);
    }

    return ret;
  }
}
```

Bingo! If we call this *wrapped_get_current_time()* instead of usual *system_get_current_time()* in all the places of our *Reactor.react()* (including *all* the functions that are called from *Reactor.react()* indirectly), it would make our implementation deterministic with regards to *system_get_current_time()*, and without any substantial code changes (besides renaming all app-level calls from *system_get_current_time()* into *wrapped_get_current_time()*[98])! Actually, this is pretty much what replay tool liblog[99] does (see [Geels, et al.] for details).

Essentially, what we're doing here is merely saying that the return value of *wrapped_get_current_time()*, while being an *output* from the point of view of this function, is actually an *input* from the point of view of our deterministic (Re)Actor. And as soon as we record this return value to *inputs-log*, we're fine from a determinism point of view; a little bit of a different perspective on the same thing can be described in terms of "isolation perimeters" (as discussed in the *On Isolation Perimeters* section below), with Call Wrapping effectively moving *system_get_current_time()* outside of the deterministic Isolation Perimeter (with the *inputs-log* frame created by *wrapped_get_current_time()* ensuring correctness of the isolation).

So far, so good — and this Call Wrapping technique does work; moreover, Call Wrapping can be used to make *any* system call deterministic.

On the other hand, for very-frequently-called functions such as *system_get_current_time()*, Call-Wrapping them has a significant caveat. If we add (or remove) any calls to *wrapped_get_current_time()* (or more generally, to any of the functions-that-record-to-*inputs-log*), the replay will fall apart. While replay will still work for *exactly* the same code base, things such as replay-based regression testing will start failing much-more-often-than-necessary in practice (and in extreme cases, replay-based regression testing can become pretty much unusable); also, existing real-world *inputs-logs* (which are an important asset of the QA team) will be invalidated much more frequently than is really necessary.

For very-frequently-called functions such as *system_get_current_time()*, Call-Wrapping them has a significant caveat.

---

98   If you prefer, it is certainly possible to avoid making *any* changes to your app-level logic (at least in C/C++), though such changing-function-without-renaming-it belongs more to the "dirty tricks" department.

99   Not to be confused with other tools with the same name; as of now, I wasn't able to find an available implementation of *liblog* as discussed in [Geels, et. al] <sad-face />.

As a result, while such Call Wrapping is a perfectly valid technique for those-calls-that-are-not-too-likely-to-be-added-or-removed (like "a call to a DB," or a pretty much any system call that is expected to modify the system in any way), frequently-called read-only functions such as *system_get_current_time()* are not exactly the best fit for Call Wrapping.

Dealing with System Calls: Pure Logic

An alternative way of making our (Re)Actor deterministic is to change the *class DoubleHit* itself so that it becomes deterministic without any Call Wrapping trickery. For example, we could change our *DoubleHit.hit()* function to the following:

```
function hit(now) {
  if(now - last_hit < THRESHOLD)
    on_double_hit();
  last_hit = now;
}
```

If we change our *class DoubleHit* in this manner, it becomes deterministic without any need to "wrap" any calls. Moreover, *DoubleHit.hit()* becomes a close cousin to "pure functions," as they're known in computer science: at least as long as we consider the current object (**this* in C++, *this* in Java, *self* in Python, etc.) as both input and return value for *DoubleHit.hit()*, it no longer has any side effects.

For time-like system calls, I like this "Pure Logic" approach better than Call Wrapping, at least because it has better resilience to modifications. However, the Pure Logic approach has some implications to keep in mind:

♦ With Pure Logic, it becomes the responsibility of the caller to provide information such as timestamps to callees.

  ▪ These *now* parameters will often go through multiple levels of calls, causing lots of typing, which quite a few developers will consider unnecessary and too bulky (and it *is* indeed boilerplate code, so I wouldn't blame them too much).

♦ Within the Pure Logic model, it becomes the responsibility of *class Infrastructure* to call *system_get_current_time()* and pass obtained value as *now* parameter to *GenericReactor.react()*.

Pure Function

A function may be considered a pure function if both of the following statements about the function hold: (1) the function always evaluates the same result value given the same argument value(s)... (2) Evaluation of the result does not cause any semantically observable side effect or output.

—**Wikipedia**

The whole chunk of processing within one *ConcreteReactor. react()* is deemed as happening at the same point in time.

- It also becomes the responsibility of *class Infrastructure* to record current time to *inputs-log* (and to handle replay too).

♦ The whole chunk of processing within one *ConcreteReactor.react()* is deemed as happening at the same point in time. While this is exactly what is desired for 99.9% of Game Logic, you still need to be careful not to miss the remaining 0.1%. In particular, most of the performance-related timestamps won't fly with Pure Logic.

A variation of Pure Logic puts *now* timestamp as a data member into our *Event* (and populates this field at the same time as described above), reading it from *Event* when necessary (via member function such as *Event.now()*). Note that I am usually firmly against making *now* a data member of *class Reactor* (as it is not an attribute of (Re)Actor); however, putting *now* into *Event* is very different and is perfectly fine. Moreover, usually *now*-as-*Event*-parameter is less verbose and less cumbersome than passing-parameters-Pure-Logic as described above.

Dealing with System Calls: TLS Compromise

As an alternative to passing parameters around, you might opt to pass parameters via TLS instead of stack. The idea is to store *now* timestamp (alongside any other parameters of a similar nature) into the TLS, and then whenever *my_get_current_time()* is called, merely read the value from TLS.

In practice, it means doing the following:

♦ You can keep your original non-deterministic logic code from *Listing 5.DoubleHit.nondeterministic* (almost) intact, just replacing *system_get_current_time()* calls with *my_get_current_time()* calls.

TLS

Thread Local Storage (TLS)... is used in some places where ordinary, single-threaded programs would use global variables but where this would be inappropriate in multithreaded cases.

—Wikipedia

♦ At exactly the same points where you'd call *system_get_current_time()* (for passing result as a parameter) in the Pure Logic model, still call *system_get_current_time()* but instead of passing the value around as a parameter, write the value-returned-by-*system_get_current_time()* to TLS[100].

♦ Implement *my_get_current_time()* as a simple read of the value from TLS.

---

100   For C++, see C++11's *thread_local* storage duration specifier, but there are usually other platform-dependent alternatives. For Java, look for ThreadLocal<T>.

With such a TLS Compromise, our *class Infrastructure* would look along the following lines:

```
//Listing 5.TLS_compromise
//PSEUDO-CODE
current_tls_time = new TLS_object();
class Infrastructure {
  GenericReactor r;//MUST have react() function

  constructor() {
    //initialize r
  }
  function run_loop(log4w) {
    //log4w is null if no recording is necessary
    while(true) {
      ev = wait_for_event();
      ev.inputs = read_inputs();
      current_tls_time = system_get_current_time();
      if(log4w) {
        ev.serializeToLog(log4w);
        log4w.write_timestamp(current_tls_time);
      }
      r.react(ev);
    }
  }
  function replay_loop(log4r) {
    while(true) {
      ev = Event.deserializeFromLog(log4r);
      current_tls_time = log4r.read_timestamp();
      r.react(ev);
    }
  }
  function my_get_current_time() {
    return current_tls_time;
  }
};
```

Let's note that such TLS-based implementations may have Big Problems™ when used outside of (Re)Actors; however, for (Re)Actors, they're perfectly safe because of (Re)Actors' inherently single-threaded nature and well-defined Event semantics. We DO know that between setting *current_time* and returning from *react()*, nobody except (Re)Actor will be able to read *current_time* (and nobody at all will be able to write it) — for the simple reason that there is nobody else in the picture.

At the time (and due to ~~developers~~ circumstances with the Big Clenched Fists™ surrounding me on my everyday job), I tend to suggest TLS Compromise for making existing projects deterministic.

This TLS-based model is a kind of compromise between the Call Wrapping and Pure Logic discussed above; while the call in TLS Compromise *looks* exactly like a Wrapped function call (and, more importantly, it doesn't need to change the original non-deterministic code), it is functionally equivalent to the Pure Logic model. As a result, TLS Compromise (unlike Call Wrapping) doesn't cause problems with *inputs-logs* becoming incompatible when somebody inserts yet another call to *my_get_current_time()* into your app code.

At the time (and due to ~~developers~~ circumstances with the Big Clenched Fists™ surrounding me on my everyday job), I tend to suggest TLS Compromise for achieving determinism for time-like functions (though if your team is okay with passing parameters or Events around using Pure Logic, it is IMO even better).

Dealing with System Calls: Pools of On-Demand Data

TLS Compromise and Pure Logic approaches work well with (Re)Actors, as long as obtaining whatever-(Re)Actor-might-possibly-need is ultra-cheap; however, obtaining *all* the potentially necessary stuff is often not feasible (or, in the case of non-idempotent calls, is not even allowed).

In some cases, however, we may be able to prepare the data in advance, store it within the *class Infrastructure*, and feed to the (Re)Actor whenever it needs the data. I've seen this model work very well for a deterministic (Re)Actor that needed real (hardware) RNG data, but we knew in advance the *maximum* amount of random data (let's name it MAX_RANDOM) that might be needed to process one single Event.

Implementation went along the following lines:

♦ Infrastructure maintained a "pool" of random data of MAX_RANDOM size. If before calling *react()*, the "pool" didn't have that MAX_RANDOM bytes of data, the missing data was replenished (in that specific case, from a system call reading from */dev/urandom*), so the "pool" always had at least MAX_RANDOM random data before each call to *react()*.

♦ Whenever (Re)Actor requested hardware RNG data, infrastructure code just extracted whatever-number-of-bytes-is-necessary from the "pool" (making the amount of data within the pool smaller, so that before the next call to *react()*, infrastructure had to replenish the "pool").

In practice, IMO such On-Demand Pools are not strictly necessary (the same results can be achieved by more generic Call Wrappers without too many downsides) but I don't see any harm in using them.

Dealing with System Calls: On-Demand Data via Exceptions

Those techniques of dealing with system calls discussed above cover pretty much all practical needs (especially as there is always a silver-bullet handling-everything Call Wrapping solution). However, there is another way of dealing with non-determinism, so at least for the sake of completeness, let's discuss it too.

Those techniques of dealing with system calls discussed above cover pretty much all practical needs (especially as there is always a silver-bullet Call Wrapping solution).

Let's consider the following scenario: your (Re)Actor *might* need some non-determinstic data, but chances of it happening are fairly slim, and requesting it before each call to *react()* would be a waste; on the other hand, the logic to determine whether the call needs the data belongs to the application level, and burdening the infrastructure-layer code with this logic does not look like a good idea. One example of such data is the same random data from a physical RNG, which we discussed above, when only a few messages will need this real-RNG data. To make things worse, we might not be able to use "pools" as described above (for example because MAX_RANDOM upper-bound is not known in advance). In this case, instead of resorting to Call Wrapping, it is apparently possible to deal with it in the following manner:

♦ Add *RNG_data*, an array with random data; it can be passed as one of the parameters to *react()* (or can be stored in TLS, or can become a data member of *class Infrastructure*), but is normally empty.

♦ Implement the function *get_random_bytes()*, which provides app-level code with random data. *get_random_bytes()* checks whether the *RNG_data* has sufficient data to satisfy the current call – and if not, it throws a special exception *NeedRNGData* (specifying the exact size of the data needed).

- ▪ This call MUST happen *before* any modification to your (Re)Actor's state has happened. This is an all-important requirement, and violating it has very severe implications. On the other hand, in certain cases, it is not *that* difficult to achieve; in particular, see the *VALIDATE-CALCULATE-MODIFY-SIMULATE Pattern* section below.

♦ Ensure that *class Infrastructure*, on catching *NeedRNGData* exception within *react()*, fills *RNG_data* from RNG source, and repeats the same call to *react()*, but using populated *RNG_data* this time; on this second attempt, the *react()* call goes exactly along the same lines as the previous one, but succeeds because *get_random_bytes()*, when called, can get necessary random data from *RNG_data*.

RAII

Resource Acquisition Is Initialization is a programming idiom used in several object-oriented languages, most prominently C++, but also D, Ada, Vala, and Rust.

—Wikipedia

This model strongly relies on the VALIDATE-CALCULATE-MODIFY-SIMULATE pattern described in the *VALIDATE-CALCULATE-MODIFY-SIMULATE Pattern* section below, and on universal use of RAII throughout your (Re)Actors; however, as you generally should do both of these things anyway, this model has been seen working in practice.

On the other hand, the semantics of this exception-based model is not really obvious with OO-based Take 3 and lambda-based Takes 4-5. Worse than that, such processing requires strict self-discipline and is rather error-prone (plus the effects of making a mistake – such as throwing an exception *after* some modification already happened – can be devastating). Based on these issues, I generally do *not* recommend exception-based processing. Still, there is one case when it *might* come in handy: when choosing between exception-based handling and Call Wrapping on the Client-Side, I *might* prefer the exception-based approach (that's because Call Wrapping happens to reveal a thing or three to the bot writers <sad-face />; more on it in Vol. VIII's chapter on Bot Fighting).

Dealing with System Calls: RPC-like Handling

Another pretty special class of cases with regards to ensuring determinism is related to those "long" calls, which we have already decided to make non-blocking (for the relevant discussion, see the *Blocking or Non-Blocking? Mostly-Non-Blocking* section above).

The good news are that such non-blocking calls are already deterministic without us doing anything special to ensure it: as these calls are non-blocking, it implies that replies to them arrive as an input event — and as we already decided to log *all* the input events, it means that we already made our system deterministic with respect to such non-blocking calls.

This approach is very practical too: I've even heard of games that ensured determinism of *all* the system calls via converting them into RPC-like ones, and it did work for them. Still, I think that Call Wrapping makes app-level code simpler (both to write and to read), so in cases when the system call is guaranteed to be short enough so that we don't want to deal with intervening events while we're waiting for the reply (see the discussion on the two different cases in the *To Block, or Not to Block, That Is the Question. Mostly-Non-Blocking (Re)Actors* section above), I tend to prefer Call Wrapping to RPC-like Calls. On the other hand, if we *do* need to handle events while waiting for the result of an outstanding system call, then, as discussed above, we *do* need to make our call non-blocking, even without taking determinism into account — and deterministic behavior will come as a really nice side effect of this effort <smile />.

Dealing with System Calls: allocations

When talking about memory allocations (including, but not limited to, *malloc(), VirtualAllocEx(), and mmap()*), we need to keep in mind that return values of these calls are not guaranteed to be the same on each program run (even less so if Address Space Layout Randomization, a.k.a. ASLR, is involved[101]). BTW, while *most* of these problems are specific to C/C++, there are cases when such

ASLR

Address space layout randomization (ASLR) is a computer security technique involved in preventing exploitation of memory corruption vulnerabilities... ASLR randomly arranges the address space positions of key data areas of a process, including the base of the executable and the positions of the stack, heap and libraries.

—Wikipedia

---

101   BTW, ASLR tends to help not only against hackers, but also against bot writers(!); so, as a rule of thumb, we do want to have ASLR enabled.

non-determinism rears its ugly head in programming languages which don't normally expose pointers to the program (more on it below).

To make allocations deterministic, strictly speaking, as with any other system call, it *is* possible to Call-Wrap all the calls to memory allocation functions.[102] On the other hand, Call-Wrapping *all* the calls to allocations is going to be a huge effort (let's keep in mind that we'll also need to Call-Wrap *operator new*, and this is not going to be a picnic, and also restoring exact pointer values during replay is not always easy); plus, it is going to cause quite a performance hit in production. Moreover, Call-Wrapping allocations, while possible in C/C++, is not really feasible in many other programming languages.[103]

Fortunately, Call-Wrapping allocations is not really necessary.

As long as

> *we're using pointers/references **only** for dereferencing (and **not** for any other purpose[104])*

our code is deterministic with respect to allocations, even without Call-Wrapping.

With respect to allocations, let's note that relying on specific pointer values, while not too frequent in real-world programs, still does happen. The two most common legitimate cases I know of are the following:

♦ Scenarios when we want to have just *some* kind of sorting. In such cases, it is tempting to use pointers as sorting keys, but while it will lead to a valid program, the program won't be deterministic (unless we Call-Wrap allocations).

♦ Using pointer as an object ID. BTW, this is quite common for several non-C/C++ programming languages such as Java or Python; in particular, the last time I checked, Java's *Object.hashCode()* was effectively relying on the memory location of the object and, as a result, wasn't deterministic.

---

102 In C/C++, that is.

103 At least without hacking into the respective VM.

104 Retrieving array element by index also counts as "dereferencing" in this case.

Overall, when it comes to pointers, below is a list of things that should be **avoided** when writing for determinism:

♦ Using non-trivial pointer arithmetic (and "non-trivial" here means "anything beyond simple array indexing"). Seriously, these things belong in Obfuscated C contest, and *should never* be used for app-level development.[105]

♦ Sending pointers over the network (and writing them to *inputs-log*), regardless of marshalling used. Again, this one should also be avoided regardless of determinism.

♦ Using pointers as identifiers (this includes implicit uses of pointers, including common implementations of *Object.hashCode()* in Java).

♦ Using pointers for ordering purposes (for example, as a key in a *std::map<>*); as noted above, even using pointers to get "just *some* kind of temporary ordering" is not good for determinism.

While this looks like quite a few items to remember, it turns out to be not that bad in practice.

Dealing with System Calls: Which System Functions Are We Talking About and What Do We Do About Them?

In general,

> *Each and every system call (including system calls made indirectly), creates the danger of your code deviating from being deterministic.*

As a result, it might seem that we will end up with millions of function calls that we need to Call-Wrap (or with millions of parameters to provide via TLS/event members/…). Fortunately, in practice, it is not *that* bad. Let's take a closer look at the question "what exactly do we usually need to wrap/provide?"

Here goes the list of the system (and alike) calls that we routinely need to use in our programs, and some of which will make your program non-deterministic (and often also non-blocking):

Let's take a closer look at the question "what exactly do we need to wrap/provide?"

105　As with anything else, there are exceptions, but in this case they're extremely few and far between. And while we're at it: if you're using stuff such as XOR-linked lists, make sure to encapsulate and hide them from app-level, for the Kernighan's sake.

	Is a "long" call?[106]	IMO the Best Implementation for Deterministic (Re)Actors[107]
Current ticks (such as *GetTickCount()* or *clock_gettime(CLOCK_MONO-TONIC, ...)*)	No	TLS-based (or placing current ticks into each Event)
Memory allocations (such as *mal-loc()*, *VirtualAllocEx()*, *mmap()*)	No	Avoiding relying on pointer values; instead, we should use pointers *only* for dereferencing
Current calendar time (such as *time()*)	No	TLS-based (or placing current time into each Event)
Time within event processing[108]	No	Call Wrapping
Implicitly-locale-dependent or implicitly-time-zone-dependent time conversion functions (such as *localtime[_s]()* and *strftime()*)	No	*Server-Side:* better to avoid if possible,[109] otherwise — Call Wrapping *Client-Side:* Call Wrapping, or exception-based processing
Both locale- and time-zone-independent time conversions (such as *sn-printf(..., "%d:%d:%d", tm.tm_hour, tm.tm_minute, tm.tm_second)*)	No	N/A (already deterministic)
File/DB access	It depends[110]	Call Wrapping or non-blocking RPC-like (the latter if you need to make the call non-blocking). Note that if reads are from well-known files (such as resources), you MAY *inputs-log* only position and size of the data read, skipping the data itself[111]
Real RNG (such as */dev/urandom* or *CryptGenRandom()*)	It depends	Call Wrapping or RPC-like (the latter if RNG call is blocking)
Pseudo-RNG	No	N/A. Usually it is better to compile it into your app (rather than rely on system-dependent library) to be 100% sure it is deterministic
C library functions implicitly using globals (such as *strtok()*, etc.)	No	Avoid (these functions tend to cause enough problems to justify writing your own replacements)
Math	No	N/A[112]

Graphic APIs (Client-Side only)	It depends	Mostly N/A[113]
Player Input	N/A	N/A, normally should be processed as input events
Network — UDP sockets	Usually no, but YMMV. As a rule of thumb, you SHOULD make even your UDP sockets non-blocking	N/A[114]
Network — TCP sockets	You MUST make your TCP sockets non-blocking	N/A
Network — *getaddrinfo()*	Blocking	RPC-like (see Take 1–Take 8 above)
RPC calls	Blocking	Non-blocking RPC
Thread APIs	SHOULD NOT appear within your (Re)Actor app-level code	N/A
Mutexes and other thread-sync primitives	SHOULD NOT appear within your (Re)Actor app-level code	N/A
Parallelizing onto multiple cores	Not really	Non-blocking RPC-like; for serious calculations- HPX (see also the *Offloading* section above)

---

106   Note that whether to consider certain functions as blocking is sometimes not that obvious, so, in some cases, YMMV. For a discussion of which calls need to be made non-blocking within our mostly-non-blocking (Re)Actor model, see the *Blocking or Non-Blocking? Mostly-Non-Blocking* section above.

107   My personal opinion, YMMV; batteries not included

108   A rare occurrence, but it might be necessary for latency-critical calculations to see "how much time still left until whatever-deadline we have."

109   At least in those cases when Clients of the same server MAY be spread over multiple time zones, formatting according to one single server time MAY be confusing.

110   Depending on the specifics of your app, you MAY or MAY NOT consider file I/O or DB access as blocking. However, you generally SHOULD consider any such access which happens over the network blocking; this usually SHOULD apply to over-the-LAN access too(!)

111   If you want to be 100% sure that nobody hacked/modded your resources on the Client-Side, you MAY additionally calculate SHA-1 of the whole file on the Client start and log it (once per file), or alternatively MAY calculate-and-log SHA-1 of each chunk you're reading.

112   Though also see the discussion about cross-platform determinism in the *Achieving Cross-Platform Determinism* section below.

113   Unless you're reading something from the graphics layer, it stays output-only and doesn't need to be written to *inputs-log*.

114   Generally, outgoing packets do not need to be written to *inputs-log*, and incoming ones should be presented as input events (and logged to *inputs-log* by framework at that point).

And that's about it. As we can see, the list of the system (and alike) function calls that may occur within our (Re)Actors is relatively limited (in particular because everything we're doing, especially on the Server-Side, is indeed pretty much "moving bits around," as discussed above).

Implementing Deterministic Logic: Other Sources of Non-Determinism

In addition to system calls, there are several other sources of non-determinism in programs. Let's take a closer look at them.

On Undefined Behavior

Some programming languages such as C++ may allow us to write a syntactically valid program, but this program, when run, can exhibit so-called Undefined Behavior (UB). Here, Undefined Behavior can mean anything (up to and including formatting the hard drive of your unfortunate user, see, for example, [Walfridsson][115]).

In general, Undefined Behavior SHOULD be avoided even in the absence of determinism. With determinism, you'll just need to be even more vigilant in this regard. One simple example: while with your usual program, reading uninitialized memory (which *is* an Undefined Behaviour) may not cause visible-enough troubles (for example, if you don't really care much about the initial state of your object), it will kill determinism by about nine orders of order of magnitude faster than you can say "Jack Robinson."

---

115   I won't go as far as saying that "it can make demons fly out of your nose"; while this behavior is indeed allowed by C/C++ standards, I am a firm supporter of the point of view that proper hardware controls should be in place to prevent misbehaving software from causing *that* much trouble (and to avoid disasters such as Therac-25).

No Access to Non-const Globals and TLS

This might go without saying, but let's make it explicit:

> *For your (Re)Actor to be deterministic, you*
> *MUST NOT use any non-const global variables within.*[116]
> *Yes, that means "No Singletons" too.*

And while we're at it, the same goes for using TLS within your (Re)Actor.[117]

Actually, "no-globals" is not just a requirement for being deterministic, but is a well-known "best practice" for your code to be reasonably reliable and readable, so please don't take it as an additional burden that you're doing just for the purpose of becoming deterministic. Following

Actually, "no-globals" is not just a requirement to be deterministic, but is a well-known "best practice," so please don't take it as an additional burden.

---

116 Technically, globals MAY be okay, as long as each is accessed from exactly one (Re)Actor. Enforcing this rule, however, is much more complicated than simple prohibition on all the non-const globals.

117 Note that "TLS Compromise," as we've discussed above, is not within (Re)Actor app-level code; using TLS in infrastructure-level code might be fine in certain very narrow and very-well-defined scenarios (such as the TLS Compromise discussed above).

this practice will make your code better in the medium and long run, even if you're not using any of the benefits provided by determinism.

The only exception to this rule is that accessing global constants is allowed without restrictions (well, as long as you don't try to modify them <wink />).

As a consequence of the rule above,

> *You SHOULD NOT use any function that implicitly uses non-const globals.*

Identifying such functions can be not too trivial, but if you need to stay deterministic, there is a requirement to avoid them. Alternatively, you may decide to Call-Wrap these calls (and write whatever-they-return into *inputs-log*) to keep your logic deterministic, but usually such artificial "wrapping" of the non-system-level code is best avoided whenever feasible.

C standard library is particularly guilty of providing functions that implicitly access globals (this includes *rand()*). Most of these functions (such as *strtok()*) should be avoided anyway due to the logic becoming non-obvious and potentially thread-unsafe on some of the platforms. One list of such functions can be found in [ARM]; note that our problem here is not limited to thread-safety, and *rand()* and *strtok()* are still non-deterministic — even on those platforms (notably Windows) — which makes them thread-safe by replacing globals with TLS-based stuff.

In general, it is better to replace *rand()* with a PRNG that resides entirely within your (Re)Actor (see the discussion in the *PRNG* section below). As for *strtok()*, etc., it is better to avoid them altogether.

Threads (at least when they're running on different CPU cores) represent a really bad source of non-determinism.

On Threads

Threads (at least when they're running on different CPU cores) represent a *really bad* source of non-determinism.[118] If we have two threads running in parallel, their relative times are not guaranteed. For example,

---

118   I don't want to get into a discussion of which of the current hardware allows for deterministic scheduling, but from the point of view of the application level that runs on top of modern desktop/mobile/server OS, threads are as non-deterministic as they get.

if on one run of the program it was thread A that grabbed the mutex first, on the second run it may be thread B doing so, with the differences between the runs starting to pile up from that point on.

Fortunately, we've already thrown away thread APIs from our (Re)Actors, so that each of our (Re)Actors is essentially single-threaded.[119]

On Determinism of the Whole Distributed Systems

BTW, the reasoning about the threads above leads to an interesting observation. While we *can* have each of our (Re)Actors deterministic (and quite easily too), it is *not* an easy task to make a system of more-than-one (Re)Actor fully deterministic as a whole.

When talking about whole-system determinism in the context of this book (for example, as we discussed it in Vol. I's chapter on Communications), we're actually talking about finding some plausible sequence of events that would make our whole system self-consistent, though without guarantees that it is *exactly* the sequence of events as they happened in the real world.[120] Even achieving such a kinda-determinism is not easy, and would amount to establishing one common time among all our (Re)Actors; this is doable, though quite cumbersome (for details, see the discussion on eliminating Server-Side uncertainty in Vol. I's chapter on Communications).

On the other hand, a lack of system-wide determinism is usually *not* a problem in practice, as long as we can make each of the system *components* deterministic, so the whole not-necessarily-deterministic system consists only of deterministic components. As soon as we achieve such *per-component* determinism, we can reap all the deterministic benefits discussed in this chapter.

---

119 Or at least "as if" it is single-threaded.

120 BTW, strictly speaking, the Special Theory of Relativity says that for distant objects, the whole concept of "simultaneity" is inherently relative <ouch! />. While physical relativity as such is not directly related to our problems here, the concepts behind STR and non-determinism of distributed systems are surprisingly similar (in a sense, we can consider our distributed system as a system which has finite and non-uniform communication speeds, which can easily happen for a physical system where the space between nodes is filled with a material with a non-uniform refractive index).

Implementing Deterministic Logic: Non-Issues

> There are three hundred and sixty-four days
> when you might get un-birthday presents,
> and only one for birthday presents, you know.
>
> — Lewis Carroll

In addition to the non-deterministic issues described above, there are also three non-issues. These things are frequently seen as potential problems for determinism at first glance, but are not really dangerous when we take a closer look. The most popular non-issues that are (erroneously) seen to prevent determinism are pseudo-random numbers, logging, and caching.

In addition to the non-deterministic issues described above, there are also three non-issues.

PRNG

Pseudo-random numbers as such are perfectly deterministic; that is, as long as you're storing the whole PRNG state as one of the members of your (Re)Actor. Instead of using non-deterministic *rand()* (which implicitly uses a global, and this global will cause quite a few problems), in theory you can implement your own linear congruential PRNG (which is literally a one-liner, but is not really good when it comes to randomicity), or use one of those Mersenne Twister classes that are dime a dozen these days (just make sure that those PRNG classes have PRNG state as a class member, not as a global).

However, as will be discussed in Vol. VI's chapter on Random Number Generators, as a rule of thumb I do *not* recommend using non-crypto RNGs for games (in short, because it may create difficult-to-spot attacks), so for not-so-RNG-critical games I suggest running your own AES-CTR PRNG; see Vol. VI for details. Note that to get your PRNG (such as AES-CTR PRNG) seeded, you still need to provide some seed that is external to your deterministic logic, but this is rarely a problem; for example, */dev/urandom* or *CryptGenRandom()* can be used for this purpose (NB: keep in mind that seed taken from */dev/urandom* or *CryptGenRandom()* needs to be saved to the *inputs-log*, using any of the methods discussed above for making system calls deterministic).

For those games that are really RNG-critical,[121] you will want to run several hardware-based RNGs and use something (such as XOR) to combine their outputs (once again, see Vol. VI for further details). From our current perspective of (Re)Actors, this combined output will be an input to our (Re)Actor, and as such will need to be *inputs-logged*.

Logging/Tracing

Logging/tracing (as in "log something to an application-level log file"), while it does interact with an outside world, is deterministic (that is, from the point of view of whoever-writes-the-log — i.e., from the point of view of our (Re)Actor). Moreover, even if your logging procedure prints current time itself (and to do so, calls *system_get_current_time()* or something else of the sort), and technically becomes non-deterministic from the "all the world outside of our (Re)Actor" point of view (this happens because its output starts to depend on the current time), it stays deterministic from the point of view of our (Re)Actor itself (as long as the (Re)Actor does not read from the log).[122]

Practical consequence: feel free to write all kinds of times to the log (such as in Node.js *time()/timeend()* pair), even if these times as such are *not* deterministic; however, make sure that the result of calling *system_get_current_time()* is not used other than to write data to the log (in particular, you MUST NOT return current time/ticks from the logging function, otherwise determinism will be broken).

Caching

Last but not least deterministic non-issue is related to caching. Caching (whether file-based or memory-based), when it comes to determinism, is quite an interesting beast.

Let's consider a database that has some data, and our own cache over this database. Now, as long as our cache works correctly, we have two choices to ensure determinism:

a) To consider the cache as part of our (Re)Actor, and to log (to *inputs-log*) all the data going from the database to the cache, but not *inputs-logging* the calls between our (Re)Actor and cache.

Last but not least deterministic non-issue is related to caching.

121 Think "stock exchanges" or "casinos."

122 I know that this explanation reads as quite ugly, but I can't find better wording; regardless of the quality of the wording, the statements in this paragraph stand.

b) To consider the cache as something external to our (Re)Actor, and to *inputs-log* all the calls between our (Re)Actor and cache, but not *inputs-logging* the calls between the cache and the database.

As long as the cache is working properly, both approaches are equivalent from a determinism point of view (though they may easily be very different, performance-wise). Moreover, even if option (a) is used, it is generally okay to drop the cache at any time. In other words, for *both* option (a) *and* option (b), it is generally acceptable *not* to serialize cache as part of the serialized (Re)Actor state[123] — and this can provide a very important performance improvement.

On Isolation Perimeters

After discussing two different ways to ensure determinism of caches, we can make one interesting observation about *any* wannabe-deterministic system:

To take advantage of determinism, we need to make an "isolation perimeter," where we control and log all the inputs.

> *to take advantage of determinism of a certain object (~="code±data"), we need to isolate it and make sure that we can control (and log to **inputs-log**) all the inputs of this object.*

In other words, we need to make an "Isolation Perimeter" where we control and log all the inputs.

Actually, the idea is well-known, though our (Re)Actors are doing it in a not-so-orthodox manner. There are quite a few systems out there (such as, for example, [Geels, et al.]) that are trying to build this Isolation Perimeter around the whole app — or even around the whole VM (as was done in the "virtual lockstep" algorithms). Actually, without access to the internals of the code, it is next to impossible for them to do anything else.

On the other hand, as we DO have access to the internals of our own code, we can build our Isolation Perimeter pretty much anywhere we want. As we can see in the example of caches discussed above, such flexibility can easily become our big advantage, performance-wise.

---

123   As discussed above in the *Going Circular* section, serializing the (Re)Actor state is necessary to get such goodies as Post-Factum Debugging and Replay-Based Regression Testing.

Implementing Deterministic Logic: Cross-Platform Determinism

Up until now, we were concentrating on the implementation of a program that exhibits exactly the same behavior when *exactly the same program* is run multiple times; [Hare, Determinism: Requirements vs Features] defines this as "same-executable determinism." However, there is also a stricter version of determinism: to have a source code, which (after it is compiled) runs exactly in the same way on different platforms; consistently with [Hare, Determinism: Requirements vs Features], we'll name it "cross-platform determinism."

Such cross-platform determinism has its own uses in games; during not-so-ancient times, there were numerous attempts to use it for multiplayer games using protocols such as deterministic lockstep. Unfortunately, these experiments have shown that achieving true cross-platform determinism is extremely difficult. The most annoying scenario occurs when you have a program that is *almost* cross-platform-deterministic, but *very occasionally* produces a slightly different numeric result; for example, due to slightly different rounding (see the discussion on rounding-related issues below). If we're relying on exactly deterministic behavior (such as in Deterministic Lockstep, etc.), this "slightly different" result will start an avalanche of results being more and more different, eventually causing a macroscopic difference between two systems, which means that determinism-based protocol has fallen apart.

On the other hand, if we're talking about cross-platform replay-based *testing* of your app (such as equivalence testing), or about cross-platform *almost-determinism*, things are not that bad. If we're trying to replay-test two systems on different platforms, and run into non-determinism, we can usually fix the issue rather easily and resume testing. Also, if we're okay with *almost-determinism* (such as in running Server-Side logic and Client-Side Prediction from the same source code), we're generally fine with the results being *slightly* different (and for Client-Side Prediction, this difference will be fixed very soon, before macroscopic effects are allowed to accumulate).

Achieving Cross-Platform Determinism

As it was already noted above, achieving cross-platform determinism is significantly more complicated than achieving just a simple same-executable kind of determinism. An in-depth discussion of those cross-platform issues that can cause slightly different behavior on different platforms is beyond our current scope, so I will merely list them.

Achieving cross-platform determinism is significantly more complicated than achieving a simple same-executable kind of determinism.

The first batch of potential problems is necessary to keep in mind, even if cross-platform *almost-determinism* is sufficient:

♦ The same functions on different platforms may exhibit subtly different behavior; moreover, both behaviors can be fully standard-compliant but different.

▪ In particular, non-ordered and partially-ordered collections may produce different results on different platforms while staying compliant. For C++, examples include iterating over hash-table-based *unordered_map<>/unordered_set<>* containers, and over tree-based partially ordered *multiset<>/multimap<>* containers.

• One funny thing about these algorithms is that they *are* indeed nothing more than "moving bits around" (which, in turn, means that they can easily be implemented in a deterministic manner); it is just that bits are moved in a slightly different (but compliant) manner for different implementations.

• It means that one way to deal with them is to write your own version (or just to compile any existing ones to all the platforms); as long as the code for all the platforms is (substantially) the same, it will compile into the code that behaves exactly the same.

• For tree-based partially ordered sets/maps, you can often make them fully ordered by adding an artificial ID (for example, incremented for each insert to the container) and using it as a tie-breaker if the original comparison returns that objects are equal. It is quite a dirty hack, but if you can ignore ID wraparounds (and this is almost universally the case if you're using 64-bit IDs), and you don't care about storing an extra ID for each item in collection, it works pretty well.

The second batch of issues plaguing cross-platform determinism, is related to floating-point arithmetic producing subtly different results on different platforms. Fortunately enough, quite often we can live with these differences when all we need is *almost-determinism*, as defined above.

In short: while floating-point operations/functions/… will return *almost* the same results on different platforms,[124] making them exactly the same across different hardware/compilers/… is very challenging at the very least; for further details, refer to [Dawson] and [Fiedler, Floating Point Determinism]. A few minor but important points in addition to the discussion in those references:

♦ There are several different sources of non-deterministic floating point behavior, including but not limited to:

  ▪ Subtly different behavior of libraries on different platforms.

  ▪ Differences in floating point implementations on different CPUs(!).

  ▪ And, last but not least, as order of calculating $a+b+c$ can be compiler-dependent,[125] and as each addition implicitly includes rounding, $a+b+c$ can result either in $round(round(a+b)+c)$, or in $round(round(b+c)+a)$, and these are not guaranteed to be equal at all.[126] This, in turn, means that compilers (as well as compiler options) can easily break cross-platform determinism.

♦ As floating-point arithmetic is once again all about "moving bits around" (it just takes some bunches of bits and returns other bunches of bits), it can be made perfectly deterministic. In practice, you can achieve it by using a software floating-point library that simulates floating-point via integer arithmetic (after all, all the floating-point stuff can be expressed in terms of integer math; see, for example, [Knuth]).

While floating-point operations/functions/… will return *almost* the same results on different platforms, making them *exactly* the same across different hardware/compilers/… is very challenging at the very least.

---

124 After all, $sin(\pi/4)$ is equal to $1/\sqrt{2}$ everywhere; it is last-bit rounding that causes all the trouble.

125 At least in C/C++, it *is* compiler-dependent.

126 Yes, it also means that addition in floating-point space is *not* associative; see, for example, [Wikipedia, Associative property].

▪ Note that such a library (if used consistently for all your platforms) does not need to be IEEE compliant; all you need is merely to get some reasonable results, and the last bit of mantissa/significand rarely matters in practice (as long as it is the same for all the platforms).

▪ Such libraries are slooooow compared to using CPU-supported floating-point; for a reasonably good floating-point emulation library (such as [Hauser, Berkeley SoftFloat]), you can expect slowdown in the order of 20–50x compared to hardware floating point.

  • OTOH, certain speedup can be expected if the library is rewritten to avoid packing/unpacking floats (i.e., that class MyFloat is actually a two-field struct separating significand and exponent), and replacing IEEE-compliant rounding with some-reasonable-and-convenient-to-implement rounding; a very wild guesstimate for such an improvement is in the order of 2x [Hauser], which is not bad, but will still leave us with at least a 10x slow-down compared to a hardware floating point.

▪ However, if you're fine with this 20x-50x-slower floating-point arithmetic (for example, because your logic performs relatively few floating-point operations), such libraries will provide you with perfect cross-platform determinism.

♦ Another deterministic alternative to floating points is to use fixed-point arithmetic; in particular, currently there is a very interesting work-in-progress within SG14 of the ISO C++ Standard Body. Among other things, it supports the so-called *elastic* fixed-point numbers, which allow to bypass quite a few limitations of traditional fixed-point. For more information – see [McFarlane, Composition of Arithmetic Types], and for current implementation – see [McFarlane, CNL: A Compositional Numeric Library for C++].

  ▪ As long as the CNL-style fixed point numbers are implemented on top of integers – they *are* perfectly deterministic. Moreover – they're generally faster than floating-point ones (speed was the main reason to develop them in the first place); of course, this comes at the cost of needing to handle fixed-point positions manually – but it is still a very viable option.

Let's also note that the difficulty of achieving cross-platform determinism significantly depends on the programming language we're using. In particular, as noted in [Ignatchenko, Deterministic Components for Interactive Distributed Systems: Benefits and Implementation], Java tends to be significantly more determinism-friendly than C/C++ (in particular, due to strict requirements on order calculations in Java specification, *and* to *strictfp* modifier); as for the other programming languages, it depends greatly on *both* the programming language as such *and* on a specific implementation.

Implementing Deterministic Logic: Summary

From the analysis above, we've found that while there are tons of places where your logic can potentially call system and system-like functions (and get something from them, making the logic potentially non-deterministic), in practice all of them can be dealt with relatively easily as described in the *Implementing Deterministic Logic: Non-Determinism Due to System Calls* section.

As for other issues (those not related to system and system-like function calls), they are also of only a very limited nature (that is, unless we're talking about cross-platform determinism). Neither a requirement to avoid globals (which is good practice anyway), nor a requirement to avoid pointer-related trickery tends to cause too many practical problems.

However, if you're going into the realm of cross-platform determinism, things may get significantly nastier (and likely will cause lots of trouble); while collection differences can be handled if you're careful enough, achieving fully cross-platform floating point calculations across different CPUs/libraries/etc. can easily become next-to-impossible. Fortunately, in quite a few cases, *almost-determinism* will be enough, and this one is *much* easier to achieve.

If you're going into the realm of cross-platform determinism, things may get significantly nastier.

Types of Determinism vs Deterministic Goodies

As mentioned above, there are at least two different types of determinism: "same-executable" determinism and "cross-platform" determinism. In addition, as mentioned in [Hare, Determinism: Requirements vs Features], there is in fact a third type of determinism, "same-platform-determinism — which stands against minor code changes." Let's give a stricter definition for each of them (and respective versions of *almost-determinism* too):

♦ **Same-Executable Almost Determinism.** Different runs of the same executable, given the same inputs, produce *almost* the same results. The "*almost*" in the name means that while the overall result is *almost* the same, some minor rounding differences (such as the difference in the last bit of the floating point output value) may be allowed. It should be noted that even this last-bit difference in floating-point value can (and most of the time will) lead to macroscopic differences further down the road, so all uses for almost-determinism SHOULD be very limited in time *and* SHOULD be self-healing. BTW, Same-Executable Almost Determinism happens quite a bit with parallelized floating-point calculations, which are very common in GPGPU, and recently there has been quite a bit of talk related to the use of GPGPU on the Server-Side (for more details, see Vol. III's chapter on Server-Side Architecture).

Same-Executable Determinism. Different runs of the same executable produce *exactly* the same results given the same inputs.

♦ **Same-Executable Determinism.** Different runs of the same executable produce *exactly* the same results given the same inputs. Quite realistic to achieve.

♦ **Same-Platform-Determinism Resilient to Minor Code Changes.** A quite special variation of Same-Executable Determinism, which is related to making our code deterministic in the face of minor code changes, and on the same platform. Such scenarios arise while using Replay-based Regression Testing, and are quite a headache (which may be made bearable though).

♦ **Cross-Platform Almost-Determinism.** The same source code, when compiled to different platforms, produces *almost* the same results on all the platforms of interest. Unlike with full-scale cross-platform determinism, achieving cross-platform almost-determinism — while being an even bigger headache than determinism-resilient-to-minor-code-changes — is still possible.

♦ **Cross-Platform Determinism**. The same source code, when compiled to different platforms, behaves *exactly* the same on all the platforms of interest. As discussed above in the *Implementing Deterministic Logic: Cross-Platform Determinism* section, Cross-Platform Determinism is extremely difficult to achieve, at least in C/C++. In particular, because of floating-point issues, achieving Cross-Platform Determinism becomes *so* difficult that it is unclear whether it is truly realistic to get a serious C/C++-based heavily-floating-point system to be perfectly deterministic over several really different platforms (though a recently-developed fixed-point CNL library *might* provide a workaround, at least for some of the use cases).

As discussed in [Hare, Determinism: Requirements vs Features] (and applying similar analysis to the other deterministic goodies not mentioned there), relations between types of determinism, and the goodies they provide, can be summarized in the following table:

	Same-Executable Almost-Determinism	Same-Executable Determinism	Same-Platform Determinism Resilient to Minor Changes	Cross-Platform Almost-Determinism[127]	Cross-Platform Determinism — most complicated
Deterministic Lockstep					Yes
Client-Side Replay					Yes
Keeping cross-platform code equivalence				Yes	Yes
Using same code for Client-Side Prediction, etc.				Yes	Yes
Replay-Based Regression Testing			Yes	Yes	Yes
Production Post-Factum Analysis		Yes	Yes	Yes	Yes
Low-Latency Fault Tolerance	Maybe[128]	Yes	Yes	Yes	Yes
(Re)Actor Migration (Better Balancing)	Maybe	Yes	Yes	Yes	Yes

---

127 For the purpose of this table, we assume that *Cross-Platform Almost-Determinism* implies *Same-Platform Determinism Resilient to Minor Changes.*

128 Strictly speaking, low-latency fault-tolerance and moving (Re)Actors around, when almost-determinism is involved, will work correctly if and only if *all* the almost-deterministic results emitted by our (Re)Actor are considered transient (i.e., subject to further revisions that will completely override all the previous results); more discussion on the effects of almost-determinism on implementations of the fault-tolerance and moving (Re)Actors around will be discussed in Vol. III's chapter on Server-Side Architecture.

Relation of Deterministic (Re)Actors to Deterministic Finite Automata

> Have it compose a poem — a poem about a haircut!
> But lofty, noble, tragic, timeless, full of love, treachery,
> retribution, quiet heroism in the face of certain doom!
> Six lines, cleverly rhymed, and every word
> beginning with the letter s!!
> — And why not throw in a full exposition of the
> general theory of nonlinear automata while you're at it?
>
> — Dialogue between Klapaucius and Trurl from
> *The Cyberiad* by Stanislaw Lem

If you're not interested in theory, you can safely skip this subsection.

NB: if you're not interested in theory, you can safely skip this subsection; for practical purposes, suffice it to say that whatever deterministic event-driven program you've-already-written is a deterministic finite automaton, so there is absolutely no need to be scared. On the other hand, if you are interested in theory, you'll certainly need much more than this subsection. The idea of this subsection is just to provide some kind of "bridge" between your uni courses and the practical use of finite automata in programming (which unfortunately differ significantly from quite a few courses out there).

First, we need to note that our *class ConcreteReactor* (a deterministic one) falls strictly under the definition of Finite Automaton (or, more precisely, Deterministic Finite Automaton) provided in Wikipedia (and in quite a few uni courses). Namely, a deterministic Finite State Machine (a.k.a. Deterministic Finite Automaton) is usually defined as follows (see, for example, [Wikipedia, Deterministic Finite Automaton]):

♦ Σ is the input alphabet (a finite, non-empty set of symbols).

  ▪ For our (Re)Actor, Σ is a set of values that a pair (now,ev) can take; while this set is exponentially huge, it is still obviously finite.

♦ S is a finite, non-empty set of states.

- In our case, it is represented by all valid combinations of all the bits forming data members of the (Re)Actor. Again, it is exponentially huge, but certainly still finite (with an upper bound for the number of different states being $2^{\text{number\_of\_bits\_in\_all\_data\_members}}$).

◆ s_0 is an initial state, an element of S.

- Whatever state results from a constructor of our (Re)Actor.

◆ δ is the state-transition function. δ: S × Σ -> S.

- In our (Re)Actors, this function is implemented as *react()*.

◆ F is the set of final states, a (possibly empty) subset of S.

- For our (Re)Actor, F is always empty.

As we can see, our *class ConcreteReactor* complies with this definition, and therefore *is* a Deterministic Finite Automaton.

Quite often[129] in university courses, state-transition function δ is replaced with a "set of transitions." From a formal point of view, these two definitions are strictly equivalent because:

◆ For any state-transition function δ with a finite number of possible inputs, we can run this function through all the possible inputs and obtain the equivalent set of transitions.[130]

◆ Having a set of transitions, we can easily define our state-transition function δ via this set.

On the other hand, if you start to define your state machine via a set of transitions in practice (and not just in theory), most likely you're starting the journey along the path which will eventually lead you to shooting yourself in the foot. When used in practice, this "set of transitions" is usually implemented as some kind of a state transition table (see [Wikipedia, State Transition Table]). It all looks very neat, and is fairly obvious. There is only one problem with table-driven finite state machines, and the problem is that they don't work for real-world app-level programming.[131]

---

129 See, for example, [Nelson].

130 Never mind that such enumeration may easily take much longer than it does for the universe to end from something such as Heat Death or the Big Rip — in math world, we don't need to restrict ourselves to such silly notions.

131 While table-driven FSMs can be fine for embedded programs with inherently-small-number-of-states, for app-level programming the number of states very rarely stops at the number that is "small enough" for table-driven FSMs.

The problem that kills this neat idea is known as "state explosion" and is all about the exponential growth of number of your states as you increase the complexity of your machine.

The problem that actually kills this neat idea is known as "state explosion," and is all about exponential growth of the number of your states as you increase the complexity of your program. I won't delve into too many details about the "state explosion," but will note that it becomes really, really bad as soon as you start to develop something realistic; even having 5 different 1-bit fields within your state leads to a state transition table of size 32, and adding anything else is already difficult; make it 8 1-bit fields (corresponding to 256 already-existing transitions), and adding any further logic has already became un-manageable.[132] In fact, while I've seen several attempts to define state machines via state transition tables at the app-level, none were able to come even somewhat-close to succeeding.

What is normally used in practice is essentially an automaton that is defined via state-transition function δ (which function δ is implemented as a deterministic function written in an imperative programming language; see, for example, our *react()* function above). Actually, such automatons are used much more frequently than developers realize that they're writing a finite automaton <wink />. To distinguish these real-world code-driven state machines from table-driven finite state machines (which are usually impractical for app-level programming), I like the term "ad-hoc state machines" (to the best of my knowledge, the term was coined in [Calderone]).

And from our perspective, we can say that our *class ConcreteReactor* clearly qualifies as such an *ad-hoc state machine*.

Deterministic Finite State Machines: Nothing New—Let's Just Start Using Them

While there is nothing new with event-driven programming (and *ad-hoc finite state machines* used for this purpose), our finite state machines have one significant advantage compared to those usually used in the industry. Our (Re)Actors a.k.a. ad hoc state machines are deterministic (at least when it comes to one single platform), and that allows for lots of improvements for debugging of distributed systems (mostly due to Replay Testing/Debugging and Production Post-Factum Analysis).

132   While hierarchical state machines may mitigate this problem a bit, in practice they become too intertwined if you're trying to keep your state machines small enough to be table-driven. In other words: while hierarchical state machines are a good idea in general, even they won't be able to allow you to use table-driven stuff at the app-level.

On the other hand, in academic circles, Deterministic Finite Automata are well known, but usually relevant academic discussions are limited to table-driven FSMs, and these don't scale well to a large number of states (due to the "state explosion" phenomenon discussed above).

On the third hand, determinism for games has been a popular topic for a while (see, for example, [Dickinson]), and in recent years has gotten a new life with MOGs and synchronous physics simulation on the Client and the Server (see, for example, [Fiedler, Deterministic Lockstep]). Oh, and BTW, at least some of the AAA companies are using deterministic automata all the way—and with Post-Factum Analysis, too (see, for example, [Aldridge]).

On the fourth hand (yes, I'm exactly halfway to becoming an octopus), if you want your game crashing 10x less frequently than the competition, do yourself and your players a favor and record production *inputs-logs* for Post-Factum Analysis purposes, as well as perform Replay-Based Regression Testing. I know I sound like a commercial, but as a gamer myself I do have a very legitimate interest in making games crash much more rarely than they do now; and I also know that for most good game developers out there, deterministic testing and post-factum analysis will help to produce more reliable programs, and will help *a lot*.

If you want your game crashing 10x less frequently than the competition, do yourself and your players a favor and record production inputs-logs for post-factum purposes, as well as perform replay-based testing.

TL;DR for Determinism Section

Phew! It was quite a long section on Determinism. Let's summarize it here:

♦ Deterministic logic is a Good Thing™, providing game-changing[133] benefits for debugging of distributed systems, including Replay-Based Regression Testing and production Post-Factum Analysis.

♦ Implementing deterministic logic requires relatively few changes in addition to the existing best practices, as long as cross-platform determinism is not required.

  ▪ Dealing with system and system-like calls in an optimal manner requires several different approaches, depending

---

133 Pun intended.

on the nature of the function we're dealing with; see the *Dealing with System Calls: Which System Functions Are We Talking About and What Do We Do About Them?* section for a quick summary of these approaches.

• Achieving full-scale cross-platform determinism can be tricky, especially because of floating-point issues.

DIVIDE ET IMPERA, OR HOW TO SPLIT ~~THE HARE~~ ~~THE HAIR~~ THE (RE)ACTOR

Divide et Impera
(Divide and Conquer)

— Philip II of Macedon, 4th Century BC

Now, as we've discussed all the goodies coming from (Re)Actors, and described the basics of their implementation, we need to consider yet another problem that comes into play as soon as our (Re)Actors become really large (and for a large game, at least some of them will).

As one all-important example, chances are that our Game World (Re)Actor is going to be huge. While all the things we wrote about still apply, a Big Fat Question™ arises: "How to write it so that the code remains manageable?" Or an equivalent "How to keep code complexity in check as the size of the (Re)Actor grows?"

BTW, in this regard I *strongly* recommend reading Chapter 7 of [Nystrom, Game Programming Patterns]. Several subsections of this book that follow are significantly influenced by that work (and by UML state machines), though (I hope) I still provide a bit of useful information beyond them.

How to keep code complexity in check as the size of the (Re) Actor grows?

On Importance of the DIY IDL Compiler

First, let's note that

> *whatever-we're-doing, **100% of** the marshalling/unmarshalling MUST be done by IDL-compiler-generated code.*

While strictly speaking, doing marshalling/unmarshalling manually might work (and I even know of a multi-million-LoC system which does just this) – such a manual approach is known to be a source of many easily-preventable time-consuming bugs. In addition, using an IDL compiler instead of manual marshalling/unmarshalling allows for certain very-important-in-practice goodies such as automated testing, and automated obfuscation (the latter being *very* important to deal with bots, more on it in Vol. VIII's chapter on Bot Fighting).

Moreover – while there are *lots* of readily available IDL compilers out there (including protobuf, FlatBuffers, and so on) – at least for gamedev I am arguing for

> *Writing your own game-tailored IDL compiler.*

Sure, it is nice to use something-which-has-already-been-developed-for-us – but unfortunately, no currently-existing IDL is IMO good enough for game development. In particular:

♦ At least for Client-2-Server communications, we need encodings which are much more sophisticated than those provided by existing IDL compilers; this includes support for delta encodings (with a reference to a previous already-acknowledged packet), fixed-point representations (without the need to convert from/to floating-point at app-level), and so on; for more discussion – see Vol. I's chapter on Communications.

♦ We DO want to specify classes/structs where the data-on-the-wire should be mapped. In particular, often we want to map marshalled data to an *existing* class, without the need to move the data manually between IDL-generated-plain-struct, and our class; for more discussion on mappings – see Vol. I. Unfortunately, currently-existing IDL compilers don't provide this capability.

As we DO expect our game to evolve, protocols are going to change

♦ Built-in versioning support. As we DO expect our game to evolve, protocols *are* going to change; as a result - versioning (with guaranteed backward-compatibility) is all-important for practical purposes (even more so if we take into account obfuscation). More discussion on it is once again available in Vol. I. Unfortunately, very few of the existing IDL compilers have even rudimentary support for versioning (and we need *much* more than that).

♦ We DO want our IDL compiler to support whatever-model-of-non-blocking-processing we prefer to use. In our Takes 1- 8 discussed above, we did assume that our IDL compiler will generate whatever-stubs-and-skeletons-we-want; in practice, having customized IDL compiler able to do it, *does* simplify writing non-blocking code greatly.

♦ We DO want our IDL compiler to generate obfuscators for our communications; it is a very important part of the Bot Fighting strategy discussed in Vol. VIII – and can be implemented quite easily as soon as we have our own IDL compiler.

The next question is *how exactly* your IDL will work for your game. At this point, I have to note that there is no one single "right" answer for this question; however - there are several common patterns which I'll briefly mention (NB: below, we'll discuss only handling of incoming events; for handling of non-blocking returns – see extensive discussion in the *Handling Returns in a Non-Blocking Way in (Re)Actors* section above).

Big-n-Ugly-Switch

```
//Listing 5.BigUglySwitch
//PSEUDO-CODE
function react(r, ev) {
  switch( ev.type ) {
    case NETWORK_PACKET_EVENT:
      switch( ev.packet.type ) {//(*)
        case MSG_ABC:
          abc = unmarshal_abc( ev.packet.body );
            //unmarshal_abc() is generated by IDL compiler
          OnMsgAbc(abc);
            //real processing,
            // hand-written member of our (Re)Actor
          break;
        case MSG_DEF:
          //pretty much the same thing,
          //  replacing "abc" with "def"...
          break;
      }
      break;
    case SOME_OTHER_EVENT:
      //...
      break;
  }
}
```

This approach does work, but boy – it *is* ugly; more importantly – it is barely readable and is cumbersome to maintain.

Generated Switch

On the other hand – while the code above is indeed ugly, realistically it matters *only* if we have to maintain this code manually. If our IDL will generate at least the-switch-on-ev.packet.type (the one marked with (*)) for us – we'll have much fewer things to care about.

To have our IDL compiler generate this switch-on-ev.packet.type – the only thing we need to do is to specify "which messages we want to handle within this generated function", that's pretty much it. Having this information, it will be trivial for our IDL compiler to generate a function implementing the inner switch.

Stream-based Unmarshalling

In the example above – we have silently assumed that all the un-marshalling happens *before* the actual *OnMsg*()* handler is called. This approach, while being certainly viable – has a potential run-time cost of (a) allocating-space-for and (b) copying the data within the network packet. If this is undesirable – a kind of "stream-based" unmarshalling can be used. In this case – some of the parameters of *OnMsg*()* function become very rudimentary "streams", with an ability to extract 'next value' out of such "stream". If present, each of these "streams" often corresponds to a collection-transferred-within-the-message.

This approach, while being *sometimes* useful (especially for rather-large-messages-with-variable-length-collections in a really-time-critical code) – should be used *very sparingly and only when it is really necessary*; otherwise – there are risks of making the code fragile without a real reason.

As we'll be moving towards more and more complicated (Re) Actors, we'll notice that in many cases our (Re)Actor can (and SHOULD) be split into several ones

Composition: (Re)Actor-within-(Re)Actor

As we'll be moving towards more and more complicated (Re)Actors, we'll notice that in many cases our (Re)Actor can (and SHOULD) be split into several ones. For example, in our Game World we'll likely have a bunch of Characters (PCs/NPCs). As a rule of thumb, each of these Characters will have its own logic and its own data, and will be self-contained enough to be represented by a (Re)Actor-within-(Re)Actor. In other words, we can implement a significant part of the logic of our *class GameWorldReactor* via a bunch of instances of *class PlayerReactor*, with each of these *PlayerReactor*s handling its own messages coming from players / AI Servers.[134]

These *PlayerReactor*s will have all the attributes of the (Re)Actor: they will have their own state, and will have their own *react()* function (or equivalent). On the other hand, with *PlayerReactor*s being a part of the *GameWorldReactor*, *class GameWorldReactor* will be able to access *PlayerReactor*s beyond *react()*. In other words, it is perfectly possible (and usually necessary) to provide *class PlayerReactor* with extra read-only functions beyond *react()* (such as, for example, *getCoordinates()*).

---

134   As discussed in Vol. I's chapter on Communications, to reduce the load on our Game World Server, it is usually desirable to run AI in separate Servers.

On the third hand (hares have at least three hands, you know <wink/>), modifying interactions between *GameWorldReactor* and *PlayerReactor* are IMO better handled via new events (such as *PlayerGotHitByArrow* event) sent by *GameWorldReactor* to *PlayerReactor*. This leads us to the rule of thumb that

> all the modifications to the **ChildReactor** are done via events (either coming from other entities and forwarded by **ParentReactor,** or coming from the **ParentReactor** directly), though reading public attributes of **ChildReactor** MAY be done directly via functions.

IMO, this approach often provides the best balance between encapsulation and convenience. On the other hand, even more so than usual, your mileage may vary, so feel free to disregard this rule of thumb if the specifics of your own system dictate otherwise.

Under the (Re)Actor-within-(Re)Actor model, *ParentReactor* (*GameWorldReactor* in our example) routes the incoming event to a *ChildReactor* (*PlayerReactor* in our example) based on some information contained within the incoming event itself; for example, for *PlayerReactors*, it can be done by source IP of the incoming packet (or, even better, by channel ID to facilitate changing IPs on the fly; see Vol IV's chapter on Network Programming for a discussion of IPs-vs-IDs).

In a sense, (Re)Actor-within-(Re)Actor is a generalization over the "Concurrent State Machines" as described in [Nystrom, State Pattern]. However, unlike "Concurrent State Machines" (and more along the lines of rather general "orthogonal regions" from [Wikipedia, UML State Machine]): (a) we're not specifying *how exactly* our *ParentReactor* should route incoming events to the *ChildReactors*; (b) we allow for an arbitrary amount of processing within *ParentReactor* before we decide whether to forward the event to *ChildReactor* (plus, events can be generated by *ParentReactor* itself); and (c) we also allow interaction between *ChildReactors*.

From my experience, *ParentReactor/ChildReactor* splits simplify development very significantly, so I *strongly* suggest looking for them, and splitting (Re)Actors along these lines wherever possible. On

From my experience, *ParentReactor/ ChildReactor* splits simplify development very significantly, so I *strongly* suggest looking for them, and splitting (Re)Actors along their lines wherever possible.

the other hand, while I am all for *ChildReactors* representing items-and-concepts-that-already-exist-in-the-original-(Re)Actor (or more generally – within GDD), I am generally against creating artificial *ChildReactors*; such artificial *ChildReactors* (i.e., those created just for the sake of splitting (Re)Actors without any "natural" objects behind them) tend to be very fragile and require too much rewriting in case of changing requirements.[135]

State Pattern

When implementing (Re)Actors, more often than not, we DO need a *state* variable, which represents the "current state" of the object. Traditionally, *state* is of enum type, but as we'll see below, it is not the only way to skin this cat.

Of course, in addition to this enumerated *state* member, our (Re)Actor will have quite a few other members (which represent the so-called "Extended State" in terms of [Wikipedia, UML State Machine]). Moreover, some parts of this "Extended State" are specific to the specific values of *state*, and this is what we're about to exploit.

State-Specific Handling

In terms of our (Re)Actors, classical State pattern (as described, for example, in [Nystrom, State Pattern]) would look along the following lines:

```
//Listing 5.StatePattern
//PSEUDO-CODE
//each of State* classes is expected to have
// enterState and exitState() members
class StateA {
  function react(ev) {
    switch( ev.type ) {//similar to Big-n-Ugly switch
                    //  discussed above
      case EV_X:
        //some code
        return null;//means 'STATE DID NOT CHANGE'
      case EV_Y:
        //some_code
```

---

135   And ever-changing requirements is one of the very few things we can rely on.

```
        return new StateB(some_params);
      //...
    }
  }
}
// other State* classes go here
class Reactor {
  constructor() {
    currentState = new someState();//one of State* objects
  }
  function react(ev) {
    newState =
            currentState.react(ev);
    if(newState) {
      currentState.exitState();
      currentState = newState;
      currentState.enterState();
    }
  }
}
```

Note that while we were using react() (and not OnMsg*()) in the example above, OnMsg*()-style handlers can be used with State pattern too. One way to implement it – is to have our IDL compiler generate the switch-calling-OnMsg*() handlers for each specific State* class.

The main point of the State pattern is to have our States completely separated, so the data members and code belonging to different States doesn't become tightly coupled without reason.

Common Data Members

Having handling of our states separated according to State pattern is all fine and dandy, but (as everything else in this world) it comes at a price. The first problem with State pattern is that it implicitly relies on the states being completely independent and not sharing anything(!). And as soon as our states DO share something (which is very common BTW), we're facing two rather bad choices:

Having handling of our states separated according to State pattern is all fine and dandy, but (as everything else in this world) it comes at a price.

♦ **Option 1.** We MAY store those data-members-which-need-to-be-shared-between-State-objects in (Re)Actor (and provide a pointer from each of the State objects back to the (Re)Actor, so that they can manipulate these shared members).

- ▪ This option will work, but the more such shared-members you have, the more encapsulation you will give away, and the more your code will become entangled, effectively defeating our original reason to separate states <sad-face />.

- ♦ **Option 2.** We MAY keep our States independent, with all the information that needs to be exchanged between them passed via parameters of those *new StateXX()* constructors.

  - ▪ This option will also work and in a sense is significantly cleaner than Option 1 above (and, more importantly, it will provide better encapsulation and separation of concerns). However, it will come at the price of the call to the constructor becoming *really* ugly and unreadable as more and more information needs to be passed.

- ♦ Of course, hybrid approaches are also possible. One such policy is to keep the stuff-that-is-common-to-*all*-the-States in the (Re)Actor and modify it via a pointer, and to keep everything-else as private members of State objects.

While each of these approaches is workable, they're different in their pros and cons, and unfortunately there is no "silver bullet" solution here. In other words, if you're going to use State pattern - you DO need to think about how you're going to handle common data members for your specific (Re)Actor.

Potentially Expensive Allocations

Another potential issue that we're introducing with State pattern, is extra allocations; as we'll see in Vol. V's chapter on C++, extra allocations tend to hurt performance significantly. On the other hand, unless we're talking about *ChildReactors*, the chances of visibly hurting performance by allocating State objects are usually pretty slim (this is because each event tends to have quite a bit of associated processing anyway, so the cost of allocation is negligible compared to the other stuff we're doing).

In any case, at least in C++, there exists a way to fight these extra allocations; see Appendix 5.A for more details. In addition, using (Re) Actor-specific non-contentious local allocators (as discussed in Vol. V's chapter on C++) tends to reduce allocation costs significantly too.

Hierarchical States

After we've discussed both (Re)Actor-within-(Re)Actor and classical State pattern, we can go a bit further and discuss Hierarchical States (in the UML world, they're known as "Hierarchically Nested States"; see, for example, [Wikipedia, UML State Machine]).

The idea goes as follows: some of the States can have their own sub-states. Then, if we're currently in a sub-state, a sub-state gets the incoming event first. However, if the sub-state doesn't handle the event, it is forwarded to the base State for processing. In [Nystrom, State Pattern], an example of PC's *DuckingState* being a subclass of an *OnGroundState* is used; I can only add that the situations when such hierarchies arise are not restricted to PCs or Characters.

As [Nystrom, State Pattern] notes, Hierarchical States fit very nicely into class hierarchies. Extending our own example above, Hierarchical States may look along the following lines:

```
//Listing 5.HierarchicalState
//PSEUDO-CODE
class StateA {
  function react(ev) {
    switch( ev.type ) {
      //...
    }
  }
}
class StateAA {
  function react(ev) {
    switch( ev.type ) {
      case EV_X:
        //some code
        return null;
      case EV_Y:
        //some_code
        return new StateB(some_params);
      //...
      default:
        return Parent.react(ev);
          //forwarding ev to base class
          // for processing
    }
  }
}
```

To avoid confusion, it should be noted that Hierarchical States are very different from the (Re)Actor-within-(Re)Actor pattern discussed above. (Re)Actor-within-(Re)Actor is about separating (Re)Actors; in contrast, Hierarchical States are dealing with separating States *within the same (Re)Actor*. In fact, there can be a (Re)Actor-within-(Re)Actor with both *ParentReactor* and *ChildReactor* using their own (and independent) Hierarchical States.

Stack-of-States

As described in [Boer] and [Nystrom, State Pattern], it is a rather common occurrence to have a "history of states." In other words, you want to enter a certain State, but when leaving that new State, you want to return not to a *predefined state,* but rather to a *previous state*.

In this case, you basically need to implement a stack of your states within your (Re)Actor, and allow your *react()* function to return a special marker meaning "return to previous State" instead of *new State*. It is not rocket science (and, unlike [Nystrom, State Pattern], I am stopping short of naming this construct a "Pushdown Automata"), but it can easily come in handy if the logic of your (Re)Actor needs such functionality.

VALIDATE-CALCULATE-MODIFY-SIMULATE Pattern

One very important practical pattern for (Re)Actors is VALIDATE-CALCU-LATE-MODIFY-SIMU-LATE.

One very important practical pattern for (Re)Actors is VALI-DATE-CALCULATE-MODIFY-SIMULATE. The idea behind this pattern is that often, when processing incoming the event/message within our (Re)Actor, we need to go through the following four stages:

♦ **VALIDATE.** Check that the incoming event/message is valid. State of the (Re)Actor is not changed (yet).

♦ **CALCULATE.** Calculate changes that need to be made to the state of our (Re)Actor. State of the (Re)Actor is still unchanged.

♦ **MODIFY.** Apply those calculated changes.

♦ **SIMULATE.** Simulate changes within our Game World. SIM-ULATE stage (unlike all the previous stages) normally does *not* depend on the nature of the incoming message/event.

When talking about VALIDATE-CALCULATE-MODIFY-SIM-ULATE, first we need to note that for *most* messages/events, certain stages of the processing can be omitted. For example, for "network tick" events in a traditional Game Loop-based simulation, there is nothing but SIMULATE (though in some cases, "network ticks" MAY include all the input packets received during the previous tick, and then we'll usually get VALIDATE-SIMULATE, with inputs taken into account within SIMULATE). On the other hand, for a Cashier (Re)Actor processing, usually there is only VALIDATE-CALCULATE-MODIFY (and no SIMULATE).

However (and probably counterintuitively), for quite a few games, all four stages may be necessary to process some of the input events. In such systems, handling of all the logic on a per-message basis turns out to be too cumbersome, so VALIDATE-CALCULATE-MODIFY stages are allowed to leave the (Re)Actor in a some kind of intermediate (though somehow consistent) state — and then the SIMULATE stage (while acting pretty much as a simulator or real-time control system) will bring it to the final state. Processing in such as SIMU-LATE-stage-coming-after-VALIDATE-CALCULATE-MODIFY can be pretty much everything: from "if there is a bullet with coordinates (X,Y,Z) and velocity (Vx,Vy,Vz), it will continue moving along the parabolic trajectory" to timeout handling. What is important, however, is that the SIMULATE stage should have nothing to do with the event that we've just processed; all the processing within the SIMULATE stage should be of the form "if we're in this state, we need to do this and that" (not referring to the reasons *why* we got into this state).

For quite a few games, all four stages may be necessary to process some of the input events.

Overall, the VALIDATE-CALCULATE-MODIFY-SIMULATE pattern is *so* generic that it covers a *vast majority* of all the processing in all the (Re)Actors; in fact, I don't remember seeing an app-level event that doesn't fit into this pattern, *ever*. As a result of this (and also because the pattern allows you to structure your code, and structuring is a good thing much more often than not), I *strongly* advocate that you use this pattern for pretty much all of your (Re)Actor processing (skipping unused stages as necessary).

VALIDATE-CALCULATE-MODIFY-SIMULATE and Exceptions

VALIDATE and CALCULATE stages

The VALIDATE-CALCULATE-MODIFY-SIMULATE pattern has quite a few useful properties; one of them is closely related to exceptions. As long as we (as advertised above) don't modify the state of our (Re)Actor within the VALIDATE and CALCULATE stages, the effects of any exception happening before the MODIFY stage are trivial: as we didn't modify anything, any exception will lead merely to ignoring the incoming message, and without any need to roll back any changes, as there were none; as for on-stack allocations, they need to be handled via traditional-and-rather-straightforward RAII (or equivalent; see also below) regardless of VALIDATE-CALCULATE-MODIFY-SIMULATE.

Exception Safety

Exception safety guarantees... are a set of contractual guidelines that class library implementers and clients can use when reasoning about exception handling safety

—Wikipedia

This effectively means that it is rather easy to ensure exception safety for VALIDATE and CALCULATE stages. Formally, for these stages we can easily provide *strong* exception safety guarantees, a.k.a. "commit-or-rollback" or "all-or-nothing". From a practical point of view, any offending incoming packet/message/event that throws an exception during the VALIDATE or CALCULATE stages can be simply thrown away *without any side effects(!)*. It means that after such an offending event, your (Re)Actor is still in a valid state, ready to process the next incoming message "as if" the offending event has never occurred. Sure, in extreme cases of a really-necessary message causing an exception, it may still lead to certain parts of your system hanging, but in practice most of the time the impact of such an exception is very limited (usually, it is *much* better to have one-Client-that-went-crazy to hang, than your whole Server to hang, to terminate, or to end up in an inconsistent state).

BTW, our exception safety guarantees for VALIDATE and CALCULATE stages cover not only our own exceptions, but also CPU-level exceptions (with dereferencing NULL pointer/*nullptr* and division-by-zero being all-time favorites). Of course, such exceptions *should not* happen – but in the real-world, just as with any other bug, they *can* happen (especially as we're dealing with the validation of completely-unknown and potentially-malicious inputs). In such a case, dropping an incoming event "as if it never happened" and continuing to work, is usually *much* preferred to killing the whole (Re)Actor; and our exception safety discussed above, provides exactly this.[136] Of course, it is certainly *not* a silver bullet (and we have to be sure to log all such occurrences and treat them as blocking bugs) – but it did save my bacon quite a few times.

To make sure that we *are* exception-safe within the VALIDATE and CALCULATE stages (and more generally – that we do NOT modify the state within these stages), we have to answer the question of "how we can *enforce* that there are no state changes before the MODIFY stage?" The answer to this question is largely programming-language-dependent (and unfortunately, most languages lack the necessary tools to enforce it or even to hint at violations), but a kinda-enforcement (assuming that there are no *deliberate* attempts to bypass it) is certainly possible at least in C++; more on it in Appendix 5.A.

dropping an incoming event "as if it never happened" and continuing to work, is usually much preferred to killing the whole (Re)Actor

MODIFY and SIMULATE stages

Up to now, we discussed exception safety only for the VALIDATE and CALCULATE stages. It still leaves us with the MODIFY and SIMULATE stages to deal with; however, the MODIFY stage is usually simple enough so the vast majority of exceptions won't happen there.

To make your MODIFY stage strongly exception-safe, you will still need to either make your modifications part of RAII, or resort to stuff such as ScopeGuard (see [Alexandrescu and Marginean, Generic: Change the Way You Write Exception-Safe Code — Forever] and [Alexandrescu, Declarative Control Flow]); fortunately, you need to do it only for your MODIFY stage <phew />.

As for the SIMULATE stage, normally there should be no legitimate exceptions within it — none whatsoever. As noted above, a problem within the SIMULATE stage would mean that the (Re)Actor has already been inconsistent before the SIMULATE stage has started, which shouldn't be possible (save for bugs, of course). From the point of view of Exception Safety, we can say that we expect the SIMULATE stage to provide the so-called "no-throw guarantee".

As for the SIMULATE stage, normally there should be no legitimate exceptions within the SIMULATE stage — none whatsoever.

---

136   With regard to CPU exceptions, exception safety stands only if you can convert CPU exception into your-language-exception; see Vol. V for details on such conversion for C++.

On the other hand, SIMULATE stage can easily be complicated enough to cause unexpected exceptions; however, as SIMULATE doesn't depend on the incoming event/message, an exception effectively means that we failed to sanitize the state before reaching SIMULATE (i.e., that we already got a bug earlier). In turn, it implies that recovery from such an exception (that is, beyond scrapping the whole offending (Re)Actor and re-creating it from scratch) will most likely be impossible, at least in a generic manner. And however cynical it may sound, IMO it is a Good Thing™ too, as we won't try to recover from inherently irrecoverable scenarios, instead concentrating on preventing them from happening in the first place. Also, let's keep in mind that separating the input validation from simulation does help the SIMULATE stage too: while at the SIMULATE stage we do need to handle all the different potential values of the current state, at least we don't need to deal with all the different input events, which tends to simplify things at least a little bit.

RAII Equivalents in Different Programming Languages

As noted above, RAII (="Resource Allocation Is Initialization") is necessary to guarantee exception safety in case of exception during the VALIDATE or CALCULATE stages (and is a Good Thing™ regardless of the VALIDATE-CALCULATE-MODIFY-SIMULATE pattern). In C++, RAII has been known for a long while (at least since the 1980s). Now, let's take a look at other programming languages.

First, let's make it very clear:

> *DON'T use finalizers (and kinda-destructors, which are called by GC when it feels like it)!*

This includes at least Java *finalize()*, C# destructor, and Python's *__del__* (also known as "destructor" in Python); however, synchronous C++ destructors are perfectly fine.

I won't discuss the problems with finalizers (including those finalizers posing as destructors) in detail here; it is already common knowledge that finalizers are evil, with the most evil thing about them being *the lack of determinism*. The finalizer is called whenever-the-garbage-collector decides to call it, which can happen "right away" for your development box, and "in the next century" for the production. And, as we've discussed above, such non-determinism means that finalizers are inherently untestable <ouch! />. There are very few things out there that are more annoying than a production crash which happened because once in a month GC decided to refrain from calling a finalizer (where you put some *file.close()*) long enough so that the next request to open the same file runs into problems.

Fortunately, garbage-collected programming languages have started to add support for RAII-like resource handling too. In particular, Java's *try-with-resources*, C#'s *using* statement, and Python's *with* statement are essentially providing RAII-like functionality (with *AutoCloseable. close()*, *IDisposable.dispose()*, or *__exit__()* called in lieu of C++ destructor).

In JavaScript, there seems to be no explicit support for RAII-like behavior, but (like pretty much everything else in JS) it can be imitated using lambdas/closures (see [Lauliac] for details).

Fortunately, garbage-collected programming languages have started to add support for RAII-like resource handling too.

Posting Messages (calling RPCs, etc.) Within VALIDATE/ CALCULATE

In your (Re)Actors, you will often need to post messages (call RPCs, etc., etc.). One of the questions that arises in this regard is whether such calls are allowed in VALIDATE/CALCULATE stages.

The answer to this question goes as follows: your first (and most obvious) option is to prohibit such calls within your VALIDATE / CALCULATE stages (and BTW this goes nicely with the logic which usually corresponds to VALIDATE and CALCULATE).

On the other hand, it *is* possible to allow such requests (as well as 'read' requests to DB/storage/etc.) to be performed in the VALIDATE/ CALCULATE stages without violating the principle of "VALIDATE/ CALCULATE stages are guaranteed to be strongly exception-safe." To achieve this guarantee, your Infrastructure Code will need to buffer all the outgoing messages that were posted from within *react()* (without actually sending them out), and to send them out only after the *react()* successfully returns (silently dropping these buffered outgoing messages in case of exception).

Divide et Impera Summary

To summarize our main observations on "how to tackle the complexity of (Re)Actors":

♦ (Re)Actor-within-(Re)Actor is an extremely powerful mechanism to control the complexity of (Re)Actors.

- Both *ParentReactor* and *ChildReactor* can use *all* the other complexity-control techniques (including further splitting).
- Separation SHOULD be done along the lines of the already-existing-entities within (Re)Actors.

♦ State Pattern is often a Good Thing™, as it allows us to reduce code spaghetti, and allows for further refinements, including such things as:

- Hierarchical States
- Stack-of-States

♦ OTOH, State Pattern has its own drawbacks (so it is not a silver bullet). Whether State pattern is worth using or not – depends a lot on many factors (including whether-your-team-likes-or-hates-it).

- In any case, it SHOULD NOT be seen as a replacement for (Re)Actor-within-(Re)Actor (instead, these patterns complement each other).

♦ VALIDATE-CALCULATE-MODIFY-SIMULATE is a pattern that covers pretty much all the (Re)Actors (at least those encountered in games).

- While not all the stages are *always* necessary, there are processing scenarios where all four stages are used.
- From what I've seen, this pattern simplifies reasoning about the code significantly.
- It simplifies life on the Server-Side after deployment too (while it is not a MUST-have, it is a very-nice-to-have).
- If you're following a VALIDATE-CALCULATE-MODIFY-SIMULATE pattern (which you SHOULD), enforcing it (for example, via *this* being *const* — as described in Appendix A for C++) is a Good Thing™.
- Following the VALIDATE-CALCULATE-MODIFY-SIMULATE pattern will allow you to safely ignore quite a few things-you-forgot-about without crashing (don't over-rely on it, though; it is not a silver bullet).

- In particular, it provides formal exception safety guarantees for the VALIDATE and CALCULATE stages.
- To achieve the Holy Grail of your whole *react()* being exception-safe, you will still need to use other techniques. However, practicality of being exception-safe beyond VALIDATE-CALCULATE is often not that obvious.

(KINDA-)SCALING INDIVIDUAL (RE)ACTORS

Our (Re)Actors are wonderful from *lots* of different perspectives, including performance (there are few thread context switches, and spatial locality tends to be very good). However, as for anything else in this

Sure, at 3GHz modern CPU can do quite a damn lot, but what if we need more than that?

world, all those goodies come at a price. For (Re)Actors, the price is that while the (Re)Actor works perfectly as long as it can be processed by one single CPU core, splitting it over several CPU cores can be quite a challenge. Sure, at 3GHz one modern CPU core can do quite a damn lot, but what if we need more than that?

We've already discussed the question of "how to split one huge Game World into independent parts" in Vol. I's chapter on Communications — and, if you're running an MMOG with all your players in one Game World, this is an exercise that you will most likely need to do on the Server-Side regardless of using (Re)Actors or not. On the Client-Side, there are also quite a few (Re)Actors that can be separated (and therefore can run in different threads/on different CPU cores); we'll discuss them in Chapter 6.

However, there are still situations (especially on the Client-Side) when one of the (Re)Actors[137] gets overwhelmed. In this section, we'll discuss how this problem of "how to scale one single (Re)Actor to several CPU cores" can be mitigated.

Keep in mind that with the techniques discussed in this section, we won't be achieving *real* scaling (as in "ability to scale our (Re)Actor into as-many-cores-as-we-want"); to get *real* scalability, you still need to split your (Re)Actors at application level (for example, along the lines of the split discussed in Vol. I's chapter on Communications). Instead, in this section we'll be talking about *(kinda-)* scaling (as in "ability to scale (Re)Actor to a just a few cores"). Still, in some scenarios (especially Client-Side ones), it may be just the ticket.

Splitting and Offloading

To really scale our (Re)Actor, the best option is to try to split it into N functionally separate Shared-Nothing (Re)Actors, which can be run in N separate threads (in fact, this model is sometimes referred to as "System-on-a-Thread"). If it is feasible, that's the best way of scaling (Re)Actors. However, quite often such splitting is not that easy, in particular because of the Shared-Nothing requirement.

---

137   Usually an Animation&Rendering one; see Chapter 6 for details.

The second common approach to (Re)Actor scaling is to try off-loading some of the calculations to another (Re)Actor (see, for example, the *Offloading* section above). Note that with Offloading, we don't really have a state for the receiving (Re)Actor, but rather transfer all the necessary data into it as an input message (and then it can do all the number crunching).

Offloading tends to work pretty well, but *only* as long as the amount of data transferred back and forth is not overly large. This effectively prevents us from using Offloading for scaling in quite a few scenarios, where one single-big-state needs to be processed by several (Re)Actors; and, unfortunately, such scenarios are quite common for game Clients.

Offloading tends to work pretty well, but only as long as the amount of data transferred back and forth is not overly large

(Re)Actor-with-Mirrored-State — Limited Relief

When the state of our (Re)Actor is really large (think "all the visible Game World State to be rendered"), we MAY start having scalability issues, and can run into a situation where splitting Game Worlds is very difficult; moreover, often Offloading doesn't help either.

In a gamedev world, one of the known ways to deal with this problem is the one when at certain points (such as "the end of each tick") our Infrastructure Code makes a copy ("mirror") of the whole Game World, so that while one (Re)Actor running on one thread/core is working on rendering, another (Re)Actor running on another thread/core can work on preparing the state of the Game World for the next tick. Such a model was, in particular, used in Halo engine, as discussed in [Chen, Silvennoinen and Tatarchuk] and [Tatarchuk].

This technique tends to work reasonably well; however, it has an obvious drawback: as there are only two threads involved, we won't be able to utilize more than two CPU cores. And if we try to make more than one copy/mirror to work on it, we'll quickly run into another problem: if our state is large enough, we may end up spending too much time just copying the data we need.[138] All of this leads us to the observation that

> *While mirroring MAY allow for up to*
> *2x improvement, using mirror to scale further*
> *is usually very difficult.*

(Re)Actor-with-Extractors

To deal with scaling issues for (Re)Actors-having-a-really-large-state further, another modification to the classical (Re)Actor can be used (as far as I know, it was first described in [Tatarchuk] with regards to Destiny engine, albeit without fancy naming). For the purpose of this book, we will name this approach "(Re)Actor-with-Extractors."

The idea of (Re)Actor-with-Extractor goes almost along the same lines as traditional (Re)Actor, with just one twist:

> *There is a special "extracting" stage within*
> *(Re)Actor processing that allows several threads/cores*
> *to "extract" (read) the data from the (Re)Actor's*
> *state, while the (Re)Actor itself is guaranteed*
> *not to modify the state.*

During this "extracting" stage, the (Re)Actor's state is guaranteed to be constant, so there is no need to synchronize access of the readers (which means that there are no locks/forced thread context switches).

During this "extracting" stage, the (Re)Actor's state is guaranteed to be constant, so there is no need to synchronize access of the readers (which means that there are no locks/forced thread context switches). This allows us to extract information very quickly, while keeping the (Re)Actor as the very same familiar-and-simple no-thread-sync game-loop-like code we've discussed above.

An example of processing flow for (Re)Actor-with-Extractors is shown in Fig 5.2:

---

138   Side consideration to be kept in mind in this regard: speed of copying is closely related to the question of "how flat is our data"; see the discussion on data locality in Vol. V's chapter on C++. In other words, the flatter our data, the faster the copying will be.

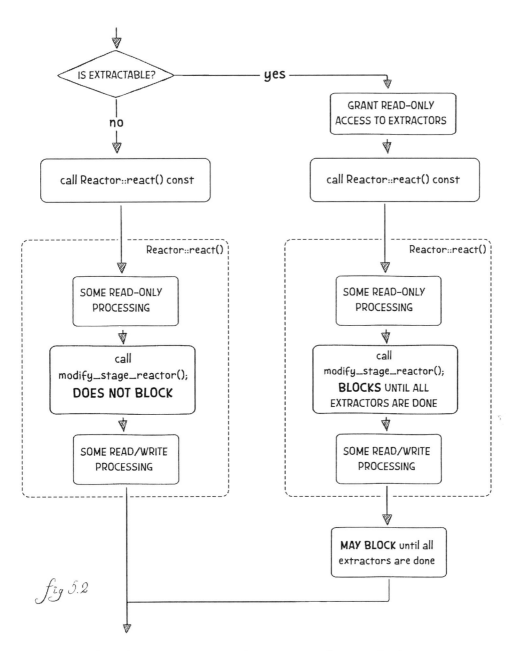

fig 5.2

NB: in the flow shown in Fig 5.2, we're assuming that our (Re)Actor is following the VALIDATE-CALCULATE-MODIFY-SIMULATE model, and calls modify_stage_reactor() to denote that it is switching from read-only processing into read-write processing.[139]

---

139 Note that while *modify_stage_reactor()* MAY be used to enforce const-ness (see the discussion in the *C++: Enforcing const-ness for VALIDATE and CALCULATE stages in VALIDATE-CALCULATE-MODIFY-SIMULATE pattern* section), it is not a requirement for (Re)Actor-with-Extractors.

As shown in Fig. 5.2, when an incoming event comes in, Infrastructure Code checks whether an incoming event[140] is "extractable"; if not, the processing goes along the usual event-processing lines outlined above.

If, however, the incoming event *is* "extractable" (i.e., it does imply that extractors need to be launched), the processing is modified. First, infrastructure code grants (read-only) access to "extractors." Then, it still may call *react()* (read-only processing is still possible while "extractors" are working). If *react()* calls *modify_stage_reactor()* (to obtain writable access to the (Re)Actor state), then in the case of an "extractable" event, Infrastructure Code should block *react()*[141] until all the extractors are done.[142] After all extractors are done, *modify_stage_reactor()* may proceed. After going out of *react()*, infrastructure code should make another check to make sure that all the extractors are done (in case if *react()* didn't call *modify_stage_reactor()*), and then the processing of the "extractable" event is over.

We were able to make our (Re)Actor app-level code *completely unaware* of the extraction (handling all the sync on the infrastructure level).

As we can see, we were able to make our (Re)Actor app-level code *completely unaware* of the extraction (handling all the sync on the infrastructure level). Among other things, it means that we still keep *most* of the (Re)Actor goodies. Of course, (Re)Actor blocking for extractors to finish their job *does* mean having a thread context switch at that point, but as long as our extraction stages are relatively rare (like "60 times per second"), costs of these very-rare-by-CPU-standards context switches won't be too noticeable.[143]

---

140   As mentioned above, pretty much anything can serve as an event trigger, including "timer event" and an event such as "we've just finished rendering of the previous frame."

141   Note that it should be *real* blocking, with a thread context switch; all the non-blocking trickery we've discussed in Take 1-Take 8 won't fly here, as there are other threads involved.

142   BTW, as extractors are read-only and do *not* use mutexes within the Reactor, it is technically possible to terminate them forcibly without affecting the Reactor; I hope that you won't need this option, but it does exist.

143   Even if the cost of the context switch is at closer-to-maximum 1M CPU cycles, and we're doing it 60 times per second, for modern 3GHz CPUs we're talking about 2% of the penalty to our single critical core, and it is not going to kill our performance. On the other hand, this calculation shows the dangers of having too many thread context switches — having as little as 50–500 context switches per frame can easily be devastating.

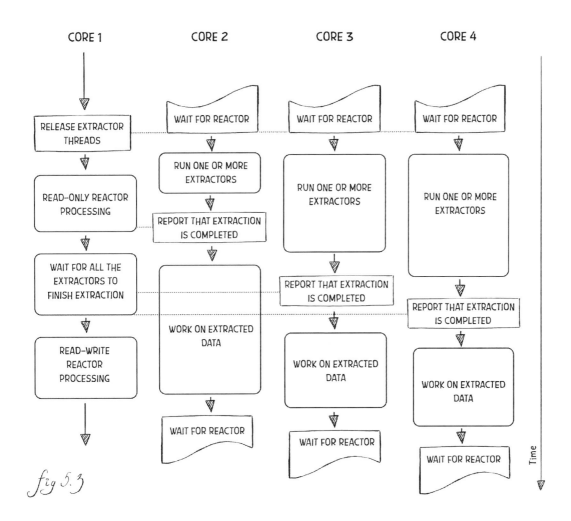

fig 5.3

Fig 5.3 demonstrates how the load is separated between different threads/ cores in the (Re)Actor-with-Extractors model. Here, Core 1 is running our main (Re)Actor itself, and other cores are running extractors and performing some additional work on the extracted data.

As noted above, one example of such a (Re)Actor-with-Extractors architecture (save for our fancy name) is currently used in Destiny engine by Bungie (see [Tatarchuk]). Very briefly: in Destiny engine, they're running their Game World in a classical game loop, and once per tick they're stopping it, running a bunch of "extractors" to get the data-necessary-for-rendering. After the "extracting" stage, they run rendering threads on the extracted data and the game loop can proceed

Memory Barrier

A memory barrier, also known as a membar, memory fence or fence instruction, is a type of barrier instruction that causes a central processing unit (CPU) or compiler to enforce an ordering constraint on memory operations issued before and after the barrier instruction.

—Wikipedia

with calculating and modifying the state of the Game World for the next tick. ~~Bingo!~~ Bungie! They have single-threaded game-level code and are using multiple cores too.

One thing to remember when implementing this model is that while the number of logical extractors (and target-(Re)Actors-they're-extracting-to) can be arbitrarily large, it is important to keep the number of threads running these extractors comparable to the number of cores on the machine your program is running on. Running hundreds of threads extracting on a 10-core box will usually cause too many unnecessary context switches and/or cache trashing.

Another potential (and very nasty one, if it hits) issue when implementing (Re)Actor-with-Extractors is related to so-called memory barriers, a.k.a. memory fences. The thing here is that, strictly speaking, we are *not* guaranteed that representations of the same portion of memory are the same for different CPU cores.[144] This MAY cause rarely occurring errors, which are extremely difficult to track. I don't want to get into a lengthy discussion of memory barriers here (if you're interested in this complicated subject, you may refer to the very practical, though maybe a bit over-generic-for-those-writing-only-for-x86/x64 [Howells, et al.]). In our case, we may say that we need the thread that runs our (Re)Actor to issue a memory fence with *release* semantics (such as *std::atomic_thread_fence(std::memory_order_release)*) *after* finishing all the modifications to the (Re)Actor state (i.e., *after* react() returns) but *before* starting to inform "extractors" that they're allowed to run; on the other hand, each of the threads running "extractors" needs to issue a memory fence with *acquire* semantics (such as *std::atomic_thread_fence(std::memory_order_acquire)*) *after* they've gotten notification that they may run but *before* starting to read the (Re)Actor's state. In most cases (especially when x86/x64 is concerned), these *memory fences* will be implicitly invoked as side effects of the synchronization calls, but to be on the safer side (and unless we're willing to *prove* that fences are called by mechanisms-used-to-allow-extractors-to-run), I would suggest having them explicit.[145]

---

144   For mutex-protected memory, memory barriers are usually called within mutex acquire/release, but as we're not using mutexes, it becomes our responsibility to deal with them.

145   And as they're going to be called only once per core per frame, the performance hit will be negligible.

Oh, and last but not least, while Bungie (as described in [Tatarchuk]) seems to use such a (Re)Actor-with-Extractor only for the Client-Side, it can have perfectly legitimate uses on the Server-Side too (in particular, to solve the same problem of extracting the data from the large state of the Server-Side Game World to send it to the Clients).

(RE)ACTOR-FEST ARCHITECTURE: PUTTING IT ALL TOGETHER

Philosophy of (Re)Actor-fest

By this point, we've discussed a lot of the details of individual (Re)Actors. Now we can proceed to the next step: discussing how to design an architecture that is not only built on top of (Re)Actors, but also *has nothing but (Re)Actors*. To reiterate:

> *In (Re)Actor-fest Architecture, all the app-level code is contained within (Re)Actors.*

While it may sound crazy, I've seen systems-with-all-the-app-level-code[146]-residing-within-(Re)Actors working in the real-world, and working really well. In particular, such systems were observed as being *much* more reliable than the competition; while it is always tempting to attribute these effects to developers being much better than the competition (especially if you were a part of the team <wink />), I am positive that using (Re)Actor-fest architecture was instrumental in this regard.

Let's also note that the bold statement above applies *only* to app-level code, and that the Infrastructure Code is exempt from the requirement to be (Re)Actor-based. While we'll discuss "full-scale" (Re)Actor-fest architectures that use nothing-but-(Re)Actors even for Infrastructure Code (in particular, in Vol. III's chapter on Server-Side Architectures), and while I personally prefer such architectures too, I have to admit

(Re)Actor-with-Extractor can have perfectly legitimate uses on the Server-Side too.

While it may sound crazy, I've seen systems-with-all-the-app-level-code-residing-within-(Re)Actors working in the real-world, and working really well

---

146 Except for database reporting.

that implementing your Infrastructure Code as (Re)Actors qualifies only as "nice-to-have"; on the other hand, *implementing your app-level code as (Re)Actors* usually qualifies as an "architecture that will give you a Big Advantage™ in the long run."

(Re)Actor-fest and Conway's Law

Back in 1967, Melvin Conway observed that

> *"Organizations which design systems (in the broad sense used here) are constrained to produce designs which are copies of the communication structures of these organizations"*[147]

which became known as "Conway's Law."

From the perspective of Conway's Law, our (Re)Actor-fest architecture tends to work very well. As we'll see in Chapter 6, on the Client-Side we'll be talking about Game Logic (Re)Actors, Animation&Rendering (Re)Actors, and various Communication (Re)Actors — and these happen to be naturally mapped into Game Logic Team, 3D Team, and Network Team. On the Server-Side, mapping between teams and (Re)Actors is also very straightforward: we'll probably have Game World (Re)Actor written by Game World Team, Database (Re)Actor (with all the SQL stuff) maintained by dedicated Database Team, very separate Cashier (Re)Actor written by Payments Team, and dealing with nothing but money and payments, Matchmaking (Re)Actor (which can easily get its own team), Facebook Gateway (Re)Actor with its own mini-team, and so on.

This, in turn, means that all the interactions between different teams will go over very-well-defined message exchanges between (Re)Actors; in other words, while we're defining inter-team interactions, we're leaving each of the teams more or less free with their implementation choices, which is a Good Thing™.

---

147 Later, Conway's Law was corroborated by several empirical studies (see [Wikipedia, Conway's Law] for a list), and, even more importantly — by my personal observations <wink />.

From a bit of a different perspective, we can say that each (Re)Actor (*if* used along the lines outlined above[148]) is highly cohesive[149] but at the same time is loosely coupled to other (Re)Actors—and this is known to be a Good Thing™.

Implementing (Re)Actor-fest

With all the preliminary work we've already done discussing individual (Re)Actors, we don't have to add much to allow for architectures that consist of (Re)Actors and nothing but (Re)Actors. In fact, I can think of the only thing missing so far: a way to create new (Re)Actors; this leads us to the discussion of (Re)Actor Factories.

(Re)Actor Factories

While quite a few of our (Re)Actors can be pre-created, very often there is the need to create instances of our (Re)Actors on demand—especially on the Server-Side. For example, if your Matchmaking (Re)Actor decides to create a Game World so that a competitive match between the teams can be played, then within our (Re)Actor-fest Architecture we'll need a way to create that Game World (Re)Actor that will handle the game.

Very often, there is the need to create instances of our (Re)Actors on demand—especially on the Server-Side.

Personally, I strongly prefer to do it via—no surprise here— (Re)Actors. Let's say that we have a special (Re)Actor, named (Re)Actor Factory, and that we always run an instance of (Re)Actor Factory on each of our physical Server boxes. Then, all our matchmaking (Re)Actor needs to do to create a new Game World on Server Box X is to issue a non-blocking RPC call *CreateGameWorld()* to the (Re)Actor Factory residing on that Server Box X, passing all the necessary info about the player IDs, game parameters, etc. as parameters of that RPC call.

On receiving the RPC call, the (Re)Actor Factory will create another instance of the Game World (Re)Actor, will probably assign some port numbers (or other kind of IDs) to this created Game World (Re)Actor,

---

148   Of course, any architecture can be abused, and (Re)Actor-fest is no exception; however, (Re)Actors *can* be used properly (and, from my experience, are pretty difficult to abuse compared to alternatives).

149   (Re)Actor-based cohesion (provided that (Re)Actors are reasonable and *not* abused) qualifies as "Communicational Cohesion" as defined in [Yourdon and Constantine], and "Communicational Cohesion" is pretty high on the list of possible reasons to create the association.

and will pass this information back to the matchmaking (Re)Actor as a reply to the RPC call. Bingo! We've just created a new instance of one of our (Re)Actors on demand.

This (Re)Actor Factory model works very well pretty much regardless of what underlying technology you're using. For example, for C++-based (Re)Actors, we can easily have the (Re)Actor Factory launch a new thread/process to run our new (Re)Actor, and in *Node.js* world, it is perfectly possible to have a Node that does nothing but wait for incoming requests, and spawn an appropriate *child_process* when such a request comes in. Also, regardless of the specific platform (but provided that your (Re)Actors are 100% blocking-free) – it might be possible to create (Re)Actors within the existing threads/processes too.

That's Pretty Much It

With individual (Re)Actors, plus (Re)Actor Factories, we can build a complete distributed system of arbitrary size, with such a system consisting of nothing but (Re)Actors. Nothing more is necessary, we're done, and that's pretty much it.

On the Client-Side, often all the (Re)Actors are pre-created (and so there is no need for (Re)Actor Factories), though I've seen a Client that did have a (Re)Actor Factory too.

On the Server-Side, the situation tends to be more complicated. Usually, on the Server-Side, the (Re)Actor-fest system starts with some pre-created (Re)Actors; at the very least, it should consist of one app-level (Re)Actor such as Matchmaking, plus (Re)Actor Factories on each of the Servers.

As Clients come in to the Matchmaking (Re)Actor, it decides to run a game, and decides which Server Box will run the game; then the Matchmaking (Re)Actor requests an appropriate (Re)Actor Factory to create a Game World (Re)Actor. After being created, the Game World (Re)Actor lives its own life according to its own logic — and terminates itself when the game is over (i.e., normally there is no need to terminate (Re)Actors forcefully).

Of course, there will be quite a bit of additional work along the way. Still, 99.9% of it will be doable without departing from the (Re)Actor-fest.

With individual (Re)Actors, plus (Re)Actor Factories, we can build a complete distributed system of arbitrary size, with such a system consisting of nothing but (Re)Actors.

For example, some addition will be necessary to balance Game Worlds. On the other hand, this is perfectly doable by staying within (Re)Actors. The simplest balancing is just to keep track of the number of Game Worlds running on each Server; the more complicated one is to measure actual load. However, whatever method you prefer, both of these things can be easily done by the same (Re)Actor Factory (Re)Actor (or a separate per-Server Load Balancing (Re)Actor).

(Re)Actor-fest and Programming Languages

Last, but not least: within our (Re)Actor-fest Architecture, nothing forces us to have all the (Re)Actors within our system written in the same programming language. In fact, as soon as we fix the protocol between our (Re)Actors (for example, using IDL), we can easily have different (Re)Actors run in different programming languages.

It does come in handy in practice, too. For example, quite often it makes sense to write your Game World (Re)Actor in C++, but your payment (Re)Actor in Java/Node.js/Python. I've seen such a multi-language (Re)Actor-fest system in a quite a large project (using a combination of C++/Java/C#) — and it worked like a charm.

Relation of (Re)Actor-Fest to Other Systems

As noted in the *Other Event-Driven Systems: GUI, Erlang, Node.js, and Java Reactor* section above, our (Re)Actors have quite a few similarities with other event-processing systems; they also have quite a bit of resemblance to the Actor Concurrency model coming from computer science. Let's take a close look at the similarities and differences of (Re)Actor-fest to these approaches.

> NB: Unless you're versed in one of the event-processing approaches, feel free to skip this section; however, if you are, it might be quite useful to see how our (Re)Actor-fest relates to familiar technologies (and even more importantly, to familiar concepts). Overall, (Re)Actors are nothing really new — it is just undeservingly-forgotten event-driven programming with a few modern tricks added, so putting (Re)Actors into context is both possible and potentially useful.

Within our (Re)Actor-fest Architecture, nothing forces us to have all the (Re)Actors within our system written in the same programming language.

Actor Concurrency Model

The actor model in computer science is a mathematical model of concurrent computation that treats 'actors' as the universal primitives of concurrent computation: in response to a message that it receives, an actor can make local decisions, create more actors, send more messages, and determine how to respond to the next message received.

—**Wikipedia**

Relation to Actor Concurrency

From a theoretical point of view, our (Re)Actor-fest architecture can be seen as a system that is pretty close to the so-called "Actor Concurrency Model," with (Re)Actor-fest's deterministic (Re)Actors being Actor Concurrency's "Actors." However, there is a significant difference between the two, at least perception-wise. Traditionally, Actor concurrency is considered a way to ensure concurrent *calculations*; that is, the thing we're usually trying to consider within Actor concurrency is usually a "pure" calculation, with all the inputs of the calculation known in advance.

With games (and interactive systems in general), the situation is very different because we don't know everything in advance (by definition); in other words, while a usual view of Actor concurrency is *calculation*-oriented, with our (Re)Actor-fest (and games in general), we're *interaction*-oriented.

Overall, it means that while the (Re)Actor is indeed a close cousin of Actor concurrency, quite a bit of the analysis made for Actor-concurrency for HPC-type tasks is not exactly applicable to inherently time-dependent systems such as games, so make sure to take it with a good pinch of salt.

Relation to Erlang Concurrency, Akka Actors, and Node.js

Akka

is… simplifying the construction of concurrent and distributed applications on the JVM. Akka… emphasizes actor-based concurrency, with inspiration drawn from Erlang.

—Wikipedia

If looking at Erlang concurrency (more specifically, at *!* and *receive* operators), at Akka's Actors, *Node.js*, or at Microsoft *Fabric Actors*, we will see that our (Re)Actors implement pretty much the same *concept* as these technologies.[150] There are no shared states, everything goes via message passing, et cetera, et cetera, et cetera.

The only significant difference concept-wise is that for (Re)Actor-fest I am arguing for determinism. In general, determinism is not guaranteed in Erlang/Akka/Node.js/etc. (at least not without DIY Call Wrapping); on the other hand, you can write deterministic actors using

---

150   While Erlang, Akka, and Microsoft zealots will argue ad infinitum that their favorite technology is much better than anything else in existence, from our perspective the differences are pretty much negligible.

these technologies the same way as in the (Re)Actor-fest. After all, determinism is just an additional restriction you need to keep in mind and enforce. Other than that, and some of those practical goodies in (Re)Actor-fest (such as recording/replay with all the associated benefits), (Re)Actor-fest looks very close to Erlang's /Akka's/Node.js/etc. concurrency from the developer's point of view.

Which can be roughly translated into the following observation:

> *To have a good concurrency model, it is not strictly necessary to program in Erlang or to use Akka or Node.js*

That being said, while the *concept* is about the same, implementations are quite different (and can cause quite a bit of trouble).

In this respect, I want to mention Erlang's "selective receive." I know that I will certainly be pummeled by Erlang fans, but I have to confess that I don't really like "selective receive" (and especially an associated "save queue"). Sure, "selective receive" *can* be used to write exactly the same things that we were discussing throughout this chapter (and it is not difficult to write a C++/Java/… library that would provide *selective receive* functionality too), but I still prefer other means to express (Re)Actors.

My main argument against using "selective receive" at the app-level of game-like processing, goes along the following lines: with "selective receive", way too much effort (and way too many discussions around recommended techniques) revolves around *NOT* processing the incoming message; in particular, if there is no match for the message, the message just sits in the queue (for our purposes, we can leave out the rather weird processing rules of the *save queue*). Moreover, as [Trottier-Hebert] puts it, "Ignoring some messages to handle them later in the manner described above is the essence of selective receives."

However, when talking about *inherently interactive* (Re)Actors such as Game Worlds, Cashiers, etc., 99% of the time we DO want to process incoming messages *right away*. There are several reasons for such processing-unless-proven-impossible paradigm: (a) very often, doing nothing while performing message processing effectively blocks the other side of communication, and blocking is bad for both performance

When talking about *inherently interactive* (Re)Actors, 99% of the time we DO want to process incoming messages *right away*.

and scalability; (b) having blocking in multi-(Re)Actor scenarios creates risks for inter-(Re)Actor deadlocks <ouch! />; (c) while scenarios when we have to delay event/message processing, DO exist — off the top of my head, I can remember only two such cases (and it was <0.1% of all the message processing cases I have seen for sure). As noted above, this doesn't mean that you *cannot* write robust non-blocking distributed programs based on "selective receive" (after all, it *is* possible to specify a catch-all pattern for "selective receive") — just that there are more convenient ways to do it (and with less risk of running into problems too).

(Re)Actors and Microservices as Close Cousins

These days, everybody and their dog talks about microservices. Well, whatever dogs can do, hare can do better <wink />, so let's say something about microservices.

The general idea of microservices as defined in [Fowler and Lewis, Microservices. a definition of this new architectural term] is all about decoupling certain parts of monolithic code, and separating them into different parts, which enables quite a few benefits, including (but not limited to) smaller, and therefore more manageable, chunks of tightly-coupled code, smaller per-service upgrades, and the ability to do per-service scaling.

Beyond this rather vague definition, the term "microservices" is not very well-defined, but of the existing interpretations, I certainly prefer the one discussed in [Bonér] (BTW, if dealing with microservices, make sure to read this freely available book — it is, IMO, by far the best discussion on microservices out there).

[Bonér] goes a bit further than [Fowler and Lewis, Microservices. a definition of this new architectural term] and discusses ways of implementing microservices; and as we've read about these ways, we're realizing that microservices and (Re)Actors are pretty much the same thing. Autonomous operation? Decoupling with the only way to interact being via published APIs? Exclusive ownership of the state? Asynchronous non-blocking message passing? Publish-subscribe mechanisms? These are the topics discussed in [Bonér], and are exactly the same as discussed in the course of this chapter.

Oh, and BTW: if talking about Event Sourcing (as discussed in [Fowler, Event Sourcing] and [Richardson]), we notice that Event Sourcing is essentially relying on the behavior of the microservice being deterministic and having a log of all input events; as such, it is a very close cousin of our recording-and-replay determinism-based techniques we've discussed above.

Event Sourcing is a very close cousin of the recording-and-replay determinism-based techniques we've discussed above.

At this point, I can see only two significant differences between microservices-as-discussed-in-[Bonér] and our (Re)Actors:

♦ First, microservices usually have some database behind; on the other hand, (Re)Actors can have either in-memory state — or a persistent one (for example, a database-based state); while we didn't discuss the latter yet, they will be discussed in Vol. III's chapter on Server-Side Architecture and Vol. VI's chapter on Databases.

  ▪ While stateful microservices (those with an in-memory state rather than DB-based state) are not unknown, they're generally frowned upon in the enterprise-app development world (where the whole microservices thing originated). This is usually done in the name of apparent scalability of stateless microservices. However, as we'll discuss in more detail in Vol. III's chapter on Scalability 101, I contend that making microservices stateless merely pushes the scalability problem to the database, and that real-world databases (in spite of what your DB sales person will tell you) do *not* scale in a linear manner unless aided by application level. To make things worse, all-stateless-microservices tend to throw too much data updates at the DB, increasing the DB load — the one that doesn't really scale well — many-fold (I've seen 30x, but if you try to make a stateless simulation game, it can get as high as 1000x). While this is clearly a Good Thing™ for DBMS vendors who can charge an arm and a leg for "enterprise" versions of their DBs, it is not necessarily so for app-devs and gamedevs. As a result, I have to insist on using *stateful* microservices/(Re)Actors at the very least as our Game Worlds; for details, see the discussion in Vol. III's chapter on Scalability. As for ways to scale the DB, this is apparently doable with (Re)Actor-style programming too; see Vol. VI's chapter on Databases for details.

♦ Second, [Bonér] doesn't specify threading models for the microservices, while our (Re)Actors are inherently single-threaded. BTW, let's note that while the very notion of a single-threaded-DB-access is almost-guaranteed to cause an enormously-angry-outburst from any enterprise-level architect (with "are you freaking crazy?" being the most polite words you'll likely hear from him), such single-writing-DB-connection architectures were observed to work very well (and *scale* very well) in the real world; these architectures and the way to scale them (proven on a real-world system processing 10+ billion real-world-transactions/year and making its owners several hundreds of millions/year as a side effect <wink />) will be discussed in detail in Vol. VI's chapter on Databases.

Physical Server — VM Docker — (Re)Actor as a Spectrum of Tradeoffs Between Isolation and Flexibility

When talking about microservices, it is common to mention application containers such as Docker. And while Docker guys do not like when Docker containers are named "lightweight VMs" (see [Coleman]), from a 50,000-foot view they, even if not exactly the same thing, are indistinguishably close.

From my perspective, the whole thing looks as follows. Originally, there were physical servers and just physical servers. Then VMs appeared, gaining in deployment-time flexibility over physical servers while giving up some isolation between different boxes (at the very minimum, VMs on the same physical box DO compete for resources). Then there was Docker (more generally – app containers), gaining more flexibility while giving up more isolation. And the last (to date) stage in improving deployment-time flexibility even further at the cost of giving up even more isolation is our (Re)Actors: after all, deployment-wise, (Re)Actors are *even more flexible than app containers* (while obviously less isolated). In other words, IMNSHO we're talking about the whole spectrum of Physical Servers — VMs — Docker Containers — (Re)Actors, with deployment-time flexibility increasing (and isolation decreasing) as we go from left to right along this spectrum.

SUMMARY OF CHAPTER 5

To summarize the main points from Chapter 5:

- ◆ (Re)Actors, Actors, event-driven programs, and ad-hoc finite state machines are pretty much the same thing under different names.

- ◆ (Re)Actors tend to provide a very good separation (with very clean interfaces) between different pieces of logic, and a very good separation between platform-independent logic and platform-specific infrastructure.

- ◆ (Re)Actors do NOT require thinking about thread sync while thinking about the logic. IMO this alone is sufficient to justify (Re)Actors.[151]

- ◆ I am arguing for mostly-non-blocking deterministic (Re)Actors, which provide numerous benefits:
    - ▪ High performance (if you do things right)
    - ▪ Replay-based regression testing
    - ▪ Production post-factum analysis (including visual post-factum analysis of the Client-Side when the player complains about lagging or something)
    - ▪ Potential for Server-Side features such as low-latency fault-tolerance, (Re)Actor migration, and almost-zero-downtime upgrades
    - ▪ Better quality of testing and better quality of code
    - ▪ And quite a few other things

- ◆ Non-blocking handling is admittedly a headache, but can be implemented in several different ways.
    - ▪ We don't really need non-blocking processing for *everything;* instead, we need to have non-blocking processing for those-potentially-long outstanding requests where we want to process intervening requests coming while we're waiting for the reply. Hence, the concept of *mostly*-non-blocking programming.

---

151   I've spent enough time working with thread sync to understand that the best way to guarantee that multi-threaded code works is to make it single-threaded.

- All the Takes discussed in this chapter with regards to handling non-blocking returns, are equivalent (in particular, none requires thread sync), but they still differ in syntax, in "how straightforward the code is compared to the original intention," and in the amount of boilerplate code.

- Personally, I prefer Take 3 (that is, if you don't have access to C++11), Take 5 (futures-based), or Take 8 (*await*, though it is limited to only a few programming languages now).

♦ Determinism in (Re)Actors can be achieved by relatively simple means, as described above.

- However, optimal methods of achieving determinism vary for different non-deterministic system calls; see the *Dealing with System Calls: Which System Functions Are We Talking About and What Do We Do About Them?* section above.

Other precautions are also necessary, though most of the time they're aligned with other existing "best practices" (see the *Implementing Deterministic Logic: Other Sources of Non-Determinism* section above).

- Achieving *cross-platform* determinism is *much* more difficult (in particular, because of the floating point issues), but is rarely necessary (that is, unless you want to rely on Deterministic Lockstep or implement User Replay).

♦ Normally the (Re)Actor doesn't scale beyond one single core. However:

- It is usually possible to split (Re)Actors, providing real scalability.

  - Moreover, this kind of scalability is Shared-Nothing Scalability, and Shared-Nothing is the only thing which *really* scales.

- In some cases, Offloading can provide real scalability too.

- If real scalability is not possible, a few (kinda-)scalability tricks can still help:

  - (Re)Actor-with-Mirrored-State (Halo-style)
  - (Re)Actor-with-Extractors (Destiny-style)

◆ When implementing (Re)Actors, there are certain common patterns to keep complexity under control:

  ▪ App-level (Re)Actors are usually NOT table-driven (due to "state explosion" problems).

  ▪ (Re)Actors-within-(Re)Actors is a Good Thing™ wherever applicable.

  ▪ State pattern MAY help to tackle complexity, but has certain drawbacks (such as shared states).

    • State pattern simplifies implementing Hierarchical States and Stacks-of-States.

  ▪ The VALIDATE-CALCULATE-MODIFY-SIMULATE pattern is generally a Good Thing™ too.

◆ (Re)Actor-fest Architecture is The Way to Go™.

  ▪ More precisely – I *strongly* advocate for using *only* (Re)Actors at app-level; as for Infrastructure Code – I still tend to prefer (Re)Actors, but have to acknowledge that they're only one of the possible ways to implement Infrastructure.

  ▪ To build (Re)Actor-fest system from individual (Re)Actors, we need to add only (Re)Actor Factory, and that's pretty much it.

Bibliography

Aldridge, David. 2011. "*I Shot You First: Networking the Gameplay of HALO: REACH.*" http://www.gdcvault.com/play/1014345/ I-Shot-You-First-Networking.

Alexandrescu, Andrei. 2015. "*Declarative Control Flow.*" CppCon. https://www.youtube.com/watch?v=WjTrfoiB0MQ.

Alexandrescu, Andrei, and Petru Marginean. 2000. "*Generic: Change the Way You Write Exception-Safe Code — Forever.*" CUJ. http://www.drdobbs.com/cpp/generic-change-the-way-you-write-excepti/184403758.

ARM. 2010-2011. "*C library functions that are not thread-safe.*" http://infocenter.arm.com/help/index.jsp?topic=/com.arm. doc.dui0492c/Chddjdaj.html.

Böck, Hanno. 2015. "*How Heartbleed could've been found.*" https://blog.hboeck.de/archives/868-How-Heartbleed-couldve-been-found.html.

Boer, James. 2005. "1.8 Large-Scale Stack-Based State Machines." In *Game Programming Gems 5.*

Bonér, Jonas. 2016. "*Reactive Microservices Architecture.*" http://downloads.lightbend.com/website/reactive-microservices-architecture/Reactive_Microservices_Architecture.pdf.

Bonér, Jonas, Dave Farley, Roland Kuhn, and Martin Thompson. 2013. "*The Reactive Manifesto.*" http://www.reactivemanifesto.org/.

Butcher, Chris. 2015. "*Learning from the Core Engine Architecture of Destiny.*" GDC. http://www.gdcvault.com/play/1022106/Lessons-from-the-Core-Engine.

Calderone, Jean-Paul. 2013. "*What is a State Machine?*" https://clusterhq.com/2013/12/05/what-is-a-state-machine/.

Chen, Hao, Ari Silvennoinen, and Natalya Tatarchuk. 2011. "*Making Games from Polygon Soup.*" https://mediatech.aalto.fi/~ari/Publications/Making_Game_Worlds_from_Polygon_Soup.pptx.

Coleman, Mike. 2016. "*Containers Are Not VMs.*" https://blog.docker.com/2016/03/containers-are-not-vms/.

Cox, Russ. 2014. "*Libtask: a Coroutine Library for C and Unix.*" https://swtch.com/libtask/.

Dawson, Bruce. 2013. "*Floating-Point Determinism.*" https://randomascii.wordpress.com/2013/07/16/floating-point-determinism/.

Dickinson, Patrick. 2001. "*Instant Replay: Building a Game Engine with Reproducible Behavior.*" http://www.gamasutra.com/view/feature/131466/instant_replay_building_a_game_.php.

Dunkels, Adam. "*Protothreads.*" http://dunkels.com/adam/pt/index.html.

Dmitry Vyukov, "*Faster Fibers/Coroutines.*" http://www.1024cores.net/home/lock-free-algorithms/tricks/fibers.

Fiedler, Glenn. 2014. "*Deterministic Lockstep.*" http://gafferongames. com/networked-physics/deterministic-lockstep/.

— . 2006. "*Fix Your Timestep!*" http://gafferongames.com/game-physics/fix-your-timestep/.

— . 2010. "*Floating Point Determinism.*" http://gafferongames. com/networking-for-game-programmers/floating-point-determinism/.

Fowler, Martin. 2011. "*Eradicating Non-Determinism in Tests.*" http://martinfowler.com/articles/nonDeterminism.html.

— . 2005. "*Event Sourcing.*" http://martinfowler.com/eaaDev/ EventSourcing.html.

Fowler, Martin, and James Lewis. 2014. "*Microservices. a definition of this new architectural term.*" http://martinfowler.com/articles/ microservices.html.

Fugal, Hans. 2015. "*Futures for C++11 at Facebook.*" https://code.facebook.com/posts/1661982097368498/futures-for-c-11-at-facebook/.

Geels, Dennis, Gautam Altekar, Scott Shenker, and Ion Stoica. 2006. "*Replay Debugging for Distributed Applications.*" *USENIX* 2006. http://www.cs.berkeley.edu/~istoica/papers/2006/liblog.pdf.

Hare, 'No Bugs'. 2016. "*Determinism: Requirements vs Features.*" *Overload* (135).

— . 2016. "*Deterministic Components for Distributed Systems.*" *Overload* (#133). http://accu.org/index.php/journals/2251.

— . 2015. "*Multi-threading at Business-logic Level is Considered Harmful.*" *Overload* (#128). https://accu.org/index.php/ journals/2134

— . 2017. " *Allocator for (Re)Actors. Part III – "Speedy Gonzales" Serializing (Re)Actors via Allocators* " *Overload* (#140).

Harrington, Dom. 2017. "*Using async/await in Node.js 7.6.0.*" https://blog.readme.io/using-async-await-in-node-js-7-6-0/

Hauser, John. "*Berkeley SoftFloat.*" http://www.jhauser.us/arithmetic/ SoftFloat.html.

— . 2016. *Private communications with.*

Henney, Kevlin. 2017. *"Thinking Outside the Synchronisation Quadrant."* ACCU 2017.

Hoskinson, Rick. 2017. *"DETERMINISM IN LEAGUE OF LEGENDS: IMPLEMENTATION."* https://engineering. riotgames.com/news/determinism-league-legends-implementation.

Howells, David, Paul E. McKenney, Will Deacon, and Peter Zijlstra. *"LINUX KERNEL MEMORY BARRIERS."* https://www.kernel. org/doc/Documentation/memory-barriers.txt.

Ignatchenko, Sergey. 1998. *"STL Implementations and Thread Safety."* C++ Report, Vol. 10, Number 7.

— . 2017. *"Deterministic Components for Interactive Distributed Systems: Benefits and Implementation."* ACCU 2017. http://ithare.com/deterministic-components-for-interactive-distributed-systems-with-transcript/

— . 2017. *"Eight Ways to Handle Non-blocking Returns in Message-passing Programs: from C++98 via C++11 to C++20"* CPPCON2017.

Ignatchenko, Sergey, and Dmytro Ivanchykhin. 2016. *"Ultra-fast Serialization of C++ Objects."* Overload (#136). http://accu.org/ index.php/journals/2317

Kaiser, Hartmut. 2017. *"The Asynchronous C++ Parallel Programming Model"*. CPPCON2017

Karjalainen, Antti. 2014. *"How we discovered Heartbleed?"* https://www.youtube.com/watch?v=ezjRv_7iZZM.

Knuth, Donald E. 1969. *"The Art of Computer Programming. Vol. 2 Seminumerical Algorithms."*

Kowalke, Oliver. 2014. *"Boost.Context Architectures."* http://www.boost.org/doc/libs/1_60_0/libs/context/doc/html/ context/architectures.html.

Lauliac, Jean. 2015. *"Looking for RAII in Javascript."* http://jeanlauliac.com/raii-in-javascript/.

Li, Chuanpeng, Chen Ding, and Kai Shen. 2007. *"Quantifying The Cost of Context Switch."* http://www.cs.rochester.edu/u/cli/research/switch.pdf.

Ligoum, Dmitri, and Sergey Ignatchenko. 2016. https://github.com/O-Log-N/Autom.cpp.

McFarlane, John. 2017. *"Composition of Arithmetic Types"*, P0554R0 http://www.open-std.org/jtc1/sc22/wg21/docs/papers/2017/p0554r0.html

— . *"CNL: A Compositional Numeric Library for C++."* https://github.com/johnmcfarlane/cnl

McShaffry, Mike, and David "Rez" Graham. 2012. *"Game Coding Complete 4th Edition."*

Nelson, Randal C. *"Finite Automata."* https://www.cs.rochester.edu/u/nelson/courses/csc_173/fa/fa.html.

Nishanov, Gor. 2017. *"Naked coroutines live (with networking)"*. CPPCON2017

Nystrom, Robert. 2014. *"Game Loop."* http://gameprogrammingpatterns.com/game-loop.html.

— . 2014. *"Game Programming Patterns."* http://gameprogrammingpatterns.com/.

— . 2014. *"State Pattern."* http://gameprogrammingpatterns.com/state.html.

Trottier-Hebert, Frederic. *"More On Multiprocessing"* http://learnyousomeerlang.com/more-on-multiprocessing

Richardson, Chris. 2016. *"Pattern: Event sourcing."* http://microservices.io/patterns/data/event-sourcing.html.

Serebryany, Kostya, and Alexander Potapenko. *"Address Sanitizer."* https://github.com/google/sanitizers/wiki/AddressSanitizer.

Jim Springfield. *"Using C++ Resumable Functions with Libuv"*. https://blogs.msdn.microsoft.com/vcblog/2017/02/02/using-ibuv-with-c-resumable-functions/

Spruiell, Mark. 2016. "*Avoiding Server-Side Garbage*." https://doc.zeroc.com/display/Ice36/Avoiding+Server-Side+Garbage.

Standard C++ Foundation. "*How do I select the best serialization technique?*" https://isocpp.org/wiki/faq/serialization#serialize-selection.

STEIIAR-GROUP. "*hpx*". https://github.com/STEllAR-GROUP/hpx

Tatarchuk, Natalya. 2015. "*Destiny's Multithreaded Rendering Architecture*." GDC. http://www.gdcvault.com/play/1021926/Destiny-s-Multithreaded-Rendering.

Walfridsson, Krister. 2017. "*Why undefined behavior may call a never-called function*." https://kristerw.blogspot.com/2017/09/why-undefined-behavior-may-call-never.html

Wikipedia. 2017. "*State Transition Table*." https://en.wikipedia.org/wiki/State_transition_table.

—. 2017. "*Associative property*."

  https://en.wikipedia.org/wiki/Associative_property.

—. 2017. "*Conway's Law*." https://en.wikipedia.org/wiki/Conway%27s_law.

—. 2017. "*Deterministic Finite Automaton*." https://en.wikipedia.org/wiki/Deterministic_finite_automaton.

—. 2017. "*UML State Machine*." https://en.wikipedia.org/wiki/UML_state_machine.

Yourdon, Edward, and Larry L. Constantine. 1978. "*STRUCTURED DESIGN. Fundamentals of a Discipline of Computer Program and Systems Design*." http://chiclassiccomp.org/docs/content/books/StructuredDesign_EdwardYourdonLarryConstantine.pdf.

Zalewski, Michal. "*afl-fuzz*." http://lcamtuf.coredump.cx/afl/.

APPENDIX 5.A. C++-SPECIFIC EXAMPLES AND COMMENTS FOR CHAPTER 5

```cpp
//Listing 5.A.Reactor
class GenericReactor {
  virtual void react(const Event& ev) = 0;
};
class Infrastructure {
  std::unique_ptr<GenericReactor> r;
  public:
  Infrastructure(std::unique_ptr<GenericReactor>& r_)
  : r(std::move(r_)) {
  }
  void run_loop() {
    while(true) {
      Event ev = wait_for_event();
      ev.inputs = read_inputs();
      r->react(ev);
    }
  }
};
class ConcreteReactor : public GenericReactor {
  public:
  void react(const Event& ev) override {
    assert(ev.type == TIMER_EVENT);
      //in real-world, most of assert()'s SHOULD be replaced
      //  with throwing-exception MYASSERT() macros, see
      //  Vol. V's chapter on C++
    process_inputs(ev.inputs);
    update();
    post_updates_to_clients();
    post_timer_event(time_left_until_end_of_network_tick);
  }
};

//Listing 5.A.Blocking.noexcept
bool CashierReactor::purchaseItem(
            int item_id, int connection_id) {
  int user_id = get_user_id(connection_id);
  //blocking RPC call to DB (Re)Actor:
  bool db_ok = dbPurchaseItem(db_reactor_id,
                              user_id, item_id);
```

```
  if(!db_ok)
    return false;
  //blocking RPC call to Game World (Re)Actor:
  gameworld_reactor_id = find_gameworld_for_user(user_id);
  bool gameworld_ok = gameworldAddItem(
                        gameworld_reactor_id,
                        user_id, item_id);

  return gameworld_ok;
}

//Listing 5.A.Take1.IDLGen
//GENERATED FROM IDL, DO NOT MODIFY!
#define CASHIER_PURCHASEITEM_REQUEST 123
#define CASHIER_PURCHASEITEM_RESPONSE 124
#define DB_PURCHASEITEM_REQUEST 125
#define DB_PURCHASEITEM_RESPONSE 126
#define GAMEWORLD_ADDITEM_REQUEST 127
#define GAMEWORLD_ADDITEM_RESPONSE 128
Msg cashierPurchaseItem_request_compose(
                        int request_id, int item_id);
//returns (request_id, item_id)
tuple<int,int> cashierPurchaseItem_request_parse(
                const Msg& msg);
Msg cashierPurchaseItem_response_compose(
                        int request_id, bool ret);
//returns (request_id,returned_value)
tuple<int,bool> cashierPurchaseItem_response_parse(
                const Msg& msg);

Msg dbPurchaseItem_request_compose(
                        int request_id,
                        int user_id, int item_id);
//returns (request_id, int user_id, int item_id)
tuple<int,int,int> dbPurchaseItem_request_parse(
                        const Msg& msg);
Msg dbPurchaseItem_response_compose(
                        int request_id, bool ret);
//returns (request_id,returned_value)
tuple<int,bool> dbPurchaseItem_response_parse(
                const Msg& msg);
Msg gameworldAddItem_request_compose(
                        int request_id,
                        int user_id, int item_id);
//returns (request_id, user_id, item_id)
tuple<int,int,int> gameworldAddItem_request_parse(
                        const Msg& msg);
```

```cpp
Msg gameworldAddItem_response_compose(
                    int request_id, bool ret);
//returns (request_id,returned_value)
tuple<int,bool> gameworldAddItem_response_parse(
                const Msg& msg);


//Listing 5.A.Take1.noexcept
//CAUTION: SEVERELY UGLY CODE AHEAD!!
struct PurchaseRqData {
  enum class Status { DBRequested, GameWorldRequested };
  Status status;
  int user_request_id;
  int user_id;
  int item_id;
  PurchaseRqData(int user_request_id_,
                int user_id_, int item_id)
 : user_request_id(user_request_id_),
   user_id(user_id_), item_id(item_id_) {
     status = Status::DBRequested;
  }
};
class CashierReactor {
  map<int,PurchaseRqData> purchase_item_requests;
  public:
  void react(const Event& ev);
};
void CashierReactor::react(const Event& ev) {
  switch( ev.type ) {
    case CASHIER_PURCHASEITEM_REQUEST:
    {
      const Msg& msg = ev.msg;
      int user_request_id, item_id;
      tie(user_request_id, item_id) =
          cashierPurchaseItem_request_parse(msg);
      int user_id = get_user_id(ev);
      int request_id = new_request_id();
      Msg msg2 =
          dbPurchaseItem_request_compose(
          request_id, user_id, item_id);
      send_msg_to(db_reactor_id, msg2);
      purchase_item_requests.insert(
          pair<int, PurchaseRqData>(request_id,
            PurchaseRqData(user_request_id,
            user_id, item_id)));
      break;
    }
```

```
case DB_PURCHASEITEM_RESPONSE:
{
  const Msg& msg = ev.msg;
  int request_id;
  bool db_ok;
  tie(request_id, db_ok) = dbPurchaseItem_parse(msg);
  auto found =
        purchase_item_requests.find(request_id);
  assert(found != purchase_item_requests.end());
  assert(found->status ==
        PurchaseRqData::Status::DBRequested);
  if(!db_ok) {
    Msg msg3 =
      cashierPurchaseItem_response_compose(
      found->second.user_request_id, false);
    send_msg_back_to(user_id, msg3);
    purchase_item_requests.erase(found);
    break;
    }

  REACTORID gameworld_reactor_id =
      find_gameworld_for_user(
      found->second.user_id);
  Msg msg4 =
      gameworldAddItem_request_compose(
      request_id,
      found->second.user_id,
      found->second.item_id);
  send_msg_to(gameworld_reactor_id, msg4);
  found->status =
      PurchaseRqData::Status::GameWorldRequested;
  break;
}
case GAMEWORLD_ADDITEM_RESPONSE:
{
  const Msg& msg = ev.msg;
  int request_id;
  bool gw_ok;
  tie(request_id, gw_ok) =
            gameworldAddItem_response_parse(msg);
  auto found = purchase_item_requests.find(
            request_id);
  assert(found != purchase_item_requests.end());
  assert(found->status ==
      PurchaseRqData::Status::GameWorldRequested);
```

```
    Msg msg2 =
           cashierPurchaseItem_response_compose(
           found->second.user_request_id, gw_ok);
    send_msg_back_to(user_id, msg2);
    purchase_item_requests.erase(found);
    break;
  }
 }
}
```

```
//Listing 5.A.Take2.IDL
//Client-to-Cashier:
void cashierPurchaseItemRequest(int request_id,
                                   int item_id);
void cashierPurchaseItemResponse(int request_id,
                                    bool ret);
//CASHIER-to-DB:
void dbPurchaseItemRequest(int request_id,
                          int user_id, int item_id);
void dbPurchaseItemResponse(int request_id, bool ret);
//CASHIER-to-GameWorld
void gameworldAddItemRequest(int request_id,
                              int user_id, int item_id);
void gameworldAddItemResponse(int request_id, bool ret);
```

```
//Listing 5.A.Take2.IDLGen
//GENERATED FROM IDL, DO NOT MODIFY!
void CashierReactor::cashierPurchaseItemRequest(
   REACTORID peer_reactor, int request_id,
   int item_id);
   //for Cashier, this is an RPC function
   // to be implemented
void CashierReactor::cashierPurchaseItemResponse(
   REACTORID peer_reactor, int request_id,
   bool ret);
   //for Cashier, this is an RPC stub
   // to be called
void CashierReactor::dbPurchaseItemRequest(
   REACTORID peer_reactor, int request_id,
   int user_id, int item_id);
   //for Cashier, this is an RPC stub
   // to be called
void CashierReactor::dbPurchaseItemResponse(
   REACTORID peer_reactor, int request_id,
   bool ret);
   //for Cashier, this is an RPC function
```

```cpp
        // to be implemented
void CashierReactor::gameworldAddItemRequest(
  REACTORID peer_reactor, int request_id,
  int user_id, int item_id);
  //for Cashier, this is an RPC stub
  // to be called
void CashierReactor::gameworldAddItemResponse(
  REACTORID peer_reactor, int request_id,
  bool ret);
  //for Cashier, this is an RPC function
  // to be implemented

//Listing 5.A.Take2.noexcept
//CAUTION: RATHER UGLY CODE AHEAD!!
struct PurchaseRqData { // same as for Take 1
  enum class Status { DBRequested, GameWorldRequested };
  Status status;
  int user_request_id;
  int user_id;
  int item_id;
  PurchaseRqData(int user_request_id_,
                 int user_id_, int item_id)
  : user_request_id(user_request_id_),
    user_id(user_id_), item_id(item_id_) {
    status = Status::DBRequested;
  }
};
class CashierReactor {
  map<int,PurchaseRqData> purchase_item_requests;
  public:
  void cashierPurchaseItemRequest(REACTORID peer_reactor,
       int request_id, int item_id );
  //...
};
void CashierReactor::cashierPurchaseItemRequest(
     REACTORID peer_reactor, int request_id,
     int item_id ) {
  int user_id = get_user_id(peer_reactor);
  int request_id = new_request_id();
  dbPurchaseItemRequest(db_reactor_id,
            request_id,
            user_id, item_id);
  purchase_item_requests.insert(
    pair<int, PurchaseRqData>(request_id,
        PurchaseRqData(user_request_id,
          user_id, item_id));
```

```cpp
}
void CashierReactor::dbPurchaseItemResponse(
     REACTORID peer_reactor, int request_id,
     bool db_ok) {
  auto found = purchase_item_requests.find(request_id);
  assert(found != purchase_item_requests.end());
  assert(found->status ==
          PurchaseRqData::Status::DBRequested);
  if(!db_ok) {
    REACTORID user_reactor =
        find_user_reactor_id(found->second.user_id);
    cashierPurchaseItemResponse(user_reactor,
             found->second.user_request_id, false);
    purchase_item_requests.erase(found);
    return;
  }

  REACTORID gameworld_reactor_id =
        find_gameworld_for_user(found->second.user_id);
  gameworldAddItemRequest(gameworld_reactor_id, request_id,
        found->second.user_id, found->second.item_id);
  found->status =
        PurchaseRqData::Status::GameWorldRequested;
}
void CashierReactor::gameworldAddItemResponse(
     REACTORID peer_reactor, int request_id,
     bool gw_ok) {
  auto found = purchase_item_requests.find(request_id);
  assert(found != purchase_item_requests.end());
  assert(found->status ==
          PurchaseRqData::Status::GameWorldRequested);
  REACTORID user_reactor =
          find_user_reactor_id(found->second.user_id);
  cashierPurchaseItemResponse(user_reactor,
               found->second.user_request_id, gw_ok);
  purchase_item_requests.erase(found);
}

//Listing 5.A.Take3.IDL, same as 5.Take1.IDL
bool cashierPurchaseItem(int item_id);
//CASHIER-to-DB:
bool dbPurchaseItem(int user_id, int item_id);
//CASHIER-to-GameWorld
bool gameworldAddItem(int user_id, int item_id);
```

```cpp
//Listing 5.A.Take3.IDLGen
//GENERATED FROM IDL, DO NOT MODIFY!
class CashierPurchaseItemReplyHandle {
  public:
  void reply(bool ret);
};
void CashierReactor::cashierPurchaseItem(
  shared_ptr<CashierPurchaseItemReply> reply_handle,
    //reply_handle MAY be copied (as shared_ptr<>),
    // if it is necessary to postpone replying
    // until later
  int item_id);
  //for Cashier, this is an RPC function
  // to be implemented
class DbPurchaseItemCallback {
  public:
  DbPurchaseItemCallback(Reactor* r);
  Reactor* get_reactor();
  void react(bool ret) = 0;
};
void CashierReactor::dbPurchaseItem(
  /* new */ DbPurchaseItemCallback* cb,
    //NOT using unique_ptr<>
    // to save on verbosity for caller
  REACTORID reactor_to,
  int user_id, int item_id);
  //sends a message, calls cb->react() when done
  //for Cashier, this is an RPC stub
  // to be called
class GameworldAddItemCallback {
  public:
  GameworldAddItemCallback(Reactor* r);
  Reactor* get_reactor();
  void react(bool ret) = 0;
};
void CashierReactor::gameworldAddItem(
  /* new */ GameworldAddItemCallback* cb,
  REACTORID reactor_to,
  int user_id, int item_id);
  //for Cashier, this is an RPC stub
  // to be called

//Listing 5.A.Take3.noexcept
//CAUTION: VERBOSE CODE AHEAD!
//TAKE 3 IS LESS ERROR-PRONE THAN TAKES 1-2,
// BUT STILL HAS LOTS OF BOILERPLATE CODE
```

```cpp
class DbPurchaseItemCallbackA
: public DbPurchaseItemCallback {
  shared_ptr<CashierPurchaseItemReply> reply_handle;
  int user_id;
  int item_id;

  public:
  DbPurchaseItemCallbackA(Reactor* r,
      shared_ptr<CashierPurchaseItemReply>& reply_handle_,
      int user_id_, int item_id_)
  : DbPurchaseItemCallback(r), reply_handle(reply_handle_),
    user_id(user_id_), item_id(item_id_) {
  }
  void react(bool db_ok) override;
};
class GameworldAddItemCallbackA
  : public GameworldAddItemCallback {
  shared_ptr<CashierPurchaseItemReply> reply_handle;
  int user_id;
  int item_id;

  public:
  GameworldAddItemCallbackA(Reactor* r,
      shared_ptr<CashierPurchaseItemReply>& reply_handle_,
      int user_id_, int item_id_)
  : GameworldAddItemCallback(r), reply_handle(reply_handle_),
    user_id(user_id_), item_id(item_id_) {
  }
  void react(bool gw_ok) override;
};
void CashierReactor::cashierPurchaseItem(
  shared_ptr<CashierPurchaseItemReply> reply_handle,
  int item_id) {
  int user_id = get_user_id(reply_handle);
  auto cb = new DbPurchaseItemCallbackA(
                this, reply_handle,
                user_id, item_id);
  dbPurchaseItem(cb, db_reactor_id,
                user_id, item_id);
}
void DbPurchaseItemCallbackA::react(bool db_ok) {
  if(!db_ok) {
    reply_handle->reply(false);
    return;
  }
  REACTORID gameworld_reactor_id =
```

```
          get_reactor()->find_gameworld_for_user(user_id);
    auto cb = new GameworldAddItemCallbackA(
                get_reactor(), reply_handle,
                user_id, item_id);
    gameworldAddItem(cb, gameworld_reactor_id,
                  user_id, item_id);
}
void GameworldAddItemCallbackA::react(bool gw_ok) {
  reply_handle->reply(gw_ok);
}

//Listing 5.A.Blocking.except
bool CashierReactor::purchaseItem(int item_id,
                                    int connection_id) {
  try {
    int user_id = get_user_id(connection_id);
    bool db_ok = dbPurchaseItem(db_reactor_id,
                user_id, item_id);
    if(!db_ok)
      return false;
    gameworld_reactor_id = find_gameworld_for_user(user_id);
    bool gameworld_ok = gameworldAddItem(
                        gameworld_reactor_id,
                        user_id, item_id);
    return gameworld_ok;
  }
  catch(const std::exception& x) {
    LogException(x);
    return false;
  }
}

//Listing 5.A.Take3a.except
//NON-BLOCKING VERSION OF LISTING 5.A.Blocking.except
//CAUTION: VERBOSE CODE AHEAD!
class DbPurchaseItemCallbackA
: public DbPurchaseItemCallback {
  shared_ptr<CashierPurchaseItemReply> reply_handle;
  int user_id;
  int item_id;

  public:
  DbPurchaseItemCallbackA(Reactor* r,
      shared_ptr<CashierPurchaseItemReply>& reply_handle_,
      int user_id_, int item_id_)
  : DbPurchaseItemCallback(r), reply_handle(reply_handle_),
```

```
        user_id(user_id_), item_id(item_id_) {
  }
  void react(bool db_ok) override;
  void except(const std::exception& x) override;
};
class GameworldAddItemCallbackA
: public GameworldAddItemCallback {
  shared_ptr<CashierPurchaseItemReply> reply_handle;
  int user_id;
  int item_id;

  public:
  GameworldAddItemCallbackA(Reactor* r,
     shared_ptr<CashierPurchaseItemReply>& reply_handle_,
     int user_id_, int item_id_)
  : GameworldAddItemCallback(r), reply_handle(reply_handle_),
    user_id(user_id_), item_id(item_id_) {
  }
  void react(bool db_ok) override;
  void except(const std::exception& x) override;
};
void CashierReactor::handleCashierPurchaseError(
      shared_ptr<CashierPurchaseItemReply> reply_handle,
      const std::exception& x) {
  LogException(x);
  reply_handle->reply(false);
}
void CashierReactor::cashierPurchaseItem(
      shared_ptr<CashierPurchaseItemReply> reply_handle,
      int item_id) {
  try {
    int user_id = get_user_id(reply_handle);
    auto cb = new DbPurchaseItemCallbackA(
                 this, reply_handle,
                 user_id, item_id);
    dbPurchaseItem(cb, db_reactor_id,
                 user_id, item_id);
  }
  catch(const std::exception& x) {
    handleCashierPurchaseError(reply_handle, x);
  }
}
void DbPurchaseItemCallbackA::react(bool db_ok) {
  try {
    if(!db_ok) {
      reply_handle->reply(false);
```

```
        return;
      }
      REACTORID gameworld_reactor_id =
          get_reactor()->find_gameworld_for_user(user_id);
      auto cb = new GameworldAddItemCallbackA(
                    get_reactor(), reply_handle,
                    user_id, item_id);
      gameworldAddItem(cb, gameworld_reactor_id,
                        user_id, item_id);
    }
    catch(const std::exception& x) {
      handleCashierPurchaseError(reply_handle, x);
    }
}
void DbPurchaseItemCallbackA::except(
      const std::exception& x) {
    handleCashierPurchaseError(reply_handle, x);
}
void GameworldAddItemCallbackA::react(bool gw_ok) {
    reply_handle->reply(gw_ok);
}
void GameworldAddItemCallbackA::except(
      const std::exception& x) {
    handleCashierPurchaseError(reply_handle, x);
}


//Listing 5.A.Take3b.except
//NON-BLOCKING VERSION OF LISTING 5.A.Blocking.except
//CAUTION: VERBOSE CODE AHEAD!
class DbPurchaseItemCallbackA
: public DbPurchaseItemCallback {
    shared_ptr<CashierPurchaseItemReply> reply_handle;
    int user_id;
    int item_id;

    public:
    DbPurchaseItemCallbackA(Reactor* r,
        shared_ptr<CashierPurchaseItemReply>& reply_handle_,
        int user_id_, int item_id_)
    : DbPurchaseItemCallback(r), reply_handle(reply_handle_),
        user_id(user_id_), item_id(item_id_) {
    }
    void react(bool db_ok) override;
    void except(const std::exception& x) override;
};
class GameworldAddItemCallbackA
```

```cpp
: public GameworldAddItemCallback {
  shared_ptr<CashierPurchaseItemReply> reply_handle;
  int user_id;
  int item_id;

  public:
  GameworldAddItemCallbackA(Reactor* r,
      shared_ptr<CashierPurchaseItemReply>& reply_handle_,
      int user_id_, int item_id_)
  : GameworldAddItemCallback(r), reply_handle(reply_handle_),
    user_id(user_id_), item_id(item_id_) {
  }
  void react(bool db_ok) override;
};
void CashierReactor::handleCashierPurchaseError(
      shared_ptr<CashierPurchaseItemReply> reply_handle,
      const std::exception& x) {
  LogException(x);
  reply_handle->reply(false);
}
void CashierReactor::cashierPurchaseItem(
      shared_ptr<CashierPurchaseItemReply> reply_handle,
      int item_id) {
  try {
    int user_id = get_user_id(reply_handle);
    auto cb = new DbPurchaseItemCallbackA(
                 this, reply_handle,
                 user_id, item_id);
    dbPurchaseItem(cb, db_reactor_id,
                 user_id, item_id);
  }
  catch(const std::exception& x) {
    handleCashierPurchaseError(reply_handle, x);
  }
}
void DbPurchaseItemCallbackA::react(bool db_ok) {
  if(!db_ok) {
    reply_handle->reply(false);
    return;
  }
  REACTORID gameworld_reactor_id =
      get_reactor()->find_gameworld_for_user(user_id);
  auto cb = new GameworldAddItemCallbackA(
                 this /*'inherits' exception handler*/,
                 reply_handle,
                 user_id, item_id);
```

```
      gameworldAddItem(cb, gameworld_reactor_id,
                    user_id, item_id);
}
void DbPurchaseItemCallbackA::except(
      const std::exception& x) {
  handleCashierPurchaseError(reply_handle, x);
}
void GameworldAddItemCallbackA::react(bool gw_ok) {
  reply_handle->reply(gw_ok);
}


//Listing 5.A.Take4.IDL, same as 5.Take1.IDL and 5.Take3.IDL
//Client-to-Cashier:
bool cashierPurchaseItem(int item_id);
//CASHIER-to-DB:
bool dbPurchaseItem(int user_id, int item_id);
//CASHIER-to-GameWorld
bool gameworldAddItem(int user_id, int item_id);


//LISTING 5.A.Take4.IDLGen
//GENERATED FROM IDL, DO NOT MODIFY!
void CashierReactor::cashierPurchaseItem(
      shared_ptr<CashierPurchaseItemReply> reply_handle,
      int item_id);
  //for Cashier, this is an RPC function
  // to be implemented
void CashierReactor::dbPurchaseItem(
      REACTORID reactor_peer,
      int user_id, int item_id,
      std::function<void(const std::exception*,bool)> cb);
  //for Cashier, this is a stub
  // to be called
void CashierReactor::gameworldAddItem(
      REACTORID reactor_peer,
      int user_id, int item_id,
      std::function<void(const std::exception*,bool)> cb);
  //for Cashier, this is a stub
  // to be called


//LISTING 5.A.Take4.except
//NON-BLOCKING VERSION OF LISTING 5.A.Blocking.except
//BEWARE: "LAMBDA PYRAMID" ROLLER COASTER AHEAD!
// NOT FOR THE FAINT OF HEART!
bool ifCashierPurchaseError(const std::exception* x) {
  if(x) {
    LogException(x);
```

```cpp
    return true;
  }
  return false;
}
void CashierReactor::cashierPurchaseItem(
      shared_ptr<CashierPurchaseItemReply> reply_handle,
      int item_id) {
  int user_id = get_user_id(reply_handle);
  dbPurchaseItem(db_reactor_id,
    user_id, item_id,
    [=](const std::exception* x, bool db_ok) {
      //same as DbPurchaseItemCallbackA::(react()+except())
      // from Take 3a
      //NB: reply_handle gets copied exactly as in Take 3
      if(ifCashierPurchaseError(x))
        return;
      if(!db_ok) {
        reply_handle->reply(false);
        return;//returns from current lambda function
      }
      REACTORID gameworld_reactor_id =
                  find_gameworld_for_user(user_id);
      gameworldAddItem(gameworld_reactor_id,
        user_id, item_id,
        [=](const std::exception* x, bool gw_ok){
          //same as GameworldAddItemCallbackA::react()
          // from Take 3
          if(ifCashierPurchaseError(x))
            return;
          reply_handle->reply(gw_ok);
        });
    });
}
```

IMPORTANT C++ note: if our lambda functions will want to modify members of our *class CashierReactor*, it will be possible (either directly or indirectly via a (member) function call) in spite of us specifying capture as *[=]*. This happens because while *[=]* in C++ means "capture everything by value," when talking about accessing members (those accessible via *this* pointer) from lambda function, it is *this* that gets captured, and while *this* is indeed captured by value, it doesn't prevent us from using it to refer to data members and modify them. Fortunately, it is *exactly* the behavior that we want.

Fortunately, it is *exactly* the behavior that we want.

```
//LISTING 5.Take4a.except
//NON-BLOCKING VERSION OF LISTING 5.A.Blocking.except
//BEWARE: "LAMBDA PYRAMID" ROLLER COASTER AHEAD!
// NOT FOR THE FAINT OF HEART!
void CashierReactor::cashierPurchaseItem(
    shared_ptr<CashierPurchaseItemReply> reply_handle,
    int item_id) {
  int user_id = get_user_id(reply_handle);
  auto catc =
    [=](std::exception& x) {
      LogException(x);
    };
  dbPurchaseItem(db_reactor_id,
    user_id, item_id,
    [=](bool db_ok){
      if(!db_ok) {
        reply_handle->reply(false);
        return;//returns from current lambda function
      }
      REACTORID gameworld_reactor_id =
                  find_gameworld_for_user(user_id);
      gameworldAddItem(gameworld_reactor_id,
        user_id, item_id,
        [=](const std::exception* x, bool gw_ok){
          reply_handle->reply(gw_ok);
        }, catc);
    }, catc);
}


//LISTING 5.A.Take5.IDLGen
//GENERATED FROM IDL, DO NOT MODIFY!
void CashierReactor::cashierPurchaseItem(
    shared_ptr<CashierPurchaseItemReply> reply_handle,
      //reply_handle MAY be copied (as shared_ptr<>),
      // if it is necessary to postpone replying
      // until later
    int item_id);
  //for Cashier, this is an RPC function
  // to be implemented
ReactorFuture<bool> CashierReactor::dbPurchaseItem(
                  Reactor* r, REACTORID reactor_peer,
                  int user_id, int item_id);
  //for Cashier, this is a stub
  // to be called
```

```cpp
ReactorFuture<bool> CashierReactor::gameworldAddItem(
                    Reactor* r, REACTORID reactor_peer,
                    int user_id, int item_id);
  //for Cashier, this is a stub
  // to be called
```

Note that our *class ReactorFuture<>* that we use here is quite different from *std::future<>* and *boost::future<>*; see the *Similarities and Differences from Existing Futures/Promises* section for a discussion of differences between futures.

```cpp
//LISTING 5.A.Take5.except
//NON-BLOCKING VERSION OF LISTING 5.A.Blocking.except
void CashierReactor::cashierPurchaseItem(
     shared_ptr<CashierPurchaseItemReply> reply_handle,
     int item_id) {
  int user_id = get_user_id(reply_handle);
  auto catc =
    [=](std::exception& x) {
      LogException(x);
    };
  ReactorFuture<bool> db_ok = dbPurchaseItem(
                    this, db_reactor_id,
                    user_id, item_id);
          //NB: infrastructure code
          // should effectively postpone
          // all the exceptions within
          // until except() handler is provided
  ReactorFuture<bool> gw_ok(this);
  db_ok.then([=](){
    if(!db_ok.value()) {
      reply_handle->reply(false);
      return;//returns from current lambda function
    }
    REACTORID gameworld_reactor_id =
                  find_gameworld_for_user(user_id);
    gw_ok = gameworldAddItem(
            this, gameworld_reactor_id,
            user_id, item_id);
  }).except(catc);
  gw_ok.then([=](){
    reply_handle->reply(gw_ok.value());
  }).except(catc);
}
```

```
//LISTING 5.A.Take5.parallel
ReactorFuture<A> a = rpcA(this);
ReactorFuture<B> b = rpcB(this);
ReactorFutureBoth<A,B> both(this,a,b);
both.then([=](){
  //...
});


//LISTING 5.A.Take6.except
//NON-BLOCKING VERSION OF LISTING 5.A.Blocking.except
void CashierReactor::cashierPurchaseItem(
      shared_ptr<CashierPurchaseItemReply> reply_handle,
      int item_id) {
  int user_id = get_user_id(reply_handle);
  ReactorFuture<bool> db_ok(this);
  ReactorFuture<bool> gw_ok(this);
  CCode code(
    ttry(
      [=](){
        db_ok = dbPurchaseItem(
                db_reactor_id,
                user_id, item_id);
      },
      waitFor(db_ok),
      [=](){
        if(!db_ok.value()) {
          reply_handle->reply(false);
          eexit();//ensures exit out of whole CCode
          return;
        }
        REACTORID gameworld_reactor_id =
                find_gameworld_for_user(user_id);
        gw_ok = gameworldAddItem(
          gameworld_reactor_id,
          user_id, item_id);
      },
      waitFor(gw_ok),
      [=]() {
        reply_handle->reply(gw_ok.value());
      }
    )//ttry
    .ccatch([=](std::exception& x) {
      LogException(x);
    }
  );//CCode
}
```

```cpp
//Listing 5.A.RecordingReplay
class Infrastructure {
  std::unique_ptr<GenericReactor> r;
  public:
  Infrastructure(std::unique_ptr<GenericReactor>& r_)
  : r(std::move(r_)) {
  }

  void run_loop(InputsLogForWriting* log4w) {
    //log4w is nullptr if no logging is needed
    while(true) {
      Event ev = wait_for_event();
      ev.inputs = read_inputs();
      if(log4w)
        Event::serializeToLog(ev, log4w);
      r->react(ev);
    }
  }
  void replay_loop(InputsLogForReading& log4r) {
    while(true) {
      Event ev = Event::deserializeFromLog(log4r);
      r->react(ev);
    }
  }
};

//Listing 5.A.DoubleHit.nondeterministic
class DoubleHit {
  private:
  const int THRESHOLD = 5;//in MyTimestamp units
  MyTimestamp last_hit;
    //actual type of MyTimestamp may vary
    // from time_t to uint64_t representing microseconds,
    // and is not important for our current purposes

  public:
  DoubleHit() {
    last_hit = MYTIMESTAMP_MINUS_INFINITY;
  }

  void hit() {
    MyTimestamp now = system_get_current_time();
      //for our current purposes, it doesn't really matter
      // which system time function we're calling here
    if(now - last_hit < THRESHOLD)
      on_double_hit();
```

```
      last_hit = now;
  }

  void on_double_hit() {
    //do something nasty to the NPC
  }
};

//Listing 5.A.call_wrapping
class Infrastructure {
  enum class Mode { NONE, RECORDING, REPLAY };
  Infrastructure() {
    //initialize log4r, log4w, mode
  }
  MyTimestamp wrapped_get_current_time() {
    if(mode == Mode::REPLAY) {
      assert(log4r != nullptr);
      return log4r.read_timestamp();
    }

    MyTimestamp ret = system_get_current_time();

    if(mode == Mode::RECORDING) {
      assert(log4w != nullptr);
      log4w.write_timestamp(ret);
    }

    return ret;
  }
};

//Listing 5.A.TLS_compromise
class Infrastructure {
  std::unique_ptr<GenericReactor> r;
  static thread_local MyTimestamp current_time;
  friend Mytimestamp my_get_current_time();
  public:
  Infrastructure(std::unique_ptr<GenericReactor>& r_)
  : r(std::move(r_)) {
  }

  void run_loop(InputsLogForWriting* log4w) {
    //log4w is nullptr if no logging is needed
    while(true) {
      Event ev = wait_for_event();
```

```cpp
      ev.inputs = read_inputs();
      current_time = system_get_current_time();
      if(log4w) {
        Event::serializeToLog(ev, log4w);
        log4w.write_timestamp(current_time);
      }
      r->react(ev);
    }
  }
  void replay_loop(InputsLogForReading& log4r) {
    while(true) {
      Event ev = Event::deserializeFromLog(log4r);
      current_time = log4r.read_timestamp();
      r->react(ev);
    }
  }
};

//Listing 5.A.BigUglySwitch
void Reactor::react(const Event& ev) {
  switch( ev.type ) {
    case NETWORK_PACKET_EVENT:
      switch( ev.packet.type ) {//(*)
        case MSG_ABC:
          auto abc = unmarshal_abc(ev.packet.body);
            //unmarshal_abc() is generated by IDL compiler
          OnMsgAbc(abc);
            //real processing,
            //  hand-written member of our (Re)Actor
          break;
        case MSG_DEF:
          //pretty much the same thing,
          //  replacing "abc" with "def"...
          break;
      }
      break;
    case SOME_OTHER_EVENT:
      //...
      break;
  }
}

//Listing 5.A.StatePattern
class State {
  public:
  virtual void enterState() {}//Enter function
```

```
    virtual void exitState() {}//Exit function
};
class StateA : public State {
  //some data members go here
  //pointer to parent Reactor also MAY be here
  /* new */ State* react(const Event& ev) {
    //you MAY want to return std::unique_ptr<>() instead,
    // but this is one case when semantics is very obvious
    // so I prefer to avoid additional verbosity and return
    // naked 'new' pointer
    switch( ev.type ) {//similar to Big-n-Ugly switch
                       //  discussed above
      case EV_X:
        //some code
        return nullptr;//means 'STATE DID NOT CHANGE'
      case EV_Y:
        //some_code
        return new StateB(some_params);
      //...
    }
  }
};
// other StateXX objects
class Reactor {
  std::unique_ptr<State> currentState;
  void react(const Event& ev) {
    std::unique_ptr<State> newState =
                          currentState->react(ev);
    if(newState) {
      currentState->exitState();
      currentState = newState;
      currentState->enterState();
    }
  }
};
```

There is a solution that allows us to have our elegant *new State()* change states, and avoid allocations.

Avoiding Expensive Allocations

As we'll discuss in Vol. V's chapter on C++, allocations are often a major source of performance problems. As a result, using *new* on each state change is something I'm usually reluctant to do. Fortunately, there is a solution that allows us *both* to have our elegant *new State()* change states, *and* to avoid allocations.[152]

---

152   Technically, we'll still be "allocating," but the way we do it will be optimized to avoid ill effects of default-allocation-from-the-global-heap.

To achieve it, we can play the following game:

♦ Add *Reactor** pointer to base *class State* (it will be necessary to implement *operator delete()* as required below).

♦ Add *static void* operator new(size_t sz, Reactor*)* and *static void operator delete(void* p)* to base *class State*.

▪ Implement allocator for these operators within the Reactor. If you're following the pattern above, then, in most cases, a very simple mechanism of having *exactly two* (more rarely – three) blocks of *uint8_t[max_size_of_your_State_objects]*[153] will do (one block is necessary to store *currentState*, and another to store *newState*, and that's it).

• This should already improve cacheability of your State objects quite significantly (compared to allocating from the global heap).

• Moreover, if you feel like it, you can even keep these blocks as members of your Reactor object, further improving locality.

▪ As you DO know that the object is derivative from *class GenericReactor*, within *delete* you can get pointer to your *class GenericReactor* from *p*.[154]

♦ To the same base *class State*, add private *static void* operator new(size_t sz)* with an *assert(false)* within to make sure that all the objects of *class State* are created <u>only</u> via *new(reactor) StateXX(...)* (and not via usual *new StateXX(...)*). Even better, if your compiler allows it, mark this *operator new(size_t sz)* with "= delete."

♦ Use *new(reactor) StateXX(some_params)* instead of former *new StateXX(some_params)* in all places.

♦ Bingo! We have our nice and readable programming model, and it will work rather fast too…[155]

---

153 Make sure to properly align these blocks using *alignas*!

154 Under the assumption that there is no multiple inheritance in sight, this is rarely a problem.

155 While the cost of the polymorphic call is still there, it is comparable to the cost of an equivalent switch; and we've improved locality to the point where ill effects due to locality being imperfect are pretty much negligible. For more discussion on data locality and performance, see Vol. V's chapter on C++.

```
//Listing 5.A.HierarchicalState
class StateA : public State {
  /* new */ State* react(const Event& ev) {
    switch( ev.type ) {
      //...
    }
  }
};
class StateAA : public StateA {
  /* new */ State* react(const Event& ev) {
    switch( ev.type ) {
      case EV_X:
        //some code
        return nullptr;
      case EV_Y:
        //some_code
        return new StateB(some_params);
      //...
      default:
        return StateA::react(ev);
              //forwarding ev to base class
              // for processing
    }
  }
};
```

C++: Enforcing const-ness for VALIDATE and CALCULATE stages in VALIDATE-CALCULATE-MODIFY-SIMULATE pattern

To rely on exception safety during the VALIDATE and CALCULATE stages with the VALIDATE-CALCULATE-MODIFY-SIMULATE pattern, it is important to enforce immutability of our (Re)Actor state before the MODIFY stage. And as it was noted in [Butcher], no rule is good if it is not enforced by code. Fortunately, at least in C++, we can enforce immutability relatively easily (that is, for reasonable and non-malicious developers).

First, let's define our task. We want to be able to enforce const-ness along the following lines:

```
//Listing 5.A.VALIDATE-CALCULATE.const-ness
void ConcreteReactor::react(Event& ev) {
  ///VALIDATE: 'this' is const
  //...validating code...

  //CALCULATE: 'this' is still const
  //...calculating code...

  //MODIFY/SIMULATE: 'this' is no longer const
  //...modifying code...
}
```

To make it work this way, for C++ I suggest the following (reasonably dirty) trick:

```
void ConcreteReactor::react(Event& ev) const {
  //yes, react() is declared as 'const'!
  ///VALIDATE: 'this' is enforced const
  //...validating code...

  //CALCULATE: 'this' is still enforced const
  //...calculating code...

  ConcreteReactor* r = modify_stage_reactor();
  //modify_stage_reactor() returns
  // const_cast<MyReactor*>(this)

  //MODIFY/SIMULATE: 'this' is still const, BUT we can use
  // non-const 'r' to modify current MyReactor object
  //...modifying code...
}
```

While not 100% neat, this trick does the trick (pun intended), and prevents accidental writing to the (Re)Actor state before *modify_stage_reactor()* is called (as the compiler will notice modifying *this* pointer declared as *const*, and will issue an error). Of course, one can still call *modify_stage_reactor()* at the very beginning of the *react()*, negating all the protection (or use one of several dozens of another ways to bypass *const*-ness in C++), but we're assuming that you do want to benefit from such a split, and will honestly avoid bypassing protection.

While not 100% neat, this trick does the trick (pun intended), and prevents accidental writing to the (Re)Actor state before *modify_stage_reactor()* is called.

On Posting messages from VALIDATE/CALCULATE in C++

If your Infrastructure Code performs the buffering described in the *Posting Messages (calling RPCs, etc.) Within VALIDATE/CALCULATE* section, in C++ it MAY declare all posting-messages functions (more generally, all having-buffered-side-effects functions) as *const* (or to have their *Reactor** parameter as *const*) to enable calling them from within VALIDATE/CALCULATE stages.[156] Otherwise (i.e., without such buffering being performed by your *class Infrastructure*), to en-force *const*-correctness of the VALIDATE/CALCULATE stages, your Infrastructure Code SHOULD declare these functions as non-*const* to prevent them being called from the VALIDATE/CALCULATE stages.

---

156 Sure, the buffer to store outgoing messages will need to be declared as *mutable*, but that's about the only complication on this way.

CHAPTER 6.
CLIENT-SIDE ARCHITECTURE

As discussed in Chapter 4, there are basically only two viable approaches for building your game: we named one an "Engine-Centric Approach" and the other a "Responsible Re-Use Approach." Which of these approaches is right for your game depends a lot on the genre and other GDD-level Requirements; the choice between the two was more or less explained in Chapter 4.

In this chapter, we'll discuss a Client-Side architecture based on the "Responsible Re-Use Approach."[157] On the other hand, if you're going to implement your game as an "Engine-Centric" one, you still need to read this chapter; while most of these decisions we're about to discuss are already made for you by your game engine, you still need to know what these decisions are (and whether you like what the specific engine has chosen for you); and whatever-your-engine didn't decide for you, will be decisions you need to make yourself. For more discussion on using an Engine-Centric Approach (as well as specific third-party game engines), see Chapter 7.

GRAPHICS 101

NB: this section is intended neither for graphics professionals nor game developers who spend half of their conscious life coding 3D; you're NOT likely to find anything new for you here. However,

This section is intended neither for graphics professionals nor game developers who spend half of their conscious life coding 3D; you're NOT likely to find anything new for you here.

---

157   As always, "Responsible Re-Use" is subject to interpretation; as I am known for leaning toward "DIY Everything," feel free to re-use more. However, for whatever you're re-using, the glue code should be yours!

for the rest of us (in particular, those coming from fields such as web development or social games), even a very cursory discussion of graphics MIGHT still be useful.

One of the first things you need when dealing with the Client-Side is the graphics engine. Here, depending on the specifics of your game, there are significant differences, but there are still a few things that are (almost) universal. Please note that at this point we're not about to discuss any implementation details of graphics engines; a bit more on graphics will be discussed in Volume V's chapter on Graphics 101, though even there please don't expect a really serious explanation of 3D stuff (there are MUCH better and more detailed books for this purpose; see the *Recommended Reading* section in the very beginning of Volume I).

For the time being, we only need to figure out a few very high-level concepts, which allow us to describe the processes involved in very general terms, and to know just enough to start drawing an overall Client-Side Architecture.

On Developers, Game Designers, and Artists

For most of the games out there, there is a pretty obvious separation between developers and artists. There is usually a kind of mutual understanding that developers do not interfere in drawing pictures (making 3D models, etc., etc.), and artists are not teaching developers how to program. This, however, raises a Big Fat Question™ about a tool-chain that artists can use to do their job. These toolchains are heavily dependent on the graphics, on the game engine you're using, etc., etc. When making decisions about your graphics, you absolutely need to realize which tools your artists will use (and which file formats they will produce, so that you can convert from these formats to whatever-formats-your-game-engine-requires).

For some genres (at least for FPS and RPG), there are usually also game designers. These folks sit in-between developers and artists, and are usually responsible for creating levels, writing quests, etc., etc. And guess what: they need their own tools too.

Actually, these toolchains are so important that I would say that at least half of the value the game engine provides to your project comes from them. If you're going to write your own engine, you need to think about these toolchains, as they can easily make-or-break your game development process. And if you're going to use a 3rd-party game engine, make sure that the toolchain it provides is understandable to and usable by both your artists and your developers (and to/by game designers too, if applicable).

Actually, these toolchains are so important that I would say that at least half of the value the game engine provides to your project comes from them.

We'll discuss more about these toolchains and, more generally, asset pipelines that use these toolchains, in Volume V's chapter on Graphics 101.

On Using Game Engines and Vendor Lock-In

These days, if you want to use a 3rd-party graphics engine, most of the time you won't find "graphics engine" as such, but will need to choose between "game engines." And "game engines" tend to provide much more functionality than just "graphics engines"—which have many positives, but there is also one negative. These additional features provided by "game engines" (in addition to pure graphic-rendering capabilities) may include such things as processing user input, support for humanoid-like creatures (which may include such things as inverse kinematics), asset management, scripting, network support, toolchains, etc., etc., etc. And guess what: most of these features even work.

So far, so great, however, there is a dark spot in this overall bright picture; exactly the same great features that tend to help a lot tend to backfire too. The thing is that the more useful features the engine has, the more you will want to use (well, they were the reason to use the 3rd-party game engine to start with). And the more features you use, the more you're tied to a specific 3rd-party game engine, and this process will very soon make it your Absolute Dependency (as defined in Chapter 4), also known as a Vendor Lock-In.

It is not that Absolute Dependencies are bad per se (and, as mentioned in Chapter 4, for quite a few games the advantages of having it outweigh the negatives), but, if you have an Absolute Dependency, it is really, really important to realize that you *are* Locked-In, and that you SHOULD NOT rely on throwing away your game engine in the future.

Just one example where this can be important. Let's consider you're writing a game with an Undefined Life Span (i.e., you're planning for your game to run for a really long while; see Vol. I's chapter on GDD for further details); then you decide (to speed things up) to make a first release of your game using a 3rd-party game engine. Your game engine of choice is very good, but has one drawback: it doesn't support one of the platforms that you do want to support (for example, it doesn't support mobile, which you want to have ASAP after the very first release). So you're thinking, "Hey, we'll release our game using this engine, and then we'll migrate our game from it (or will support another graphics engine for those platforms where it doesn't run, etc.)".

In theory, it all sounds very good. In practice, however, you'll find yourself in hot water. By the time you want to migrate away, your code and game in general will be *that* much intertwined and interlocked with the game engine that separating your code from your game engine will amount to a full rewrite (which in turn is rarely possible within the same game without affecting too many subtle gameplay-affecting issues that make or break your game). It means that in our hypothetical example above, you won't be able to support mobile devices *ever* (well, unless you scrap the whole thing and rewrite it from scratch, which will almost inevitably require a re-release at least on a different set of servers, if not under a different title).

If you're using only a graphics engine (as opposed to a full-scale game engine, or are using your game engine only as a graphics engine), you MAY be able to avoid it becoming your Absolute Dependency. However, even in such cases, to avoid being Locked-In, you'll need to be extremely vigilant at limiting the features you're using. As a very rough rule of thumb: whatever-feature-affects-only-rendering without information ever going back to your code is okay, but any use of the features that provide you with some feedback from a supposed-graphics engine is a Big No-No™. This automatically rules out (that is, if you want to avoid being Locked-In) using a 3rd-party engine for physics (even as simple as collision detection); on the other hand, in the Authoritative-Server model, you won't be able to use a graphics engine for physics anyway.

If you're using only a graphics engine (as opposed to a full-scale game engine, or are using your game engine only as a graphics engine), you MAY be able to avoid it becoming your Absolute Dependency.

Let's re-iterate:

> *Having an Absolute Dependency is not necessarily evil, but, if you have one, you'd better realize it and also think of worst-case scenarios.*

As noted above, this is especially important for games with an Undefined Life Span.

Types of Graphics

Now, let's start considering different types of graphics that you may want to use for your game.

Games with Rudimentary Graphics

First, let's see what happens if your game requires only minimal graphics (or none at all).

Contrary to popular belief, you *can* build a game without any graphics at all, or with very rudimentary ones. When talking about rudimen-

Contrary to popular belief, you *can* build a game without any graphics at all, or with very rudimentary ones.

tary graphics, I mean static graphics, without animation — just pictures with defined areas to click. Such games-with-rudimentary-graphics are not limited to obvious examples like stock exchanges, but also include some games that are doing it with great success (one such example being the quite popular Lords & Knights).

If your graphics are nonexistent or rudimentary, you can (and probably should) write your graphics engine all by yourself. It won't take long, and having a dependency on a 3rd-party engine merely to render static images is usually not worth the trouble.

The artists' toolchain is almost nonexistent, too; all the artists need to work with rudimentary graphics is their favorite 2D graphics editor (which usually happens to be Photoshop) to provide you with bitmaps of sizes-that-you-need.

Games with 2D Graphics

In general, when you're making a 2D game, your development process, while more complicated than for games with rudimentary graphics, will still be much, much simpler than that of a 3D game.

The next step on the ladder from nonexistent graphics to the holy grail of realistic ray-traced 3D[158] is 2D graphics. 2D graphics is still very popular, especially for games oriented toward mobile phones, and for social games (also social games tend to have a mobile phone version, so there is a strong correlation between the two). This section also covers 2D engines used by games with pre-rendered 3D graphics.

In general, when you're making a 2D game, your development process, while more complicated than for games with rudimentary graphics, will still be much, much simpler than that of 3D games.[159] First, 2D graphics (unlike 3D graphics) are rather simple, and you can easily write a simple 2D engine yourself (I've seen a 2D engine with double-buffering and virtually zero flickering written from scratch within 8-10 man-weeks for a single target platform; not too much, if you ask me). Actually, in Vol. V's chapter on Graphics 101, we'll discuss pretty-much-everything you need to develop your own 2D engine; TBH, it is not much: sprites and double-buffering will get most 2D games running (and the rest can be added as you need it). On the other

---

158   I do know that nobody does ray tracing for games (yet), but who said that we can't daydream a bit?

159   Hey, isn't it a good reason to scrap all 3D completely in the name of time to market? Well, probably not.

hand, you may want to go further and to use the GPU to render your 2D graphics (with shaders etc.); we'll briefly discuss related techniques in Vol. V's chapter on Graphics 101.

Alternatively, you can use one of the many available "2D game engines"; however, you need to keep in mind the risk of becoming Locked-In (see the *On Using Game Engines and Vendor Lock-In* section above). In particular, if you're planning to replace your 2D game engine in the future, you should stay away from using such things as "2D Physics" features provided by your game engine, and limit your use of the game engine to rendering only. In practice, with 2D engines it is usually not-too-difficult to avoid Vendor Lock-In (and keep your option to migrate from this 2D engine, or add another 2D or even 3D one alongside it, etc.); while it still requires you to be extremely vigilant, at least it has been done and is usually doable.

One good example of a 2D game engine (which is mostly a 2D graphics engine) is [Cocos2D-X]. It is a popular enough cross-platform engine (including support for iOS, Android, and WinPhone, and going mobile is one-really-popular-reason for creating a 2D game these days), and has an API that is good enough for practical use. If you're developing only for iOS, SpriteKit [Apple] is another popular choice. BTW, if you're vigilant enough in avoiding dependencies, you can try making your game with Cocos2D-X, and then support SpriteKit for iOS only (doing it the other way around is also possible, but is usually riskier unless you're absolutely sure that most of your users are coming from iOS).

> NB: *if you're serious about such cross-engine development, make sure to implement a Logic-to-Graphics API as described in the "Generic Client Architecture" section below.*

About using 2D functionality of the primarily 3D engines such as Unity or Unreal Engine: personally, I would stay away from them when it comes to 2D development (for my taste, they are way too locking-in for a task as relatively simple as 2D). Such engines would have a Big Advantage™ for quite a few genres *if* they could support both 2D and 3D "views" on the same Game World, but to the best of my knowledge, none of the major game engines provide such support.

About toolchains for 2D development. For 2D, artists' toolchains are usually fairly simple, with artists using their favorite animation editor. As a result of their work, they will usually provide you with sprites (for example, in a form of series of .pngs-with-transparency, or "sprite sheets"). More on example toolchains in Volume V's chapter on Graphics 101.

On Pre-rendered 3D

Now, let's see what happens if your game is supposed to *look* like a 3D game. In this case, first you need to think whether you really need to do 3D rendering in real-time, or if you will be fine with so-called pre-rendered 3D.

When talking about pre-rendered 3D, the idea is to create your 3D models and 3D animations, but then, instead of rendering them in real-time using OpenGL or DirectX, to pre-render these 3D models and animations into 2D graphics (often, into 2D "sprites"); this pre-rendering is usually done in the comfort of the artist's own environment, with all the sophisticated rendering stuff (such as ray tracing) she or he may prefer to use. Then, we'll ship this pre-rendered 2D graphics with your game instead of shipping full 3D models, and then will render them with a 2D graphics engine.

Fully 3D pre-rendered games allow you to avoid running a 3D engine on Clients, replacing it with a much simpler (and much less demanding) 2D engine.

Fully 3D pre-rendered games[160] allow you to have graphics that look like 3D, while avoiding running a 3D engine on Clients, replacing it with a much simpler (and much less demanding) 2D engine.

Usually, full 3D pre-rendering won't work for first-person games (such as MMORPG/MMOFPS), but it may work reasonably well even for (some kind of) MMORTS, and for many other kinds of popular MMO genres too. Full 3D pre-rendering is quite popular for platforms with limited resources, such as in-browser games, or games oriented toward mobile phones.

Technically, fully pre-rendered 3D development flow consists of:

♦ 3D design, usually made using a readily available 3rd-party 3D toolchain. For this purpose, you can use tools such as Maya,

---

160   In fact, partial 3D pre-rendering is also perfectly viable, and is used a lot in 3D games that do have a 3D engine on the Client-Side, but this is beyond the scope of our discussion until Vol. V's chapter on Graphics 101.

3D Max, Poser, or — for really adventurous ones — Blender. 3D design is not normally done by developers, but by 3D artists. It includes both models (including textures, etc.) and animations.

♦ Pre-rendering of 3D design into 2D graphics, such as sprites. Usually implemented as a bunch of scripts that "compile" your 3D models and animations into 2D graphics, including animated sprite sequences; the same 3D tools that were used for 3D design are usually used for this 3D-to-2D rendering. Using the same 3D tools for both design and rendering is one Big Advantage™ of this approach; it allows you to avoid compatibility issues between your 3D modeling tools and your 3D engine, which will otherwise plague your game development.

♦ Rendering of 2D sprites on the Client, using a 2D graphics engine.

As an additional bonus, with 3D pre-rendering, you normally don't need to bother with optimizing your 3D models to be low-poly, and can keep your 3D models in as high a number of polygons as you wish. Granted, these high-poly models won't usually make any visual difference (as each of the 2D sprites is commonly too small to notice the difference, though YMMV), but at least you won't need to bother with polygon number reduction (and you can be sure that your 3D artists will appreciate it, as achieving low-poly-but-still-decent-looking 3D models is well-known as a Big Headache™).

3D pre-rendering is certainly not without disadvantages. The two biggest problems of 3D pre-rendering that immediately come to mind are:

♦ First, you can pre-render your models only at specific angles; it means that if you're showing a battlefield in isometric projection, pre-rendering can be fine, but doing it for a MMOFPS (or any other game with a first-person view) is usually not an option.

♦ Second, if you're not careful enough, the size of your 2D sprites can easily become huge.

On the positive side, if you can survive 3D pre-rendering without making your game unviewable (and without making it too huge in size), you can make your game run on the platforms that have no 3D at all (or their 3D is hopelessly slow to do what-you-need); I'm mostly

If you can survive 3D pre-rendering without making your game unviewable (and without making it too huge in size), you can make your game run on the platforms that have no 3D at all (or their 3D is hopelessly slow).

talking about smartphones here (while smartphones have made huge improvements in 3D performance, they are still light years away from PCs — and it will probably stay this way for a long while, so if you want to show a thousand units at the same time, well, you'll probably be out of luck with 3D on a smartphone).

The second big benefit of 3D pre-rendering (compared to real-time rendering) is a clean separation of the artist's toolchain. In general, artists' toolchains are usually not a problem for pre-rendered 3D; artists are pretty much free with regards to what they use (though it is still advisable to use one tool across the whole project); it can be anything ranging from Maya to Blender, with 3D Max in-between. In most cases, for 3D pre-rendering, your job as developer in this regard is limited to making artists use some kind of source control system, and writing the scripts for the automated "build" of their source files (those in 3D Max or whatever-else-they're-using) into 2D sprites.

Bottom Line about pre-rendered 3D: whether you want/can switch your game to 3D pre-rendering depends, but at least you should consider this option (that is, unless your game has a first-person view). While this technique is often frowned upon (often, using non-arguments such as "it is not cool"), it might (or might not) work for you.

If you're lucky enough to be able to exploit pre-rendering, you shouldn't miss the opportunity.

Just imagine: there is no need to make those low-poly models; no need to worry that your models become too "fat" for one of your resource-stricken target platforms as soon as you throw in 100 characters within one single area; no need to bother with texture sizes; and so on. It *does* sound "too good to be true" (and in most cases it will be), but if you're lucky enough to be able to exploit pre-rendering, you shouldn't miss the opportunity.

Last, but not least: if you manage to get away with pre-rendered 3D, make sure to read the section on 2D graphics above (as you'll still need to render 2D within your Client).

Games with 3D Graphics

— But first you must put on the spectacles.

— Why?

— Because if you did not wear spectacles the brightness and glory of the Emerald City would blind you. Even those who live in the City must wear spectacles night and day.

They are all locked on, for Oz so ordered it when the City was first built, and I have the only key that will unlock them.

— Wizard of Oz

If you have found that your 3D game is not a good match for pre-rendered 3D, you will probably need to have a 3D rendering engine on the Client-Side. This tends to unleash a whole lot of problems, from weird exchange formats between the toolchain and your engine, to implementing inverse kinematics (if applicable). We'll discuss some of these problems in Vol. V's chapter on Graphics 101; for now, let's just write down that non-pre-rendered 3D is a Big Pain in the Neck™ (compared to the other types of graphics discussed above). If you do need a 3D rendering engine on the Client-Side, you basically have two distinct options.

Making 3D work is not easy, but making it look good is a major challenge.

Option 1 goes along "DIY" lines, with you writing your own rendering engine over either OpenGL or DirectX. In this case, be prepared to spend a lot of time making your game look somewhat reasonable. Making 3D work is not easy to start with, but making it *look good* is a major challenge. In addition, you will need to implement the artist's toolchain; at the very least, you'll need to provide a way to import and use files generated by popular 3D design programs (hint: supporting import from Wavefront .obj won't be enough; you'll generally need to dig much deeper into the specifics of the 3D-program-you're-supporting and its formats, and whenever formats go beyond Wavefront, things start to get ugly).

On the plus side, if you manage to survive this ordeal and get reasonable-looking graphics with your own 3D engine, you'll get a solid baseline that will give you a lot of flexibility (and you may need this flexibility, especially if we're talking about the games with Undefined Life Span).

Option 2 is to try using some "3D game engine" as your "3D rendering engine." This way, unless you've already decided that your game engine is your Absolute Dependency, is rather risky – though you still have a fighting chance.

The problem you'll be facing is that 3D game engines tend to be very complicated, and have lots of interaction with the game. This means that to prevent your 3D engine from becoming your Absolute Dependency a.k.a. Vendor Lock-In, you'll need to be extremely vigilant when it comes to dependencies. In particular – you have to restrain *all* interactions with your 3D engine to the Logic-to-Graphics API as discussed in the *Logic-to-Graphics API* section below, otherwise you will almost certainly won't be able to replace the engine later. Once again, I am not saying that ~~Wizard-of-Oz~~ Vendor Lock-In is necessarily a bad thing, but if you're going along this Yellow Brick Road toward the shiny Emerald City of <whatever-3D-engine-you-want-to-use>, you do need to realize that there are very few forks in this road, and only a small portion of them can possibly get you out of being forced to wear green spectacles (without any chance of taking them off).

GENERIC CLIENT ARCHITECTURE

> How do you program an elephant? One byte at a time!
>
> — (Almost) proverb

Okay, after all the preliminaries, we're now ready to draw our first Client Architecture Diagram. At this point, I don't want to go into any details, so it is bound to be extremely generic (and of limited use):

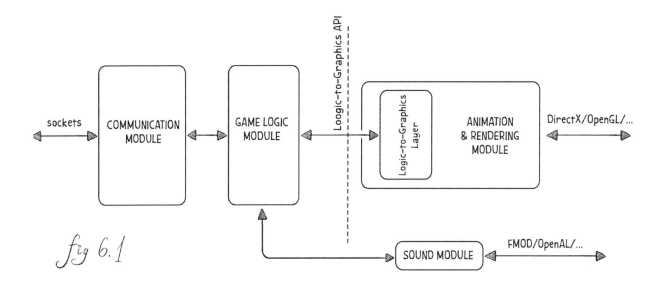

fig 6.1

Fig 6.1, in spite of being very generic, still provides *some* valuable information. In particular, it demonstrates that even on the Client-Side (and contrary to the beliefs of many indie gamedevs), it is necessary to split your program into several loosely coupled (and highly cohesive) Modules. In particular, as a Big Fat Rule of Thumb™, I insist on:

♦ Separating your Communication Module from your Game Logic Module. Doing otherwise would keep your Game Logic cluttered with communication stuff <big-ouch />. *NB: if you're using something like Unity HLAPI or UE4 networking, this separation will be more or less done for you by the engine <phew />.*

♦ Separating Animation&Rendering from Game Logic. More on it in the *Logic-to-Graphics API* section below.

♦ Separating the Sound Module from everything else (that is, if sounds for your game go beyond "start playing this sound now.")

These separations are extremely important (and having very clean, very-well-defined interfaces between the Modules is very important too). The reason is that if you don't have even a very basic separation, you'll for sure end up with a huge monolith of spaghetti code, which will become a guaranteed disaster as soon as your project grows to about 100K–200K LOC (which is not much for a game).

LOC

Lines of Code is a software metric used to measure the size of a computer program by counting the number of lines in the text of the program's source code.

—Wikipedia

Logic-to-Graphics API

Of all the separations in Fig. 6.1, arguably the most important is the separation between your Game Logic Module and your Animation&Rendering Module. In Fig 6.1, it is shown as a "Logic-to-Graphics API," followed by a "Logic-to-Graphics Layer." Note that, strictly speaking, the Logic-to-Graphics Layer is optional, and in some cases its functionality can be performed by the Animations&Rendering Module itself; however, the *Logic-to-Graphics API* is of paramount importance and most of the time I *insist* on having it.

Let me explain the concept in one simple example. If your game is blackjack, Client-Side Game Logic needs to produce rendering instructions to your graphics engine. Usually, naïve implementations will just have Client-Side Game Logic issue instructions, such as "draw such-and-such bitmap at such-and-such coordinates." This approach works reasonably well, until you need to port your Client to another device (in an extreme case, from PC to phone — with the latter having much less screen real estate, and the coordinates being very different too).

In contrast to this naïve approach, with a Logic-to-Graphics API expressed in terms of Game World, your blackjack Game Logic will issue rendering instructions NOT in terms of "draw 9S.png at the point (234,567) on the screen," but rather in terms of "place the card 9S in front of player #3 at the table." Then it becomes the job of the Logic-to-Graphics Layer (or, more generally, the Animations&Rendering Module) to translate this instruction into screen coordinates.

For a 3D simulation such as a first-view RPG, Game Logic should prepare a 3D scene in physical world coordinates, and again the translation from physical world coordinates into screen coordinates should be done by the Animation&Rendering Module.

Of course, the Logic-to-Graphics layer is not limited to blackjack, and is applicable pretty much across the board. If your game is a strategy, Client-Side Game Logic should issue instructions in terms of "move unit A to position (X,Y)" (with the coordinates expressed in terms of simulated-world coordinates, not in terms of on-screen coordinates(!)), and, again, the translation between the two should be performed by our Logic-to-Graphics Layer. And for a 3D simulation such as a first-view RPG, Game Logic should prepare a 3D scene in physical world coordinates (based on information from the Server, plus Client-Side Interpolation/Extrapolation/Prediction; see Vol. I's chapter on Communications for details), and again the translation from physical world coordinates into screen coordinates should be done by the Animation&Rendering Module (ideally – by a separate Logic-to-Graphics layer).

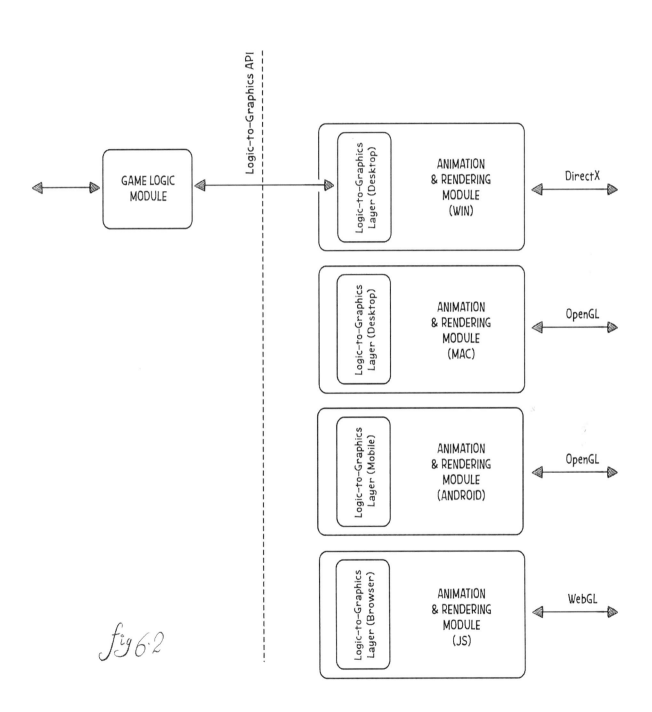

fig 6.2

Fig 6.2 illustrates how screen-independent and Game-World-oriented Logic-to-Graphics API can facilitate vastly cross-platform Clients. As screen real estate is very different on desktops and mobile devices, screen coordinates will be very different too; on the other hand, Game Logic in Fig 6.2 can stay exactly the same regardless of running on a desktop or mobile device (or even on a browser; more in the *Big Fat Browser Problem* section below). After all, all Game Logic does is just issue instructions in terms of the Game World, not in terms of screen coordinates. This, in turn, has been observed as an extremely important factor when trying to maintain[161] your Game Client across different platforms.

Naïve vs Logic-to-Graphics for Cross-Platform Development

Let's compare these two approaches — the "naïve" one and Logic-to-Graphics one — in the context of cross-platform development.

Having more than one code base has been observed as being devastating for maintainability.

In naïve implementations without Game-World-oriented Logic-to-Graphics API, your whole Game Logic would become platform-specific; and Game Logic is the thing that tends to be changed a *lot*. Which means that without Logic-to-Graphics API expressed in terms of Game World, you'll need to maintain two substantially similar, but technically different, code bases for your Game Logic Module. This, in turn, leads to a very serious problem, as having more than one code base has been observed as being devastating for maintainability. I've seen a game that tried to release a Mac Client in addition to an already-existing PC Client — using two separate code-bases for PC and Mac. The whole process went as follows:

♦ First, they released a shiny new Mac Client alongside the PC Client.

♦ Then, over the next few months, the PC Client was modified (with support of new game rules, new Game World entities, new UI, etc.), and the Mac Client began to fall behind the PC Client.

♦ And at around six months after the initial release, the Mac Client became so out-of-sync with Servers that it wasn't playable anymore, and the Mac Client was abandoned completely.

---

161   A euphemism for "keep modifying."

A competing game went the way of Logic-to-Graphics API (and the associated Logic-to-Graphics Layer), working in terms of Game World. It took longer to implement the Mac Client there (as it required quite a bit of preliminary work to make a clean separation along the lines of Logic-to-Graphics API). On the other hand, after the separation was completed, everything worked like a charm. The frequently changing piece of code — Game Logic — was identical for PC and Mac, so maintaining it didn't cause any trouble. As for the Logic-to-Graphics Layer and the Animation&Rendering Module: they happened to be changed *much* less frequently than the Game Logic, which means that they stayed pretty much without changes for long periods of time (and when they were changed, all the changes were very straightforward). Moreover, later the very same game was ported with relatively little effort to tablets and mobile devices (with updates to all the Clients across four platforms released within 1-2 days).

Moreover, the amount of work involved tends to be *much* higher for the naïve approach even if we don't take the costs of keeping-different-pieces-of-code-in-sync into account. From a formal point of view, in "naïve" implementations with per-platform code bases, *any* change concerning *either* Game Logic *or* Animation&Rendering needs to be duplicated on *all* the P platforms we want to support. It means that the amount of work for a new release with G changes in Game Logic and A changes in Animation&Rendering is $(G+A)*P$ (let's name it *naïve_work*).

On the other hand, for games with a Logic-to-Graphics layer, the amount of work for the same new release will be $G+A*P$ (let's name it *LtG_work*), so we have pure savings of $(G-1)*P$ compared to the naïve approach. Furthermore, as usually at the later-stages-of-game-development[162] A happens to be much smaller than G, the ratio of *naïve_work/ LtG_work* $= ((G+A)*P)/(G+A*P)$ becomes pretty close to P (with $A<<G$, $((G+A)*P)/(G+A*P) \sim= G*P/G = P$).

I rest my case.

---

162 And especially after deployment, which is a critical part of an MOG life cycle.

First, you will have a very clear separation between the different layers of the program, which tends to help a whole lot in the long run.

Logic-to-Graphics Benefits

Overall, when keeping your Logic-to-Graphics API Game-World-oriented, you'll get quite a few benefits.

First, you will have a very clear separation between the different layers of the program, which tends to help a whole lot in the long run.

Second, even if you're supporting only one platform now, with a Logic-to-Graphics layer you're leaving the door open for adding support for all the platforms you might want to support in the future. This includes such things as adding a 3D-rendered version to your currently-2D-only game, and an in-browser version (more on it in the *Big Fat Browser Problem* section below). And with regard to cross-platform support: as discussed above, Logic-to-Graphics-based architectures beat naïve ones hands down.

Third, with a Logic-to-Graphics layer you don't have a strong dependency on any graphics engine, so if in five years from now a new, much-better engine arises, you'll be able to migrate there without rewriting the whole thing.

Fourth, due to making the monolithic-block-of-code-around-your-Game-Logic smaller, Logic-to-Graphics separation tends to enable more sophisticated Game Logic; this is especially important if you need to implement complicated features such as Client-Side Extrapolation and/or Prediction (see Vol. I's chapter on Communications for details). In addition, having your Game Logic cross-platform enables code re-use between the Server and the Client (which is often a Good Thing™, especially for Client-Side Prediction).

Logic-to-Graphics Costs

By now, we've discussed the benefits of Game-World-oriented Logic-to-Graphics API, but what about the cost? In fact, I can only think of two realistic negatives of Logic-to-Graphics:

♦ There is a certain development overhead that is necessary to achieve this clean separation. I'm not talking about performance overhead, but about development overhead. With Logic-to-Graphics being used, if the Game Logic developer needs to get something from the graphics engine, he can't just go ahead and call the graphics-engine-function-that-she-wants. Instead, an interface to get whatever-she-needs should be created, has to be supported by all the engines, etc., etc. It's all easily doable, but it introduces quite a bit of mundane work. On the other hand, I contend that in the long run, such clean interfaces provide much more value than this development overhead takes away; in particular, clean interfaces have been observed as a strong obstacle to the code becoming "spaghetti code," which is already more-than-enough to justify them.

♦ A learning curve for those game developers coming from traditional limited-life-span (and/or not-massively-multiplayer) 3D games. In these classical games (I intentionally don't want to use the term "old-fashioned" to avoid being too blunt about it <wink />) everything revolves around the 3D engine, so for such developers moving toward the model with clean separation between graphics and logic can be rather painful. However, for most of the games with Authoritative Servers, you need to move away from 3D-engine-centric approach anyway (we have to sep-arate Server-Side decision-making from Client-Side rendering), so I would say that this drawback shouldn't be attributed solely to the Logic-to-Graphics Layer.

The benefits of Logic-to-Graphics happen to greatly outweigh the costs for the vast majority of major distributed systems, IMNSHO.

Overall, the benefits of Logic-to-Graphics happen to greatly outweigh the costs for the vast majority of major distributed systems, IMNSHO.

Dual Graphics, Including 2D+3D Graphics

In some cases, you may need to support two substantially different types of graphics. One such example arises when you need to support your game both for PC and phone; quite often, the difference between available screen real estate is too large to keep your layout the same, so you usually need to redesign not only the graphics, but also redesign the layout.

In such cases of dual graphics, it is paramount to have your Logic-to-Graphics API expressed in terms of the Game World.

In such cases of dual graphics, it is paramount to have your Log-ic-to-Graphics API expressed in terms of Game World, as described above. As soon as you have your Logic-to-Graphics API work in terms of Game World, adding a new type of graphics becomes a breeze. You just need to add another implementation of your Animation&Render-ing Module (re-using your Logic-to-Graphics Layer if applicable), and there is no need to change Game Logic at all(!). These two different implementations of the Animation&Rendering Module may have different APIs on the boundary with graphics engines, but they always have the same API on the boundary with Game Logic (and this is possible because the API actually has nothing to do with graphics). The latter observation will allow you to keep development of your Game Logic without caring about the specific engines you're using.

Of course, if you need to add a new instruction that comes from Game Logic to the Animation&Rendering Module (for example, if you're adding a new graphical primitive), you will still need to modify both your implementations of the Animation&Rendering Module. However, if your Logic-to-Graphics API is clean enough, you will find rather soon that such changes (while still happening and causing their fair share of trouble) are, by orders of magnitude, rarer than changes to the Game Logic; this difference in change frequencies makes the difference between workable workflow and an unworkable one.

An extreme case of dual graphics is dual 2D+3D graphics. Not all game genres allow it (for example, first-person shooters usually won't work too well in 2D <wink />), but *if* your game genre is okay with it, *and* you have a Logic-to-Graphics separation layer, this becomes perfectly feasible. You just need to have two different graphics engines: a 3D one and a 2D one (they can be in separate Clients, or even switchable in run-time), and an implementation of the Animation&Rendering Module for each of them (both using the same Logic-to-Graphics API to communicate with the Game Logic). As soon as you have this — Bingo! — you've provided your players with a choice between 2D and 3D graphics (depending on their preference, or platform, or whatever else). Even better, when using a clean Logic-to-Graphics API, you can start with the type of graphics that is simpler/more important/etc., and add alternative graphics later.

Modules and Their Relationships

Now, as we've finished discussing Logic-to-Graphics API and its benefits, let's take a look at Fig 6.1 once again, and explore a probable separation of the responsibilities between different modules for a more or less "typical" game. As always, YMMV (and in this case, even more than usual), so the separation above may or may not apply to your specific game; still, chances are that at least some of the modules won't be too different.

Game Logic Module

Game Logic Module is the one that makes most of the decisions about your Game World. More strictly, these are not exactly decisions about the Game World in general (as this one is maintained by our Authoritative Server), but about the *Client-Side copy* of the Game World. In some cases, it can be almost trivial, though in other cases (especially when Client-Side Prediction is involved) it can be very elaborate.

Game Logic Module is likely to keep a copy of the Game World from the Game Server as part of its state.

In any case, the Game Logic Module is likely to keep a more-or-less up-to-date copy of the Game World State (or of the relevant portion of the Game World State) from the Game Server. However, as we discussed in Vol. I's chapter on Communications, there can be up to *three* different states in our MOG: Server-Side State (often represented by ultra-low-poly meshes without textures, which are sufficient for simulation but not for rendering), Publishable State (the one usually expressed in terms such as "there is a PC standing at position (X,Y) in the Game World coordinates, facing NNW," or "there are cards AS and JH on the table"), and "Client-Side State" (sufficient for rendering, so high-poly meshes, textures, and lots of other stuff is necessary). As we have *three* different Game World States – a question arises "which one of these Game World States should be within our Game Logic?"

Usually, however counterintuitively it may sound, Game World State within Game Logic Module *should not* correspond to the Client-Side State; normally, the Client-Side State belongs to the Animation&Rendering Module (and *only* there). And within the Game Logic Module, we'll usually have either the Publishable State, *or* the Server-Side State (the latter is common if we want to run the Client-Side Prediction). This separation between Game Logic Module and high-poly Client-Side State is important to facilitate a clean separation along the lines of the Logic-to-Graphics API (and also has side benefits such as the re-use of Server-Side code for Client-Side Prediction).

Game Logic Module & Graphics

Probably the most closely related to the Game Logic Module is the Animation&Rendering one. Most of the interaction between the two goes in the direction from Game Logic to Animation&Rendering, using Logic-to-Graphics API commands. As a rule of thumb, the Game Logic Module will instruct Animation&Rendering Module to construct a portion of its own copy of the Game World State as a (2D or 3D) scene, and then will instruct it to update Animation&Rendering copy as its own copy of the Game World State changes.

In addition, the Game Logic Module is going to handle (but not render) UI, such as HUDs, and various UI dialogs (including the dialogs leading to purchases, social stuff, etc.). As long as it is possible, this UI handling should be implemented in a very cross-platform manner. All APIs or messages intended for UI handling, just as anything else going over Logic-to-Graphics API, should be expressed in very graphics-agnostic terms, such as "show health at 87%" or "show the dialog described by such-and-such resource."

To handle UI, the Game Logic Module might need to issue a request (for example, make an API call or send a message) to the Animation&Rendering Module asking for information such as "what object (or dialog element) is currently in the crosshair (or under the cursor)". On receiving a reply, the Game Logic Module may decide to update HUD, or do whatever-else-is-necessary (more on it in the *UI Interaction Example* section below).

If Client-Side Prediction is involved, it might be tempting to request other services from the Animation&Rendering Module, such as "notify me when the bullet hits the NPC." However, most of the time I argue against such a dependency of Game Logic from Animation&Rendering, and argue instead for implementing *all* the physics (such as Client-Side Prediction etc.) *completely* within the Game Logic Module; in quite a few cases, it can/should be done by re-using some parts of the Game Logic from the Server-Side (see the *Game Logic Module: Client-Side Prediction and Simulation* section below for further discussion).

Overall, there can be quite a few interactions between the Game Logic Module and the Animation&Rendering Module. Still, while it may be tempting to combine the Game Logic Module with the Ani-

While it may be tempting to combine the Game Logic Module with the Animation&Rendering Module, I usually *strongly* advise against it.

mation&Rendering Module, I usually *strongly* advise against it for the reasons discussed at length above.

Game Logic Module: Client-Side Prediction and Simulation

One practically important case for a Game Logic Module is when it needs to implement Client-Side Prediction (for a discussion on Client-Side Prediction, see Vol. I's chapter on Communications). Very briefly – with Client-Side Prediction, for those actions coming from our own player, we will be *both* sending them to the Server-Side, *and* at the same time will start simulating them right away on the Client-Side. The idea of Client-Side Prediction is to reduce *perceivable* lag, i.e. the way the player can *observe* the lag (and BTW, lag happens to be most visible exactly for player's own actions). On the negative side, with Client-Side Prediction there is a risk that the authoritative picture of the Game World (coming later as an update from the Server-Side) will look different from our Client-Side Prediction – and in this case the so-called "reconciliation" has to be used, to make Client-Side consistent with Server-Side, which is not that easy (to complicate things further, a good reconciliation process has to do things smoothly, avoiding any "sudden jumps").

To implement Client-Side Prediction, the Game Logic Module will need to simulate the Game World (including physics and maybe some AI, but not rendering). In quite a few cases, simulation within the Game Logic Module will mimic certain parts of the Server-Side logic (after all, Client-Side Prediction is nothing more than an attempt to "predict" what the Server-Side would decide anyway); on the other hand, care needs to be taken not to make significant decisions (such as "the opponent is dead") on the Client-Side, as reversing such significant decisions during reconciliation will look way too counterintuitive to the player.

Simulating physics means that in certain cases our Game Logic Module may need to use some meshes (though not textures). On the other hand, its meshes should be as simple as possible, and they usually will be the same kind of meshes used by the Server-Side — the ones with characters represented by cubes or hexagonal prisms (see Vol. I's chapter on Communications for a discussion of the Server-Side State and its meshes), and *not* high-poly meshes used for rendering purposes.

When it happens, simulation Game Loop within Game Logic Module will be separate from the rendering Game Loop in Animation&Rendering Module.

This means that meshes SHOULD NOT be shared between the Game Logic Module and the Animation&Rendering Module, which further facilitates very clean separation between the two.

Game Logic Module: Game Loop

If your Game Logic Module is running Client-Side Prediction (or any other kind of simulation), it is likely running a Game Loop. When it happens, this simulation Game Loop within the Game Logic Module will be *a separate one* from the rendering Game Loop in the Animation&Rendering Module. In addition, as noted below, most of the time you'll want to run Game Loop within your Animation&Rendering Module at the refresh rate of the monitor; on the other hand, updates from the Server-Side will come to your Game Logic Module on network ticks. It means that you'll face a question: whether your simulation Game Loop (the one within Game Logic Module) needs to run at the speed of the network ticks, or at the refresh rate of your monitor.

As it often happens in real-world, there is no once-and-for-all answer to this question (="you'll need to figure it out yourself").

What is obvious is that we *will* need to synchronize two simulations running with two different and unrelated frequencies ("network tick rate" and "monitor refresh rate"),[163] or more generally – with different time steps (as at least in theory we can use variable time steps for any of the Game Loops). As as frequencies/time-steps are not related – we'll likely need to perform some kind of interpolation (see, for example, [Fiedler], and also Client-Side Interpolation in Vol. I's chapter on Communication) regardless of our choice between two frequencies for our Game Logic Module; the only question is whether this synchronization+interpolation will happen (a) on the boundary between messages-coming-from-Server-Side and our Game Logic Module, or (b) on the boundary between the Game Logic Module and the Animation&Rendering Module.

---

163   BTW, if V-Sync is involved, even typical frequencies of 20fps for "network ticks" and 60fps for "monitor refresh rate" *are* unrelated <sad-face />.

Game Logic Module: Keeping it Cross-Platform

Last but not least about the Game Logic Module. If your game has even the slightest chance of becoming cross-platform, you MUST keep your Game Logic Module truly platform-independent. While all the other Client-Side Modules MAY be platform-specific (and separation between Modules along the lines described above facilitates platform-specific development when/if it becomes necessary), you should make all effort possible to keep your Game Logic the same across all your platforms. The reason has already been discussed in detail, and it is mostly about Game Logic being the most-frequently-changing part of your Client-Side code; usually, it changes so often that you won't be able to keep several code-bases-supposedly-doing-the-same-thing reasonably in sync.

You should make all effort possible to keep your Game Logic the same across all your platforms.

Animation&Rendering Module

The Animation&Rendering Module is more or less similar to the rendering part of your usual single-player game engine. Usually, at the heart of the Animation&Rendering Module, there is a more or less traditional Game Loop. How to implement it depends on the further specifics of your Client-Side architecture; we'll discuss implementing Game Loop for (Re)Actor-fest Client in the *Animation&Rendering (Re)Actor and Game Loop* section below.

If your game is a 3D one, then in the diagram above,

> *It is the Animations&Rendering Module that keeps and cares about all the renderable meshes, textures, and animations;*[164] *as a Big Fat Rule of Thumb™, nobody else in the system (including the Game Logic Module) should know about them.*

Going against this advice and sharing renderable meshes with the rest of the Client would kill our clean separation between Modules (and, unless we want to incur the heavy penalties of inter-thread-synchronization, would prevent us from running each Module in its own thread). As, in addition to causing problems, such sharing is usually

---

164 As noted above, even if the Game Logic (Re)Actor uses some meshes, they are usually ultra-low-poly Server-Side meshes rather than renderable Client-Side meshes.

unnecessary—keeping renderable meshes to the Animation&Rendering Module becomes a no-brainer.

Communications Module

Another Module that is all-important for your MOG is the Communications Module. The idea here is to keep all the communications-related logic in one place. This may include very different things, from plain socket handling to such things as connect/reconnect logic,[165] connection quality monitoring, encryption if applicable,[166] etc., etc. Also, implementations of higher-level concepts such as generic publisher/subscriber, generic state synchronization, etc. (see Vol. I's chapter on Communications for further details) also generally belong here.

For most of (if not "all") the platforms, the code of the Communications Module can (and SHOULD) be kept the same.

For most of (if not "all") the platforms, the code of Client-Side Communications Module can (and SHOULD) be kept the same. In particular, all the input packets (and/or messages over TCP stream) are usually considered input events for our Module (and therefore, can be logged, etc.).

To send packets/messages by the Communications Module, it will normally use some kind of socket-related API (for C/C++, it is going to be something like Berkeley Sockets' *send()/sendto()*). On the other hand, I suggest that you use your own (however thin) wrapper around these functions to account for platforms with some peculiar ideas about sockets (*errno* vs *WSAGetLastError()* anyone?).

Sound Module

The Sound Module handles, well, sound. In a certain sense, it is somewhat similar to the Animation&Rendering Module, but for audio. If your sound is at least somewhat non-trivial, the interface of the Sound Module will usually need to be implemented via some kind of "Logic-to-Sound API."

This "Logic-to-Sound" API should be conceptually similar to the "Logic-to-Graphics API"; in particular, similar to the Logic-to-Graph-

---

165 BTW, handling connect/reconnect will be most likely needed even for UDP.

166 And more often than not, you DO need encryption — at least to prevent proxy bots; more on it in Vol. VIII's chapter on Bot Fighting.

ics API, the Logic-to-Sound API should be Game-World-oriented; in other words, commands going from the Game Logic Module to the Sound Module should be expressed in terms of "play this sound at such-and-such a volume coming from such-and-such a position within the Game World" (with all the further translation happening within the Sound Module, and potentially in a system-dependent way).

Relation to MVC

When looking at Fig 6.1, we can observe rather obvious similarities to a Model-View-Controller model (the one that is very-widely-used at least in the non-gamedev world). In the case of Fig 6.1, the Game World State of the Game Logic Module acts as an MVC Model, and the Animation&Rendering Module and the Sound Module act as MVC Views. As for the MVC Controller, the situation is a bit less obvious: for MOGs it is the Server (not shown in Fig 6.1) that acts as an MVC Controller.

If looking at it this way, we can see that player inputs go to the Server (MVC Controller), then changes caused by player inputs return to the MVC Model (Game World State maintained by Game Logic Module), which in turn notifies the Animation&Rendering Module (MVC View) so it can show whatever is necessary to the player.

If we take into account Client-Side Prediction (see the *Game Logic Module: Client-Side Prediction and Simulation* section above), we will notice that we have two different data flows (and, as a result, two separate MVC Controllers within our system). The first flow goes as before: via the Server as an MVC Controller, to the MVC Model within the Game Logic Module, and to the Animation&Rendering Module as an MVC View. The second flow goes a shorter way: directly to the Game Logic Module (which acts as a second MVC Controller in this case), then to the same MVC Model within the Game Logic Module, and to the Animation&Rendering Module as an MVC View.

Not that this relation to MVC is really important *per se*, but for those-coming-from-traditional-business-programming where MVC is ubiquitous, it may clarify a thing or two.

MVC

Model–view–controller (MVC) is a software architectural pattern for implementing user interfaces. It divides a given software application into three interconnected parts, so as to separate internal representations of information from the ways that information is presented to or accepted from the user.

—**Wikipedia**

The idea of the diagram in Fig 6.1 can be seen as having 90% of your existing "3D engine as you know it" with all the 3D stuff as a basis for the "Animation&Rendering Module."

Differences from Classical 3D Single-Player Game

If you're coming from single-player game development, you may find the whole diagram in Fig 6.1 confusing; this may be especially true for the inter-relation between the Game Logic Module and the Animation&Rendering Module.

From the point of view of single-player gamedev who wants to make an MOG out of her single-player game, the idea of the diagram in Fig 6.1 can be seen as having 90% of your existing "3D engine as you know it" with all the 3D stuff as a basis for the "Animation&Rendering Module." You will just need to separate Game Logic (the one that makes decisions about gameplay, including physics if applicable — and it needs to be moved to the Server-Side anyway[167]), and UI logic (which will go into the Game Logic Module), and that's pretty much it.

As discussed above, all the mesh-related stuff should stay *exclusively* within the Animation&Rendering Module; i.e., even Game Logic Module should know absolutely nothing about renderable meshes, vertexes, and textures.

Interaction Examples in 3D World: Single-Player vs MOG

By now, we have more-or-less defined our Modules; however, as usual, without concrete examples there is lots of potential for misunderstandings. To be a bit more specific, let's consider how a few typical (and not-so-trivial) interaction examples can be implemented over the modular Client-Side Architecture shown in Fig 6.1.

Let's consider an MMOFPS example when Player A presses a button to shoot with a laser gun, and Game Logic needs to perform a raycast to see where it hits and what else happens.

MMOFPS Interaction Example (Shooting)

First, let's consider an MMOFPS example when Player A presses a button to shoot with a laser gun, and Game Logic needs to perform a raycast to see where it hits and what else happens. In single-player, all this usually happens within a 3D engine. For an MOG, it is more complicated:

---

167 Also, it may be partially duplicated to the Game Logic Module too for Client-Side Prediction purposes.

- Step 1. Button press goes to our Authoritative Server as a message.

- Step 2. Authoritative Server receives the message, performs a raycast, and calculates where the shot hits (all within its Server-Side ultra-low-poly Game World).

- Step 3. Our Authoritative Server expresses "where it hits" in terms such as "Player B got hit right between his eyes"[168] and sends it as a message to the Client (actually, to all the Clients, usually as a (kinda-)Broadcast message; see Vol. I's chapter on Communications for details).

- Step 4. This message is received by the Game Logic Module and translated into the commands of Logic-to-Graphics API (still without meshes and triangles; for example, "show laser ray from my gun to the point right-between-the-eyes-of-Player B," and "show laser hit right between the eyes of Player B"), which commands are sent (as messages) to the Animation&Rendering Module.

- Step 5. The Animation&Rendering Module can finally render the whole thing.[169]

While the process is rather involved, most of the steps are inherently inevitable for an MOG; the only thing that you could theoretically save compared to the procedure described above is merging step 4 and step 5 (by merging the Game Logic Module and the Animation&Rendering Module), but I advise against it as such merging would introduce too much coupling, which will haunt you in the long run. Doing such different things as parsing network messages and rendering within one tightly coupled module is rarely a good idea, and it becomes even worse if there is a chance that you may ever want to use some other Animation&Rendering Module (for example, a newer one, or the one optimized for a different platform).

---

168 This is generally preferable to player-unrelated "laser hit at (X,Y,Z)" in case of Client-Side Prediction; of course, in practice you'll use some coordinates, but the point is that it is usually better to use player-related coordinates rather than absolute Game World coordinates — as in case of discrepancies it is more important to see that it was the *player* who got hit, and not a bullet hit in a technically correct place but outside of the player.

169 I won't try to teach you how to render things; TBH, if you're from the 3D development side, you already know much more about it than me.

MMORPG Interaction Example (Ragdoll)

In a typical MMORPG example, when an NPC is hit for the 93rd time and dies as a result, ragdoll physics is activated. And in a typical single-player game, once again the whole thing is usually performed within a 3D engine. And once again, for an MOG, the whole thing will inevitably be more complicated:

♦ Step 1. Button press (the one that will cause NPC death) goes to the Authoritative Server.

♦ Step 2. Server checks attack radius, calculates chances to hit, finds that the hit is successful, decreases health, and finds that NPC is dead.

♦ Step 3. Server performs ragdoll simulation in the Server-Side 3D world. However, the Server doesn't need to send it to the Clients as a complete vertex-based animation. Instead, the Server can usually send to the Client only a movement of "center of gravity" of NPC in question (calculated as a result of 3D simulation). This movement of "center of gravity" is sent to the Client (either as a single message with the whole animation or as a series of messages with the "current position" of each).

   ▪ As an interesting side effect: as the whole thing is quite simple, there may be no real need to calculate the whole limb movement on the Server-Side, and it may suffice to calculate just a simple parabolic movement of the "center of gravity," which MAY save you quite a bit of resources (both CPU and memory-wise) on the Server-Side.

♦ Step 4. Game Logic Module receives the message that describes "center of gravity" movement and translates it into Logic-to-Graphics commands. This doesn't necessarily need to be trivial, and may include simulating the whole ragdoll movement (including limbs movement) while keeping center-of-mass movement as prescribed by the Server; OTOH, in most cases, simulation of the limbs' movement during ragdoll will be delegated to the Animation&Rendering Module.

♦ Step 5. The Animation&Rendering Module gets the movement, performs ragdoll simulation if necessary (="if simulation wasn't performed by Game Logic Module"), and then renders the whole thing.

In a typical MMORPG example, when an NPC is hit for the 93rd time and dies as a result, ragdoll physics is activated.

Ragdoll physics

In computer physics engines, ragdoll physics is a type of procedural animation that is often used as a replacement for traditional static death animations in video games and animated films.

—Wikipedia

- It should be noted that when using this approach to ragdoll animation, fine details of the ragdoll simulation MAY be slightly different on the Server-Side and the Client-Side; however, if there are any discrepancies, Client-Side simulation will eventually correct coordinates so that "center of gravity" is adjusted to the position sent by the Server, and this is the only thing that really matters for an RPG. For a typical RPG, nobody really cares about exact movement of limbs during ragdoll; what is really important is where the NPC eventually landed — here or over the edge of the cliff — and this is guaranteed to be the same for all the Clients, as they're synchronized to the final position of the "center of gravity," which comes from the Server Side.

UI Interaction Example

In a typical RPG game, a very common task is to show object properties when the object is currently under cursor. For the diagram in Fig 6.1 above, it can be implemented as follows:

What is the object ID of the object under the cursor?

♦ Step 1. Game Logic Module sends a request to the Animation&Rendering Module: "what is the object ID of the object under the cursor?" ("…in the crosshair?" etc.)

♦ Step 2. Animation&Rendering Module processes this (trivial) request and returns object ID back.

♦ Step 3. Game Logic Module finds object properties by ID, translates them into text, and instructs Animation&Rendering Module to display object properties in HUD.

While this may look like overkill, the overhead (both in terms of the developer's time and CPU time) is negligible, and the good old rule of "the more cleanly separated parts you have, the easy is further development is" will more than compensate for the complexities of such separation in the long run.

Pre-alloc Everything

Another difference of an MOG over classical single-player games is related to the concept of "pre-allocating all the resources you will need" for an upcoming "game event."

It is usually better to allocate *all* the resources needed for a certain "game event" than to risk that your player's PC runs out of resources right in the middle of the "game event."

The point here is that in a multi-player game, it is usually better to allocate *all* the resources needed for a certain "game event" than to risk that your player's PC runs out of resources right in the middle of the "game event." For example: if your game is a 2D MOBA, it is usually better to pre-allocate *all* the resources you will need (such as bitmaps, memory, GPU resources, etc., etc.) than to risk that you face resource-allocation-failure in the middle of a MOBA match. Of course, we still need to check for resource allocation failures, but if we allocate (and therefore detect allocation failure) *before* the MOBA match starts, we can often prevent the player from entering that-MOBA-match-that-he's-going-to-lose-anyway-because-of-a-lack-of-resources (!).

Contrast it with single-player games, where resource allocation failure, however unpleasant, doesn't usually cause effects such as "losing that ranking match the player was preparing for a month," or "losing that artifact that is worth $10K on eBay."

Some notes about pre-allocating everything in advance:

♦ In a real-world game, such a "preallocate everything" approach has been seen to reduce the number of Client-Side in-game failures (IIRC, the reduction was over 2x). Measuring (and attributing) improvement in player satisfaction is much more difficult, but I am sure that there was quite a bit of it; in short, I am sure that *pre-allocation did make business sense.*

♦ I do *not* mean that we should load *all* the bitmaps, etc. into RAM; rather, we should have enough bitmap objects of sufficient size to load everything-we-might-need-to-have-loaded-at-the-same-time. The rationale for it is simple: from what I've seen in the real world, the chances of the file becoming suddenly unavailable are extremely slim; however, the chances of the player running a hundred other programs that already ate all the resources so there is nothing left for our Client is much *much* higher (and BTW, doesn't depend on how-powerful-modern-machines-are).[170]

▪ More generally, we MUST be *very* careful about all the resources we're using, and bring them *to the absolute minimum.* On the other hand, after we have reached this *absolute minimum* – it is usually fine to pre-allocate it.

---

170 As computers become more powerful, programs become more resource-hungry. As a result, in a shared environment such as the Client-Side Device, the problem of insufficient resources isn't going to go away any time soon (if ever).

♦ Sure, the "preallocate everything" approach inevitably means that our Client effectively becomes a "resource hog"; however, if we'd make a player survey asking what they'd prefer, have the gameplay *guaranteed* while consuming more resources, or risking that during the all-important-match we won't be able to render the enemy, we can be pretty sure of the answer (and it is the player who we should make happy).

Progressive Downloading

One technique that is not 100% MOG-specific, but is still pretty new (and relies on the Internet being always-available) is so-called "progressive downloading" (also known as the "file streaming" flavor of the "cloud gaming" buzzword).

> NB: unlike "pixel streaming" or "video streaming"-based "cloud gaming," "progressive downloading" can be made viable with existing technologies (more on the difference between the two in Vol. VII's chapter on Preparing for Deployment).

The idea behind Progressive Downloading is to download a small part of the game first, and to proceed with downloading of parts-likely-to-become-necessary, as the game goes on. Business-wise, Progressive Downloading aims to achieve "instant gameplay," which in turn can become a competitive advantage (whether it is worth the trouble is a different story that needs to be decided at the GDD level; see Vol. I's chapter on GDD).

Progressive Downloading aims to achieve "instant gameplay," which in turn can become a competitive advantage.

Architecture-wise, Progressive Downloading consists of two big parts:

♦ Making your Client work with only *some* of the necessary files (for example, your Client may start running with just a few meshes/textures/etc., as long as it knows *for sure* that for the upcoming "game event" it won't need anything else).

> NB: for "seamless worlds," it might be difficult to achieve, but for games with discrete "game events" (such as MOBAs with different maps, etc.) it can be done for sure.

▪ For the time being, this "work with only *some* of necessary files" is the only thing that you need to think about.

♦ Online download while playing. Implementing concurrent download that doesn't interfere with gameplay can be a non-trivial exercise, but, fortunately, we don't need to deal with it right now; this topic will be discussed in Vol. V's chapter on Client Updates.

(RE)ACTOR-FEST CLIENT-SIDE ARCHITECTURE

While the diagram in Fig 6.1 above is pretty good, it has one obvious drawback: it is too generic to be practical without further clarifications and specifications.

First, let's note that there are many different ways to implement Game Client while staying within very generic boundaries of Fig 6.1, and (Re)Actor-fest Client-Side Architecture, which we'll discuss in this section is just one of these ways. Still,

> *(Re)Actor-fest is the way I recommend architecting your Game Client (and I have Good Reasons™ to do it).*

On the other hand, if you *really* hate (Re)Actors, it is not the end of the world; doing things in a different manner will most likely cost you (especially when you start deploying your game into the real world), but, well, it *might* still be workable. However, even if you do NOT like (Re)Actors, make sure to follow generic advice with respect to generic architecture in Fig 6.1 above; it applies pretty much across the board regardless of using or not using (Re)Actors.

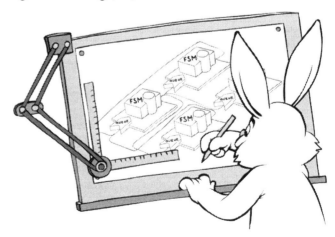

(Re)Actor-fest Client Architecture

> Do not communicate by sharing memory;
> instead, share memory by communicating.
>
> — *Effective Go*

Fig. 6.3 shows a diagram that depicts one of the possible implementations of the Client under (Re)Actor-fest architecture.

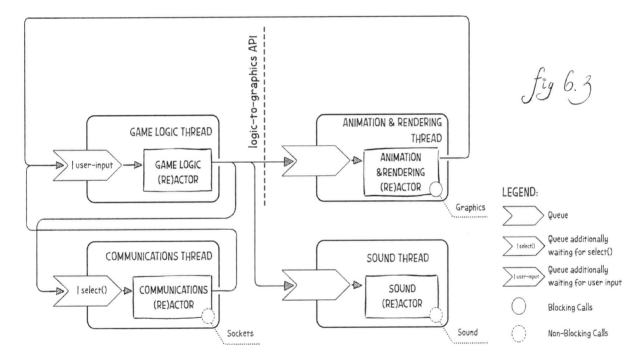

Of course, as noted above, such a (Re)Actor-fest Client Architecture is (by far) not the only possible one, and even not the most popular one, but this architecture and its variations have been seen to produce games with extremely good reliability, extremely good decoupling between parts, and very good maintainability (for a very detailed discussion of the benefits coming from (Re)Actors, see Chapter 5). On the minus side, I can list only a bit of development overhead due to the message-based exchange mechanism, but from my experience it is more than covered with better separation between different parts (supported by very-well-defined interfaces), which leads to development speedups

even in the medium run (and is even more important in the long run to avoid spaghetti code). Throw in the ability of "replay-based regression testing" and "replay-based post-factum debugging" in production, and it becomes a solution for lots of real-world problems.

> *In short, I'm a very strong advocate of this architecture (and its variations described below), and don't know of any practical cases when it is not the best thing you can do.*[171] *While it might look over-engineered on first glance, it pays off in the medium and long run.*

On the minus side, I can list only a bit of development overhead due to the message-based exchange mechanism, but from my experience it is more than covered with better separation between different parts and very-well-defined interfaces, which leads to development speedups even in the medium run.

I hope that the diagram in Fig 6.3 is more or less self-explanatory, but I will elaborate on a few points that might not be too obvious:

♦ Ideally, each of the (Re)Actors is a mostly-non-blocking deterministic (Re)Actor as described in Chapter 5.

▪ While being deterministic is not a strict requirement, implementing your (Re)Actors this way will make your debugging and post-factum analysis much, *much* easier.

♦ All the exchange between different (Re)Actors is message-based. Here "message" is a close cousin of a network packet; in other words, it is just a bunch of bytes formatted according to some convention between sending and receiving thread.

▪ There can be different ways of passing these messages around; examples include explicit message posting, or implementing non-blocking RPC calls instead. While the idea behind the (Re)Actor-fest architecture won't change because of the way the messages are posted, convenience and development time may change quite significantly. Still, while important, this is only an implementation detail (with a detailed discussion on the ways to implement it available in Chapter 5).

Still, while important, this is only an implementation detail.

▪ For the messages exchanged between the Game Logic Thread and the Animation&Rendering Thread, the message format/API should be along the lines of "Logic-to-Graphics API," as

---

171 As usual, "I don't know of any cases" doesn't provide guarantees of any kind, and your mileage may vary. However, before throwing this architecture away and doing something-that-you-like-better, please make sure to read the rest of this section, where quite a few of the potential concerns will be addressed.

described in the *Generic Client Architecture* section above. In short: it should be all about logical changes in our Game World, along the lines of "NPC ID=ZZZ is currently moving along the path defined by the set of points {(X0,Y0),(X-1,Y1),...} with speed V" (with coordinates being game-world coordinates, not screen coordinates), or "Player at seat #N is in the process of showing his cards to the opponents."[172]

♦ Each thread has an associated Queue, which is able to accept messages, and provides a way to wait on it as long as the Queue is empty.

▪ Queues of Game Logic Thread and Communications Thread are rather unusual. They're waiting not only for usual inter-thread messages, but also for some other stuff (namely input messages for the Game Logic Thread, and network packets for the Communications Thread). More on implementing such Queues in Vol. V's chapter on C++.

• In most cases, at least one of these two particular queues will be supported by your platform.

• For those platforms that don't support such queues, you can always use your-usual-inter-thread-queue (once again, the specifics will be discussed in Vol. V), and have an additional thread that will get user input data (or call *select()*), and then feed the data into your-usual-inter-thread-queue as yet another message. This will create a strict functional equivalent of the two specific Queues mentioned above.[173]

♦ The architecture is "Shared-Nothing." It means that there is no data shared between threads, and the *only* way to exchange data between threads is via Queues and messages-passed-via-the-Queues.

▪ Shared-Nothing means no thread-synchronization problems (there is no need for mutexes, critical sections, etc., etc. outside of your Queues). This is a Really Good Thing™, as trying to handle thread synchronization with any frequently changeable logic (such as the one within at least

The architecture is "Shared-Nothing." It means that there is no data shared between threads, and the only way to exchange data between threads is via Queues and messages-passed-via-the-Queues.

---

172 Yes, I know I've repeated it quite a few times already, but it is *that* important that I prefer to risk being bashed for annoying you rather than being pounded by somebody who didn't notice it and got into trouble.

173 Performance-wise, having an additional thread is not ideal, but TBH, on the Client-Side the difference will be very small.

some of the (Re)Actors) inevitably leads to lots and lots of problems (see, for example, [Hare]).

▪ Of course, while we're implementing Queues, we still need to use inter-thread synchronization, but this is a one-time effort and has been done many times before, so it is not likely to cause too much trouble; see Vol. V's chapter on C++ for further details on implementing Queues in C++.

▪ As a nice side effect, Shared-Nothing architecture means that whenever you want it, you can deploy your threads into different processes without changing any code within your (Re)Actors (merely by switching to an inter-process implementation of the Queue). In particular, it can make answering very annoying questions such as "who's guilty for the memory corruption" much easier; I've also seen it handy to deal with stuff such as Vista-and-later process permissions (which may need to be different for different parts for your Client).

▪ One possible exception to this Shared-Nothing approach is related to using "(Re)Actor-with-Extractors" (see the *Parallelizing Client-Side (Re)Actors* section for relevant discussion).

♦ All the threads on the diagram (with one possible exception being the Animation&Rendering Thread; see below) are NOT tight-looped, and unless there is something in their respective Queue, they just wait on the Queue until some kind of message comes in (or *select()* file descriptor becomes "ready").

▪ While "no-tight-loops" is not a strict requirement for the Client-Side, wasting CPU cycles in tight loops without a Really Good Reason™ is rarely a good idea, and might hurt quite a few of your players (those with weaker rigs).

▪ The Animation&Rendering Thread is a potentially special case, and MAY use tight loop; see the *Animation&Rendering (Re)Actor and Game Loop* section below for further discussion.

♦ To handle delayed actions (at least in other-than-Animation&Rendering Thread), Queues should allow (Re)Actors to post some kind of "timer message" to their own thread. In practice, it is not a problem to implement it.

(Re)Actor Specifics

Fig. 6.3 shows four different (Re)Actors; they directly correspond to Modules we've discussed above, so *all* the discussions in the *Generic Client Architecture* section about Modules apply to respective (Re)Actors too. Still, there are a few notes that are specific to (Re)Actors:

♦ It is possible to run several (Re)Actors within the same thread (and without changing the (Re)Actor code at all).

- Still, even if running two or more (Re)Actors from the same thread, I *strongly* suggest keeping the (Re)Actors separate. It is both cleaner and leaves you more flexibility in case one core proves to be insufficient. In other words: even if you decide to run two (Re)Actors from the same thread, do yourself a favor and keep the (Re)Actors separate; some months down the road, you'll be very happy that you kept your interfaces clean and different Modules nicely decoupled.[174]

Even if you decide to run two (Re)Actors from the same thread, do yourself a favor and keep the (Re)Actors separate.

- As a rule of thumb, (Re)Actors that are using blocking calls SHOULD NOT run within the same thread as the other (Re)Actors.

- See the *Variations* section below for further examples.

If by any chance one of your (Re)Actors becomes *that* CPU-consuming that one single CPU core won't cope with it, in most cases it can be addressed without giving up the goodies of the (Re)Actor-based system; see the *Scaling (Re)Actor-fest Architecture* section below.

Now, let's discuss (Re)Actor-related specifics on a per-(Re)Actor basis.

Animation&Rendering (Re)Actor and Game Loop

As noted above, our Animation&Rendering Module (and therefore our Animation&Rendering (Re)Actor) will usually contain some kind of Game Loop.

---

174   Or you'll regret that you didn't do it <sad-face />.

And as described in Chapter 5, Game Loops usually looks as follows:

```
//Example 6.1 (taken from Chapter 5)
while(true) {
  process_input();
  update();
  render();
}
```

All the decision-making is moved at least to the Game Logic (Re)Actor, with most of the decisions actually being made by our authoritative server.

When applying this classical Game Loop to our Animation&Rendering (Re)Actor, we can move an inner part of this loop into the *react()* function of our Animation&Rendering (Re)Actor, taking into account the following considerations:

♦ Just like the inner part of the game loop above, *react()* consists of calls to *process_input()*, *update()*, and *render()*.

- *process_input()* function, instead of processing user input, processes instructions coming from the Game Logic (Re)Actor.

- *update()* function updates only the 3D-scene-to-be-rendered, and not the Game Logic's representation of the Client-Side Game World; all the decision-making is moved at least to the Game Logic (Re)Actor, with most of the decisions actually being made by our Authoritative Server.

- *render()* works pretty much the same as it worked for a single-player game.

♦ After the Animation&Rendering (Re)Actor's *react()* function returns, the Animation&Rendering Thread may deal with timestep as it sees fit (in particular, *any* classical timestep mentioned in Chapter 5 can be implemented).

♦ Then, the Animation&Rendering Thread goes back to the very beginning (back to checking if there is anything in its Queue), which completes the infinite Game Loop.

As noted in Chapter 5, all the common variations of Game Loop (and timesteps) can be implemented via (Re)Actors if you want it.

On the other hand, *if* you're not a 3D guru yet, I would suggest to start with running your Animation&Rendering (Re)Actor at the fixed rate, which is equal to your monitor's refresh rate and is synchronized with V-Sync (more on V-Sync in Vol. V's chapter on Graphics 101). While it is certainly not the only way to shoe this horse, it is known to provide decent results without too much complications.

As discussed in [Nystrom] and [Fiedler] (and briefly mentioned in Chapter 5), for single-player games it is common to run your rendering at one fixed rate, and your physics timestep at a different fixed rate. This is exactly what will happen in our case (though, for us, network timestep will usually be *slower* than frame rate). For a more detailed discussion on timesteps and their implications, see [Fiedler] and [Nystrom].

One further variation of the Animation&Rendering (Re)Actor that is not commonly mentioned in the context of games is a simple event-driven thing that you would use for your usual Windows programming; in this case, delays in Game Loop under Windows can be implemented via *WM_TIMER*,[175] and 2D drawing via something like BitBlt(). While usually woefully inadequate for any serious frames-per-second-oriented games, it has been seen to work very well for social- and casino-like ones (and interestingly, it still maps to our (Re)Actor-fest very well).

Overall, IMO one of the best things about our Client-Side (Re)Actor-fest Architecture shown in Fig 6.3 is that the architecture as a whole doesn't really depend on timestep choices made for rendering; you can even make different timestep choices for different platforms and still keep the rest of your code (beyond Animation&Rendering Thread) intact.

Our (Re)Actor-fest Architecture as a whole doesn't really depend on timestep choices for rendering; you can even make different timestep choices for different platforms and still keep the rest of your code intact.

Communications (Re)Actor and Blocking/Non-Blocking Sockets

The diagram in Fig. 6.3 shows an implementation of the Communications (Re)Actor that uses non-blocking socket calls. For the Client-Side, it is perfectly feasible to keep the code of the Communications (Re)Actor exactly the same, but to deploy it in a different manner, simulating non-blocking sockets via two additional threads (one to handle reading and another to handle writing), with these additional threads communicating with the main Communications Thread via Queues (using the Communication Thread's existing Queue, and one new Queue per new thread).[176] BTW, it illustrates an all-important point: with (Re)Actors properly separated

---

175   Yes, this does work, despite being likely to cause ROFLMAO syndrome for any game developer familiar with serious game engines.

176   For the Server-Side, however, these extra threads are not advisable due to the performance overhead. See Vol. III's chapter on Server-Side Architecture for more discussion on, well, Server-Side architectures.

from infrastructure code, we can easily have non-blocking (Re)Actors while serving them with blocking sockets; more generally, the (Re)Actor being non-blocking doesn't necessarily imply using only non-blocking calls at the system level.

One more thing to keep in mind with regard to blocking/non-blocking Berkeley sockets is that the *getaddrinfo()* function,[177] which is commonly used for DNS resolution, is usually blocking, with many platforms having no non-blocking counterpart. However, for the Client-Side, in most cases it is a non-issue unless you decide to run your Communications (Re)Actor within the same thread as your Game Logic (Re)Actor. In the latter case, calling a function with a potential to block for minutes can easily freeze not only your game updates (which is inevitable anyway in the case of connectivity problems), but also game UI (which is not acceptable, regardless of network connectivity). To avoid this effect, you can always introduce yet another thread (with its own Queue) with the only thing for this thread to do being to call *getaddrinfo()* when requested, and to send results back as a message when the call is completed.[178]

Other (Re)Actors

While not shown in Fig 6.3, there can be other (Re)Actors within your Client. Usually, such (Re)Actors may run in their own threads, but other variations are also possible.

One practical example of such a Client-Side (Re)Actor (which was implemented in practice) was "update (Re)Actor," which handled an online download of DLC (a.k.a. "progressive download") while making sure that the gameplay delays were within acceptable margins (see more on Client updates in general and updates-while-playing in particular in Vol. V).

In general, *any* kind of entity that performs mostly-independent tasks on the Client-Side can be implemented as an additional

---

177   As well as an older *gethostbyname()* function.

178   Alternatively, it is also possible to create a new thread for each *getaddrinfo()* call (with such a thread performing *getaddrinfo()*, reporting the result back, and terminating). This thread-per-request solution would work, but would be a departure from (Re)Actor-fest architecture, and it can lead to creating too many threads in some fringe scenarios, so I usually prefer to keep a specialized thread intended for *getaddrinfo()*, staying within a pure (Re)Actor-fest model.

(Re)Actor. While I don't know of practical examples of extra Client-Side (Re)Actors other than "update (Re)Actor" as described above, it doesn't mean that your specific game won't allow/require any, so make sure to keep your eyes open.

On (Re)Actors and Latencies

One question that often arises when discussing queue-based architectures and fast-paced games is related to latencies introduced by those additional Queues. The question is usually asked along the lines of "Hey, why have all those queues if we need absolutely the best possible latency?"

Why have all those queues if we need absolutely the best possible latency?

Sure, we do want to show the data to the user as fast as possible. However, my experience shows that[179] with queues, we're talking about additional latency[180] of the order of single-digit microseconds. This number can probably be lowered further into a sub-microsecond range by using less trivial non-blocking queues, but this I'm not 100% sure of because of the relatively expensive allocations usually involved in marshalling/unmarshalling; for further details on implementing high-performance low-latency queues in C++, please refer to Vol. V's chapter on C++. As this single-digit-microsecond delay is at least three orders of magnitude smaller than an inter-frame delay of 1/60 sec or so, I am arguing that nobody will ever notice the difference, even for single-player or LAN-based games; for Internet-based MOGs the absolute best we can hope for is delays in the order of dozens of milliseconds, which makes this additional microsecond-level latency even less relevant.

On the other hand, *if* our thread/(Re)Actor is overloaded (so the queue starts to grow), it *can* cause additional latencies, and very easily too. However, this type of delay is not specific to (Re)Actors; if we'd implement the same thing with a large mutex on the same state as the (Re)Actor, we'd only make the situation worse.[181]

---

179   Assuming that the thread is not busy doing something else, and that there are available CPU cores to run it.

180   Introduced by a reasonably well-designed message marshalling/unmarshalling + reasonably well-designed inter-process single-reader queue.

181   Strictly speaking, there *may* be situations when splitting one big (Re)Actor state into two smaller sub-states, each sub-state protected with its own mutex, can help to reduce the bottleneck; however, splitting one big (Re)Actor into two independent Shared-Nothing (Re)Actors along the same lines will help even more. Moreover, in all-real-world-cases-I've-seen, whenever a split of (Re)Actor state was possible, splitting to two (Re)Actors was also possible (and was universally the only viable option, at least for app-level code).

To summarize:

♦   I don't think the additional single-digit-microsecond delay due to Queues can possibly have any effect that is visible to the end-user.[182]

♦   If the (Re)Actor gets overloaded, it *can* cause lots of latencies. This effectively means that the (Re)Actor's state needs to be split, and the best way to do so is usually via splitting the overloaded (Re)Actor into two Shared-Nothing (Re)Actors.

(Re)Actor-fest Variations

Fig 6.3 shows each of the (Re)Actors running within its own thread. On the other hand, as noted above, each of the (Re)Actors can be run in the same thread as the Game Logic (Re)Actor. In the extreme case, it results in a system where all the (Re)Actors are running within a single thread, and a corresponding diagram is shown in Fig 6.4:

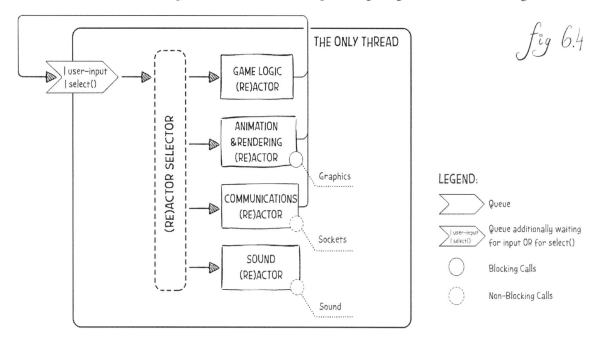

Each and every one of the (Re)Actors in Fig 6.4 is *exactly* the same as a corresponding (Re)Actor in Fig 6.3; moreover, logically these two diagrams are exactly equivalent (and the "recording" made within

---

182   That is, if queues are implemented properly, *and* if there are idle cores most of the time.

the architecture on Fig. 6.3, can be "replayed" on architecture shown in Fig. 6.4 and vice versa). The only difference in Fig 6.4 is that we're using the same thread (and the same Queue) to run all our (Re)Actors. (Re)Actor Selector here is just a very dumb piece of code, which looks at the destination-(Re)Actor field (set by whoever-sent-the-event) and routes the event accordingly.

This kind of threading could be quite practical, for example, for a casino or a social game. However, not all the platforms allow you to wait for the *select()* in the main graphics loop, so you may need to resort to another variation, shown in Fig 6.5:

Logically, Fig 6.3 and 6.4 are exactly equivalent.

fig 6.5

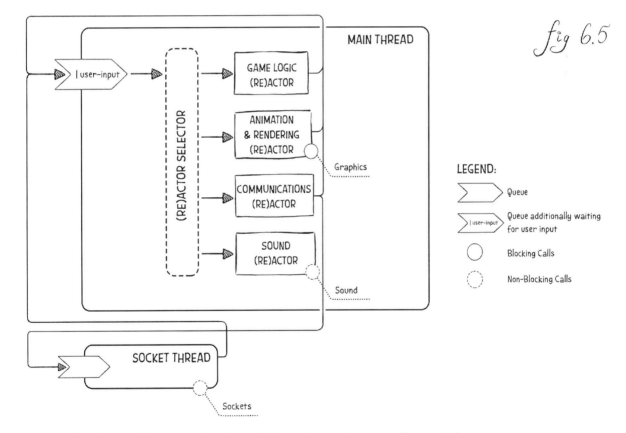

Here Sockets Thread is very simple and doesn't contain any substantial logic; all it does is merely push whatever-it-got-from-Queue to the socket, and pushing whatever-it-got-from-socket to the Queue of the Main Thread; all the actual processing will be performed there, within the Communications (Re)Actor.

An architecture shown in Fig 6.5 (and its variation with Communications (Re)Actor moved to Socket Thread) will work for a social or
casino-like game on Windows, with Main Thread in Fig 6.5 being your
usual Windows UI thread, and all the communications with it going via
Windows messages.[183]

On the other end of the spectrum of different Client-Side variations
of the (Re)Actor-fest architecture lie such heavyweight implementations as the one shown in Fig 6.6:

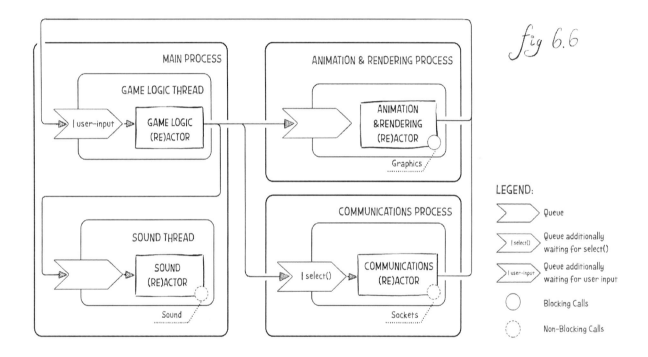

Here, the Animation&Rendering (Re)Actor and the Communications
(Re)Actor run within their own processes. This approach might be useful
during testing (in general, you may even run (Re)Actors on different developers' computers if you prefer this kind of interactive debugging); in particular,
I observed it to be useful to answer a pretty nasty and fingerpointing-risky

---

183   While on Windows it is easy to create both "|select()" and "|user-input" queues, creating one
single queue that will be both "|select()" and "|user-input" simultaneously is not that trivial — which
makes configurations such as the one in Fig. 6.5 quite a logical choice. For more details on implementing
these and other queues, see Vol. V's chapter on C++.

question of "which of the (Re)Actors is responsible for memory corruption." However, for production, it is better to avoid such configurations, in particular as inter-process interfaces may help bot writers.

Overall, the whole point of the variations shown above is not to demonstrate *all* the viable configurations, but rather to demonstrate that:

a) There are lots of different configurations that we can build using exactly the same (Re)Actors.

b) That with (Re)Actors, configurations can be changed as desired at later stages of development and deployment (among other things, it means that our current choice is not *that* important, as it can be easily changed later).

c) That different configurations can be useful in practice.

There are lots of different configurations that we can build using exactly the same (Re)Actors.

From a practical perspective (and keeping (b) in mind), what really matters is that

> *As long as you're keeping your development model (Re)Actor-based, you can deploy it any way you like without any changes to your (Re)Actors.*

In practice, this property has been observed as providing quite significant help in the long run. While this effect has significantly more benefits on the Server-Side,[184] it has been seen to aid Client-Side development too; for example, different configurations for different platforms do provide quite a bit of help. In addition, situation-dependent configurations have been observed to help a bit during testing (including in-production testing).

On Code Bases for Different Platforms

As mentioned above, you SHOULD keep your Game Logic (Re)Actor the same for all the platforms (i.e., as a single code base). Otherwise, given the frequent changes to Game Logic, all-but-one of your code bases will most likely start to fall behind, to the point of being completely useless.

---

184   Which will be discussed in Vol. III's chapter on Server-Side Architecture.

But what about those other (Re)Actors? Do you need to keep them as a single code base? The answer here is quite straightforward:

While the (Re)Actor-fest Architecture shown above allows you to make non-Game-Logic (Re)Actors platform-specific, it is usually better to keep them the same — as long as possible.

For example, if your game is graphics-intensive, there can be really good reasons to have your Animation&Rendering (Re)Actor different for different platforms; for example, you may want to use DirectX on some platforms, and OpenGL on other platforms (granted, it will be quite a chunk of work to implement both, but at least it is possible with the architecture above, and under certain circumstances it MAY become a potentially viable business choice, especially as the OpenGL version and DirectX version can be developed in parallel).

On the other hand, chances that you will need the platform-specific Communications (Re)Actor are much lower.[185] Even if you're writing in C/C++, usable implementations of Berkeley sockets exist on most (if not on all) platforms of interest. Moreover, the behavior of sockets on different platforms is quite close from the game developer's point of view (at least with regard to those things that we are able to affect).

As a result, while such choices are obviously specific to your specific game, statistically there should be more Animation&Rendering (Re)Actors than Communications (Re)Actors — and, in a heavy cross-platform development, using the same Communications (Re)Actors across different platforms can save you a bit of work too.

Scaling (Re)Actor-fest Architecture on the Client

If your existing 3D engine is too CPU-hungry to fit on one single CPU core, and either your Game Logic Thread or your Animation&Rendering Thread become overloaded, you might need to introduce an additional thread or five into the picture. This is especially likely for the Animation&Rendering Thread/(Re)Actor if your game uses serious 3D graphics. While complexities of the threading model for serious 3D

If your game is graphics-intensive, there can be really good reasons to have your Animation&Rendering (Re)Actor different for different platforms.

If your existing 3D engine is too CPU-hungry to fit on one single CPU core, you might need to introduce an additional thread or five into the picture.

---

185   I don't count conditional inclusion of *WSAStartup()*, and wrapping error handling as being really platform-specific.

graphics engines are well beyond the scope of this book, I will try to provide a few hints for those who're just starting to explore that direction.

As usual with multithreading, if you're not careful, things can easily become ugly, so in this case:

> ### First, take another look if you have some gross inefficiencies in your code.

It is usually *much* better to remove these inefficiencies rather than trying to parallelize. For example, if you're performing an $O(N^2)$ sort over a 10K-element collection, it is *much* better to switch to some $O(N*logN)$ algorithm rather than try getting more and more cores working on unnecessary stuff. On the other hand, I am not talking about 20% optimization here — such relatively minor gains are unlikely to prevent the need to parallelize in the long run; however, any potential improvement of 2x and more (and in the big-O example above, the difference was in thousands) does have the chance to save you from multi-threading.

If all the algorithms are already within reason, we're more or less bound to parallelize. However, when doing it, we need to keep in mind that *any* additional threads *add* to the overhead; in other words, most often *throughput_of_your_algo_on_N_cores* will be *less* than *N*throughput_of_the_same_algo_on_single_core*. In the real world, I've even seen implementations where *throughput_on_N_cores* was *less* than throughput on a single core(!). And it wasn't a part of the exercise in malicious coding; it just so happened that thread-switching overhead was too large compared to the useful tasks (which happened to be very small).

This leads us to one all-important observation:

> ### To be efficient, parallelism SHOULD be coarse-grained.

As noted in [Li, Ding and Shen], a context switch can easily cost as much as 100K-1M CPU clock cycles. It means that if you will try to perform a calculation worth 1K CPU cycles in a separate thread, overheads are likely to be *huge*. Even if your calculation-to-be-performed-in-a-separate-thread is worth 1M CPU cycles, you still may feel the overhead (though TBH, for real-world tasks and computing 1M-cycle chunks, it is quite unlikely). *NB: for GPGPU programming things are very different and outside the scope of our current discussion.*

Parallelizing Client-Side (Re)Actors

In some cases, you may be able to split your CPU-hungry (Re)Actors into several less CPU-hungry ones, and limit interaction between them to messages.

By this point, you have already established that you DO need some kind of parallelization. As discussed in Chapter 5, there are several different options to scale/parallelize your (Re)Actors. Let's see how these options apply to our Client-Side (Re)Actor-fest architecture.

Option A. System-on-a-Thread. In some cases, you may be able to split your CPU-hungry (Re)Actors into several less CPU-hungry ones, and limit interaction between them to messages. In fact, we've already done a bit of it in our (Re)Actor-fest architecture as shown in Fig. 6.3, separating our Client into several (Re)Actors (which can run in separate threads, and which can be executed on different CPU cores). In practice, for the Client-Side this is not that likely to work beyond what is shown in Fig. 6.3, due to an observation that most of our CPU-hungry calculations will need access to pretty much the same Game World States[186] (and copying major parts of the game state via messages-sent-on-each-frame can be rather inefficient).

Option A1. System-on-a-Thread with Mirrored State. This option involves keeping not one, but two copies of the Game State. While one copy is being modified, another is being rendered. In the 3D world, this approach is well-known and was used in particular in Halo engine by Bungie ([Chen, Silvennoinen and Tatarchuk], [Tatarchuk]). Essentially, with Mirrored State (and one mirror), we can use up to two cores (one core working with one copy of Game State, and another core working with another copy).

Option A2. System-on-a-Thread with (Re)Actor-with-Extractors. In a further improvement over State Mirroring, we can use the (Re)Actor-with-Extractors, which was discussed in Chapter 5. It is the architecture that was used in the Destiny engine by Bungie [Tatarchuk]. The idea here is to keep Game State as read-only for some time once per tick, allowing several "extractors" to work in parallel on the Game State and to extract whatever information they need. Then, after the extraction phase is completed, threads that ran extractors may proceed

---

186   Usually, the Server-Side State for Game Logic (Re)Actor, and usually-the-even-larger Client-Side State for the Animation&Rendering (Re)Actor.

with their work (NOT touching the Game State anymore), while the main thread may proceed with modifying the Game State. For a more detailed description of this approach, see Chapter 5.

One Good Thing™ about *all* the System-on-a-Thread approaches (with or without State Mirroring or (Re)Actor-with-Extractors) is that System-on-a-Thread is inherently coarse-grained. Good for us, for performance, and (arguably) for the environment.[187] Oh, and System-on-a-Thread keeps all the (Re)Actor-based goodies mentioned in Chapter 5, too (including but not limited to "replay testing" and production post-factum analysis).

Option B. Offloading. A subtly different option is to "offload" some of the processing to a different "calculating" thread, with this "calculating" thread being just as all the other threads in Fig 6.3; in other words, it should have an input queue and a (Re)Actor within. This directly corresponds to "Task-Based Multithreading" described in [Fosner].

The idea here is that whenever our main (Re)Actor thread (the one running one of those CPU-hungry (Re)Actors) has something to calculate, it can send a message to the "calculating" thread, "offloading" the calculation there. And after doing its (very isolated) part of the job, a.k.a. "task," the calculating thread may report back to whichever-thread-has-requested-its-services.

In a sense, "offloading" can be seen as an incarnation of System-on-a-Thread, with the (Re)Actor dedicated for use for offloaded calculations, and effectively having no state (as all the data necessary to perform calculations is passed to it via the messages).

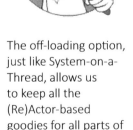

The way "task offloading" is done depends on the implementation specifics. In some implementations, we MAY use data-driven pipelines (similar to those described in [Fosner]) to enable dynamic task balancing, which allows us to optimize core utilization on different platforms. For serious calculations, we can even use a library such as HPX (for a discussion on HPX, see Chapter 5). However, from what I've seen, implementations based on simple non-blocking RPC calls (using one of the ways described in Chapter 5) are usually more popular.

The off-loading option, just like System-on-a-Thread, allows us to keep all the (Re)Actor-based goodies for all parts of your Client.

---

187   Well, those CPU cycles burned by unnecessary overheads do contribute to unnecessary energy consumption, and to global warming too. If our game burns 10 unnecessary watts per Client, and we have a million simultaneous players, we're talking about 10 MW of unnecessary power consumed, which roughly corresponds to 65'000 metric tons of CO_2 per year, or to yearly emissions from 14'000 cars [EPA].

The offloading option, just like System-on-a-Thread, allows us to keep all the (Re)Actor-based goodies for all parts of your Client. However, coarse-grain parallelism, while encouraged by offloading, tends to be a bit worse than with System-on-a-Thread. On the plus side (compared to System-on-a-Thread), offloading tends to allow for simpler (or better) load balancing between different CPU cores.

Option C. Traditional Multi-Threading. The third option we have is to throw away all the "replay debugging" and post-factum analysis benefits for one specific too-heavy-for-one-single-core (Re)Actor, and to implement *this single (Re)Actor* using multi-thread in-whatever-way-you-like (for example, using traditional inter-thread synchronization stuff such as mutexes, semaphores, or Dijkstra forbid, memory fences etc., etc.).

This is a very dangerous option, and my advice is to avoid it for new development as long as possible. However, if you have an existing 3D rendering code base that already works, well, this option may become rather viable.

If you want to use Option C for your Game Logic, think twice, and then twice more.

Also, if you want to use Option C for your Game Logic, think twice, and then think twice more. As Game Logic is the one that changes a damn lot, with Option C this has all the chance of becoming unmanageable (see, for example, [Hare]). It is *that* bad that if your Game Logic needs to run over multiple cores, and without ability to use System-on-Thread or Offloading, I would seriously think whether the Game Logic requirements are feasible to implement (and maintain) at all.

In any case, if going the way of Option C, your multi-threaded Option-C Module SHOULD look as a normal (Re)Actor from the outside. In other words, multi-threaded implementation SHOULD be just this: an implementation detail of this particular kinda-(Re)Actor, and SHOULD NOT affect the rest of your code. This is useful for two reasons. First, it decouples things and creates a clean, well-defined interface; and second, it allows you to change implementation of this specific kinda-(Re)Actor (or add another one — for example, for a different platform) without rewriting the whole Client.

With this in mind, it should be noted that even in case you're forced to use Option C, you should be losing (Re)Actor-related benefits (such as "replay testing" and post-factum analysis) only for that specific kinda-(Re)Actor, which uses Option C; all the other (Re)Actors will still remain deterministic (and therefore, easily testable) <phew />.

Summary of (Re)Actor-fest Architecture on the Client-Side

Let's summarize our findings about the (Re)Actor-fest Architecture for the Client-Side, as shown in Fig 6.3 (as well as variations from Fig 6.4-Fig.6.6). Overall, it is quite an interesting beast.

First, let's note that while it does ensure a clean separation between parts ((Re)Actors in our case), it tends to go against (IMNSHO rather outdated) API separation techniques of COM-like components. The key difference between (Re)Actors and COM-like components is that COM-like components are essentially based on blocking RPC, so after you called a COM-like RPC, you're blocked until you get a reply. With (Re)Actor-based architecture from Fig 6.3-6.6, even if you're requesting something from another (Re)Actor, you still can (and usually should) process events coming while you're waiting for the reply. For further details, see the detailed discussion on non-blocking processing in Chapter 5.

From my experience, while developers usually see this kind of (Re)Actor-based programming as somewhat more cumbersome than usual procedure-call-based programming, after trying it most agree that it is beneficial in the medium to long run. As advantages of our (Re)Actor-fest architecture, we can list:

Most developers agree that (Re)Actor-based programming is beneficial in the medium to long run.

♦ Very good separation between different modules ((Re)Actors). With the only way of communication being via message-oriented APIs, (Re)Actors tend to be isolated very nicely (sometimes even *a bit too nicely*, but this is just another way to see the "somewhat more cumbersome" negative mentioned above).

  ▪ Each of the modules is very much self-contained, which helps to both (a) separate the work of different teams and (b) organize testing.

♦ Goodies such as "replay-based regression testing" and post-factum analysis. See Chapter 5 for details.

♦ Very good performance. The point here is that with a (Re)Actor-fest architecture, context switches are kept to the absolute minimum, and each thread is working without any unnecessary pauses (and without any overhead associated with these pauses) as long as it has something to do.

- On the flip side, the (Re)Actor-fest doesn't provide inherent capabilities to scale each (Re)Actor beyond one single core; however, scaling a (Re)Actor-fest to a limited number of CPUs (like scaling to 4-6 cores), even for a single Game World, is perfectly achievable — in particular, along the lines of the (Re)Actor-with-Extractors described above.

PROGRAMMING LANGUAGE FOR GAME CLIENT

All those diagrams and discussions are grand and dandy, but we still need something-to-write-our-Game-Client-with. In other words: we need to choose a programming language for our Client.

Some of you may ask "what is the Big Fat Hairy Difference™ between choosing a programming language for the Game Client, and choosing a programming language for any other programming project?" Fortunately or not, in addition to all the usual language holy wars,[188] there are some subtle considerations that make programming language choices for the Game Client different; we'll discuss some of these peculiarities below.

---

188 Between strongly typed and weakly typed programming languages, between compiled and scripted ones, and between imperative and functional languages, just to name a few.

One Language for Programmers, Another for Game Designers (MMORPG/MMOFPS etc.)

First, let's note that in quite a few (or maybe even "most") development environments, there is a practice of separating game designers from programmers (see the *On Developers, Game Designers, and Artists* section above). This practice is pretty much universal for MMORPG/ MMOFPS, but can be applicable to other genres too (especially if your game includes levels and/or quests that are designed by hand).

In such cases, it is quite common to use two different programming languages for the Game Client. One of these programming languages is (roughly) intended for programmers, and another is (even more roughly) intended for game designers. For example, Unreal Engine 4 positions C++ for developers, and Blueprint language for game designers. Amazon Lumberyard[189] goes further and supports three(!) different languages: C++, Lua, and Flowgraph. And just for the record (and as our micro-overview of popular game engines won't be complete without it), it is worth noting that while Unity 3D doesn't insist on using different languages for programmers and designers (so you can use C# as a scripting language), pretty often you'll still use C# for programming and UnityScript/JavaScript for designer-written scripts.

It is quite common to have two different programming languages for the Game Client: one (roughly) intended for programmers, and another (even more roughly) intended for game designers.

While having two programming languages within your Game Client is not fatal, it has some important ramifications. In particular, you need to keep in mind that whenever you have two programming languages, the cheater (bot writer/reverse engineer/etc.) will usually attack you through the weakest one. In other words, if you're using both C++ and JavaScript within your Client, it is JavaScript that will be reverse-engineered (that is, if JavaScript allows us to manipulate those things that are needed for the bot writer — but usually it does).

Let's also note that at least in theory, as long as you're using (Re)Actor-fest architecture, you MAY use different programming languages for different (Re)Actors (and quite easily too). However, doing so would mean having more-than-one language for *programmers* (and in addition to any programming language(s) for designers), and this has its drawbacks for the Game Client (in particular, it would further

---

189   Inheriting it from CryEngine, which Lumberyard is based on.

facilitate reverse-engineering attacks, and also additional overall complexity is rarely worth doing it this way — on the Client-Side, that is). On the other hand, *if* your languages on the Client-Side and Server-Side are different, *and* you need to re-use some Server-Side code on the Client-Side (for example, because you're using Client-Side Prediction), your best option MIGHT be to do exactly this; more discussion on it in the *On Consistency Between Client-Side and Server-Side Languages* section below.

A Word on CUDA and OpenCL

I wanna show you something. Look, Timon. Go on, look.
Look out to the horizon, past the trees, over the grasslands.
Everything the light touches...
[sharply] belongs to someone else!

— Timon's mom, *Lion King 1½*

GPGPU

General-purpose computing on graphics processing units (GPGPU, rarely GPGP or GP²U) is the use of a graphics processing unit (GPU), which typically handles computation only for computer graphics, to perform computation in applications traditionally handled by the central processing unit.

—Wikipedia

If your game is an inherently 3D one, it normally means that you have a really powerful GPU at your disposal on each and every Client. As a result, it can be tempting to try using this GPU as a GPGPU, utilizing all this computing power for your purposes (for example, for physics simulation or for AI).[190]

Unfortunately, on the Client-Side, players' GPU is usually already pushed to its limits (and often beyond), even when all it does is rendering. This means that if you try using GPU for other purposes, you're likely to sacrifice fps, and this is usually a Big No-No™ in 3D game development. This is pretty much why while in theory CUDA (and/or OpenCL) is a great thing to use on the Game Client, it is rarely used for games in practice. In short, don't hold your breath about using available GPU power as a GPGPU; not because this power is insufficient (it is not), but because it is already used.

On the other hand, let's keep in mind that the question of using CUDA/OpenCL on the Server-Side is different; we'll discuss it a bit in Vol. III's chapter on Server-Side Architecture.

---

190   And yes, I've heard this argument quite a bit — at least from indie developers.

Different Languages Provide Different Protection from Bot Writers

As was discussed in Vol. I's chapter on Cheating, as soon as your multiplayer game becomes successful, it becomes a target for cheaters. A short recap. For an MMORPG, you can be pretty sure that there will be people writing bots; these bots will "grind" through your RPG, will collect some goodies you're giving for this "grinding," and will sell these goodies, say, on eBay. And as soon as there is a financial incentive for cheating (and selling on eBay certainly creates one), cheaters will be abundant. For other genres, such as MMOFPS or casino multiplayer games, bots (including aimbots, wallhacks/maphacks, grinding bots, etc.) tend to be at least as popular.

And if cheaters are abundant, *and* cheaters have significant advantage over non-cheating players, your whole game becomes at risk (in the ultimate case, your non-cheating players will become so frustrated that your game is abandoned). As a result, you will find yourself in an unpleasant, but necessary, role of policeman who needs to pursue cheaters so that regular non-cheating players are not at a significant disadvantage.

The problem of bot fighting is extremely common and well-known for MOGs; unfortunately, there is no "once and for all" solution. In the *best* case,[191] bot fighting is a two-way battle, with bot writers inventing a way around the MOG defenses, and then MOG developers striking back with a new defense against the most recent attack; rinse and repeat.

We'll discuss bot fighting in detail in Vol. VIII's chapter on (not too surprisingly) Bot Fighting, but, at the moment, we won't delve into the details of this process; all we need at this point is two observations:

- For bot fighting, every bit of protection counts (this can be seen as a direct consequence of the battle going back and forth between bot writers and MOG developers).
- Reverse engineering is a cornerstone of bot writing.

From these, we can easily deduce that

> *For the Game Client, the more resilient the programming language against reverse engineering, the better.*

Game Bot

is a type of AI expert system software that plays a video game in the place of a human.

—**Wikipedia**

Bot fighting is always a two-way battle, with bot writers inventing a way around the MOG defenses, and then MOG developers striking back with a new defense against the most recent attack; rinse and repeat.

---

191 I.e. *after* you did your homework, and did spend time to architecture and implement your game properly.

Resilience to Reverse-Engineering of Different Programming Languages

Now let's take a look at different programming languages and their resilience to reverse engineering. In this regard, most practical programming languages can be divided into three broad categories.

Compiled Languages[192]

Whether as a developer you like compiled languages or not, they clearly provide the best protection from reverse engineering.

From all the popular compiled languages, C++ tends to produce the binary code that is the most difficult-to-reverse-engineer.

And from all the popular compiled languages, C/C++ languages tend to produce the binary code, which is the most difficult-to-reverse-engineer (that is, provided you have turned all the optimizations on, disabled debug info, are not using DLLs, and are doing a dozen of other things; more on it in Vol. VIII's chapter on Bot Fighting). If you have ever tried to debug at assembly level your "release" (or "-O3") C/C++ code, compiled with a modern compiler, you've certainly had a hard time understanding what is going on there; this is even with you being the author of the source code! C/C++ compilers are using tons of optimizations that make machine code less readable; while these optimizations were not intended to obfuscate, in practice they're doing a wonderful job in this regard just as a very-nice-for-our-purposes side effect <smile />. Throw in the heavy use of allocations typical for C/C++,[193] and you've produced a binary code that is among the most obfuscated out there.

One additional phenomenon that helps C++ code to be rather-difficult-to-reverse-engineer is that even a single-line change in C++ source code can easily lead to a vastly different executable; this is especially true when the change is made within an *inline*'d function, or within a C++ *template*.

BTW, if we try to compare C with C++ from the point of view of reverse engineering, we'll see that while C++ kinda-aids attackers with RTTI and virtual method table pointers, C++ templates tend

---

192 Strictly speaking, protection is not related to programming language as such, but applies to each compiler/interpreter separately. Still, for the sake of keeping things readable, let's use the term "language" for our purposes (with an understanding that there is compiled-to-native-code Java, which is different from compiled-to-bytecode-Java, etc.).

193 In practice, it may be a good idea to throw in a randomized allocator, so that memory locations differ from one run to another; ideally, it should be done *in addition* to any ASLR in use. More on it in Vol. VIII's chapter on Bot Fighting.

to make the life of the attackers *much* more difficult. In other words – anti-reverse-engineering-wise it is all about *how* we program in C++, and we'll briefly discuss it in Vol. IV's chapter of Things to Keep in Mind, and in *much* more detail – in Vol. VIII's chapter on Bot Fighting.

Compiled languages other than C/C++ tend to provide good protection too, though the following observation usually stands. The less development time has been spent on the compiler, the less crazy optimizations are usually present in generated binary code, and therefore the more readable and more easy-to-reverse-engineer the binary code is. In other words: it usually makes sense to pick the compiler that has a looong development history behind it.

One last thing to mention with respect to compiled languages is that while C++ usually provides the best protection from reverse engineering from the programming language side,

> ### *Using C++ doesn't mean that your code won't be cracked.*

Anything that resides on the Client-Side *is* crackable by definition; the only question is *how long* it will take attackers to do it (and there is a big practical difference between being cracked in two days and being cracked in two years, especially as we can usually release updates every few weeks). Therefore, making all the other precautions against bot writers, mentioned in Vol. IV's chapter on Things to Keep in Mind (and discussed at length in Vol. VIII's chapter on Bot Writing), is still necessary, even if you're using C++. Moreover, even if you do everything that I've mentioned in this book to defend yourself from bot writers, most likely there still will be bot writers able to reverse engineer your Client (or at least to simulate user behavior on top of it); however, with bots, it is not the mere fact of their existence, but their numbers that count, so every bit of additional protection does make a practical difference (for further discussion on it, see Vol. I's chapter on Cheating).

Languages That Compile to Bytecode

Compiling to bytecode (with the runtime interpreting this bytecode in some kind of VM) is generally a very useful and neat technique.

High-level bytecode tends to be reverse engineered *much* more easily than a compiled binary code.

However, as a Big Fat Rule of Thumb™, high-level bytecode tends to be reverse engineered *much* more easily than a compiled binary code (that is, *unless* you're using a special closed-source anti-reverse-engineering-VM with opcodes frequently changing and other obfuscation techniques in use). There are many reasons for (well-known) bytecode being *less* resilient to reverse engineering than machine code; for example, function boundaries tend to be better visible within the bytecode than with compiled languages, and in general bytecode operations tend to have higher-level semantics than "bare" assembler commands, which makes reverse engineering substantially easier. In addition, some bytecode-executing VMs (notably JVM) have to verify the bytecode, which makes it much more formalized and restricted (which in turn limits options available for obfuscation).

It should be noted that JIT compilers don't help to protect from the reverse engineering; however, so-called Ahead-of-Time (AOT) Compilers, such as GCJ[194] or Excelsior JET, which compile source code into binary instructions, do help against reverse engineering (effectively moving your language from a "Byte-Compiled" into "kinda-Binary-Compiled" category). What really matters here is what you ship with your Client: machine binary code or bytecode; if you're shipping machine code, you're better than if you're shipping byte code. This also means that those "compile to .exe" techniques that essentially produce .exe consisting of JVM and bytecode (such as *jar2exe*), do not provide much protection. Moreover, the "bytecode encryption" feature in such .exes is still a Security-by-Obscurity feature,[195] and (while being useful to scare away some novice bot writers) won't withstand an attack by a dedicated attacker (in short: as decryption key needs to be within the .exe, it can be extracted, and as soon as it is extracted, all the protection falls apart; moreover, with Java custom class loaders, it is usually easy to find the point where "decryption" is performed).

JIT

Just-in-Time (JIT) compilation, also known as dynamic translation, is compilation done during execution of a program – at run time –rather than prior to execution.

—**Wikipedia**

One pretty-weird-but-seemingly-working trick that *MAY* help to improve the resilience of bytecode to reverse engineering is to recompile your byte code into C++ source code, and then further compile this generated C++ source code using a regular C++ compiler. This trick is *so* important in practice that it is officially supported by Unity

194 Unfortunately, discontinued in 2016.

195 In fact, "scrambling" would be a fairer name for it.

via their *IL2CPP* compiler (though not because of anti-cheating). After applying *IL2CPP*, you can expect resilience-to-bot-writers, which is substantially better than that of the bytecode-given-to-the-Client, but is still substantially worse than "native" C++ code (especially if we use all the hardening trickery that we'll discuss in Vol. VIII's chapter on Bot Fighting). Oh, and while we're at it: when going this way, make sure that you are compiling/linking your *libil2cpp statically*(!) — it is really important for making a whole bunch of attacks more difficult.

Scripting/Interpreted Languages

From a reverse engineering point of view, scripting/interpreted programming languages provide almost-zero protection. The attacker essentially has your source code, and understanding what you've meant there is only a matter of (quite a little) time. Ironically, the better your scripting code is (i.e., the easier it is to read and maintain your code), the easier it becomes for the attacker to reverse engineer.

From a reverse engineering point of view, scripting/interpreted programming languages provide almost-zero protection.

Obfuscators, while improving protection a little against a casual observer, are no match against dedicated attackers. <Bummer />. As a rule of thumb, if you have interpreted language in your Client, you will assume that whatever interpreted code is there will be reverse engineered, and modified to the bot writer's taste. Oh, and don't think that "we will sign/encrypt the interpreted code, so we won't need to worry about somebody modifying it"— exactly like with "bytecode encryption," it doesn't really provide more than a scrambling (and to make things worse, this scrambling can be broken at one single point).

On asm.js, wasm, and Emscripten

While all the discussion above about scripting or bytecode-compiled languages being easily crackable stands firmly in general, fortunately for us there is one very interesting (and very practical) exception.

If we take C++ code, we can use *Emscripten* to compile our C++ into a special kind of kinda-assembler (such as *asm.js* or *wasm*). Then, this *asm.js*/*wasm* can be run within some kind of browser's VM (JS VM for *asm.js*, and special *wasm* VM for *wasm*), effectively allowing us to run C++ within the browser (!).

As a rule of thumb, while *asm.js* is able to run on pretty much any reasonably-modern browser, without special optimizations (those taking into account the type information) it will be excruatingly slow (and running *wasm* on a browser without special support for it, is outright impossible). On the other hand, as of mid-2017, *all* the major browsers (Chrome, Firefox, Safari, and Edge) *do* support *both* optimized-asm.js *and* wasm; *wasm* performance on the major browsers is usually within 2x from "native" C++ performance on the same platform [Zakai] [Krause].[196]

As the icing on our current anti-reverse-engineering cake — with *emscripten*, we can get obfuscation, which is even a bit better than that of the traditional bytecode-compiled programming languages (the difference compared to other bytecode-compiled programming languages is that *asm.js* and *wasm* code tends to be more low-level than them, *and* also enjoys most of the ~~obfuscations~~ optimizations provided by a very mature Clang compiler). On the other hand, *asm.js/wasm* resilience to reverse engineering is still lacking compared to real C++-compiled-to-machine-code.

With emscripten, we can get obfuscation, which is even a bit better than that of the traditional bytecode-compiled programming languages

A few notes in this regard:

♦ While *emscripten* is pretty good for obfuscation purposes, I have no idea how other compilers (such as Cheerp) are doing in this regard. At least some versions of Cheerp were mapping C++ structures into JS structures – and this practice, while potentially having other virtues, leads to a *reduction* in anti-reverse-engineering capabilities <sad-face />. On the other hand – this field is evolving very rapidly, so it is always better to double-check it yourself.[197]

♦ Compared to native binary-code C++, *asm.js/wasm* will still provide substantially worse obscurity[198] — in particular, due to:

■ Obvious function boundaries.

---

196 Surprisingly, *asm.js* performance is in the same ballpark, but (a) *asm.js* suffers from significantly longer startup times (due to parsing), and (b) performance tends to vary more significantly between different browsers.

197 At least you should look at the generated code and try to understand what it does; if all you can see is about as low-level as your usual *asm* — it should be okay.

198 While being orders-of-magnitude better than any other JS.

- Less (if any) asm operator rearranging happening within LLVM *asm.js/wasm* back ends compared to x64/ARM/... back-ends.
- Simpler-to-identify interactions with the rest of the system.
  - In particular, *malloc()* is often mapped directly to the JS-level APIs. *NB: this can be mitigated by using our own sub-allocator on top of malloc() calls (in a sense – using JS-level malloc() instead of mmap()/ VirtualAllocEx()), but it requires quite a bit of work.*

♦ If you encrypt your traffic (which you SHOULD, at least to deter proxy bots; see the discussion in Vol. VIII's chapter on Bot Fighting), you will face a dilemma: either use browser-provided TLS (which will weaken your obfuscation greatly), or try compiling your TLS library with *emscripten* (which has been reported to work, but make sure to test its performance while a computation-heavy public crypto is executed when establishing TLS connection; also make sure to restrict your TLS to only one protocol, and to disable as much unnecessary stuff as you can during compile-time, to reduce the footprint of your TLS library).

♦ All the usual C++ obfuscation measures (such as using STL, templates, inlines, and custom allocators, and avoiding globals and externalized functions) still apply; more on "how-to-make-your-C++-code-more-difficult-to-reverse-engineer" will be discussed in Vol. IV's chapter on Things to Keep in Mind (and in Vol. VIII's chapter on Bot Fighting).

Summary

Our observations about the resilience of various programming languages to reverse engineering can be summarized in the following Table 6.1 (all numbers are subjective and not to scale; they're provided merely to give an extremely rough idea of some relations between different programming languages anti-reverse-engineering-wise):

Programming Language	Resilience to Reverse Engineering (Subjective Guesstimate); on a scale from 1 to 10 (with 10 being "not able to break at all")
C++ with heavy use of templates, lots of force-inlines, no RTTI, and limited virtual functions (Release/-O3, no debug info, no DLLs)	8 🙂
C (Release/-O3, no debug info, no DLLs)	7.5 🙂
C++ with limited templates, with lots of virtual functions, and with RTTI	7 🙂
C++ compiled to *asm.js/wasm* (Emscripten)	6 🙂
C# recompiled into C++ using *IL2CPP*	5-6 😐
Java or C# (compiled to binary with an AOT compiler)	5–6 😐
Java or C# (compiled to byte code, obfuscated, and scrambled)	4 😠
Java or C# (compiled to byte code)	3 😠
JavaScript (obfuscated)	2 😡
JavaScript	1 😡

Note that in this table, I'm not trying to compare any of the other advantages/disadvantages of the listed programming languages; the point of this exercise is to emphasize *one single* aspect that is very important for game Clients, but which is overlooked way too often — and it is resilience to reverse engineering. Also, just to avoid any doubts, I'm not trying to say that you MUST program your Client in C++ no-matter-what; what you should do, however, is take this table into account when choosing programming language for your Game Client.

Language Availability for Client-Side Platforms

The next very important consideration when choosing a programming language is "whether it will run on all the platforms you need." While this requirement is very common not only for games, it still has certain specifics in the game-development world. In particular, the list of the Client platforms is not that usual.

In Table 6.2 below, I've tried to gather as much information as possible about the support of different programming languages for different Client-Side game platforms.

Will it run on all the platforms I need?

	Windows	Mac OS X	PS4[199]	XBox One [199]	iOS [199]	Android	Browser
C/C++[200]	Native ☺	Native ☺	Native ☺	Native ☺	Native ☺	Native[201] ☺	Emscripten ☺
Objective C	GNUStep 😐	Native ☺	No 😠	No 😠	Native ☺	No 😠	No 😠
Java	Oracle, can be distributed with the game ☺	Oracle, can be distributed with the game ☺	Not really[202] 😠	Not really[202] 😠	Oracle MAF 😐	Native, ☺ Oracle MAF 😐	Oracle, usually requires separate install, 😠 or GWT 😐
C#	Native ☺	Mono ☺	Monogame 😐	Native ☺	Xamarin 😐	Xamarin 😐	JSIL, 😐 Bridge.NET, 😐 or IL2CPP+Em-scripten 😐
HTML 5/ Java Script[203]	Native 😐	Native 😐	Native 😐	Native 😐	Native 😐	Native 😐	Native 😐

199 Not accounting for jail-broken devices.

200 Caution required to achieve cross-platform code; see Vol. IV's chapter on Things to Keep in Mind.

201 Via NDK.

202 Well, you can write your own JVM and push it there, but…

203 Compatibility and capabilities are still rather poor.

Note that Flash, once the king of browser-based development, has already gone from "pretty much dead" into the "officially pronounced dead" category, so it is not even in the table above (~="I certainly don't recommend it for any kind of new development").

On Garbage Collection

These days, most programming languages out there are garbage collected (with C/C++ and Rust being the only exceptions I know of). I don't want to start yet another flame-infested debate of "whether garbage collection is a Good Thing™ or a Bad Thing™", and will just mention that IMO, the pros and cons of GC'd programming languages vs non-GC'd programming languages are well-balanced. In particular, GC pros include:

♦ Shorter learning curve (to start programming, that is)

♦ Faster development (as a rule of thumb)

♦ No syntactic memory leaks (though see below on semantic memory leaks)

♦ No dreaded memory corruptions that are next-to-impossible to find

However, these pros are quite well-balanced with GC cons (that's even if you're NOT using *finalize() / Finalize() / __del__()* etc., which you *really* shouldn't; see a bit of discussion on it in Chapter 5):

♦ Significantly higher risk of "semantic memory leaks," especially by those-programmers-who-skipped-the-long-learning-curve.

▪ For a discussion on the differences between "syntactic" and "semantic" garbage and memory leaks, see, for example, [Wikipedia, Garbage (computer science)].

▪ Sure, these leaks are avoidable, but avoiding them requires the effort that is IMNSHO comparable to the effort to avoid syntactic memory leaks in C/C++ (after all, placing = *null* all over the code is not that much different from placing *delete*s in more or less the same places).

▪ In practice, it often leads to an outright memory bloat (*OpenHAB* or *Eclipse* anyone?)

♦ Stop-the-World problem:

- As we'll see below, avoiding it for fast-paced games will often require very significant efforts.

While most of the items are self-explanatory, the Stop-the-World one is unusual enough (and is very important especially in the context of fast-paced games) to discuss in more detail.

On "Stop-the-World" Problem

One thing that plays quite a significant role when choosing a programming language for a really fast-paced game (think first-person shooter) is garbage collection and the "stop the world" (STW) problem.

Very briefly: if your programming language is garbage-collected, you may face an unpleasant problem when programming your fast-paced game. The problem is that *most* garbage collector implementations out there are using so-called "stop-the-world" garbage collection, at least at some points in their life cycle.

In short: from time to time, the whole runtime needs to be stopped for some milliseconds (or seconds(!)) to collect your garbage (or at least to *start or stop* collecting your garbage). This, in turn, causes "micro-freezes" to your game code. If your game is not too fast, you won't even notice these micro-freezes (your threads will be just silently suspended for the duration of STW, and the only thing that changes is wall-clock time). However, if we're talking about MMOFPS, or a fast-paced MMORPG, STW can easily kill player experience unless it is kept in check.

From time to time, the whole runtime needs to be stopped for some milliseconds to collect your garbage, which causes "micro-freezes" for your game.

First, let's note that

> *Some production-level Garbage Collectors can easily cause STW pauses as long as single-digit-seconds(!!)*

That-long-STW-times were a Really Big Problem™ fifteen years ago; these days, quite a few runtimes (especially those for Java and C#) do provide garbage collectors that are trying to push *most* of the GC work into the other threads, therefore reducing (though usually not completely eliminating) time for stopping the world. By mid-2010s, *the best* of the "stock" garbage collectors[204] for Java/C# improved STW pauses to about 50-150ms[205] (see, for example, [Shaya], and [Warren, Measuring the impact of the .NET Garbage Collector]+[Warren, Measuring the impact of the .NET Garbage Collector - An Update]). BTW, as a rule of thumb, the smaller the STW pauses are, the less GC performance is (and a 20% performance penalty in exchange for smaller STW is not unheard of).

It should be noted that it *is* possible to reduce STW times further. In particular, Zing Java runtime (see [AZUL Systems]) claims to reduce STW times down to single-digit *milliseconds*. Still, while I agree that their approach (as discussed in [Tene, Iyengar and Wolf]) *seems* to be solid, I didn't try their implementation, so I cannot vouch for it. Even more importantly, they support only Linux (and as they *seem* to require a kernel-level driver to work(!), cross-platform support doesn't look likely), so for our current Client-Side discussion it is not really applicable. In theory, there is also a Metronome family of "incremental" GCs (see [Bacon, Cheng and Rajan]) (with the idea behind to make each change very small, so that collection never causes an STW for more than a few hundred microseconds), but I don't know of their use for games either.

In short: as of 2017, if we're on the Client, it *seems* that we're still more or less stuck with STW pauses of around 50-150ms; however, if taking a closer look, we'll notice that these STW times are inevitable only when we're talking about pretty big apps having multi-gigabyte memory usage and lots of allocations/deallocations. Apparently, we *can* reduce STW times by the way we program, so for *our* game STW times will be lower.

If our game won't tolerate 150ms delays while we still want to use a garbage-collected language, we can (and usually SHOULD) do the following:

Apparently, we *can* reduce STW times by the way we program, so for *our* game STW times will be lower.

◆ Avoid swapping. For most GC implementations out there, swapping is an absolute killer (a 5-minute swap isn't that rare, especially when it comes to GC). To avoid swapping, I know of two very different approaches:

- Good One™. Reducing memory consumption by your program (which is a good thing, even without the risk of swapping, though TBH, on Client devices we *always* have such risk[206]). In turn, reducing memory footprint (when going beyond an obvious "don't allocate whatever-you-don't-need") for GC-ed languages often involves at least two different techniques (both essentially aiming to remove those *semantic memory leaks* that tend to plague GC-ed programs so much):
  - The Big One. Assigning *null* to those data members that are no longer necessary (or removing the no-longer-necessary reference from collection). The problem we're addressing here is that whenever we're leaving no-longer-necessary data with a reference to it, by the very idea of GC it causes the data to be kept while the reference to that not-necessary-any-more-object still exists. In practice, these no-longer-necessary references is one of the largest sources of those semantic memory leaks mentioned above.
  - In a sense, assigning *null* as soon as the object is no longer needed is very similar to C++'s *delete* (it happens at the same places, causes pretty much the same results, etc.). So in case you thought that in GC'ed language there is no need to do manual memory management, think again </trolling> (see also below on weak references).
  - I've heard arguments that manual assignment of *nulls* is no longer necessary (because the newer, better compiler will handle it for you automatically); well, it still is (and there is no foreseeable way to avoid it in the future; moreover, as [Wikipedia, Garbage (computer science)] says, identifying semantic garbage in a general case is an undecidable problem).[207]

---

206   Except for some of the consoles.

207   What DID improve is automated *null*-ifying of no-longer-used *local* (on-stack) references, which is trivial and can indeed be done automagically; however, automated *null*-ifying of on-heap references is a *semantic* issue, which cannot possibly be solved by the compiler (it just cannot possibly know whether you will need a referenced object in the future, unless you tell it explicitly by removing the reference).

Weak refs (actually, in Java it is soft refs) can be used to implement caches-that-are-automagically-dropped when you're running out of RAM.

- A useful-but-more-tricky technique involves using weak/soft references. In general, weak references can be used to avoid some of the semantic memory leaks (which effectively leads to reducing the memory footprint and avoiding swapping) — though, keep in mind that weak refs, when used to avoid semantic leaks, require a very good understanding of what-is-going-on (otherwise they can backfire, removing that-object-that-you-need, earlier than you expect). NB: in addition to removing semantic leaks, weak refs (actually, in Java it is soft refs) can be used to implement caches-that-are-automagically-dropped when you're running out of RAM; however, you need to be very careful when using such caches for fast-paced games (if you're dropping caches, you're slowing down some part of the system, so you may need to account for significantly slower loads from your caches in some cases).

  - Bad One™. Locking pages in memory (using *mlock()* or *VirtualLock()*), or disabling swapping system-wide, which has very similar effects. While these techniques are often useful for soft-real-time Servers such as Game World Servers, locking pages on Client PC (or asking the player to disable swapping) is quite problematic. Oh, and BTW: if you didn't reduce memory consumption, then trying to lock your whole multi-gigabyte working set into RAM won't work, so we're pretty much back to square one.

- Make sure to use GC, which at least *tries* to reduce STW pauses.

  - To make a shortlist of GC candidates, you may use data from [Shaya] and [Warren, Measuring the impact of the .NET Garbage Collector]+[Warren, Measuring the impact of the .NET Garbage Collector - An Update].

  - Make sure that good-enough GCs are available for *all* our platforms.

  - Make sure to test your GC-of-choice yourself (things *do* change, and not always for the better), and on *all* your platforms.

- Moreover, we need to make sure to run ongoing tests with GC STW measurements (methodics for STW measurements can be found in the articles mentioned above) while our game is being developed. It is pretty difficult to judge the amount of "stutter" within your own game (especially when most of the time it is run in debugger), so we need to test it objectively and, moreover, there is nothing worse than running such a test after your game is finalized — and realizing that the results are pretty bad (which in turn can require quite a bit of rewriting along the lines discussed here).

◆ Reduce the number of allocations/deallocations (especially of long-term allocations) as much as possible. Note that this point is subtly different from reducing-the-memory-footprint discussed above; here we're talking about reducing the *number* of allocations/deallocations, even if they're not leaks and even if the total memory footprint is the same. For example, if the same amount of RAM can be allocated in two chunks or in one, we should prefer the latter.

- If you're writing a fast-paced game using a GC-collected programming language, this should become a part of the programming culture across the whole gamedev project.[208]

- Note that depending on the specifics of GC used, reducing the number of allocations may either reduce STW times or reduce the frequency of STW pauses, while keeping STW pauses the same.

◆ Reduce the size of our garbage-collected heaps by splitting one single heap into several. Doing so will reduce the amount of work to be done on collection (in each of the heaps, that is), and will shorten that dreadful STW time.

- Just as one example: if you run different processes, they generally will use different instances of GC, which will lead to smaller STW times for each.

To reduce STW time, we can try to reduce the size of our garbage collected heaps (by splitting one single heap into several).

---

208 Well, actually, even if you're writing your fast-paced game in C/C++, avoiding allocations should also be a part of your coding culture, though for slightly different reasons (more on it in Vol. IV's chapter on Things to Keep in Mind). Still, it is worth noting that C/C++ developers — who got used to manual memory management from the very beginning — tend to use significantly fewer allocations to start with.

This goes very well alongside the Share-Nothing (Re)Actors discussed in the context of (Re)Actor-fest architecture above (by running some (Re)Actors within a separate process. While on Clients you still MAY have one of the (Re)Actors with a large state (usually an Animation&Rendering one; see also the *Scaling (Re)Actor-fest Architecture on the Client* section below), you still MAY get a bit of STW time improvement by separating all the other (Re)Actors into a separate process (with its own GC).

♦ In some cases, you *may* be able to get away with allocating some of your objects using some C/C++ (which in turn will allow you to move these objects to a separate heap — which doesn't need to be GC-ed); this is doable at least in C# (via unmanaged code, BTW this — to the best of my knowledge — is more or less what Unity is doing), and in Java (via JNI).

♦ I've also heard about people trying to delay garbage collection until "later" (to avoid stopping it "right now"), but I've never heard of anything good coming from it. Very briefly, in a fast-paced game there aren't usually any "safe points" when it is safe to stop-the-world.[209]

All in all, I've heard of decent fast-paced games written in the GC-collected programming languages (at least Game Logic Module, that is); however, when speaking to those developers who have done it, way too often it became a story of "how we've spent several months wrestling GC to work without STW pauses being noticeable" — and I've even heard of games that were abandoned because of such problems. On the other hand, the whole STW problem doesn't apply to slower-paced games (at least those where the occasional 100ms delay is not a problem).

To GC or Not to GC?

Personally, as a developer with a C++ background, I usually prefer to have everything in my own hands (and avoid depending on GC, which is a big and IMO rather unpleasant dependency).

---

209 Strictly speaking, such "safe points" DO usually exist; they're just way-too-far from "right now" to be of any practical use. For example, for MOBA, such a "safe point" will certainly come at the end of match — but it can be as far as an hour from "now," so delaying GC for such a long time is rarely feasible (that is, unless you're doing your own allocation and avoiding GC allocations during this time altogether, but this is pretty much hopeless for most of the GC'd languages out there).

However, I won't say that GC-collected languages are inherently bad; in recent years, GCs have made significant improvements with regards to the STW problem, and you MIGHT be able to find con-current-enough implementations for all your platforms, which in turn MIGHT enable you to develop your fast-paced games in garbage-collected language without *too much* trouble.

Bottom line:

> *When answering "to GC or not to GC," do what you're more comfortable with.*

However, if using GC'd language for a fast-paced game, make sure to test your game on ALL your target platforms ASAP; otherwise, you still may be facing some quite nasty surprises, if on one of your must-have target platforms there is no decent GC implementation (and/or if your own code is not STW-friendly).

And even more importantly: keep in mind that most of the time "to GC or not to GC" is not the most important question to ask when choosing your programming language for the Client-Side; in particular, issues such as availability-on-all-your-platforms and resilience-to-reverse-engineering play an extremely important role when making this all-important choice.

Most of the time, "to GC or not to GC" is not the most important question when choosing your programming language for the Client-Side.

On Consistency Between Client-Side and Server-Side Languages

One not-so-usual consideration when choosing a programming language for your MOG is related to the observation that there might be some benefit in keeping programming languages the same for your Client and your Server. Having them different is certainly not the end of the world, but it might mean certain issues with integration (which is usually not that big a deal), and with inter-team communication (and this one might be more significant in the long run, though still unlikely to be fatal).

In addition, if you have your Client-Side and your Server-Side programming languages the same, you often will be able to use two important parts of your code both on the Client and the Server:

♦ Communication Module

♦ Parts of Game Logic Module

  ▪ The latter can become Really Important™ if you are doing Client-Side Prediction, which is often best implemented via running the same simulation code on both the Server-Side and the Client-Side.

    • If you're NOT using the same language for the Client-Side and the Server-Side, this need to re-use may even call for using two programming languages on the Client-Side (one to re-use a portion from the Server-Side, and another to code your Client-Side specific stuff, such as rendering).

      · At least with (Re)Actors, it is doable.

      · OTOH, due to increased exposure to reverse engineering, it is usually not too desirable (though not really fatal either).

How important these considerations are in your context depends on the specifics of your game, but they *might* play an important role for your project, so it is better to take them into account sooner rather than later.

Sprinkle with All the Usual Considerations

We've discussed several peculiarities of the programming languages when it comes to games. In addition to these not-so-usual things to be taken into account, all the usual considerations still apply. In particular, you need to think about:

♦ Is your-language-of-choice used long enough to be reasonably mature (so you won't find yourself fixing compiler bugs — believe me, this is not a task that you're willing to do while developing a game)?

♦ Are available tools/libraries/engines sufficient for your game?

♦ Is your programming language readable? More specifically: "is it easily readable to the common developer out there?" (the latter is necessary so that those developers you hire later won't have too much trouble jumping in).

♦ How comfortable are your team's feelings about it?

♦ How difficult is to find developers *willing* to write in it?

   ▪ Note that I'm not talking about "finding somebody with five years of experience in the language"; I'm perfectly sure from my own twenty years of experience as an architect and a team lead that any (half-)decent programmer with any real-world experience in more than one programming language can start writing in a new one in a few weeks without much problem. [210,211] It is frameworks that usually require more knowledge than languages, but the chance of finding somebody who is versed in your specific framework is usually small enough to avoid counting on such miracles.

   ▪ On the other hand, if your programming language of choice is a COBOL, Perl, FORTRAN, or (Ritchie forbid!) assembler, you may have difficulty finding developers *willing* to use it.

Any (half-)decent programmer with any real-world experience in more than one programming language can start writing in a new one in a few weeks without much problem.

♦ Do you have at least one person on the team with substantial real-world experience in the language, with this person developing a comparable-size project in it. Right above, I was arguing that in general language experience is not really necessary, but this argument applies only when the developer comes to a well-established environment. And to build this well-established environment, you need that "at least one person" with an intimate knowledge of the language, environments, their respective peculiarities, and so on.

♦ Is it fast enough for your purposes? Here it should be noted that performance-wise, there are not that many tasks that are time-critical on the Client Side. Traditionally, with games, time-critical stuff is pretty much restricted to graphics, physics, and AI. With an MOG, however, most of the physics and AI normally need to be moved to the Authoritative Server, leaving graphics and rendering pretty much the only Client-Side time-critical thing.[212]

---

210 BTW, feel free to pass this message on to your hiring manager; while he or she might not trust you that easily, in certain not-so-hopeless cases, a quote from a book might help.

211 That is, if the new language is not an exotic one such as LISP, PROLOG, or Haskell.

212 In case of Client-Side Prediction, however, you may need to duplicate some or even most of the physics/AI on the Client-Side; see the *Game Logic Module: Client-Side Prediction and Simulation* section for the relevant discussion.

- Sure, 3D rendering *is* usually damn important, performance-wise; however, if you have delegated rendering to a 3rd-party rendering engine, it is out of the picture, and then it might (or might not) happen that all your Game Logic is not time-critical. And if it isn't time-critical, you can pretty much forget about the performance of your programming language (though you still need to remember not to do crazy things such as using $O(N^3)$ algorithms on million-item containers).

And just for the sake of completeness, here is the list of questions that are NOT to be taken into account when choosing your programming language:

♦ Is it "cool"?

♦ How will it look on my resume after we fail at this project?[213]

♦ Is it the #1 language in popularity ratings? (while popularity has some impact on those valid questions listed above, popularity as such is still very much irrelevant, and choosing programming language #6 over language #7 just because of its position in the ratings is outright ridiculous).

How will it look on my resume after we fail this project?

♦ Is the code short? As code is read much more often than it is written, it is "readability" that needs to be taken into account, not the "amount of stuff that can be fit into 10 lines of code." Also note that while way too often "brevity" is interpreted as "expressiveness," they're not the same.

C++ as a Default Game Programming Language

Given our analysis above, it is not at all surprising that C++ is frequently used for game Clients. Just a few years ago, it was pretty much the only programming language used for serious game development (with some other language often used at the game-designer level). These days, there is a tendency toward introducing other programming languages into gamedev; in particular, Unity is pushing C# (and quite successfully too).

---

213 If you succeed with your MOG project, the project itself will be much more important for your resume than the language you've used, so the only scenario when you should care about "language looking good on resume" is when you're planning for failure.

However, we should note that while C# may[214] speed up your development, it comes with several significant (albeit non-fatal) caveats. First, as noted above, C# apps (at least when they are shipped as byte code) have a lower resilience to bot writers. Second, you need to keep an eye on the platforms supported by C#/Mono. Third, as a GC'd language, it comes with a whole bunch of pros and cons (see the *On Garbage Collection* section above), which also need to be taken into account.

Bottom line: C++ is indeed a default programming for game Clients, and there are both objective and subjective/historical reasons for it. On the other hand, your team might benefit from using alternative languages such as C#; however, make sure to take a look at the issues discussed above to make sure that they won't affect your specific game too much.

Big Fat Browser Problem

As we can see from Table 6.2 above, if you need to run your game *both* on a browser, *and* on some other platform, you have quite a problem on your hands. First, let's see more-or-less viable options available in this case.

Dropping browser as a platform. While very tempting technically, business-wise it might easily be unacceptable.

Usually-Not-Really-an-Option 0 would be to... drop support for the browser — or, for everything-except-for-the-browser as a platform for your Client. While very tempting technically ("hey, we can stay with C++/C#/.../JS then!"), business-wise (and GDD-wise) it might easily be unacceptable. <Bummer />

BTW, even if your game is okay to be browser-only, still make sure to keep reading (Option 3 may especially be of practical interest).

Option 1. Write downloadable Client in Other-Language plus browser-based one in HTML5/JS. The idea here is to keep two separate code bases for "Other-Language" (for downloadable/installable Clients) and HTML5/JS (for browser-based Clients). In theory, it may even work. However, in practice, there are three Big Fat Problems™ with this approach.

First, despite all the improvements with JavaScript, it is still one big can of worms with lots of browser compatibility problems trying to get

---

214 And usually, though not necessarily, will.

out of the can right in the face of your unfortunate player. While development of simpler games in JS may be viable (see, for example, [Bergström]), as the complexity of your game grows, problems will mount exponentially. While HTML5/JS might become a viable technology for larger games at some point, right now it is still not there.

Second, even if/when JS-based development does become viable, you need to keep in mind that protection of JS from being hacked tends to be very low (see Table 6.1 above), and that all your protocols — according to "the weakest link" security principle — will be hacked using JS code base, which means that resilience of your whole Client to reverse engineering will become pretty much non-existent <very-sad-face />.

And third, in practice, Clients with two separate code bases are known to fail pretty badly. You may still try it, but don't tell me that I didn't warn you. For a real-world horror story about a Client with two separate code bases, see the *Logic-to-Graphics API* section above.

Clients with two separate code bases are known to fail pretty badly.

It should be noted that the third problem *can* be mitigated by (a) writing your Client with a Logic-to-Graphics API as discussed above, (b) using the "1.5 code bases" technique (discussed in Vol. IV's chapter on Things to Keep in Mind) for Game Logic, and hopefully also for the Communication Module, and (c) having two separate code bases for the Animation&Rendering Module. Such an approach, if executed correctly, *will* effectively remove *most* of the third problem, and will even make code maintenance viable; however, the first and second problems mentioned above will still haunt you pretty badly.

Option 2. Write non-browser Client in Some-Other-Language, using Logic-to-Graphics API — and then run Game Logic on the Server Side using a "Client-on-Server" trick, essentially passing Logic-to-Graphics commands from the Server Side to a dumb HTML5/JS front-end. Details of the "Client-on-Server" approach will be discussed in the *Client-on-Server Trick* section below.

The disadvantages of this option are mostly related to (a) potentially vastly different experiences for different Clients, and (b) scalability. On the other hand, on the plus side, you can stay with single-code-based Other-Language for your Game Logic, *and* you can keep your Other-Language reasonably protected from bot writers (that is, if you are not too concerned about bots coming from JavaScript Clients, which may happen if player capabilities for JS and non-JS versions are different, and JS Client is actually just a "teaser" for the main downloadable Client).

Option 3. Write your Client in C++ (once again, with a Logic-to-Graphics API) and use *emscripten* to re-compile your code into *asm.js*/wasm for the browser-based version.

With Option 3, you can develop your Client along the following lines:

- You develop your non-browser Client in C/C++ — *and* with Logic-to-Graphics API.
- You recompile the same Game Logic (and hopefully also Communication Module) into *asm.js* or *wasm* using *emscripten*; at the same time, you'll most likely need to re-implement your Animation&Rendering Module under JS — and that's where your Logic-to-Graphics API will come in handy (allowing you to change *only* your Animation&Rendering Module, without rewriting the rest of your Client).
  - In practice, make sure to do this recompile-into-*asm.js*-or-*wasm* ASAP; the longer you wait, the more (solvable, but cumbersome) problems will occur when trying to recompile, so it is better to align your different versions as early as feasible.

This model is free of the problems of Options 1 and 2, and provides pretty good protection from reverse engineering (it is pretty much the best you can get when using browser[215]). The only potential problem with *asm.js* / *wasm* is performance – but, as noted above, as of 2017 it is usually within 2x from native C++ (which is not bad at all, though you still *may* have to sacrifice *some* of less-powerful Client-Side devices as your Clients).

Side notes:

- Unity allows to use C# instead of C++ to compile into asm.js. When Unity compiles C# into JS, first they're converting C# (or, more precisely, .NET's Intermediate Language) into C++, using the

emstripten+asm.js/ wasm model is free of the problems of Options 1 and 2, and provides pretty good protection from reverse engineering.

---

215 Except for Google NaCl, which is somewhat-better reverse-engineering-wise, but is deprecated now

IL2CPP compiler, and then are going along the very same route as discussed for our Option 3 above. Overall, I don't see *too many* problems with this approach, though reverse-engineering-wise it is not perfect <sad-face />.

♦ before 2017, Google NaCl/PNaCl was competing with *asm.js/ wasm*; however, in May 2017, Google has officially announced the deprecation of (P)NaCl, leaving *asm.js/wasm* as the only viable option for running C++ code within the browser.

Choosing the Right Option. Which of the options above will suit your game better is your decision, and it depends on the specifics of your game (and even more so on the specifics of your GDD and monetization). Still, personally, if facing the task of developing a game-that-needs-both-browser-and-downloadable-Clients, I'd very seriously consider Option 3 (*emscripten+asm.js/wasm*).

Client-on-Server Trick

One of the cross-platform options discussed in the *Big Fat Browser Problem* section above mentioned the "Client-on-Server" trick. While with the advent of *emscripten*, Client-on-Server is usually not the most viable option, let's still take a quick look at it.

Let's assume that you already have a working code in some programming language (such as C++), and want to create a browser-based Client. Assuming that your working code is cross-platform (and that it has that Logic-to-Graphics API we've discussed above), such a browser-based Client might be implemented along the following route:

♦ Make your Client-written-in-C++ (or whatever other language) run on the Server, but without graphics (i.e., with dummy implementation Logic-to-Graphics API doing nothing).

♦ Write a Logic-to-Graphics Layer, which will simply send Logic-to-Graphics commands to a really-dumb-Client over the network.

♦ Write a really-dumb-Client in HTML5/JS. This really-dumb-Client should just receive rendering commands (which go along the lines of Logic-to-Graphics API, as discussed above) from the network and render them.

To be honest, given the progress with *emscripten*, I am no longer a fan of this approach (especially if you're planning for a dual downloadable/browser Client from the very beginning). In particular, with Client-on-Server, the player experience on browser platforms may be *much* worse than that of a downloadable one; also, Server resources necessary to run Clients are going to be significant (as logic on Clients is rarely optimized for the Server-Side). However, in certain cases of converting the existing game into the browser, Client-on-Server still *might* happen to work for you.

ON UI DIALOGS

One Client-Side issue that traditionally looks minor in the Grand Scheme of Things™, but which tends to cause quite a bit of trouble later down the road, is UI Dialogs. Most of the time, even for a multiplayer game, you will need at least *some* dialogs (at the very least, settings and purchases[216]) — and starting off implementing them on the wrong foot will have pretty unpleasant implications in the long run.

One Big Fat Rule of Thumb™ about UI dialogs is

> *DON'T use UI dialogs with fixed layout. DO use HTML (or HTML-like) layouts.*

Dialogs with fixed layout (like thirty-year-old Windows-resources-based ones) tend to work okay at first, but become a nightmare very quickly as soon as you either (a) try to make your game cross-platform, *or* (b) try to make your game internationalized.

Fixed layouts — Way to Disaster

While a detailed discussion of i18n won't happen until Volume IX,[217] UI dialogs is one of those things we need to think about from the very beginning to avoid expensive rewrites in the future. And from those real-world translation efforts I've seen, while it is very easy to find

To be honest, given the other options currently available, I am no longer a fan of the Client-on-Server approach.

---

216 As discussed in Vol. I's chapter on GDD, you DO need to make money from your game to at least pay for Servers.

217 There also will be a brief mentioning in Vol. IV's chapter on Things to Keep in Mind.

With a fixed-layout approach, a simple addition of one checkbox to one of the dialogs would result in 125(!) dialog layouts in need of being manually adjusted, which would pretty much be a non-starter.

Pseudo-localization

is a software testing method used for testing internationalization aspects of software. Instead of translating the text…, the textual elements of an application are replaced with an altered version of the original language.

—Wikipedia

translation folks to translate a bunch of *strings*, the same folks won't adjust layouts (it is not their job, they don't have the tools, etc., etc.).

As a result, with fixed a-la Windows dialog layouts (and an approach of "hey, we'll just put resources for each language, with the resources including dialog layouts too") you'd end up having a special person on the team who will just monitor translation changes (and translations happen to be adjusted all the time) and change fixed layouts accordingly (and for *all* the supported platforms). Given enough languages and enough platforms, it simply doesn't work.

I've seen a game that supported twenty-five different languages over five different platforms; for such a game, with a fixed-layout approach, a simple addition of one checkbox to one of the dialogs would result in 125(!) dialog layouts in need of being manually adjusted, which would pretty much be a non-starter.

Way Out—HTML-Like Flexible Layouts

As a rule of thumb, a *much* better alternative is to use flexible HTML-like layouts; in this case, most of the time translations will be readjusted automatically, and without too much hassle to change layouts. Sure, there will be languages-that-have-too-long-translations to fit into the existing layout (out of European languages, I've heard that Norwegian and German are two of the most likely offenders, though YMMV), but as soon as you have plenty of reserves (which can be done by using pseudolocalization with, say, 1.5x of the original English symbols), the whole thing tends to work pretty well (while there are occasional hiccups here and there, they're usually not *too* bad).

BTW, I am *not* saying that you MUST use a fully HTML5-compliant engine to render your UI dialogs. Instead, pretty much anything that allows for flexible layouts will do; in particular, wxWidgets' *wxHTML* or *litehtml* will usually be fine (NB: you still MAY use a full-scale HTML/Web engine; it is just not a firm requirement).

On Modal Dialogs and MOGs

One further issue that is rather common with quite a few of the existing UI Dialog libraries is the way they handle so-called modal dialogs. By definition, a modal dialog is "something that blocks underlying UI," and it works nicely for a usual business app.

However, for MOGs, at least those that allow invoking dialogs over updatable-from-Server-Game-World, it is not that simple. In such cases, while the dialog is open, we usually still need to handle those Server updates and draw the things *underneath* our supposedly-modal dialog(!). While such handling *is* doable in pretty much any modal-dialog implementation I know, it is way too inconsistent across different implementations, so going cross-platform quickly starts to cause way too many problems. In particular, I've seen that those Windows-like systems-that-create-second-event-handler-for-modal-dialog-while-still-running-the-first-one (i.e., they have *more than one* event loop on the program stack at the same time) tend to be very difficult to port.

As a result, I usually prefer to treat *all* your dialogs *as if* they're modeless. It means that there is no such thing as an event-handler-running-on-top-of-event-handler on your program stack <phew />; instead, all your processing is good ol' event-driven processing with *all* the events handled at the same level (if you're using (Re)Actors, within the same (Re)Actor[218]). While this programming style is usually more cumbersome for UI developers, it tends to pay off very well as soon as you need to migrate your code to the second substantially different platform.

To simplify work for your developers, make sure to have a library that *simulates* modal behavior while staying within single-level event handling; if using (Re)Actors, such a library will be very similar to the non-blocking (Re)Actor handling (which was discussed ad nauseam in Chapter 5).

ON USING BROWSER WINDOW ALONGSIDE THE CLIENT

As mentioned in Vol. I's chapter on GDD, for MOG development, quite often it is tempting to use our-own-downloadable-Client for receiving-and-rendering our Game World in real-time, and to use a traditional

It is tempting to use our-own-download-able-Client for receiving-and-rendering our Game World in real-time, and to use a traditional browser window to implement all the other boring stuff.

---

218   Though this (Re)Actor MAY be split using (Re)Actor-within-(Re)Actor, as discussed in Chapter 5.

browser window (speaking to a traditional-web-server-on-the-Server-Side) to implement all the other boring stuff. Overall, it is a perfectly viable technique to speed up your development; the only question here is "how to do it in a way that won't haunt you for years to come."

Implementation-wise, separating some stuff into a web-driven part can be done in a number of different ways; let's see what each of them means in practice. BTW, to be clear: for the time being, we'll be talking *only* about using-HTML-to-show-our-own-stuff (leaving aside integration with 3rd-party sites — most importantly, 3rd-party logins).

To show our-own-stuff using HTML, we have at least the following options.

Downloadable Client + Completely Separate Web Site

Our very first and most obvious option is to use a downloadable Client alongside a completely separate web site; it means separate logins into the Client and into the site, etc.

As was already discussed in Vol. I's chapter on GDD, personally, as a player, I *hate* such things (I want to feel my game as a whole, and not as a bunch of unconnected pieces; also a requirement to login twice is an unnecessary burden for me as a player – and exposes me to phishing too). Still, it is a GDD-level decision, so if your GDD is fine with such an IMO-abomination, you're fully within your rights to use it.

Technically, it is certainly the simplest option; however, it has several important drawbacks:

♦ As noted above, as the separation is obvious to the end-user, it may create the feeling of being half-baked, cumbersome, etc., etc.

♦ Separate logins represent a significant problem from a security point of view.

  ▪ In particular, they increase the chance of phishing attacks to succeed by orders of magnitude.

  ▪ In addition, it makes your web server an additional attack surface on your whole system (and, as a rule of thumb, web servers are much easier to attack compared to Game Servers).

♦ As interactions between the Client and web browser are completely open to the potential cheater, it MAY be used to mount certain cheating attacks (in particular, receiving feedback to see whether the attack is doing fine can be *much* easier this way). While I didn't see *too bad* cheats using this attack vector, as a rule of thumb, pretty much *any* weakness along these lines can be abused (eventually, pretty badly).

♦ As the UI and browser connections are completely separate, it will be extremely difficult to implement throttling-down-heavy-download (such as DLC or theme) while a time-critical game is in progress. This can easily lead to a degraded experience for your players (and you can be sure that they *will* complain about your game lagging, even if it is them who caused it in the first place).

♦ Potential inter-browser compatibility issues require you to be careful with your site (keeping to testing it everywhere), though not more so than for a usual website.

Downloadable Client with a System-Provided In-App Browser

The second option we have to allow us to leverage existing web infrastructure for a not-so-time-critical part of our MOG, is to use a system-provided in-app browser. In this case, at least you'll be able to make the player experience (including login) seamless <phew />.

Still, I don't like this option either, in spite of it being quite popular. My concerns about using a system-provided in-app browser go along the following lines:

At least you'll be able to make the player experience seamless <phew />.

♦ System-provided browsers have (not really surprisingly) system-specific APIs for our Client to interact with them.

  ▪ This instantly creates a Big Headache™ for cross-platform development.

  ▪ It becomes even worse as these APIs tend to change way too often.

♦ In addition, from what I've seen, these APIs (and surrounding-those-APIs-implications) are often buggy-as-hell.

  ▪ Once upon a time, I saw a competitor's game that used

a system-provided in-app browser. And it happened to crash when being run on systems with exactly-one-specific-version-of-IE-installed (all other versions, both before and after, were perfectly fine). Testing for this kind of thing is one of the worst possible nightmares for the developer.

♦ As now we pretend that the browser window is actually *our* window, any browser incompatibility will be perceived as an *outright bug within our Client*, so we need to test the whole thing *even more vigorously*. And with more-than-one-platform to be supported, it will become a never-ending nightmare (heck, even for one single platform, it can easily become a very serious issue; see the example above about Client-crashing-when-player's-system-had-one-exact-version-of-IE).

♦ As interaction API between Client and web parts is well known, cheating is still simplified.

♦ Web server is still an additional attack surface.

♦ Throttling down in-game downloads is still very difficult.

Downloadable Client with an Embedded Web Engine

The next option we have to delegate some of our MOG development to the well-known web infrastructure is to integrate a 3rd-party-web-engine into our Client. *Now we're talking.* In general, if the engine is good enough (and assuming that we can get it running on all the platforms of interest), we can avoid most of the compatibility problems and issues listed above; in particular, we can test our website only once (in our own Client), and that's it.

Is there a *good enough* web engine available for easy embedding?

However, all the beauty of this approach hinges on the question of "is there a *good enough* web engine available for easy embedding?"—and fortunately, there is such an engine: *WebKit. NB: from what I've seen myself and heard from others, I'd stay away from trying to integrate/ embed Gecko; last time I looked at its code, it was quite a mess from an integration perspective, without clear separation between those-parts-we-want-to-use and those-parts-that-are-irrelevant-for-embedding-engine-into-app.*

Taking all the considerations into account, I DO like this approach; however, when using it, a few (admittedly rather minor) issues still remain:

♦ Throttling competing traffic is usually still complicated.

♦ The web server is still an additional attack surface.

Embedded HTML Engine but Own Communications

To deal with these issues, I usually suggest going a little bit further. More specifically, if we integrate a 3rd-party-web-engine along the lines above, *while implementing a network layer for that web engine ourselves*, we'll be able to solve those remaining problems listed above.

If you decide to go this way, it should be done more or less along the following lines:

♦ Intercept all the network/URL accesses coming from your 3rd-party-web-engine (which still runs within your Client).

♦ Tunnel them through your own communication channels (including authentication etc.).

♦ On the Server-Side, get the requests out of the tunnel and feed them to your usual web servers (more on using web servers in MOGs will be discussed in Vol. III's chapter on Server-Side Architecture).

The only disadvantage of this approach compared to a web-engine-without-communications is the additional work involved (especially if the rest of your game is UDP-based); whether it is worth it for your game depends, though personally I don't really like going for in-Client web without it. Still, it is certainly not a black-and-white decision whether to do it.

Last but not least: when using such an HTML-engine-with-our-own-communications, we can use much lighter engines than a full-scale *WebKit*, and *wxHTML* and *litehtml* are immediately coming to mind; what exactly to choose depends on your specific requirements (do you need JavaScript within your HTML, or HTML+a-bit-of-CSS will be fine?), but it is still nice to have such an additional option.

The only disadvantage of a 3rd-party-HTML-engine with DIY-communications compared to a web-engine-without-communications is the additional work involved; whether it is worth it for your game depends.

On Embedding and emscripten

When going the route of embedding a web engine (especially a full-scale one such as *WebKit*) into your Client, and *if* we want to have our downloadable Client run under a browser using *emscripten* (see the *On asm.js, wasm, and Emscripten* section above), we may end up running *WebKit*-compiled-with-*emscripten*-running-under-browser's-*Webkit* — and it sounds outright crazy.

TBH, I never run into such scenarios (and have even never heard of somebody running into them), so all I'll be saying below is outright speculation. Still, in such a case, you have three rather obvious options:

♦ Try to compile *WebKit* under *emscripten*. While this sounds even more crazy than usual *emscripten*, and is going to be tough — but *if* you manage to do it and it works — well, you just got away without any changes to your Client (and kept all the anti-cheating defenses up too).

♦ Use significantly lighter *wxHTML/litehtml* rather than *WebKit*. IMO this option is the best bet in this case — that is *if* you can afford to drop those-features-available-in-*WebKit*-but-unavailable-in-*wxHTML/litehtml* (and unfortunately, there are quite a few of them).

♦ For a browser-based Client, replace your embedded-*WebKit* with using the browser itself (while still using embedded *WebKit* for a downloadable Client). While it is quite an obvious approach, it is going to be a significant headache (among other things, you will need to test the web part of your app on all the browsers), and, depending on your game and information-that-is-provided-via-web-interface, MAY lower your resilience to certain cheats. Still, it *can* be made to work, and if nothing else works for you it MAY be your only option (and not *that* bad of one, TBH).

Integrating with 3rd-party Websites. 3rd-party Logins

Up until now, we discussed only those scenarios when our Client needed to show only the data coming from *our own* Servers. When we need to deal with some information coming from a *3rd-party* website (to perform a 3rd-party login, or to perform a payment, or invite a friend from Facebook), the whole thing is turned upside down, and none of our previous arguments stand anymore.

Whenever we need to integrate with a 3rd-party website (especially for the purposes of logging in/socializing/payments),

> *The most important thing is to use the same browser that the player routinely uses for regular web browsing.*

If we're doing it in any other manner, our players, when opening a 3rd-party web page in some-other-browser (whether system-provided or our-own embedded one), won't be able to use their saved passwords/auto-filled forms/existing-login-sessions, which will put *so* much unnecessary pressure on our players that up to a half of them[219] will leave without logging in/referring-a-friend/paying, etc.

Our players, when opening a 3rd-party web page, won't be able to use their saved passwords/auto-filled forms.

Most of the time, our best bet is just to use some OS API that is supposed to open OS default browser (while not ideal, it is still by far the best way I know). Depending on the specific platform, it can be *ShellExecute()*, or *openURL*, or *Intent.ACTION_VIEW*, etc.

At this point, two different data flows can occur. The simpler one does *not* require the browser to return anything to our Client; while such a simple workflow is often possible with asking-to-share and sometimes is possible for payments (for payments, we might be able to obtain a "payment completed" confirmation from our own Server-Side), it is rarely (if ever) a viable option for logins.

Whenever we DO need a confirmation back from the browser window, it is going to be quite a headache to say the least. Still, it *is* doable, and the most bulletproof (and most cross-platform) solution I know goes along the following lines:

♦ First, our Client app gets a random one-time *our_own_token* from our Server. Ideally – it should be an at-least-128-bit-long crypto-quality random number (for a discussion on random numbers, see Vol. VI's chapter on RNGs).

  ▪ The server stores information that "this *our_own_token* was given to *such-and-such Client* at *such-and-such time*."

---

219   And potentially even more (unless our game is already a household word).

♦ Then, our Client opens *our own* URL (i.e., URL residing on our own web server), using some "open URL in default OS browser" APIs, and passing *our_own_token* as a part of this URL.

NB: yes, we're not opening the 3rd-party site directly.

♦ The web page sitting on our-own-URL — just as any other web site — performs a standard web login procedure with a 3rd-party web site;[220] as this is usually the most common use scenario for 3rd-party logins, it tends to work very smoothly (at least much more smoothly than anything else).

♦ As a result of this 3rd-party login, our own web server (the one handling our-own-URL) usually gets some kind of *access_token*, which (a) indicates that the user is authenticated, and (b) can be used to access some of the social-platform goodies (e-mail address, friends list, etc.).

♦ After the login process is completed, our own web server pushes this *access_token* alongside *our_own_token* to our Server (the one where our Client is connected).

♦ Our Server pushes this information to our Client (or our Client may poll our Server instead[221]).

▪ In this process, *our_own_token* is used to identify our Client among all the Clients waiting for login.

• Note that using ClientID (or anything else but a randomized one-time *our_own_token)* for the purposes of such matching is risky and is likely to cause some kind of trouble down the road. In particular, security implications can be pretty bad depending on specifics (while one-time *our_own_token* tends to be safe for pretty much any use).

♦ Bingo! We've got our 3rd-party login working — all while using the default OS browser (i.e., all the passwords and forms will be auto-filled for our player) — *and* without any special support from the 3rd-party (just using their ubiquitous 3rd-party-login-from-web-site feature).

There are other approaches out there (ranging from running-some-JS-within-web-browser and communicating back via scanning cookie folder,

We've got our 3rd-party login working — all with passwords and forms auto-filled — *and* without any special support from the 3rd-party.

---

220 Or performs a payment, etc., etc.

221 While in general I hate polling, this is one case when you MAY need it.

to running-webserver-locally-and-accessing-it-via-localhost), but most of them are usually way too unreliable when trying to run it on millions of different player PCs with different browsers/personal firewalls/etc.

One other way of receiving-reply-back-from-login-process that works is to use officially-supported 3rd-party login APIs for apps (or, for devices, see, for example, [Facebook]); if such an API is supported for your platform, it is surely your best bet; however, when there is no such API, you will likely need to resort to the above cumbersome-but-working solution.

BOTTOM LINE FOR CHAPTER 6

Phew, it was another rather long chapter. On the other hand, we've managed to provide a 50,000-feet (and 30,000-word) overview of the MOG Client-Side architectures, both in a generic form, and as my favorite (Re)Actor-fest Architecture. To summarize and re-iterate my personal recommendations in this regard:[222]

♦ Think about your graphics, in particular whether you want to use pre-rendered 3D or whether you want/need dual graphics (such as 2D+3D); this is one of the most important questions for your Game Client.[223]

- ▪ If your game is an MMOFPS or an MMORPG, most likely you do need fully-fledged Client-Side 3D, but even for an MMORTS the answer can be not that obvious.

♦ Writing your code as a deterministic event-driven (Re)Actor (as described in Chapter 5 in nauseating detail) tends to help, and to help a *damn lot*.

- ▪ (Re)Actor-fest is not the only viable architecture, and you may be able to get away without it. However, at the very least you should consider it and understand why you prefer an alternative before throwing the (Re)Actor-fest away.

  - • Keep in mind that massive multithreading stuff with mutex-based inter-thread synchronization doesn't really work reliably in larger projects (and doesn't scale well either, at least in game-like environments).

---

222   As always, YMMV; all responsibility disclaimed, and batteries not included.

223   Yes, I know I'm putting on my Captain Obvious hat once again.

- As for message-passing approaches that are not (Re)Actors, they MAY work (though I still happen to prefer (Re)Actors).

  - Having a deterministic (Re)Actor has *lots* of useful features, including post-factum analysis of the problem-your-real-player-complains-about.

  - Keep all your (Re)Actors perfectly self-contained in a Shared-Nothing model. It will help in quite a few places down the road.

  - Feel free to run multiple (Re)Actors in a single thread if you think that your game and/or current platform is a good fit, but keep those (Re)Actors separate; it can really save your bacon a few months later.

  - Keep one single code base for your Game Logic (Re)Actor. For other (Re)Actors, you may make different implementations for different platforms, but do so only if it becomes really necessary.

- When choosing your programming language, think twice about resilience to bot writers, and also about those platforms you want to support. While the former is just one of those things to keep in mind, the latter can be a deal-breaker when deciding on your programming language.

- Usually, C++ is quite a good all-around candidate for the Game Client, but there are other options out there too.

- Running Game Client on a web browser is a known problem, but *emscripten+asm.js/wasm* DO provide an interesting (and often practical) way of handling it.

- Make sure to use a flexible layout (such as HTML) for your UI dialogs; otherwise, i18n and ports will cause many more headaches than is necessary.

- Running a non-time-critical part of your game using web browsers/web servers is possible, *but* you DO need to be careful. IMNSHO, the best option is to have a 3rd-party web engine (such as *WebKit/wxHTML/litehtml*) embedded into your Client.

  - Keep in mind that interactions with 3rd-party web sites (for logins, payments, etc.) is a very different beast, and with very different solutions.

Bibliography

Apple. "*SpriteKit.*"
    https://developer.apple.com/spritekit/.

AZUL Systems. "*Zing.*"
    https://www.azul.com/products/zing/.

Bacon, David F., Perry Cheng, and V.T. Rajan. 2003. "*The Metronome: A Simpler Approach to Garbage Collection in Real-Time Systems.*"

Bergström, Sven. 2013. "*Real Time Multiplayer in HTML5.*"
    http://www.htmlgoodies.com/html5/client/real-time-multiplayer-in-html5.html.

Chen, Hao, Ari Silvennoinen, and Natalya Tatarchuk. 2011. "*Making Games from Polygon Soup.*" https://mediatech.aalto.fi/~ari/Publications/Making_Game_Worlds_from_Polygon_Soup.pptx.

Cocos2D-X.
    http://www.cocos2d-x.org/.

EPA. "*Greenhouse Gas Equivalencies Calculator.*" https://www.epa.gov/energy/greenhouse-gas-equivalencies-calculator

Facebook. 2017. "*Facebook Login for Devices.*"
    https://developers.facebook.com/docs/facebook-login/for-devices.

Fiedler, Glenn. 2006. "*Fix Your Timestep!*" http://gafferongames.com/game-physics/fix-your-timestep/.

Fosner, Ron. 2010. "*Task-based Multithreading - How to Program for 100 cores.*" http://www.gdcvault.com/play/1012321/Task-based-Multithreading-How-to.

Hare, 'No Bugs'. 2015. "*Multi-threading at Business-logic Level is Considered Harmful.*" http://accu.org/index.php/journals/2134.

Krause, Stefan. 2017. "*A first look at WebAssembly performance*"
    http://www.stefankrause.net/wp/?p=405

Li, Chuanpeng, Chen Ding, and Kai Shen. 2007. "*Quantifying The Cost of Context Switch.*" http://www.cs.rochester.edu/u/cli/research/switch.pdf.

Nystrom, Robert. 2014. "*Game Loop.*" http://gameprogrammingpatterns.com/game-loop.html.

Shaya, Daniel. 2015. "*Starting out with jHiccup.*" http://www.rationaljava.com/2015/02/starting-out-with-jhiccup.html.

Tatarchuk, Natalya. 2015. "*Destiny's Multithreaded Rendering Architecture.*" GDC. http://www.gdcvault.com/play/1021926/Destiny-s-Multithreaded-Rendering.

Tene, Gil, Balaji Iyengar, and Michael Wolf. 2011. "*C4: The Continuously Concurrent Compacting Collector.*" ACM SIGPLAN Notices. http://www.azulsystems.com/sites/www.azulsystems.com/c4_paper_acm.pdf.

Warren, Matt. 2014. "*Measuring the impact of the .NET Garbage Collector - An Update.*" http://mattwarren.org/2014/06/23/measuring-the-impact-of-the-net-garbage-collector-an-update/.

— . 2014. "*Measuring the impact of the .NET Garbage Collector.*" http://mattwarren.org/2014/06/18/measuring-the-impact-of-the-net-garbage-collector/.

Wikipedia. 2017. "*Garbage (computer science).*" https://en.wikipedia.org/wiki/Garbage_(computer_science)

Zakai, Alon. 2017. Quote: "*Usually [wasm] code is around half as fast as native, or better, but some things are currently much slower, like C++ exceptions and SIMD.*" https://github.com/WebAssembly/binaryen/issues/1070

CHAPTER 7.

CLIENT-DRIVEN DEVELOPMENT:

UNITY, UE, LUMBERYARD, URHO3D, AND 3RD-PARTY NETWORK LIBRARIES

ON CLIENT-DRIVEN VS. SERVER-DRIVEN DEVELOPMENT WORKFLOWS

As we already mentioned in Volume I's Chapter on GDD, there are two rather different approaches to MOG development, which we've named "Server-Driven Development Workflow" and "Client-Driven Development Workflow." While in this chapter we'll mostly concentrate on Client-Driven Development Workflow, let's first briefly discuss Server-Driven one.

On Server-Driven Development Workflow

One common game development scenario occurs when the logic of your MOG does not require access to game assets. In other words, it happens when the gameplay is defined by some internal rules, and not by object geometry or levels. Examples of such games include stock exchanges, social games, casino-like games, some simpler simulators (maybe a snooker simulator), and so on.

What is important for us in this case is that you can write your Game Logic (the one that will run on your Authoritative Server) without any 3D models, and without any involvement of graphics artist and level designer folks. It means that for such development, Server-Side has no dependencies whatsoever, and Server-Side becomes a main driver of game development, plain and simple. And the 3D stuff acts as a mere rendering of the Server-Side world, without any ability to affect it.

With Server-Driven development workflow, game designers are working on Server logic, and can express their ideas without referring to essentially-3D or essentially-graphical things such as game levels, character geometry, etc.

If your game allows it, Server-Driven development is a Good Thing™ — and whenever possible, it is generally simpler and more straightforward than Client-Driven. Developing, say, a social game the other way around usually qualifies as a pretty bad idea. However, not all MOGs are suitable for such Server-Driven development, and quite a few require a different development workflow.

Client-Driven Development Flow

For those games where your Game Designers are not only laying out the game rules, but are also involved in developing graphical things such as game levels, Server-Driven Development Workflow as described above tends to fall apart fairly quickly. The problem lies with the fact that when designing game levels, Game Designers shouldn't (and usually couldn't) think in terms of coordinates (which are required to describe your game in Server-Driven terms). Instead, Game Designers tend to (and *should*) think in terms of *pictures (or other visualizable entities)* — and this is extremely difficult (to "outright impossible") to do while staying completely on the Server-Side.

Two examples of games that almost universally won't work well with Server-Driven development flow (and will require a Client-Driven approach, as described below) are MMORPGs and MMOFPS.

Games that almost universally won't work well with Server-Driven development flow are MMORPGs and MMOFPS.

Implementing Client-Driven Workflows

Definitions aside, we can start discussing *implementing* Client-Driven Workflows.

As mentioned in Vol. I's chapter on GDD, one way to implement Client-Driven Workflow is to create a full-scale toolchain integrating *both* the game-level design tools *and* the authoritative Server-Side. However, while an AAA game development studio can afford to take this effort, for indie gamedevs it is very rarely an option, so they need to stick to existing tools.

Acknowledging that not all the gamedev companies are AAA (with their own game engines and toolchains), for the rest of this chapter we will concentrate on ready-to-use 3rd-party game engines (either 2D or 3D) — and the ways an MOG can be developed with your Game Designers using these 3rd-party game engines (all without developing your own full-scale toolchains). In Chapter 4, this was referred to as the "Engine-Centric Approach."

One practical problem in this regard is that popular 3D engines (such as UE or Unity) are actually centered on the Client-Side — and their capabilities with regard to the Server-Side (and especially networking) are rather limited <sad-face />.

The rest of this chapter is not intended for developers coming from AAA gamedev companies — unless, of course, you are going to use a 3rd-party game engine.

Single-player Prototype and "Continuous Conversion"

As discussed in Vol. I's chapter on GDD, to deal with these limitations, the following approach (which we named "continuous conversion") is used pretty often with varying degrees of success:

♦ First, develop a game prototype using the existing game engine "as if" it is a single-player game.

- It means that both Game Designers and 3D artists can work within a familiar environment and are able to test things — as well as fix them — right away.

- At this stage, there is no need to deal with the network at all: in particular, there are no *[SyncVar]*s, no RPCs — nothing of the sort.

♦ At a certain point, start a parallel project to "convert" your single-player game into an MOG. This process is going to be rather involved (and can be done in at least two different ways, as discussed in more detail below).

While the Client-Driven Development Process as described above is no picnic, it is IMHO the best you can do for such games given the tools currently available (and without writing the whole toolchain integrating your Server into it). Such a process does allow Game Designers to avoid thinking in terms of coordinates (which would be outright crazy), and also isolates them from most of the complexities related to state synchronization, RTTs, and latencies; while certain network-related issues such as "what should happen with a player when she gets disconnected" will still appear in the Game Designer space, it remains much better than making your Game Designers *think all the time* about Clients and Servers.

How to do this "conversion" is actually the subject of this whole chapter <smile />. However, whichever way you want to "convert" your game,

> *Make sure to start "conversion" to the Server-Side as soon as possible, which is "as soon as some playable prototype becomes available." Moreover, ensure that it is a "**continuous** conversion."*

Starting conversion ASAP is necessary because "conversions" from single-player are never obvious and tend to cause quite a bit of trouble, so the sooner you can have your "converted" game playtested,[224] the better; you'll find quite a few nasty things that you need to fix. Moreover, sometimes these multiplayer-specific restrictions can even affect your game rules — and sometimes in a drastic manner; as a result, it may take a while to find proper game balance after you change them.

On the other hand, this process of "conversion" should never end. As your designers will ask for some new logic (and they will), at least this new logic will need to be converted to the Server-Side again (and, even more importantly, your game should be re-tested as a whole; you never know where latencies can hurt your gameplay, even after the most innocent-looking change in the logic).

Starting conversion ASAP is necessary because "conversions" from single-player are never obvious and tend to cause quite a bit of trouble, so the sooner you can have your "converted" game playtested, the better.

Engine-Provided Server vs. Standalone Server

Using such a "continuous conversion" process is more or less common across the board.[225] However, while staying within a "continuous conversion" development model, there are at least two distinct ways to implement your Server.

The first option for implementing your Server is to use the capabilities provided by your 3rd-party engine;[226] this also usually implies using engine-provided network capabilities and protocols. Let's name this approach an "Engine-Provided Server."

The second option for implementing your Server[227] while using a 3rd-party game engine is to have a completely standalone Server — with 100% of the Server-Side code being brand new and unrelated to the 3rd-party game engine you're using. In other words, when using this Standalone Server option, your Client will be still developed using a 3rd-party game engine,[228] but your Server will be (almost) completely separated — and can use *any* networking libraries, protocols, programming languages, etc.

---

224   And using latency/packet loss simulators too(!).

225   That is for games that require Client-Driven Development Workflow and without writing your own toolchain.

226   In Vol. I's chapter on GDD, we named it "Option 1a."

227   Referred to as "Option 1b" in Vol. I's chapter on GDD.

228   Though both the Client and the Server *may* use a 4th-party network library.

Note that for such a Standalone Server approach to work, you'll need to make a special converter, which will take all those levels designed by your Game Designers, and will convert the levels into some kind of format your Standalone Server is able to understand.

Important Clarification: Development Workflow vs Data Flow

One important thing to note is that regardless of *game development workflow* being Server-Driven or Client-Driven, from a technical point of view the *data flow* in our completed Authoritative-Server game will always be Server-Driven: as our Server needs to be authoritative, all decisions are always made by the Server and are propagated to the Clients, which merely render things as prescribed by the Server (see more discussion on different data flows in Vol. I's chapter on Communications).

Regardless of *game development work-flow* being Server-Driven or Client-Driven, from a technical point of view the *data flow* in our completed Authoritative-Server game will always be Server-Driven.

MOST POPULAR 3RD-PARTY GAME ENGINES

Now, as we're done with discussing generic concepts, we can start reviewing specific network-oriented setups, which are based on popular game engines such as Unity or UE. In this process, we'll try to cover *both* Engine-Provided Servers *and* Standalone Servers as defined above.

Overall, there are lots of game engines out there, so — being limited by space — we'll consider only three commercial engines that are the most popular ones as of 2017, plus one open-source engine. Specifically, those lucky ones are Unity 5, Unreal Engine 4, Amazon Lumberyard, and Urho3D.[229] For these engines, we'll consider *both* their built-in network capabilities *and* 3rd-party network libraries that can be used to make an MOG with these game engines.

Note that comparing the graphics-related advantages and disadvantages of Unity vs. UE vs. Cryengine/Lumberyard vs. Urho3D, as well as the graphics performance differences etc., etc., are beyond the scope of

---

229   As noted in *The engine that didn't make it — Source* section below, Source engine didn't make it into this comparison, as Source 1 was already badly outdated and Source 2 wasn't yet available as of the time of writing.

this book; if you want to find discussion on these issues, Google "Unity 5 vs. UE4" ("Unity vs. Cryengine," etc.) and you will easily find a ton of comparisons of their non-network-related features. We, however, are more interested in network-related topics, and such comparisons are not that easy to find (to put it mildly). So, let the comparison of different *network*-related features of Unity 5, UE4, Amazon Lumberyard, Urho3D, and related libraries begin!

Unity 5

Unity 5 is a very popular (arguably *the most* popular among indie developers) 3D/2D game engine. It supports tons of different platforms (HTML5 support via *IL2CPP+emscripten* included), uses .NET CLI/CLR as a runtime, and supports C#/JS/Boo (whatever the last one is) as a programming language. One thing about Unity is that it targets a very wide range of games, from first-person shooters to social games (i.e., "pretty much anything out there").

As usual, support for CLI on non-MS platforms requires *Mono*, which is not exactly 100% compatible with CLR, but from what I've heard, most of the time it works (that is, as long as you adhere to the

As usual, support for CLI on non-MS platforms requires Mono, which is not exactly 100% compatible with CLR, but from what I've heard, most of the time it works.

"write once—test everywhere" paradigm). As for running Unity on top of *.NET Core* instead of *Mono*, this looks unlikely [Peterson], and Unity team *seems* to concentrate on supporting *.NET Standard* instead (see [Landwerth]; very briefly, *.NET Standard* is intended to become an underlying library for *all* of the *.NET Framework*, *.NET Core*, *Xamarin*, and *Mono*) instead of supporting *.NET Core*.

Another thing to keep in mind when dealing with Unity is that CLR (as pretty much any garbage-collected VM; see discussion in Chapter 6) suffers from certain potential issues. These issues include the infamous "stop-the-world"; for slower games it doesn't really matter, but for really fast ones (think MMOFPS) you'll need to make sure to read about mitigation tricks, which were briefly mentioned in Chapter 6, *and* test your game often to make sure you're not running into this problem.

Event-Driven Programming/Reactors

Like most of the game engines out there, Unity is event-driven by design <smile />. Normally, Unity's Game Loop is hidden from sight, but it does exist "behind the scenes," so everything basically happens in the same thread.[230] As a result, you don't need to care about inter-thread synchronization. From our point of view, Unity can be considered pretty much a (Re)Actor (as defined in Chapter 5).

With regards to handling non-blocking stuff, Unity supports coroutines. Unity coroutines[231] are executed within the same thread, so inter-thread synchronisation is still unnecessary when using them <phew />. Referring to our eight Takes from Chapter 5, Unity's coroutines are roughly analogous to Take 5 (which isn't too bad to start with).

In addition, at least when using C# for Unity, it *seems* possible to use an even-better *async/await* with Unity [Vermeulen], with the potential to serialize *await* frames as well [Wischik]. *If* both async-instead-of-coroutines, *and* serializing of async-frames in C# really do work in practice[232], it would mean that we have the ability to serialise the program state, enabling such (Re)Actor goodies discussed in Chapter 5

---

230   Or at least "as if" it happens in the same thread; what is important for us now is that thread-sync issues can be safely ignored.

231 As coroutines should, and unlike goroutines.

232   Unfortunately, I didn't have an opportunity to check it

as production post-factum analysis, low-latency server-fault tolerance, and certain aspects of replay-based testing. IMNSHO, having these abilities is very important, especially when it comes to the post-deployment debugging of games, so that we can fix those problems which manifest themselves only in production (see Chapter 5 for the relevant discussion); as a result – I suggest to at least try playing with *async/await* in Unity (and whatever the results are – please let me know <wink />).

Built-In Communications: HLAPI (for Engine-Provided Server)

Communication support in Unity 5 is known as UNet, and is split into two separate API levels: High-Level API (HLAPI) and Transport-Level API (LLAPI). Let's first take a look at HLAPI.

First, let's note that high-level APIs (such as HLAPI) are usually pretty difficult to use for Standalone Servers. In particular, state synchronization is usually quite an involved protocol, and re-implementing a compatible version of it on your Standalone Server is rarely worth the trouble. As a result

> *As a rule of thumb, HLAPI[233] is only usable for the Engine-Provided Server.*

Now to the specifics of HLAPI. One potential source of confusion when using HLAPI is the HLAPI term "Local Authority" as used in [Unity Technologies, Unity 5 Network System Concepts]. When the game runs, HLAPI says that usually a Client has "authority" over the corresponding PC. It might sound like a bad case of violating the Authoritative Server principles (that we need to avoid cheating; see Vol. I's chapter on Cheating), but in fact it isn't. In HLAPI-speak, "client authority" just means that the Client can send [Command] requests to the Server (more on [Command]s below) about this specific object — that's pretty much it — so it doesn't really give any decision-making authority to the Client <phew />.

You SHOULD NOT use Command requests to allow the client to modify the state of the PC on the Server directly.

On the other hand, you *should not* use [Command] requests to allow the Client to modify the state of the PC on the Server directly; doing so

---

233   As well as other high-level APIs.

will violate Server Authority, widely opening a door for cheating. For example, if you're allowing a Client to send a [Command] that sets the PC's coordinates directly and without any Server-Side checks, you're basically inviting a trivial attack when a PC controlled by a hacked Client can easily teleport from one place to another. To avoid it,

> *Instead of making decisions on the Client-Side and sending coordinates calculated from the player's inputs, you should send the player's inputs to the Server and let the Authoritative Server simulate the world and decide where the player really goes as a result of the simulation that uses those inputs.*[234]

State Synchronization

In HLAPI, you basically have two major communication mechanisms: "state synchronization" and RPCs.

State synchronization is Unity's incarnation of the Server State -> Client State synchronization process, which we discussed in Vol. I's chapter on Communications. In Unity 5, state synchronization can be done via the simple addition of a [SyncVar] tag to a variable [Unity Technologies, Unity 5 State Synchronization]; it is as simple as that.

As discussed in Vol. I, for quite a few games you will need to implement Interest Management. Not only does it help reduce traffic, but it is also necessary to deal with "see through walls" cheats, a.k.a. wallhacks, and "lifting fog of war" cheats, a.k.a. maphacks.

Importantly, Unity does provide support for both distance-based and custom Interest Management. Distance-based Interest Management is implemented via *NetworkProximityChecker*, and a custom one via *RebuildObservers()* (with related *OnCheckObservers()/OnRebuildObservers()*).

Also, on top of [SyncVar]s, you *may* need to implement some (or all) of the Client-Side stuff discussed in Vol. I's chapter on Communi-

---

234 As an unfortunate side effect of this approach, you *may* get additional perceived latencies on the Client-Side; to deal with these additional latencies, you may need to use Client-Side Prediction as discussed in Vol. I's chapter on Communications. Still, however bulky this approach might look on first glance, it is widely recognized as *the only* viable way to implement a multiplayer game that goes beyond playing with friends.

cations (up to and potentially including Client-Side Prediction); one implementation of Client-Side Prediction for Unity is described in [Arellano].

So far so good, but the real problems will start a bit later. In the long run, there are two significant problems with [SyncVar]s in HLAPI:

♦ Unity-provided synchronization mechanisms are usually quite inefficient traffic-wise. While Unity *seems* to use Whole-Field Delta Compression (or a reasonable facsimile), its default serialization can't implement most of the compression mechanisms that we discussed in Vol. I. In particular, Incremental Delta Compression and restricting precision of Publishable State variables are not possible (the latter in turn makes bitwise streams pretty much useless). Of course, you can create a separate set of variables just for synchronization purposes (effectively creating a Publishable State separate from your normal Server State), but even in this case[235] you won't be able to implement many of the traffic compression techniques that we discussed in Vol. I.

♦ Even worse: HLAPI as such doesn't seem to support encryption. And as a lack of encryption enables fundamentally undetectable proxy bots, it is usually a Big No-No™ to release any production game with more than a few thousand players without encryption.

This doesn't mean that HLAPI is bad; however, it does mean that before going into production, you *should* switch from [SyncVar]s to using "custom serialization" functions (*OnSerialize()/OnDeserialize()*).

Using custom serialization instead of [SyncVar]s will allow you to:

♦ Improve compression. It should be noted, however, that the custom serialization model in HLAPI is relatively limited; in particular, it does not support the concept of "difference from any previous state," and always refers to the "immediately previous state" instead. In turn, it implies that HLAPI's state sync cannot use the "Low-Latency Compressed State Sync" method as described in Vol. I's chapter on Communications; instead, HLAPI needs to rely on some kind of "reliable UDP," which tends to exhibit substantially worse latencies in case of lost packets.

While Unity does use Whole-Field Delta Compression (or a reasonable facsimile), its default serialization cannot possibly implement most of the compression mechanisms that we discussed in Vol. I.

---

235 Which BTW will require quite an effort, as well as being a departure from HLAPI philosophy, even if you're formally staying within HLAPI.

♦ Enable encryption (sort of). With custom serialization, it *is* possible to implement kinda-encryption at serialization level. On the other hand, it should be understood that implementing encryption via customized serialization is pretty difficult, very cumbersome and error-prone, and is somewhat limited.[236] Also, let's keep in mind that if implementing encryption on top of HLAPI, we should make sure to encrypt RPCs too (separately).

As a result, custom serialization, while being significantly better than a built-in one, will still lose (both compression-wise and anti-cheating-wise) to a well-designed marshalling library of your own.

RPCs (a.k.a. "Remote Actions")

In Unity 5, RPCs were renamed "Remote Actions." However, in reality, not much has changed compared to Unity 4 — except that now there is a [Command] tag for Client-to-Server RPC and [ClientRpc] tag for Server-to-Client RPC, so it is still the same RPCs albeit under a different name.

Unity RPCs still *must* be void.

In any case, Unity RPCs still *must* be *void*. As we've seen in Chapter 5, this implies quite a few complications when you're writing your code. For example, if you need to query the Server to get some value, then you need to have an RPC call ([Command] in Unity) going from the Client to the Server, and then you'll need to use something like *Networking.NetworkConnection.Send()* to send the reply back (not to mention that all the matching between requests and responses must be done manually, and it will quickly become a major headache; see Chapter 5's Take 2 for examples). In my book,[237] it qualifies as "damn inconvenient" (though you certainly *can* do things this way).

Of the more serious negatives of HLAPI's RPCs, we should mention:

♦ Lack of encryption. Adding encryption to HLAPI RPCs, while possible, would be quite an effort. To do so, generally we'd need to replace all specific [Command]s going from the Client to the Server, with one single call *SendSomethingToServer()* having the only

236 At least boundaries between messages will remain unencrypted. Strictly speaking, it is unclear whether this is inherently exploitable; what *is* clear is that building a solid encryption schema at this level, even if possible, is non-trivial and error-prone.

237 Pun intended.

byte-array parameter (with *SendSomethingToServer()* performing encryption — and calling a special [Command] that will just send the encrypted data). And to get all the different RPC calls into this *byte-array* parameter, we'll need to use our own marshalling (and do so manually for all the [Command]s <ouch/>). And then, we'll need to do the same thing for all the [ClientRpc]s (replacing them with *SendSomethingToClient()* function, calling a special [ClientRpc] within) <double ouch />.

♦ Lack of support for Server-to-Server communications — and it is a significant limitation for serious games. As we'll see in Volume III's Chapter on Server-Side Architecture, having your Server-Side split into some kind of modules, microservices, or, even better, Node.js-style nodes is a must for pretty much any sizeable Server-Side development; as a result, having your network/game engine support interactions between these nodes/modules is extremely important. Sure, you can use another library (such as ZeroMQ, or maybe even a DIY library) for Server-to-Server communications; however, doing so is a headache, and integrating it with Game Logic is even more of a headache <sad-face />. Once again, while it is certainly doable, implementing it is going to be rather cumbersome and time-consuming in practice.

Lack of support for Server-to-Server communications is a significant limitation for most serious games out there.

HLAPI Summary

As discussed above, HLAPI comes with quite a few limitations; from my perspective, the worst is the lack of encryption — and this is going to be a *Big Problem*™ for serious games out there (that is, as soon as they reach enough popularity to attract cheaters). In addition, for quite a few simulation games, HLAPI's [SyncVar] won't provide "good enough" traffic compression and optimization. As a result,

> *While HLAPI can be convenient for prototyping, you **do** need to think about its limitations ASAP. For your production game, at least, you should use custom serialization instead of [SyncVar]s, **plus** implement custom marshalling for [Command]s and [ClientRpc]s. At most, you should switch to LLAPI.*

In other words, HLAPI's [SyncVar]s and RPCs are reasonably good for prototyping and the early stages of development, speeding development up. And then you should be able to rewrite [SyncVar]s and RPCs into something more efficient (and encrypted(!)) using custom serialization *plus* custom RPC marshalling, or (IMO better) using LLAPI. It is not going to be a picnic, and you need to allocate enough time for this task, but it can be done.

As a Big Fat Rule of Thumb™, this rewriting into customized-HLAPI or LLAPI should be started pretty soon in the development cycle (IMO, as soon as the first multiplayer prototype is up and somewhat-running). In other words, while it might be a good idea to start your "continuous conversion" from a single-player game into a multi-player one using HLAPI, I would suggest starting to convert it further into custom-ized-HLAPI or LLAPI *as soon as you can see that your game is really playable as a multi-player game after conversion from a single-player one.*[238]

Answering the question of whether custom serialization/marshalling should be done on top of HLAPI or LLAPI: IMO, writing custom serialization/marshalling around HLAPI, while possible, *should* be avoided for new development (however, if you are already using HLAPI extensively, and want gradual migration, customizing HLAPI *may* be a viable approach). For new projects, instead of customizing HLAPI, I would suggest using LLAPI; with the need to implement marshalling yourself anyway, this seems to be the most straightforward and flexible approach.

Built-In Communications: LLAPI (Both for Engine-Provided Server and Standalone Server)

Just as advertised, Unity Transport Layer API (a.k.a. LLAPI) is an extremely thin layer on top of UDP.

Just as advertised, Unity Transport Layer API (also known as LLAPI[239]) is an extremely thin layer on top of UDP. There is no RPC support, no authentication, not even IDL or marshalling. On the other hand, in certain use cases this lack of built-in marshalling can be seen as a blessing (in particular, it allows you to use *any* kind of marshalling, which in turn enables you to use it with Standalone Servers).

---

238 With simulated packet loss, but probably without real-world bandwidth limitations at this point.

239 Don't ask why "Transport-Level API" is abbreviated "LLAPI" and not "TLAPI."

For me, the biggest practical problems with LLAPI are the following:

◆ Lack of IDL (which means manual marshalling for any not-so-trivial case, and discrepancies between marshalling of different communication parties tend to cause a lot of unnecessary trouble).

  ▪ This, however, can be mitigated by using a 4th-party IDL compiler. In theory -.NET *BinaryFormatter* or Google *Protocol Buffers* can be used for this purpose; however, at least for Client-2-Server communications – I suggest writing an IDL compiler yourself.

◆ IP:Port addressing model. Having to keep track at application level of all those IP/port numbers is a significant headache, especially as they can (and will) change.

◆ Lack of explicit support for state synchronization, and lack of RPCs (even void-only RPCs are better than nothing from a development speed point of view).

Still, while each of these problems is somewhat annoying (and all of them together are *quite* annoying), neither qualifies as a showstopper.

On the positive side: LLAPI provides you with pretty much all the capabilities in the world — that is, as long as you do everything-you-need yourself <wink />. Once again, we can think of LLAPI as a pretty thin layer on top of UDP, so we need to do pretty much everything that-goes-beyond-sending-and-receiving-UDP-packets ourselves.

When implementing your own protocol on top of LLAPI, I *strongly* suggest that you write your own IDL compiler, supporting both state sync and RPCs (ideally, non-void ones). For more discussion on IDL compilers, see Vol. I's chapter on Communications, and Vol. IV's chapter on Marshalling and Encodings.

3rd-party Communications for Unity: Photon Server

After we discussed built-in communication support in Unity itself, let's proceed with discussing 3rd-party network/communication libraries for Unity. The most popular of such libraries is probably Photon Server.

One restriction of Photon Server is that its Server-Side always runs on top of Windows .NET.

Photon Server is positioned as an "independent network engine," and does as advertised — adds its own network layer to Unity (or to Unreal). On the Client-Side, it integrates with Unity (i.e., the Client will use Unity's graphics and most of the scripting); on the Server-Side, in our terms, it is a Standalone Server (i.e., it uses pretty much nothing from Unity Client). As a result, it doesn't need to care about graphics etc., and can spend more effort on MOG-specific tasks such as load balancing and matchmaking service.

One restriction of Photon Server is that its Server-Side always runs on top of Windows .NET and APIs are written with C# in mind (I have no idea how it feels to use other .NET languages with Photon, and it *seems* that Photon doesn't support Linux[240]). For the Client-Side, however, Photon supports pretty much every platform you may want; so as long as you're okay with your Servers being Windows/.NET, you should generally be fine (though keep in mind additional costs of Windows licenses as discussed in Volume VII's chapter on Preparing for Deployment).

Functionally, the Photon Server is all about simulated worlds consisting of multiple relatively small rooms; while it is a restriction, this is actually how most MOGs out there are built anyway, so it is not as limiting as it may sound. For example, if you want to develop an MMORPG with a seamless world, then, as we discussed briefly in Vol. I's chapter on Communications, you'll need to split it into multiple zones to be able to cope with the load.

Within Photon Server, there are two quite different flavors for networked game development: Photon Server SDK and Photon Cloud (the latter includes Photon PUN and Photon Realtime).[241]

First, let's see how Photon organizes its Server-Side; this includes both Photon Server SDK and Photon Cloud, though the latter only if you can run your own Server-Side plugin, which, in turn, requires an Enterprise Cloud.

---

240   According to Exit Games, the Photon Server itself is written in C++, but is based on IO Completion Ports, so it is not easily portable to Linux (if at all).

241   Recently, Photon has added Bolt and TrueSync to the mix of its cloud-based offers. Staying true to the spirit of Authoritative Servers (as discussed in Vol. I's chapter on cheating), we won't discuss Bolt (which is mostly peer-2-peer technology, and as such is inherently vulnerable to rampant cheating), and TrueSync (which is lockstep protocol, and as such is wide-open to Information Leak attacks, not to mention severe problems with over 4-6 players playing within the same Game World).

As far as I understand, on the Server-Side, Photon uses thread pooling (more specifically – I/O Completion Ports), but it serializes calls of its Server-Side plugins to Game Worlds ("rooms" in Photon-speak). This is an architecture that is pretty much indistinguishable[242] from event processing/(Re)Actors, which is a Good Thing™ (in particular, because you don't need to care about thread sync <phew />). On the other hand, performance-wise it is not that obvious how well Photon synchronization works in practice (there are ways of implementing it in a good way, and ways to implement it in a pretty performance-hitting way too <sad-face />). Still, IMO what matters is that the plugin API is good in this regard (guaranteeing that no-thread-sync will ever be necessary) — and synchronization issues, if present, can be optimized by Photon guys without affecting plugins.

Photon Server SDK

IMPORTANT: Photon Server SDK is not to be confused with Photon Cloud/PUN, which will be discussed below.

Necessary disclaimer. Unfortunately, personally, I didn't see any real-world projects implemented over Photon Server SDK, and documentation on Photon Server SDK is much less obvious than on Photon Cloud, so I may be missing a few things here and there, but I will try my best to describe it.

Photon Server SDK doesn't explicitly support the concept of synchronized state.

When looking at Photon Server SDK, we'll notice that it doesn't explicitly support the concept of synchronized state. Instead, you can *BroadcastEvent()* to all connected peers and handle this broadcast on all the clients to implement state synchronization. Note that while *BroadcastEvent() can* be used to implement synchronized state, there is a substantial amount of work involved in making your synchronization work reliably (I would estimate the amount of work required to be of the same order of magnitude as implementing synchronised states on top of Unity's LLAPI). In addition, keep in mind that when relying on *BroadcastEvent()*, most compressions we discussed in Vol. I's chapter on Communications won't really work (because with broadcasts, we won't be able to adjust packets to account for some Clients having received the previous packet and some of the Clients not receiving

---

the same packet). Moreover, relying on broadcasts precludes Interest Management — and this is usually a Pretty Bad Thing™ for most of the games out there — both because of sending unnecessary traffic and because of wallhacks/maphacks (see Vol. I's chapter on Communications for the discussion). As a result, you will probably need to send events to individual clients (via *SendEvent()*), effectively using Photon SDK exactly as a low-level API such as LLAPI.

From an RPC point of view, the Photon Server has kinda-RPC. Actually, while it is named *Photon.SocketServer.Rpc*, it is more like a message-based request-response than a remote procedure call, as we usually understand it. In other words, within Photon Server (I'm not talking about PUN) I didn't find a way to declare a function as an RPC, and then to call it with all the stubs being automagically generated for you. Instead, you need to create a peer, send an operation request over the peer-to-peer connection, and while you're at it, register an operation handler to manage operation response.

This approach is more or less functionally equivalent to the simplistic Take 1 from Chapter 5; as Take 1 is not the most convenient thing to use (this is putting it mildly), it will become quite a hassle to work with directly (on the other hand, void RPCs, which are typical for the other libraries, correspond just to Take 2 out of 8, and are not *that* much better). In addition, I have my concerns about *Peer.SetCurrentOperationHandler()* function, which *seems* to restrict us to one outstanding RPC request per peer; this in turn creates additional (and IMHO unnecessary) hassles.

On the positive side (and unlike all the network engines discussed before), Photon Server does support such features as Server-to-Server communication and Load Balancing.

On the positive side (and unlike all the network engines discussed before), Photon Server does support such all-important-for-any-serious-MMO-development features as Server-to-Server communication and Load Balancing. While I didn't try them and so cannot talk about how well they're implemented (and implementing Load Balancing is a non-trivial exercise), at least there is a chance <smile />.

Photon Cloud (PUN and Realtime)

IMPORTANT: Photon Cloud is not to be confused with Photon Server SDK, which is discussed above.

The second flavor of Photon-based development is Photon Cloud; in turn, Photon Cloud-oriented Clients can use either Photon Unity Networking (PUN), or Photon Realtime. While Photon Cloud is implemented on top of Photon Server (which was discussed above), the way Photon Server is deployed for Photon Cloud is very different from the way you would develop your own Authoritative-Server game on top of Photon Server SDK.

The key problem with Photon Cloud is that basically you're not allowed to run your own code on the Server.[243] While there is an exception for so-called "Photon Plugins," they're relatively limited in their abilities, and what's even worse, they require a "Photon Enterprise Cloud" (which as of 2017 doesn't even have pricing published, instead saying "contact us" <ouch />).

And as long as you're not allowed to run your own code on the Server-Side, you cannot make your Server authoritative, which makes dealing with cheaters next-to-impossible. That's the reason I cannot recommend any kind of the Photon Cloud for any serious MOG development, at least until you (a) realize how to deal with cheaters given limited functionality of Photon Plugins, and (b) get a firm quote from Exit Games regarding their "Photon Enterprise Cloud" (as noted above, they don't provide pricing for the Enterprise Cloud, and the lack of a publicly available quote is usually a pretty bad sign of it being Damn Expensive™ <sad-face />).[244] In addition, it *seems* that to support encryption of the *whole* game traffic in PUN, we'd need to implement it ourselves — and at a rather inconvenient level (pretty much at the same level as for HLAPI).

These cheater-related potential issues are a pity, as the rest of Photon Cloud[245] is quite easy to use (more or less in the same range as Unity HLAPI, but with manual serialization of synchronization states). Still, unless you've managed to figure out how to implement an Authoritative Server over PUN or Realtime (and how to pay for it), I'd rather stay away from Photon Cloud because IMNSHO any sizeable game without an Authoritative Server carries way too much risk of becoming a cheaterfest.

Any game without an Authoritative Server carries way too much risk of becoming a cheaterfest.

---

243   To the best of my understanding.

244   BTW, I do sympathize with Chris Wegmann in this regard and do realize that allowing foreign code on your server boxes opens more than just one can of worms, but still having an Authoritative Server is *that* important that I cannot really recommend anything-without-the-ability-to-implement-Authoritative-Servers for any serious MOG.

245   At least as long as we're talking about PUN

3rd-party Communications for Unity: SmartFoxServer

Photon Server is not the only product within the niche of "Stand-alone Servers for Unity," and there is a competitor: SmartFoxServer. SmartFoxServer is a Java-based server, which allows different types of Clients — including the ones based on Unity.

My biggest complaint about SmartFoxServer is that instead of being Game Loop/Reactor based,[246] it is thread-pool based. Moreover, it is not just thread-pool based (well, under the hood, Photon Server is thread-pool-based too, but nobody can really see it), but SmartFox pushes all the complexity of the inter-thread sync into the face of the unlucky gamedev. In other words, with SmartFoxServer it is your responsibility as a gamedev to write all those mutexes, locks, and whatever-other-thread-sync-things-you-need to guarantee that your Game World State remains consistent, even under a heavy load.

Being an active opponent of mixing app-level logic with thread sync for many years (see, for example, [Hare]), I cannot agree with using thread sync within such a crucial part as Server Game Logic <sad-face />. For a more detailed discussion of the advantages of (Re)Actors/Game Loops over massive thread-pooling, see Chapter 5; a short summary goes along the following lines: (a) (Re)Actors/Game Loops are *much* simpler to code and maintain than mutex-ridden programs; (b) (Re)Actors/Game Loops are testable (while in general, explicitly thread-synced programs aren't), and this may enable production post-factum analysis and replay-based testing; (c) last but not least: (Re)Actors/ Game Loops tend to perform better (for about the same reasons nginx tends to perform better than Apache).

Of course, it is possible to simulate kinda-(Re)Actors based on SmartFoxServer (by protecting the state of the corresponding (Re)Actor with a mutex, and locking it for each and every method call that goes from SmartFox to our Game Logic[247]), but the efficiency of such an approach will inevitably be lacking (especially under a higher load and especially on typical NUMA server boxes). In addition, having

---

246   As discussed in this chapter, most other game-oriented network libraries *are* Game-Loop based.

247   In Java-speak, it is done via using a *synchronized* keyword that acquires a lock on 'monitor' of the object, but is still the same good old mutex.

the ability to "optimize" your code by rearranging mutex locks or using atomics can easily push you onto a slippery road of mutex-and-atomics-ridden code, and such code is inevitably very deadlock-and-race prone <very-sad-face />; of course, it is possible to avoid it (just by providing a wrapper locking the mutex before your Game Logic and saying "we never ever use mutexes and other thread-sync primitives in our Game Logic"), but doing so will require a certain level of self-discipline.

To summarize my feelings about massively multithreaded servers with thread sync exposed to the Game Logic: while they are not necessarily fatal (you still can create a wrapper that will eliminate thread sync at Game Logic level), IMNSHO they're pretty bad for the health of your game (as they push you into a very wrong direction, and resisting the temptation to bend the rules "just this once" will be difficult).

To summarize my feelings about massively multithreaded servers with thread sync exposed to the game logic: while they are not necessarily fatal, IMNSHO they're pretty bad for the health of your game.

The second significant drawback of SmartFoxServer is that while the newer SmartFoxServer seems to kinda support UDP, this support still feels like the kind of support Cinderella's sisters provided to her — just enough to *claim* that such support does exist (and lacking any desire to understand her or do anything real).[248] And as UDP is still a cornerstone for many games out there (in particular, it is pretty much a must for any game that has characteristic times below 100ms), I tend to see a lack of UDP understanding as a major disadvantage, at least for faster-paced games.

Other than that unfortunate decision to go massively multithreading (and pushing all the sync complexities to the gamedev instead of taking responsibility itself) and lacking support for UDP, SmartFoxServer follows pretty much the same patterns as the rest of the high-level libraries. It seems to support a concept of "sync state" (via "Room Server Variables"), though in absence of IDL, or equivalent, API to manipulate these variables is quite cumbersome; also SmartFoxServer has a way to add custom serialization (which is a Good Thing™ in general, as built-in serializations tend to be lacking).

---

248 When official "SMARTFOXSERVER 2X FPS TUTORIAL", while discussing a first-person shooter(!), claims that *"UDP was invented in a different millennium to run games over 14.4k modems,"* you cannot really expect much in terms of UDP understanding <sad-face /> or reasonable support for it. To see why this point of view is *dead* wrong – see Vol. IV's chapter on Network Programming, in particular, the discussion on Head-of-Line Blocking.

Instead of RPCs, SmartFoxServer has Requests; just as with Photon Server SDK — while these are functionally similar to RPCs, they're actually message-exchange mechanisms — which are quite cumbersome (though I have to admit that traditional void RPCs are not that much better).

On the plus side: SmartFoxServer *does* support encryption for all traffic; as it was one of my quite serious complaints about Photon, I am certainly happy to see encryption in SmartFox.

Overall, while I really dislike SmartFoxServer's approach to pushing mutexes/*synchronized* objects to a Game Logic level, if you make a framework which wraps *all* the calls to your Game Logic (synchronizing on a mutex/Java monitor *before* you enter Game Logic), IMO for slower-paced games SmartFox *might* become competitive with Photon Server SDK. What is important to note though is that both Photon Server SDK and SmartFoxServer have a killer advantage over non-Enterprise Photon Server Cloud — namely, both allow all-important Authoritative Servers. In addition, if your game calls for a Web Deployment Architecture, as discussed in Volume III's chapter on Server-Side Architectures, SmartFoxServer may fly too (along the lines of Web Deployment Architecture, as discussed in Vol. III, but using SmartFoxServer protocol instead of the usual-for-web-architectures HTTP).

3rd-party Communications for Unity: uLink

uLink [MuchDifferent] *seems* to be quite an interesting beast. It is a high-level API (effectively competing with Unity's own HLAPI), and from uLink documentation it *seems* that uLink folks know significantly more about the network than Unity developers. uLink guides (in particular, specific recommendations on implementing Authoritative Servers) also look very reasonable.

On the other hand, there are some rants about uLink (in particular, [Newman] makes me rather uneasy), and more importantly, as of the time of this writing, uLink is no longer updated for four-plus years (which is never a good sign <sigh />). As a result, I cannot really recommend uLink for new development. As for its technical properties, see the comparison table below.

3rd-party Communications for Unity: DarkRift

DarkRift is another interesting horse out of the stable of Unity networking libraries. What I like about it:

♦ It is explicitly oriented toward Authoritative Servers.

    ■ In particular, it means that the separation between Server and Client is very explicit, so the Client and Server are decoupled in a very clean manner.

    ■ Also, the concept of Server Plugins is good (actually, let's make it Very Good™).

♦ It is lean and mean.

    ■ And its protocol is reportedly reasonably lean and mean too.[249]

With DarkRift, the Client and Server are decoupled in a very clean manner.

However, nothing is perfect in this imperfect world, and DarkRift has two *very* significant drawbacks <sad-face />. My biggest complaint about DarkRift is the same as about SmartFoxServer: both are massively multithreaded, pushing all the thread-sync complexity into the gamedev's face (and believe me, you as gamedev will have lots of other things to care about besides mutexes). On the other hand, just like with SmartFoxServer, it is possible to create a framework that will ensure proper synchronization, so this IMO-very-significant drawback does *not* qualify as a showstopper.

Another big drawback of DarkRift (which is promised to be fixed in the long-promised DarkRift 2) is a lack of support for UDP.[250]

BTW, here go two rants about DarkRift marketing claims. First, in spite of DarkRift guys claiming that DarkRift is "as fast as server solutions can get," I have to note that (Re)Actor-based apps will generally beat massively multithreaded mutex-synchronized apps;[251] moreover,

---

249 Though, from what I know, using the compression techniques discussed in Vol. I's chapter on Communications, it is beatable.

250 Is it only me, or does DarkRift look like a C# incarnation of SmartFoxServer — or vice versa? On the other hand, on the plus side for DarkRift 2, it seems that understanding of UDP by DarkRift 2 folks is significantly better than that of the SmartFoxServer folks (though DarkRift 2, just as any other UDP-based system out there, still seems to lack support for "Low-Latency State Sync" discussed in Vol. I's chapter on Communications).

251 Under load, high-contention mutexes cause lots of thread context switches, and context switches are Damn Expensive (up to 1M CPU cycles <ouch! />). As a practical manifestation of the same thing, we can observe that non-blocking *nginx* does outperform massively-multithreaded *Apache*.

if we consider what is "fast" from the player's perspective, we'll see that with only TCP being supported by DarkRift, latency spikes over packet-losing Internet are going to be pretty bad (mostly due to head-of-line blocking; more in Vol. IV's chapter on Network Programming). Second, DarkRift promo materials seem to imply that "multithreaded API" is a good thing (and even a selling point); well, having (co-)architected a stock exchange and a game that runs 400K+ players simultaneously with 99.98% reliability, I contend that "multithreaded API" is a Really Bad Thing™ (note that "support for multicore processing" is a very different story and *is* necessary; it is just "multithreaded APIs" that need to be well-hidden from the view of the app-level developer).

Overall, I would be happy to recommend DarkRift (it does have a straightforward architecture, and good ideas), but this multithreading-exposed-to-app-level approach (coming right from the pre-nginx Dark Ages of Massively-Multithreaded Inquisition in the early 2000s) prevents me from suggesting it for Classical Deployment Architectures (see Vol. III's chapter on Server-Side Architecture for details); lack of UDP support is also a Really Bad Thing™ for fast-paced games such as FPS.

On the other hand, if your game is asynchronous, then DarkRift can be used to make an architecture similar to "Web Deployment Architecture" (in the same manner as SmartFoxServer; see above).

Also, I'd suggest keeping an eye on DarkRift 2's underlying library (*Hazel*); it is still under development, but may be just the ticket for C#-based Clients such as Unity (though more as a "lower-level" library than a full-scale Standalone Server).

Multithreading-exposed-to-app-level approach (coming right from the pre-nginx Dark Ages of Massively-Multithreaded Inquisition in the early 2000s) prevents me from suggesting DarkRift for Classical Deployment Architectures.

3rd-party Communications for Unity: Lower-Level Libraries

If you didn't see anything you like in the list above,[252] keep in mind that it is possible to use lower-level libraries (either C# ones or C++ ones) with Unity engine.

In particular, there is a whole bunch of "Reliable UDP" (RUDP) game-oriented libraries, and another bunch of socket-wrapper

---

252 I didn't <sad-face />.

libraries. Most of such libraries are C/C++, but there are a few C# libraries too (such as the aforementioned *Hazel* by *DarkRift* folks, and *LiteNetLib*).

At this point, we need to make one all-important observation about Clients: any call to a DLL inherently represents a very good attack point for bot writers,[253] so as a Big Fat Rule of Thumb™, DLLs on the Client-Side are to be avoided. On the other hand, for low-level DLLs such as RUDP (and provided that encryption happens *before* your call to the RUDP DLL), it is usually not *that* big a deal. Still, to avoid chances that you'll be inadvertently using encryption-within-your-DLL (which would hurt your anti-bot efforts *badly*), or any other similar issues, I would still suggest using pure C# libraries (rather than C/C++ libraries) from C# Clients.

Still, using a C++ library is possible from Unity. For a discussion on C++ libraries as such, see the *UE Networking: Lower-Level C/C++ Libraries* section below. Also, keep in mind that calling C/C++ from Unity is rather cumbersome; while it is certainly possible, you'll need to jump through quite a few hoops, first making a DLL out of your C/C++ library, and then explaining to Unity how to integrate that DLL into C# (see [Unity Technologies, Native Plugins] for details).

In addition, whether your library is C# or C++, make sure to read the *UE Networking: Lower-Level C/C++ Libraries* section below for a discussion about glue level and its API; to be honest, this is potentially even more important than bot-fighting considerations (at least, it is much more difficult to fix later).

Unity 5 Summary

When trying to summarize using Unity for MOG development, we have to note that from the point of view of MOGs, Unity as such has a significant drawback. As Unity is using C# on the Client-Side, and C# (as pretty much any other bytecode-compiled language) stands pretty poorly against bot writers (see Chapter 6 for a detailed discussion of this topic), it means that as soon as your game reaches 10K+ players, you're risking becoming a bot-writer paradise.

---

253 We'll discuss more of it in Vol. VIII's chapter on Bot Fighting.

To address this problem to *some* extent, it *might* be possible to recompile your Client-Side Unity code into C++ (via Unity's *IL2CPP*), but it still will certainly be less protected than native C++.[254] Still, it is very important to remember that

> *If using Unity, make sure to compile your game*
> *with **IL2CPP** as soon as possible.*

While I'm stopping short of saying that "you *must not* release a Unity-based game without being recompiled by *IL2CPP*," it is *very* likely that you'll need that additional protection provided by *IL2CPP*. As a result, making sure that you DO have this option is a very good thing; also, it is extremely important to avoid any kind of code that may break this capability (and there were quite a few such things reported to do so <sad-face />). In addition, while we're at it, I'll repeat a piece of advice from Chapter 6 to use *libil2cpp* as a static one (and NOT as *DLL/.so*) — it is *really* important for resilience to reverse engineering.

As for Unity networking, all in all, Unity 5/UNet does a decent job if you want to try converting your existing single-player game into a low-player-number multiplayer one. On the other hand, if you're into serious MOG development (with thousands of simultaneous players), you're going to face quite a few significant issues; while not showstoppers, they're going to take a lot of your time to deal with (and if you don't understand what they're about, you can easily bring your whole game to its knees).

With regard to 3rd-party networking frameworks aiming at Unity, well, most of them have their own deficiencies, and unfortunately, pretty bad ones at that; in particular, as discussed above, Photon Cloud (though not Photon Server) has problems with implementing Authoritative Servers, uLink is not updated for several years, and SmartFoxServer and DarkRift suffer from a massive multithreading programming paradigm (and a lack of decent UDP support, limiting their use for fast-paced games).

All in all, Unity 5/ UNet does a decent job if you want to try converting your existing single-player game into a low-player-number multiplayer one.

---

254 Assuming that in your native C++, you're following all the hardening guidelines from Vol. VIII's chapter on Bot Fighting.

For fast-paced games (such as shooters), it essentially leaves us with the choice of:

♦ Engine-Provided Server
  ▪ Unity's HLAPI and/or LLAPI. I have to admit that Unity's HLAPI is not my favorite way of doing things (beyond prototyping; see the *HLAPI Summary* section above for a relevant discussion). Still, with custom serialization and custom RPC marshalling, it *might* be made usable — though I still prefer LLAPI.

♦ Standalone Server
  ▪ Unity's LLAPI
  ▪ Photon Server SDK
  ▪ Lower-level libraries

For slower-paced games (think casinos, though some RPGs *might* be able to use them too), Standalone Servers based on DarkRift and SmartFoxServer might work; however, for both I have to insist on creating a framework that hides inter-thread synchronization from the application level.

Now, let's take a closer look at these options.

Engine-Provided Server. HLAPI Now, Probably LLAPI Later

As discussed above, one option for Client-Driven Development is to use Engine-Provided Server. For Unity, it pretty much means taking quite a big chunk of your existing single-player Client Logic and running it on your Server. Usually, this is not the most optimal path, but there are ways to make it work.

One way of doing it is to take your single-player Client and move all the decision-making logic to your Authoritative Server (sending player inputs there via RPC calls)[255]. After Server processes inputs, it will change the state and will publish it via HLAPI/[SyncVar] variables. Then Clients will get the current state of your game via these [SyncVar] variables — and display it. Bingo! You've got your MOG. Sort of…

More specifically, what you've got is certainly an MOG; however, you'll likely need to make quite a few refinements to make it work over

What you've got is certainly an MOG; however, you'll likely need to make quite a few refinements to make it work over the Internet for many thousands of players.

---

255 Don't forget to do it as early as possible in your development process — that's Damn Important™.

the Internet for many thousands of players. In particular, the following improvements are likely to be necessary (though YMMV depending on the nature and specifics of your game):

♦ Most likely, you'll want to use severely simplified 3D models on your Server-Side. As a Big Fat Rule of Thumb™, no textures are necessary on the Server-Side; moreover, the number of polygons in your meshes can be severely reduced (for example, for most RPGs out there, it is sufficient to describe a PC/NPC as a hexagonal prism or even box, and each of the rooms as a mere box with openings for doors).

  ▪ Ultra-low-res meshes tend to reduce the amount of work on the Server-Side many-fold (100x anyone?) — and as on the Server-Side, you need to run more than one Game World per Server; it comes in Very Handy™.

  ▪ Though it is not too likely, low-res meshes can affect playability, so it is paramount to start doing it (and testing it) ASAP.

♦ If your game is fast-paced, you may want to implement stuff such as Client-Side Interpolation/Extrapolation/Prediction, which were discussed in Vol. I's chapter on Communications. Before implementing these things, our game corresponds to "Take 1" of the flow diagram discussed in Vol. I, and if our game is an FPS, we'll likely need to get it all the way to "Take 3" (and maybe even beyond, into rather controversial Lag Compensation).

♦ Make sure to add encryption (as noted above, encryption is *very* important to deal with proxy bots[256]). This can be done in at least two different ways:

  ▪ Via encrypting your data before feeding it to HLAPI. As discussed above, it can be done within custom serialization *plus* via custom encrypted marshalling for HLAPI RPC calls — and is very cumbersome to say the least.

  ▪ By migrating to LLAPI, and implementing encryption there.

  ▪ In any case, I *strongly* suggest writing your own IDL compiler (see Vol. I's chapter on Communications and

---

256 And they're a very important class of bots/cheaters.

Vol. IV's chapter on Marshalling and Encodings for further discussion).

♦ If you multiply traffic generated by HLAPI-based implementation by the number of players you want to run on your Servers (and by the cost per Megabyte), chances are that you'll find it way too expensive. Alternatively, you may find that HLAPI-generated traffic for the individual player won't fit into a typical ADSL channel.[257] In this case, the following optimizations *might* help:

You may find that HLAPI-generated traffic for individual player won't fit into a typical ADSL channel.

- Make sure to create a separate Publishable State (see Vol. I's chapter on Communications for a discussion about the differences between the Server State, Publishable State, and Client State).

- If applicable, make sure to implement Interest Management as discussed in Vol. I.[258]

- Rewrite state sync (of that separate Publishable State) using custom serialization or LLAPI, using some or all compression techniques discussed in Vol. I.

  - While you're at it, pay special attention to rounding: not only does it reduce the number of bits, but it also reduces the amount of "white noise" in your communications — and any "white noise" is non-compressible by any further compression you may want to use.

Of course, this is only a very sketchy description, but I hope you've got the overall direction.

Standalone Server with Export from Unity

A second distinct option for working with Client-Driven Development Workflow (i.e., being able to use Unity's level editor) goes along the following lines (once again, we're assuming that single-player prototype is already working):

♦ Make a script to export data from Unity-level editor into a format that can be understood by your Standalone Server.

---

257 And most likely, as of 2017, your GDD still says that you DO need to support ADSL.

258 Or at least to understand why Interest Management doesn't apply to your game.

♦ Write a Standalone Server that will work with this exported level data and will use this data for simulation.

  ▪ For communication purposes, pretty much anything can be used, including LLAPI, Photon Server SDK, and low-level libraries of all sorts. It means that you'll need to implement all the state sync stuff yourself, but, on the other hand, while doing it, you will have complete flexibility (and will be able to implement all the stuff you may need, including all the optimizations described for the Engine-Provided Server above).

  ▪ As your Server will be standalone and unrelated to the Client:

    • As a benefit compared to the Engine-Provided Server, you'll get *much* cleaner decoupling between the Client and the Server (and *much* less trouble dealing with removing all the Client-Side stuff from the Server-Side).

    • On the other hand, additional care will be necessary to deal with the Client-Side Prediction (in many cases it is desirable to re-use Server-Side simulation code for Client-Side Prediction, so clean reusable API and cross-platform implementation will probably be necessary).

Engine-Provided vs Standalone: Which One Is Better?

Unfortunately, I can't tell which option — Engine-Provided Server or Standalone Server — is better; it depends on too many factors, and I don't know the processes well enough to generalize experiences I know about. However, I need to say that I've heard about games that are successfully implemented via *both* these options.

As for Server-to-Server communications (and you *will* need them; see for example Vol. I's chapter on Communications), neither of the ways described above will provide much help <sad-face />. However, it is not rocket science (and you can implement them on top of good ol' TCP sockets, or on top of LLAPI, or on top of a 3rd-party library such as ZeroMQ).

Unreal Engine 4

Unreal Engine 4 is a direct competitor of Unity, though it has some-what different positioning. Unlike Unity (which tries to be a jack of all trades), Unreal Engine is more oriented toward first-person games, and (arguably) does it better. Just like Unity, UE also supports a wide range of platforms (with the differences from Unity being of a marginal nature), and does have the support for HTML (again, using *emscripten*).

For UE4, supported programming languages are C++ and UE's own Blueprints. At some point, Mono team has tried to add support for C# to UE4, but dropped the effort shortly afterward <sad-face />.

Unreal Engine is more oriented toward first-person games, and (arguably) does it better.

It should be noted that UE4's variation of C++ has its own garbage collector (see, for example, [Epic Games]). Honestly, I don't really like hybrid systems that are intermixing manual memory management with GC (they introduce too many concepts that need to be taken care of, and tend to be rather fragile as a result), but Unreal's is reported to work pretty well.

Event-Driven Programming/Reactors

Unreal Engine is event-driven by design. As with Unity, normally game loop is hidden from sight, but you can override and extend it if necessary. And exactly as with Unity or (Re)Actors, everything happens within the same thread, so (unless you're creating threads explicitly) there is no need for thread synchronization.

Support for non-blocking processing in UE4 does exist, but you have to be very careful here, as there are several different (and often rather bulky) concepts involved. In particular, one has to be very careful with offloading, which is implemented via FAsyncTask<>; the problem here is how to return the data to the main game thread without crashing, and TBH, calling CreateAndDispatchWhenReady(…, ENamedThreads::GameThread) to execute a task in the main thread is *not* the most intuitive way of doing it. As for UE4 RPCs, just as with Unity, they're non-blocking but void-only, with all the relevant implications.

With regard to serializing the state of the Game World – in yet another similarity with Unity, such serialization *seems* to be doable, but (also like with Unity) it is going to be rather cumbersome.

UE for MOG

Moving our discussion on UE towards our primary subject of "using UE for MOGs," first we have to observe that pretty much like Unity, UE as such doesn't really provide a way to implement a clean separation between the Client and the Server code (while there is a *WITH_SERVER* macro for C++ code, it is far from being really cleanly separated). Now, let's take a bit closer look at UE networking.

UE Networking: Very Close to Unity 5 HLAPI

Just like Unity, at a higher level of abstraction, UE4 provides two primary communication mechanisms: state synchronization ("Replication" in UE-speak) and RPCs. There is not much to discuss here, as both replication and RPCs are very close to the Unity counterparts discussed above.

Replication in UE4 is conceptually very similar to Unity's [SyncVar]s.

In particular, replication in UE4 is conceptually very similar to Unity's [SyncVar]s (with a different syntax of *UPROPERTY(Replicated)* and *DOREPLIFETIME()*). UE4's RPCs (again having a different syntax of *UFUNCTION(Client)*/*UFUNCTION(Server)*) are again very similar to that of Unity HLAPI (with the only-void restriction, no support for addressing and for Server-to-Server communications, and so on).

Interest Management in UE4 is based on the concept of being "network relevant" and is dealt with via *AActor::NetCullDistanceSquared()* and *AActor::IsNetRelevantFor()* functions (ideologically similar to Unity's *NetworkProximityChecker* and *RebuildObservers()* respectively).

Being so close to Unity 5 ideology means that UE4 also shares all the drawbacks described above for Unity HLAPI; it includes sub-optimal traffic optimization for replicated variables, void-only RPCs, and a lack of support for Server-to-Server communications; see the *HLAPI Summary* section above for further discussion.

On the minus side, compared to Unity 5, UE4 doesn't provide LLAPI, so bypassing these drawbacks as was suggested for Unity is a tad more difficult (though still possible).

Most Popular 3rd-party Game Engines · **381**

UE Networking: Lower-Level C/C++ Libraries

While UE4 doesn't have a direct counterpart to Unity's LLAPI, it does provide classes to work directly with sockets (look for *FTcpSocketBuilder/FUdpSocketBuilder*), and using Berkeley sockets *seems* to be possible too. And as soon as we have some kind of sockets, implementing an (very thin) analogue of LLAPI is pretty easy.

Moreover, UE4 comes with an added (though relatively minor) benefit: UE4 is C++-based, and it is much easier to find 3rd-party C++ network libraries than C# ones. In general, I try to separate these C++ libraries into two broad categories: (a) reliable UDP libraries and (b) socket wrapper libraries. And as for OO-like libraries/frameworks such as *CORBA/DCOM/ICE*, I do NOT recommend them (and in spades too) for any over-the-WAN interaction; see the discussion in Chapter 5 for details.

As for C++ libraries, I try to separate them into two broad categories: reliable UDP libraries, and socket wrapper libraries.

Reliable UDP Libraries

The idea of a Reliable UDP (RUDP) library is pretty much as it says on the tin: it creates a reliable UDP channel to facilitate reliable exchanges without incurring TCP-style latencies.

There is a wide-spread perception that "RUDP provides better latencies than TCP;" however, it is *really* important to realize that retransmits and Head-of-Line blocking[259] are still necessary to achieve reliable-ordered delivery, whether we're using TCP or RUDP. As a result, when talking about reliable-and-ordered RUDP channels compared to TCP, latency improvements are mostly related to subtle reductions of retransmit timing (including the potential to avoid TCP-style "exponential backoff").

In fact, *significantly* better latency improvements from using UDP can be achieved when we implement UDP-based Low-Latency Compressible State Sync (which was discussed in Vol. I's chapter on Communications), but, unfortunately, I don't know of a single RUDP library that supports this concept out of the box <sad-face /> (though you can implement it yourself on top of the unreliable portion of RUDP library, or on top of plain UDP sockets for that matter). For more discussion on

---

259   As discussed in Vol. IV's chapter on Network Programming.

TCP, UDP, and their respective latencies, please see Vol. IV's chapter on Network Programming.

There are quite a few well-known RUDP libraries out there, including *Enet*, *UDT*, and *RakNet*; we'll discuss them in more detail in Vol. IV's chapter on Network Programming, but for the time being let's note that they give or take provide the same functionality (that is, unless you need "NAT punchthrough," but for Authoritative Servers hosted in datacenters and having static IP addresses, you don't really need it). One big problem with these three libraries is that they're not really developed/supported anymore; and while they're still working (there are no changes in the Internet infrastructure that can really break basic UDP) — the question of how optimal they still are may not be as obvious (as fine-tuning of the Internet, such as typical over-the-Internet delays and the reasons behind dropping packets, does change over time). IMO it is not *that* big a deal, but as there are newer alternatives, I'd prefer to use them <smile />.

Among newer libraries, there are two rather interesting ones. One is *proto-quic* [Google], which is essentially latency-optimized reliable streams by Google. In general, *proto-quic* (and QUIC in general) is intended as a latency-optimized multistream replacement for TCP+TLS — and should be treated exactly as such. In other words, do not expect major improvements latency-wise[260] (except for the initial handshake, where improvement is indeed significant), but it will provide *a bit* of latency improvement without significant changes to your TCP-oriented code (i.e., pretty much for free); it also allows for multiple streams, which allows you to prioritize your traffic within a single QUIC connection.

Another new kid on the block is *libyohimbo* by a recognized game networking guru, Glenn Fiedler.

Another new kid on the block (and a much more game-oriented one too) is *libyohimbo* [Fiedler] by a recognized game networking guru, Glenn Fiedler. I see *libyohimbo* as a more traditional RUDP library such as *RakNet* etc., but with encryption thrown in. And as (a) encryption is *really* important to deal with cheaters (more on it in Vol. VIII's chapter on Bot Fighting), and (b) as UDP encryption is non-trivial to implement (we'll discuss it in more detail in Vol. IV's chapter on Basic Security), well, built-in encryption *is* certainly a Good Thing™. If Glenn would

---

260　In particular, Head-of-Line Blocking is still there; more on it in Vol. IV's chapter on Network Programming.

also add support for state-sync (allowing for custom inter-packet compression and keeping track of already-acknowledged packets; see the discussion of Low-Latency Compressible State Sync in Vol I's chapter on Communications), I'd even stronger recommend *libyohimbo* <wink />.

Regardless of specific RUDP library you're using, I would argue that such libraries (while certainly very useful) are generally too low-level to be used directly by your Game Logic. Instead, most of the time a glue level sitting between your code and lower-level library is necessary;

> *Moreover, app-facing API of this glue level MUST be expressed in terms of your app needs (such as "let's update this variable on all the Clients") rather than in terms of capabilities of the underlying library (such as sending packets).*

This all-important rule makes sure that your game developers can concentrate on the Game Logic, while your network developers can concentrate on translating needs of Game Logic into underlying packets (reliable/unreliable connections, etc. etc.). Even if it is the same person who is writing both layers – this separation of concerns is still necessary; at least, it will allow to avoid thinking about both things at the same time (which almost-universally leads to cognitive overload and violation of the all-powerful "7±2" cognitive limit).

Socket Wrapper Libraries

The second large family of lower-level libraries lies even lower than RUDP, and are basically merely wrappers for UDP and/or TCP sockets. However, there are three important observations about mere wrappers:

(a) Using any 3rd-party socket library — including 3rd-party wrappers — *directly* from your Game Logic code qualifies a Pretty Bad Idea™; this means that you'll need your own wrapper library around a 3rd-party library anyway.

(b) Mere wrappers do *not* provide any additional functionality (instead, they often *lose* some functionality that the wrapper writer considered unimportant); contrast it with RUDP libraries, which *do* provide "reliable UDP" as a significant added-value.

Most of the time, I do **not** recommend using 3rd-party merely-wrapping libraries (writing your own mere wrapper is a very different story—these **are** useful, even very useful).

(c) It is usually a bit simpler to wrap system calls than to wrap 3rd-party wrappers (as system calls are usually better documented; and when talking about Berkeley sockets, well, they're *extremely* well-documented).

As a result, most of the time, I do *not* recommend using 3rd-party merely-wrapping libraries (writing *your own* wrapper-tailored-for-needs-of-your-app is a very different story—these *are* useful, even "very useful").

Examples of such merely-wrapping libraries include *PocoProject* and *boost::asio* (the latter, while providing non-blocking programming interface, is still too low-level to be used in Game Logic code, and tends to add unnecessary overheads in infrastructure-level code).

UE4 Summary: Engine-Provided and Standalone Servers

Now, we can try to summarize my ranting on UE4 in the context of MOGs. Overall, to convert an UE4 single-player game into a multi-player one, just as with Unity, there are the same two approaches of Engine-Provided Server and Standalone Server.

Using Engine-Provided Server means starting with splitting the single-player logic into Client-Side and Server-Side using an UE4-provided state sync and RPC, getting the whole thing running in this mode, and converting to custom-written state sync later (when/if it becomes necessary—though most of the time it will, sooner or later). The whole process is very similar to the one described for Unity in the *Engine-Provided Server. HLAPI Now, Probably LLAPI Later* section above, so make sure to refer there for a list of potentially important optimizations. One substantial difference from Unity is that for rewriting state sync (and potentially RPC) under UE4, you can do one of the following (a) use low-level UE4 functions such as *FUdpSocketBuilder* (and build your own stuff on top of it); or (b) use an RUDP library discussed above (however, you'll still need to write state sync yourself).

The Standalone Server approach for UE4 is also conceptually similar to the Standalone Server described for Unity 5 above. The idea is to use some kind of export from the UE4 (to obtain level information to be used by your Standalone Server), and then to write a standalone Server from scratch—either on top of plain sockets, or using one of the lower-level libraries discussed above.

Amazon Lumberyard

A relatively recent development in the field of major single-player engines that allow for MOG development is Amazon Lumberyard. Looking at it from 30,000-feet, we can consider Amazon Lumberyard a well-known CryEngine, *plus* added network support (and also with full source code, etc., etc.). Moreover, it's free (well, sort of; see below).

A Choice Between Amazon-Only Hosting—and (Hopefully) Co-Location

Amazon Lumberyard can be seen as a well-known CryEngine, with network support added.

> The only free cheese is in the mousetrap
>
> — Proverb

Disclaimer: I am not a lawyer, and the analysis below is just my personal speculations, and does not represent any attempt to provide any kind of legal advice. Make sure to seek professional advice in all legal matters such as licenses, copyrights, etc.

If you think that an AAA-grade engine for free "is too good to be true," well, indeed it is. The trick is that

> *The license of Amazon Lumberyard (at least as I read it) prevents you from running your Lumberyard-based game on leased servers (or cloud services) other than Amazon ones.*

For details, it is better to refer to the original authoritative source [Amazon, AWS Service Terms], with the most-interesting-for-us point being found in paragraph 57.4. Moreover, if you're serious about using Lumberyard, it is better still to have your *lawyer* read the whole agreement (and you may also want to ask Amazon more specific questions about what is allowed and what is not).

My understanding of paragraph 57.4 from [Amazon, AWS Service Terms] is that you're still free to run your-game-using-Lumberyard-engine on the servers that "you own and operate." From a very unofficial discussion in [Amazon, Two questions about Lumberyard licensing], it *seems* that:

♦ Amazon is not okay with you running a Lumberyard game on traditional rented servers, or cloud servers (that is, unless it is Amazon cloud).

♦ Amazon *seems* to be okay with you purchasing servers (to "own" them), and then co-locating them.

▪ Whether it is okay to use your-colocating-ISP guys to install and plug in your servers, and to act as "remote hands" is still not 100% clear, but at least there is a chance (and in a really extreme case, you could go to your ISP yourself once to connect the servers; as we'll see in Vol. VII's chapter on Preparing for Deployment, with the right choice of servers, 99.99% of the server administration beyond connecting Ethernet cables can and should be done remotely).

This basically *seems* to leave you with two options:

♦ Run your game on Amazon EC2. This, however, has two important drawbacks:

▪ As we'll see in Vol. VII's chapter on Preparing for Deployment, virtualization tends to lead to increased latencies and latency spikes (which BTW tend to be very important for shooters, which is *exactly* the kind of game aimed at by Lumberyard). This is not a problem for social games, but can become a big deal for shooters and MOBAs.

• While this problem can be avoided by using "bare-metal cloud servers," last time I checked, Amazon didn't provide such an option <sad-face />.

▪ As we'll see in Vol. VII, pricing of the cloud services tends to be higher-than-rented-servers for quite a few games out there (optimal configurations tend to go along the lines of "handling constant load on rented servers, and handling load spikes on the cloud servers"). [261]

Pricing of the cloud services tends to be higher-than-rented-servers for quite a few games out there.

---

261 As of 2017, the typical price difference between a per-month lease of a "dedicated server" and comparable "cloud server" for the same time period is about 4x (i.e. the "cloud server" is 4x more expensive than the "dedicated rented server"). While the price difference can be compensated by elasticity of the cloud, for quite a few typical game load patterns elasticity is not sufficient to compensate for the 4x price difference (and the best option price-wise is usually a hybrid one, with the "flat" portion of the load handled by per-month leased servers, and load spikes handled by the cloud servers). For a detailed discussion, see Vol. VII's chapter on Preparing for Launch.

- In addition, if not for the co-location option, staying with EC2 forever-and-ever would mean an *Absolute Vendor Lock-In* (and I am very, *very* cautious of such lock-ins, at the very least for Games with an Undefined Lifespan).

♦ Run your game from co-location. This also has a drawback, related to the costs and complications of co-location. We'll discuss it in Vol. VII's chapter on Preparing for Deployment, but very briefly: with co-location we'll need to handle (and pay for) all server upgrades ourselves, will need to store some spare parts (or keep whole servers in reserve to account for multi-hour hardware-fix times by vendors), won't get any benefit from discounts-that-big-providers-get-for-the-same-hardware, and so on.

Overall, you *may* be able to run your Lumberyard-based game smoothly (for example, using co-location for DB Servers and "flat" load+EC2 cloud for load spikes[262]), but keep in mind that due to the licensing restrictions, doing so may cause significantly more trouble than non-Lumberyard-based games. *Whether the benefits of the Lumberyard as an engine are worth the trouble depends entirely on your priorities. If for any reason you feel that you cannot live without CryEngine/Lumberyard, I believe it should be possible to use them; just make sure that you know ALL the implications of doing this, including licensing ones.*

One thing to keep in mind if your balance of pros and cons shows that you *do* want to use Lumberyard:

> *Make 100% sure that if necessary you **will** be able to use co-location, even if you do **not** plan to use co-location in the foreseeable future.*[263]

To achieve it, I *strongly* advise that you at least (a) obtain an official response from Amazon about co-location (and about permission for ISP folks to connect cables to your Servers without violating the Lumberyard license), and (b) have your lawyer read Amazon's response to make sure that your intended usage of Lumberyard doesn't contradict their license terms.

---

262   And it will likely be the best approach price-wise regardless of Lumberyard license restrictions, though beware of cloud latencies.

263   With Games with an Undefined Lifespan, you never know what changes will come five years down the road, and Absolute Vendor Lock-In is damn dangerous, even when you're locked-in by Amazon.

With all the lawyer-speak about licenses aside, we can finally get to more interesting stuff.

Amazon Lumberyard: General

With all the lawyer-speak about licenses aside, we can finally get to more interesting stuff.

From what I was able to find out (with all the usual disclaimers that it is just one rabbit's opinion), Amazon Lumberyard is not that much different from the other engines we have discussed above. As a result, I won't repeat the same things over and over again, but instead will try to describe *differences* between *Lumberyard* and *Unity/UE4. Please also note that information on Lumberyard is relatively scarce, and that I didn't have a chance to play with it myself — so please take all my analysis with even bigger pinch of salt than usual.*

Amazon Lumberyard: Platforms, Programming Languages, and Event-Driven Programming

In a similar manner to the other game engines, Amazon Lumberyard supports multiple programming languages (C++ and Lua). Note though that unlike UE4, Lumberyard *seems* to rely on traditional-for-C++ manual memory management (rather than introducing some kind of garbage collection like UE4 does).

With regards to platform support, Lumberyard is a bit more limited than Unity/UE4; and while all the major desktop/console/mobile platforms are supported (and a lack of support for MacOS/Wii/WinPhone is usually not *that* important for modern games), an inability to release an HTML5/browser-based version of your game *may* be a negative (depending on the specifics of your game, marketing plans, and GDD; for more discussion, see Vol I's chapter on GDD).

As for event-driven programming, at heart Lumberyard[264] is essentially an event-driven program. In addition, an equivalent of off-loading capabilities discussed in Chapter 5 is supported (see, for example, [Amazon, Physics Scripting Guide]).

Amazon Lumberyard Networking: GridMate

The communication layer for Amazon Lumberyard is known as "Amazon GridMate" and again, its concepts are quite similar to other

---

264   As is Unity/UE4.

high-level communication systems discussed above. In particular, GridMate provides both synchronized states and void RPCs.

Synchronized states in GridMate are known as "replicas." And while GridMate uses an-IMO-rather-outdated concept of "replica ownership,"[265] it *seems* that if you keep all your replicas owned by the Server-Side, it will allow you to make your Server an Authoritative one <phew />. One thing that I have not the slightest idea about is how efficient GridMate's state sync really is; on the positive side, GridMate seems to support custom serialization (via custom *Marshalers*), so even if the built-in one is not good enough for your purposes, you will be able to provide your own one.

As for void RPCs, they are also present in GridMate, though in a somewhat unusual manner. In particular, within GridMate, RPCs are seen primarily as ways to manipulate replicas (and are actually executed in the context of replicas); still, in spite of this peculiarity, it doesn't seem to be *too* big a deal for our purposes.

Of the unique features of GridMate, I need to mention their support for encryption[266] — and, as I noted earlier more than once, encryption is a prerequisite for robust anti-cheating. On the other hand, at the moment GridMate seems to limit encryption to Win64-only(!)[267] — and this pretty much negates most of the good things provided by built-in encryption (as we'll discuss in Vol. III's chapter on Server-Side Architecture, in most cases we don't want to run Windows-based Servers, and limiting Clients to desktops-only is not always feasible either).

At the moment GridMate seems to limit encryption to Win64-only.

AWS Integration: Amazon GameLift

With Amazon being a major cloud provider, it would be quite strange if they wouldn't provide integration with their cloud ecosystem in their Lumberyard. Such an integration service is known as Amazon GameLift.

Very, very roughly: GameLift is intended to help you run your Game World Servers (known simply as "Game servers" in Amazon

---

265 Which IMO comes from the Dark Ages of Authoritative Clients.

266 For other engines, you will need to encrypt the traffic yourself.

267 Which is IMO quite strange: saying *"OpenSSL"* and *"Win64-only"* in the same breath doesn't make much sense TBH.

GameLift), to allocate and destroy new cloud instances as necessary, to load-balance them, and even to optimize player experiences geographically (see [Amazon, Game Architecture with Amazon GameLift] for a discussion on GameLift architecture). How good GameLift is for these purposes is still unclear to me; my own extremely wild guess is that: (a) GameLift is better than what-most-of-us-would-do from our very first attempt at writing such a system; (b) taking specifics of our game into account, we should be able to beat GameLift efficiency-wise[268] sooner rather than later. Still, having the *option* to launch our game without knowing much about multi-datacenter hosting certainly qualifies as a Good Thing™.

Oh, and one more thing: GameLift seems to be heavily oriented toward games-with-lots-of-small-Game-Worlds, so if your game is an MMO with larger and/or seamless Game Worlds, make sure to study whether it will work for you.

Amazon Lumberyard: Summary and Engine-Provided/Standalone Servers

As the bottom line for Amazon Lumberyard: personally, I am quite cautious of their license agreement; however, *if* co-location is indeed allowed, it *can* be made viable. Other than that, Lumberyard support for network stuff *seems* to be pretty much along the same lines as Unity and UE4 (with an added benefit of GameLift).

As for options to organize your Client-Driven Development Flow around Lumberyard, once again, the same options of Engine-Provided Server and Standalone Server are possible. Same old, same old...

As for options to organize your Client-Driven Development Flow around Lumberyard, once again, the same options of Engine-Provided Server and Standalone Server are possible.

To get Engine-Provided Server, you can start moving your Game Logic to the Server, starting with naïve marshalling (to improve it later). If you prefer Standalone Server, you can try exporting your levels (which I hope is possible) and then proceed to write your Standalone Server (without actually using any of GridMate, but rather relying on 3rd-party libraries or on system-provided sockets). Same old, same old...

Urho3D

After we spent this much time discussing commercial game engines, we need to mention that there are also open-source ones (and usually they're free, *both* as in "free beer" *and* in "free speech"). At the very least, it is next-to-impossible to beat them in terms of license price <smile />. On the other hand, open-source engines tend to be less popular than their commercial counterparts, tend to have less polished development UIs, and, probably most importantly, they often fall behind in advanced 3D graphics capabilities when compared to AAA-level engines, such as UE and CryEngine/Lumberyard.[269] This price-vs-capabilities choice creates a kind of balance between the commercial and open-source game development worlds.

Of open-source engines, we will discuss Urho3D; of course, it is certainly not the only open-source 3D engine out there, but from my mostly-network-oriented perspective I happen to like it more than the competition (in particular, unlike some other not-named-here open-source engines, Urho3D devs seem to understand the importance

---

269   To be honest, 3D graphics provided by good open-source engines such as Urho3D is beyond *my own* capabilities with regards to 3D graphics, so it wouldn't be a limiting factor for me personally. Still, capabilities of the relevant *teams* are a completely different story.

of Authoritative Servers, know what Interest Management is about, etc. — and this is always a good sign).

Once again, within this book we will *not* discuss aspects such as graphics and toolchains (instead, we'll concentrate on the overall architecture and networking features). In addition, as differences between different engines at the concept level are not too drastic, I won't repeat the same things again and again, and will refer to *differences* from previously discussed engines instead.

Urho3D: Supported Platforms, Programming Languages, and Event-Driven Programming

Urho3D, being an open-source engine, has platform preferences that are quite different from commercial ones. In particular, in Urho there is no support for consoles, but there is support for Client-Side Linux. HTML5 via *emscripten* is also supported.

As for programming languages, Urho3D supports C++ and AngelScript (which is apparently quite popular among serious gamedevs).

When it comes to event-driven programming, Urho3D (just like all the other engines we've seen) *is* event-driven (and, of course, has Game Loop — known as "main loop" in Urho3D). To utilize multi-core, Urho3D also supports a version of Off-Loading (via *WorkQueue*).

Urho3D Networking

Urho3D networking is very much centered on Authoritative Servers.

As noted above, Urho3D networking is very much centered on Authoritative Servers (and, as we discussed in Volume II's chapter on Cheating, Authoritative Servers are *a must* for serious MOG development). What's good about Urho3D networking is that it will be very difficult for you to depart from the Authoritative Server paradigm (which is a Good Thing™, as such departures will cause *lots* of trouble down the road).

To implement networking, Urho3D provides "scene replication" [Urho3D]; moreover, it *does* support distance-based Interest Management. As for the other types of Interest Management, it is unclear whether they are officially supported; however, my wild guess is that even if they're not, it should be possible to support them, given the open-source nature of the engine. In addition, while Urho3D doesn't support Client-Side Prediction by itself, it does provide hooks (referred to as "intercepting network updates") for doing it yourself.

As for point-2-point communications, Urho3D departs from the usual-for-other-game-engines concept of void-only RPCs, preferring plain message exchanges. IMNSHO, it is not *that* much different from void-only RPCs (TBH, both are rather ugly; to see the difference yourself, you can compare Take 1 and Take 2 in Chapter 5).

Under the hood, Urho3D used to use *kNet*, but very recently it *seems* Urho3D devs have switched to *RakNet*.

Urho3D: Summary and Engine-Provided/Standalone Servers

Overall, of the open-source game engines I've seen, Urho3D developers *seem* to be the most aware of the typical problems that arise in the MOG environment. As a result, if opting for open-source, Urho3D is the engine that I'd currently recommend for MOG development.

As for the Engine-Provided Server and Standalone Server options, exactly as with other engines, both of these options *seem* to be workable for Urho3D.

Of the open-source game engines I've seen, Urho3D developers *seem* to be the most aware of the typical problems that arise in the MOG environment.

The Engine That Didn't Make It—Source

In addition to Unity, UE, and Lumberyard, there is another major game engine that is worth mentioning, but which didn't make it to our comparison. I am referring to Source engine.

At the time of this writing (late-2017) Source engine was in a state of "Source 2 engine long-announced but not released to the public"; as a result, it doesn't make much sense to review the outdated Source engine, and is not possible yet to review Source 2. As soon as Source 2 is released (though it is not clear when—or even if—it will happen), I would certainly like to review it, but for now I don't have such an opportunity <sad-face />.

Comparison Table

The discussion above (plus some subtle additional details) is summarized in the table below.

Features (those IMO most important ones are in bold)	Unity 5 (HLAPI)	Unity 5 (LLAPI)	Photon Server SDK	Photon Cloud	SmartFoxServer 2X	uLink
General						
Price	Unity Free: Free, up to $100K revenue Unity Pro: $125/seat/month, unlimited revenue ☺	Free: Free, up to 100 simultaneous connections Unlimited: $175/month, unlimited☺. Unity price extra		Hosting included ☺ $185/month/1000 simultaneous connections ☺ (no Authoritative Servers)😡 Unity price extra☺	100CCU: EUR250, up to 100 connections. Unlimited: EUR3000, unlimited connections. Unity price extra☺	EUR550 / game title ☺
Last Update[271]	Less than a month ago☺	5 months ago☺			4 months ago ☺	3 years ago😡
Platforms						
Desktop	Win/MacOS/SteamOS☺	Win/MacOS☺			Win/ MacOS ☺	Win/ MacOS/ SteamOS☺
Consoles	PS/Xbox/Wii☺	PS/ Xbox/Wii☺			?[272] ☺	PS/Xbox/ Wii ☺
Mobile	IOS/Android / WinPhone☺	iOS/Android/ WinPhone☺			iOS/ Android ☺	iOS/ Android/ WinPhone☺
HTML5	Yes/Websockets ☺	Yes/Websockets☺			Yes/Websockets ☺	Yes/ Websockets☺
Server	Windows/ Linux ☺	Windows Only😠			Windows/ Linux☺	Windows/ Linux☺

---

270 As of mid-2017, DarkRift Networking 2 wasn't available, so I'm listing properties of DarkRift Networking 1.

271 As of September 2017.

Disclaimer: all information below is "to the best of my understanding"; having some mistakes in this table is very likely; before relying on anything, make sure to double-check it yourself.

DarkRift[270]	Unreal Engine 4	RUDP Libraries	Amazon Lumber-yard	Urho3D	My ideal DIY network engine (along the lines of this book)
Free: up to 20 simultaneous connections, Extreme: $100 / Server: unlimited connections☺	5% of revenue 😐	Free☺	Free if you're running on AWS or on "owned and operated hardware". Not available otherwise😠	Free (both as in "free beer" and "free speech"☺	N/A
1 month ago☺	1.5 months ago ☺	From "less than a month ago" for *libyohimbo*☺, to "over 3 years ago" for UDT😠	Less than a month ago☺	Less than a month ago☺	N/A
Win/ MacOS☺	Win/ MacOS/ SteamOS☺	Depends	Win😐	Win / MacOS / Linux☺	Whatever tickles your fancy☺
?	PS/XBox☺	Depends	PS / XBox☺	None😠	Whatever floats your boat☺
?	iOS/ Android☺	Depends	iOS / Android☺	iOS / Android ☺	Whatever butters your biscuit☺
No😠	Yes/Websockets ☺	No😠	No😠	Yes☺	Yes☺
Windows☺/ Linux😐[273]	Windows/ Linux ☺	Windows / Linux ☺	Windows / Linux ☺	Windows / Linux☺	Windows / Linux ☺

272 Issues were reported when trying SmartFox on consoles, but supposedly fixable or even fixed.

273 Via Mono.

Features	Unity 5 (HLAPI)	Unity 5 (LLAPI)	Photon Server SDK	Photon Cloud	SmartFox Server 2X	uLink
Programming Languages						
C/C++	Sort Of [274] 😐		Client Only[275] 😐		Client Only 🙂	Client Only 🙂
Garbage-Collected	C#/CLI 🙂		C#/CLI 🙂		Java 🙂	C#/CLI 🙂
Scripting	JS/CLI, Boo/CLI 🙂		Client Only 🙂		Client Only 🙂	Client Only 🙂
Best-possible resilience to bot writers[279]	5-6/10 🙂 (C# with *IL2CPP*)		N/A[280]			
Programming Model						
Event-Driven Programming without app-level Thread Sync	Yes 😃	Yes 🙂	Sort of[281] 🙂	Sort Of[281] 🙂	No[282] 😐	Yes 🙂
Deterministic Goodies[284]	No 😠	No 😠	No 😠	No 😠	No 😠	No 😠
void non-blocking RPCs	Yes 🙂	No 😐	No 😐	Yes 🙂	No 😐	Yes 🙂
non-void non-blocking RPCs	No 😠	No 😠	No 😠	No 😠	No 😠	No 😠
Futures for RPCs	No 😠	No 😠	No 😠	No 😠	No 😠	No 😠
Co-routines	Yes 🙂	Yes 🙂	Yes 🙂	Yes 🙂	No 😠	Yes 🙂
Clear Client-Server Separation	No (favors Engine-Provided Server)		Yes (favors Standalone Server)	No (favors Engine-Provided Server)	Yes (favors Standalone Server)	No (favors Engine-Provided Server)
Graphics						
3D	Unity 🙂		Unity 🙂		Unity 🙂	Unity 🙂
2D	Unity 🙂		Unity, Cocos2D 🙂		Unity, Flash, etc. 🙂	Unity 🙂
2D+3D Views on the same game[288]	No 😠	No 😠	DIY 🙂	No 😠	No 😠	No 😠
Networking — General						
Support for Authoritative Server	Yes 🙂	Yes 🙂	Yes 🙂	No[289] 😐	Yes 🙂	Yes 🙂

274 Unmanaged code is possible, but cumbersome.

275 On Server-Side, unmanaged C++ might work.

276 Actually, UE4 is using a somewhat-garbage-collected dialect of C++.

277 Mono tried to add support for C# in UE4, but this effort looks abandoned.

278 As noted above, UE4 has their own garbage collection for C++.

279 Based on the best programming language available, with per-language resilience to bot writers taken from Table 6.1.

280 Depends on the engine used for the Client.

281 While strictly speaking, Photon plugins are not event-driven, they're guaranteed to be serialized "as if" they're in the same thread.

DarkRift	Unreal Engine 4	RUDP Libraries	Amazon Lumberyard	Urho3D	My ideal DIY network engine
Client Only[275] 😐	Yes[276] ☺	Yes ☺	Yes ☺	Yes ☺	Yes ☺
C#/CLI ☺	No[277,278] 😠	No 😠	No 😠	No 😠	C#/Any, Java/Any, etc. ☺
Client Only ☺	"Blueprint" 😐	No 😠	Lua ☺	AngelScript ☺	JS/Any (incl JS/V8 and Node.js), Python/Any, etc. ☺
	7.5/10 ☺ (C++)	N/A[280]	7.5/10 ☺ (C++)	7.5/10 ☺ (C++)	7.5/10 ☺ (C++)
No[282] 😐	Yes ☺	Agnostic[283]	Yes ☺	Yes ☺	Yes ☺
No 😠	No 😠	N/A	No 😠	No 😠	Yes[285] ☺
No 😐	Yes ☺	N/A	Yes ☺	No 😐	Yes ☺
No 😠	No 😠	N/A	No 😠	No 😠	Yes ☺
No 😠	No 😠	N/A	No 😠	No 😠	Yes[285] ☺
Yes ☺	No 😠	N/A	No 😠	No 😠	Yes[285] ☺
Yes (favors Standalone Server)	No (favors Engine-Provided Server)	Yes (favors Standalone Server)	No (favors Engine-Provided Server)	Yes (favors Standalone Server)	Whatever you prefer ☺
Unity ☺	UE4 ☺	Any[287] ☺	CryEngine ☺	Urho3D[286] 😐	Any[287] 😐
Unity ☺	UE4 ☺	Any[287] ☺	No	Urho2D ☺	Any[287] 😐
No 😠	No 😠	N/A	No 😠	No 😠	Yes ☺
Yes ☺	Yes ☺	Agnostic	Yes ☺	Yes ☺	Yes ☺

282 Can be kinda-simulated but performance is likely to be hit.

283 It is possible to do event-driven programming using lower-level libs, but it is beyond their scope.

284 Replay testing, production post-mortem, server fault tolerance, etc.

285 Restrictions apply; batteries not included. See Chapter 5 for details.

286 While reasonably good, it still cannot really compete with UE4 or CryEngine <sad-face />.

287 Integrating with the editor is difficult.

288   Note that this is *different* from 2D+3D "hybrid" games.

289 Photon Plugins *may* allow for a way out, but this needs separate analysis.

Features	Unity 5 (HLAPI)	Unity 5 (LLAPI)	Photon Server SDK	Photon Cloud	SmartFox Server 2X	uLink
Networking — Marshalling/IDL						
IDL	In-Language ☺	No 😠	No 😠	In-Language[290] ☺	No 😠	In-Language[290] ☺
State Synchronization	Yes ☺	DIY 😐	DIY 😐	DIY 😐	Yes ☺	DIY 😐
Clear Server-State — Publishable State Client State separation	No[291] 😐	N/A 😠	N/A 😠	No[291] 😐	No[291] 😐	No[291] 😐
Cross-language IDL	No 😠	N/A 😠	N/A 😠	No 😠	N/A 😠	No 😠
IDL Encodings	No 😠	N/A 😠	N/A 😠	No 😠	N/A 😠	No 😠
IDL Mappings	No 😠	N/A 😠	N/A 😠	No 😠	N/A 😠	No 😠
Interest Management	Yes ☺	DIY 😐	Yes ☺	Yes ☺	DIY 😐	DIY 😐
Client-Side Interpolation	DIY ☺	DIY ☺	DIY ☺	DIY ☺	DIY ☺	DIY ☺
Client-Side Extrapolation	DIY ☺	DIY ☺	DIY ☺	DIY ☺	DIY ☺	DIY ☺
Client-Side Prediction	DIY ☺	DIY ☺	DIY ☺	DIY ☺	DIY ☺	DIY ☺
Delta Compression (whole fields)	Automatic ☺	DIY 😐	DIY 😐	DIY 😐	DIY 😐	Automatic (reliable stream only) 😐
Delta Compression (field increments)	DIY 😐	DIY 😐	DIY 😐	DIY 😐	DIY 😐	DIY 😐
Variable Ranges, Rounding-when-Transferring, and Bit-Oriented Encodings	DIY 😐	DIY 😐	DIY 😐	DIY 😐	DIY 😐	DIY 😐
Dead Reckoning	DIY 😐	DIY 😐	DIY 😐	DIY 😐	DIY 😐	DIY 😐
Sync of Arbitrary Trees (see Vol. I's chapter on Communications)	DIY 😐	DIY 😐	DIY 😐	DIY 😐	DIY 😐	DIY 😐
VLQ	DIY 😐	DIY 😐	DIY 😐	DIY 😐	DIY 😐	DIY 😐
Huffman Coding	DIY 😐	DIY 😐	DIY 😐	DIY 😐	DIY 😐	DIY 😐
IDL support for backward compatibility	No 😠	N/A 😠	N/A 😠	No 😠	N/A 😠	No 😠

290 Last time I checked, Photon PUN and uLink had only RPC part as declarative IDL; Publishable State was via manual serialization.

DarkRift	Unreal Engine 4	RUDP Libraries	Amazon Lumberyard	Urho3D	My ideal DIY network engine
No 😠	In-Language 🙂	No 😠	In-Language 🙂	No 😠	Yes 🙂
No 😠	Yes 🙂	No 😠	Yes 🙂	Yes 🙂	Yes 🙂
N/A 😠	No[291] 😐	N/A 😠	No[291] 😐	No[291] 😐	Yes 🙂
N/A 😠	No 😠	N/A 😠	N/A 😠	N/A 😠	Yes 🙂
N/A 😠	No 😠	N/A 😠	N/A 😠	N/A 😠	Yes 🙂
N/A 😠	No 😠	N/A 😠	N/A 😠	N/A 😠	Yes 🙂
DIY 😐	Yes 🙂	DIY 😐	DIY 😐	Yes 🙂	Yes 🙂
DIY 🙂	DIY 🙂	DIY 🙂	DIY 🙂	DIY-with-Helper 🙂	DIY-with-Helper 🙂
DIY 🙂	DIY 🙂	DIY 🙂	DIY 🙂	DIY-with-Helper 🙂	DIY-with-Helper 🙂
DIY 🙂	DIY 🙂	DIY 🙂	DIY 🙂	DIY-with-Helper 🙂	DIY-with-Helper 🙂
DIY 😐	Automatic 🙂	DIY 😐	DIY 😐	DIY 😐	Controlled 🙂
DIY 😐	DIY 😐	DIY 😐	DIY 😐	DIY 😐	Yes 🙂
DIY 😐	DIY 😐	DIY 😐	DIY 😐	DIY 😐	Yes 🙂
DIY 😐	DIY 😐	DIY 😐	DIY 😐	DIY 😐	Yes 🙂
DIY 😐	DIY 😐	DIY 😐	DIY 😐	DIY 😐	Yes 🙂
DIY 😐	DIY 😐	DIY 😐	DIY 😐	DIY 😐	Yes 🙂
DIY 😐	DIY 😐	DIY 😐	DIY 😐	DIY 😐	Yes 🙂
N/A 😠	No 😠	N/A 😠	No 😠	N/A 😠	Yes 🙂

291 It is possible to separate them, but requires substantial additional efforts.

Features	Unity 5 (HLAPI)	Unity 5 (LLAPI)	Photon Server SDK	Photon Cloud	SmartFox Server 2X	uLink
Networking — Addressing/Authentication						
Addressing Model	"Client"/ "Server"[292] ☻	IP- :Port[293] ☺	IP:Port[293] ☺	"Client"/ "Server"[292] ☹	"Client"/"- Server"[292] ☹	"Client"/"Serv- er"[292] ☹
Player Authentica- tion	DIY☺	DIY☺	DIY☺	DIY☺	DIY☺	Yes☺
Encryption[294]	Limit- ed[295] ☹	DIY☺	DIY☺	Limited[295] ☹	Yes[296] ☺	Yes☺
Server-to-Server Communications	No[297] ☹	DIY☺	Yes☺	No[297] ☹	No[297] ☹	No[297] ☹
Networking — Supported Protocols						
UDP	Yes☺	Yes☺	Yes☺	Yes☺	Lacking☹	Yes☺
TCP	Low-Lev- el Only[299] ☺	Yes☺	Yes☺	Yes☺	Yes☺	No[300] ☹
Websockets	Yes (only for WebGL apps?)☺	Yes☺	Yes☺	Yes☺	No☹
HTTP	Low-Level Only[299] ☺	Yes☺	Yes☺	Yes☺	No☹
Scalability/Deployment Features						
Load Balancing	DIY☺	DIY☺	World-to -Serv- er Only☺	World-to -Serv- er Only☺	DIY☺	Special Case for seamless worlds: PikkoServer☺
Integration with Cloud	DIY☺	DIY☺	DIY☺	DIY☺	DIY☺	DIY☺
Front-End Servers	No☹	No☹	No☹	No☹	No☹	No☹

292   I.E., there is no way to address anything except "Client" on Server and "Server" on Client; this addressing model is too restrictive, and effectively excludes Server-to-Server communication.

293   Implementing IP-independent addressing (which is usually necessary) is rather cumbersome.

294   Very important to prevent cheating; see Vol. VIII's chapter on Bot Fighting for a detailed discussion.

295   It is possible to do encryption on top of Unity 5, PUN, and UE4—but it is cumbersome, error-prone, and limited.

296   TCP and Websockets only.

DarkRift	Unreal Engine 4	RUDP Libraries	Amazon Lumberyard	Urho3D	My ideal DIY network engine
"Server", By ID for Clients 😊	"Client"/"Server"[292] ☹️	IP:Port[293] 😐	Session-Oriented 😐	IP:Port[293] 😐	By server name for servers, player ID / "connected client" for players 😊
DIY 😐	DIY 😐	DIY. 😐 Yes for *libyohimbo* and proto-quic 😊	Yes 😊	DIY 😐	Yes 😊
DIY 😐	Limited[295] ☹️	DIY. 😐 Yes for libyohimbo and proto-quic 😊	Win64-only 😐	DIY 😐	Yes 😊
No[297] ☹️	No[297] ☹️	No ☹️	No[297] ☹️	No[297] ☹️	Yes 😊
No[298] ☹️	Yes 😊	Yes 😊	Yes 😊	Yes 😊	Yes 😊
Yes 😊	Low-level Only[301] 😐	No[300] ☹️	No[300] ☹️	No[300] ☹️	Yes 😊
No ☹️	No ☹️	No ☹️	No ☹️	No ☹️	Yes 😊
No ☹️	No ☹️	No ☹️	No ☹️	Yes 😊	Yes 😊
DIY 😐	DIY 😐	DIY 😐	World-to-Server Only 😊	DIY 😐	Both World-to-Server and Client Load Balancing 😊
DIY 😐	DIY 😐	DIY 😐	Amazon AWS 😊	DIY 😐	Yes 😊
No ☹️	No ☹️	No ☹️	No ☹️	No ☹️	Optional 😊

297 There is always an option to use another 3rd-party library for Server-to-Server.

298 Promised in DarkRift 2.

299 There are low-level socket/HTTP classes, but there is no easy way to integrate into [SyncVar], etc.

300 3rd-party library or sockets are still an option.

301 While there are classes like *FTcpSocketBuilder,* they are more like Unity's LLAPI, without an easy way to integrate into UPROPERTY, etc.

In this table, the rightmost column represents what I would like to see from my own (hypothetical) DIY game network engine. In this case, while the network engine itself is DIY, there is a big advantage of pushing all these things into the network engine (in terms of Chapter 5, known as "Infrastructure Code"), separating them from the Game Logic. The more things that are separated via well-defined interfaces, the less cluttered your Game Logic code becomes, and the more time you have for really important things such as gameplay; in extreme cases, this difference can even mean the difference between the life and death of your project. Also keep in mind that if going a DIY route, for any given game you won't need to implement *all* the stuff in the table; think about what is important for your game, and concentrate only on those features that you really need. For example, UDP support and dead reckoning are not likely to be important for a non-simulation game, and HTTP "long polling" isn't likely to work for an MMOFPS.

SUMMARY FOR CHAPTER 7

Summarizing the discussion in Chapter 7:

- There are quite a few games out there that require Game Designers to use level editors.
  - Such games very often require what we name Client-Driven Development Workflow.
- For games that require Client-Driven Development Workflow, it is usually an essentially-single-player game that Game Designers are working with, plus "continuous conversion." To implement "continuous conversion", two approaches are possible:
  - Engine-Provided Server. Essentially, moving Client-Side Game Logic to the Server, using engine-provided means.
  - Standalone Server. Completely separate development of the Server, using exported game levels from the game engine.
- When choosing between network layers of Unity/UE4/Amazon Lumberyard/Urho3D — when looking at the concepts involved, all are surprisingly similar. Still, lots of differences of different magnitude exist; for these, see the huge table above.
  - Two pretty big obstacles when trying to use high-level APIs is that most of the time they (a) have not-so-efficient mar-

shalling, and are (b) non-encrypted[302] — and encryption is a
very important tool for cheating prevention.

♦   As for third-party libraries and frameworks, they're more diverse.
The issues that concern me the most are:

- Thread synchronization exposed to game-logic level (IMNSHO,
it is a Big No-No™, so if your library requires it, you *must* make
a wrapper that entirely hides thread sync from app-level).

- Lack of UDP support (which makes the library unsuitable
for fast-paced games).

- Lack of encryption (this is more a problem for frameworks,
as for lower-level libraries it can be added relatively easily).

♦   Overall, I clearly do *not* want to recommend any of the listed
technologies over the others *unconditionally*. There are many
all-important factors to consider, including those that are not
included in the table above; however, before finalizing your choice
of 3rd-party game engine and your network libraries for your
MOG, make sure to take a look at the table above, and think about
your development flow too.

Bibliography

Amazon. 2017. *"AWS Service Terms."* https://aws.amazon.com/service-
terms/.

—. 2016. *"Two questions about Lumberyard licensing."*
https://gamedev.amazon.com/forums/questions/10112/two-
questions-about-lumberyard-licensing.html.

—. *"Physics Scripting Guide."* http://docs.aws.amazon.com/lumberyard/
latest/developerguide/physics-scripting-threads.html.

—. *"Game Architecture with Amazon GameLift."* http://docs.aws.amazon.
com/gamelift/latest/developerguide/gamelift-architecture.html.

Arellano, Christian. 2015. *"UNET Unity 5 Networking Tutorial Part 2
of 3 - Client Side Prediction and Server Reconciliation."*
http://www.gamasutra.com/blogs/ChristianArellano/20151009/
255873/UNET_Unity_5_Networking_Tutorial_
Part_2_of_3__Client_Side_Prediction_and_Server_
Reconciliation.php.

---

302   Except for Lumberyard.

Epic Games. "*Garbage Collection Overview.*" https://wiki.unrealengine.com/Garbage_Collection_Overview.

Fiedler, Glenn. "*libyojimbo*" https://github.com/networkprotocol/libyojimbo.

Google. "*proto-quic.*" https://github.com/google/proto-quic.

Hare, 'No Bugs'. 2010. "*Single-Threading: Back to the Future?*" Overload.

Landwerth, Immo. 2016. "*Introducing .NET Standard.*" https://blogs.msdn.microsoft.com/dotnet/2016/09/26/introducing-net-standard/.

MuchDifferent. 2013. "*uLink Overview.*" http://developer.muchdifferent.com/unitypark/uLink/uLink.

Newman, Garry. "*Network Recode.*" https://playrust.com/friday-devblog-4/.

Peterson, Josh. 2016. "*Unity3D Sripting - .NET Core 1.2 replacement of Mono.*" https://forum.unity3d.com/threads/unity3d-sripting-net-core-1-2-replacement-of-mono.439826/#post-2860076.

Unity Technologies. 2017. "*Unity 5 Network System Concepts.*" http://docs.unity3d.com/Manual/UNetConcepts.html.

—. 2017. "*Unity 5 State Synchronization.*" http://docs.unity3d.com/Manual/UNetStateSync.html.

—. 2017. "*Native Plugins.*" https://docs.unity3d.com/Manual/NativePlugins.html.

Urho3D. 2017. "*Networking.*" https://urho3d.github.io/documentation/1.5/_network.html.

Vermeulen, Steve. 2017. "*Async-Await instead of coroutines in Unity 2017*" http://www.stevevermeulen.com/index.php/2017/09/using-async-await-in-unity3d-2017/

Wischik, Lucian. 2016. "*Async workflow [how to hibernate async methods, part 2]*" https://blogs.msdn.microsoft.com/lucian/2016/04/20/async-workflow-2/

VOL. II
SUMMARY

In this volume, we started with Chapter 4, briefly arguing what-we-should-do-ourselves and what-we-should-re-use.

Then, in Chapter 5, we presented my favorite way of implementing distributed systems — (Re)Actors (a.k.a. event-driven programs, a.k.a. Game Loops, a.k.a. ad-hoc Finite State Machines, et cetera, et cetera). While (Re)Actors are not *strictly* required to get your game flying, for medium- and larger-sized games, they tend to get you there *much* faster (and tend to result in *much* more reliable programs).

First, we mentioned that (Re)Actors can be seen as a generalization of the good ol' Game Loop, and discussed how it can be improved to obtain certain goodies (such as production post-factum debugging and replay-based regression testing).

One such improvement is non-blocking handling of RPC returns, and we considered *eight* different ways to do it; the second improvement is determinism, and we spent quite a bit of time deliberating on its specifics (in particular, on cross-platform determinism vs same-executable determinism).

Last but not least for Chapter 5, we discussed ways to scale (Re)Actors — and the ways to organize the code within (Re)Actors.

Chapter 6 was dedicated to Client-Side Architecture. Within Chapter 6, we started with a very generic Client-Side architecture and then proceeded to discuss (Re)Actor-fest Client-Side Architecture as my-favorite way to implement the generic one. In addition, we also addressed the questions of choosing a programming language for the Client-Side (including the resilience of different programming languages to bot writers, and the ways to use C++ for browser) and integrating web-based stuff with downloadable Clients.

In Chapter 7, which concludes Vol. II, there was an examination of the different ways of "how 3rd-party game engines can be used to build your MOG." In particular, special attention was paid to comparing the three most popular commercial game engines (Unity, UE, and Lumberyard) and one open-source engine (Urho3D) and also the associated network technologies and libraries (including the Photon and RUDP libraries).

WHAT'S NEXT

After discussing issues related to the Client-Side, it is only logical to proceed to the significantly different world of the Server-Side (however, I have to note that my beloved (Re)Actors are IMNSHO even more applicable there <wink />).

Development and Deployment of

MULTIPLAYER ONLINE GAMES

Volume III: Scalability, Server-Side Arch., Fault Tolerance

In Vol. III, we'll start our discussion on Scalability 101 in Chapter 8. We'll discuss both common topics such as Scaling Up vs Scaling Out, and MOG-specific issues such as a general desire to roll back to the beginning of the Game Event in case of crash (which, in turn, has serious implications on MOG Scalability and architecture).

Then, we'll proceed to a large Chapter 9, discussing many aspects of Server-Side Architecture. In particular, we'll discuss issues related to different deployment architectures (both Web-Based and Classical, with a Front-End Server twist), their respective scalability, as well as the choice of operating system and programming language for the Server-Side.

Then, in Chapter 10, we'll briefly address ways of dealing with various failures, ranging from failure containment to full-scale fault tolerance (with the most practical ways to implement it being VM-based, and DIY (Re)Actor-based). A discussion of "how improperly implemented fault tolerance *reduces* MTBFs" will be included too.

In Chapter 11, we'll discuss all those boring things that are necessary before starting coding. This discussion will include source control (including certain peculiarities for gamedev), issue tracking, coding guidelines, and so on.

This will conclude Vol. III — and also Part ARCH (devoted to Architecture and Pre-Coding).

INDEX

Symbols

A

B

C

LETTER FROM THE AUTHOR

Hello, fellow game developer!

I hope you've found something of interest (and maybe even useful) within all my barely coherent blabbering. And I hope that you're going to get your hands on Vol. III of this epic work.

For the time being, chapters of the 1st beta of Vol. III–VII are available on ithare.com/category/dnd-of-mogs-volII-1st-beta/, with more added every week. If you have any comments or criticism, please e-mail me at nobugs@ithare.com, or comment right on the site. For this volume, Vol. II, comments from website readers (and on Reddit) have helped add a lot of previously missing things, and have fixed quite a few mistakes of varying severity. THANKS A LOT to everybody who pointed out omissions and mistakes (and I hope for further comments to also make future volumes better)!

Last but not least:

> ### Please consider reviewing this book on Amazon

(or Goodreads, if you already have an account). It will help both me (the author) and others who could benefit from reading this book. The landscape of even-somewhat-useful books on multiplayer game programming is IMO really barren these days, so letting others know that there is something worth reading is really important.

Best regards (and thanks for reading this far <smile/>),

No Bugs' Hare